THATCHER

THATCHER

E.H.H. GREEN

Hodder Arnold

A MEMBER OF THE HODDER HEADLINE GROUP

First published in Great Britain in 2006 by
Hodder Education, a member of the Hodder Headline Group,
338 Euston Road, London NW1 3BH

www.hoddereducation.com

Distributed in the United States of America by
Oxford University Press Inc.
198 Madison Avenue, New York, NY10016

British Library Cataloguing in Publication Data
A catalogue record for this book is available from the British Library

Library of Congress Cataloging-in-Publication Data
A catalog record for this book is available from the Library of Congress

ISBN-10: 0-340-75977-1
ISBN-13: 978-0-340-75977-6

1 2 3 4 5 6 7 8 9 10

Typeset in 10.5 on 12.5 Garamond by Phoenix Photosetting, Chatham, Kent
Printed and bound in Malta

What do you think about this book? Or any other Hodder
Education title? Please send your comments to the feedback
section on www.hoddereducation.com.

For C.J.A.

Contents

Abbreviations

BSC	British Steel Corporation
CCO	Conservative Central Office
CDU	Christian Democratic Union
CPA	Conservative Party Archive
CPC	Conservative Political Centre
CPS	Centre for Policy Studies
CRD	Conservative Research Department
EC	European Council
EDU	European Democratic Union
EEC	European Economic Community
EMS	European Monetary System
ERG	Economic Reconstruction Group
ERM	Exchange Rate Mechanism
IRA	Irish Republican Army
KJP	Keith Joseph Papers
MTFS	Medium Term Financial Strategy
NCB	National Coal Board
NEDC	National Economic Development Council
NUM	National Union of Mineworkers
PCNI	Policy Committee on the Nationalized Industries, 1950s
PGNI	Policy Group on the Nationalized Industries, 1960s and 1980s
PLDF	People's League for the Defence of Freedom
TP	Thatcher Papers
TUC	Trade Union Congress
UN	United Nations

Acknowledgements

I would like to extend my thanks to the Humanities Division and the Modern History Faculty of the University of Oxford, and to the President and Fellows of Magdalen College, who granted me special sabbatical leave to complete this book. I would also like to thank the Thatcher Foundation and the Modern Records Centre at Churchill College, Cambridge, and their archivists, Chris Collins and Andrew Riley, for granting me access to the Thatcher Archive. Maria Tippett, with characteristic generosity, provided me with the opportunity to see that archive for the first time. The Bodleian Library, notably the staff of Room 132 and the Conservative Party Archive, especially Colin Harris and Emily Tarrant, have been friendly, efficient and effective in providing access to papers that complemented the vast Thatcher holdings. My editor at Hodder Arnold, Michael Strang, was patient, and then still more so, for which I am very grateful, and, in the same company, Tiara Misquitta was also a great help.

This study covers selected and specific themes and has consciously avoided some areas – notably Thatcher's view of and relations with the Civil Service and her approach to public services, especially the NHS. These topics are not addressed because they are being or have been covered in detail by other scholars – notably by Rodney Lowe, in his forthcoming official history of the Civil Service, and by Charles Webster, in his similarly authorized and authoritative study of the NHS. Furthermore, this book has examined policy creation and has not focused on the details of policy implementation. Its unconscious omissions are doubtless more legion than its conscious ones, and the author can only offer anticipatory apologies to readers.

It could be said that I have been working on this book throughout my adult life, in that I was 16 when Margaret Thatcher became leader of the Conservative Party and 32 when she resigned. Most of my research has been devoted to the Conservative Party and Conservatism, and Thatcher's importance to both led my research inexorably to her. I have shared the process of thinking about and working on Thatcher and Thatcherism with many friends and colleagues. In particular, my exchanges with Peter Clarke on Thatcher began at the outset of her premiership and have continued ever since, and both our conversations and his own work on Thatcherism have helped to shape my thoughts on the subject. I have been fortunate that my colleagues at Magdalen, Laurence Brockliss, John Nightingale and Nick Stargardt, have supported me and tolerated my lengthy absences. Other friends and colleagues at Magdalen have shared thoughts on Thatcherism, and I have profited hugely from many discussions, in college and over drinks, with Stewart Wood and Michael Wheeler-Booth. My colleagues in the faculty have also been very generous, and I have benefited particularly from the ideas of Roy Foster, Jose Harris and Ross Mckibbin. Further afield, David Howell, Jim Cronin, Peter Weiler, Steven Brooke, Jon Schneer and Bob Dewey have offered intellectual stimulation and personal generosity in great measure. The critical observations of a fellow scholar of Conservatism, Clarisse Berthezène, helped me to rethink the history of Conservative ideas and place Thatcherism in perspective.

I have been fortunate as a Fellow of Magdalen to teach a series of exceptional students, some of whom have become politically active in think tanks and in government. 'Talking Thatcherism' with Sarah Fitzpatrick and Sophia Parker has been a constant source of critical inspiration. The questioning thoughts of Hester Barron pressed me to consider the long-term historical background to the 1984–85 miners' strike and Thatcherite ideas about class politics and the idea of community. Other good friends, both inside and outside academia, have been essential to my work, Rob Hughes, Zoe Penn, Charlie and Caroline Jenne have provided moments of calm as the storms of ill health have set in, and Steve Baxter has been not only a brilliant source of stories from an era I never studied – and now wish I had – but a great friend as I try to adjust to life on wheels. Lizzie Melville has been a constant source of support and amusement, and Ninon Vinsonneau, Jonathan Magidoff, Pauline Lavagne, Benoit Rossel, Kath Aubert, Julien Gaisne, Sonia Eap and Christèle Dedebant all helped to create an environment that made research and writing a great deal easier. Stefanie Shaver was an important presence 'offstage'.

As I set out on the path less travelled I look over my shoulder to the paths to Pen y Fan and to the Shenandoah Valley, and hope that 'one day'...

Oxford, October 2004

Introduction

Margaret Thatcher was one of the most important figures in British political history in the twentieth century. She was the first and only woman to lead a major political party and Britain's first female prime minister. She led the Conservative Party for 15½ years and was prime minister for 11½ years, making her the longest-serving party leader and the longest-serving prime minister of the century. Indeed, she had the longest uninterrupted tenure of the premiership since Lord Liverpool.[1] This book is not a biography. Any readers who were expecting or hoping that it would be will be disappointed. There are 25 biographies of Thatcher available, and the latest, completed by Britain's leading political biographer, is a study of Margaret Thatcher's political reputation, and its aims are different from those of a work in the biographical genre. It may seem that to divide biography from the study of political reputation is to make a distinction without a difference, but this is not the case. A political reputation is necessarily a *public construction*. It may be constructed both by and for a range of different publics, but that merely means that a political reputation is a complex construction rather than making it any less public. Biography necessarily places emphasis upon the individual and, in the case of political biography, frequently seeks to explore the personal motivations that led a politician to choose a particular course of action. This is an important area of study, but it necessarily runs a risk of, as it were, placing the text above the context. For the purposes of this exploration context is the overriding concern. The focus of this book will be Margaret Thatcher's *political, public* reputation as it evolved over the period from her first ventures into politics in the mid- to late 1940s to her position as an 'elder statesman' in the early twenty-first century.[2] Matters relating to her personal life, including her family background, education, career before entering politics, and personal matters and relationships, are considered only in terms of their contribution to the shifting construction of her political reputation by both herself and others.

A reputation in the making

Politicians who enjoy an extended period of high office have their reputations repeatedly assessed, reassessed, assailed and defended, both during and after their careers. Margaret Thatcher is no exception to this rule, for she attracted and continues to attract praise and opprobrium in equal measure. To her supporters and admirers her 'conviction' politics allowed her to define problems with clarity and to pursue her prescribed solutions with equal straightforwardness – whether it was the problem of economic decline, overmighty trade unions, domestic and international Socialism, aggressive South American or Middle Eastern dictators or empire-building Eurocrats. Thatcher, to acolytes in her party and supporters in the electorate, removed the grey from politics in favour of black and white. To her opponents on the Left she appeared ruthless – seemingly indifferent to the poor and disadvantaged, and to social problems, especially unemployment. Moreover, they regarded her international outlook as either simplistic or dangerously atavistic, whether in the context of heightening cold war tensions or disrupting European diplomacy. Opposition to Thatcher from within her own party was complex. Initially she attracted criticism from those labelled 'Wets', who regarded her 'socially divisive' policies as a betrayal of 'true' Conservatism and its socially integrative traditions. In the latter period of her ascendancy she was upbraided by former close allies, who had become critical of her 'dictatorial' style of leadership. Whether Thatcher was loved or loathed, few in the political spectrum doubted that she had successfully defined, or perhaps redefined, the agenda of British politics. George Urban, one of Thatcher's policy advisers, remarked that, 'For good or evil, she impinged on every aspect of British self-understanding and on the understanding of the British abroad',[3] while *Guardian* journalist Peter Jenkins, a critic of Thatcher, stated that 'History will surely recognize her achievements as Britain's first woman Prime Minister, a leader with the courage of her convictions, who assailed the conventional wisdom of her day, challenged and overthrew the existing order, changed the political map, and put her country on its feet again'.[4]

In 1970 Thatcher was appointed Minister of Education, and it was in this post that she 'enjoyed' what was, at that point, her greatest public recognition. The 1972 decision to abolish free milk for schoolchildren saw her labelled 'Margaret Thatcher – Milk Snatcher', and led the *Sun* to describe her in November 1972 as 'The most unpopular woman in Britain'.[5] However, following the Conservatives' second electoral defeat of 1974 in October of that year, Thatcher became Robert Carr's deputy in the Conservative Shadow Treasury team, and 'she developed . . . a formidable reputation' as a member of the parliamentary standing committee on the Budget.[6] It was partly as a consequence of her success in this role that she became a candidate for the Conservative leadership in January 1975, but it was not widely thought that she would secure the position. On the Labour benches Barbara Castle noted, shortly before the first round of the contest, that she expected Heath to retain his position, not because he was popular but because 'You can't find two Tories to agree on an alternative to him'.[7] Castle was not alone in thinking along such lines, for on the Conservative side R.A. Butler stated, 'We don't have to take this Thatcher thing seriously, do we?'[8] But Castle, Butler and many other commentators overestimated Heath's position, for he was a three-time electoral loser and was not liked by many in the parliamentary party. That Heath lost to Thatcher by 11 votes was not wholly surprising and it was fatal to his leadership, but it was by no means a ringing endorsement of his opponent. The second ballot, which saw Thatcher achieve a majority of 18 over the combined votes of the other candidates, was more convincing, but both ballots indicated that much of the parliamentary party, especially, it seems, its senior figures, had their reservations. Intriguingly, Thatcher's Labour opponents were initially more impressed with her than her own colleagues. Barbara Castle noted soon after Thatcher's election that 'She is so clearly the best man among them',[9] and, likewise, Tony Benn reflected, 'I think it would be foolish to suppose that Mrs Thatcher won't be a formidable leader'.[10]

In the light of subsequent developments one might see Castle and Benn possessing prescient insight of the kind attributed to James Callaghan. The Labour prime minister stated on the eve of the general election in 1979 that Thatcher and the Conservatives were benefiting from the fact that 'There are times, perhaps once every thirty years, when there is a sea change in politics. It then does not matter what you say or what you do. There is a shift in what the public wants and what it approves of.'[11] But tempting though it may be, attributing prescient wisdom to such comments would be a mistake, for they seem insightful only *because* of subsequent events. In late 1979, just months after the Conservatives had achieved their handsome election victory under her leadership, Alan Clark described Thatcher as a beleaguered prime minister who enjoyed neither the support nor respect of her Cabinet. In so far as Thatcher's first Cabinet contained a majority of 'Heathites', who had not supported her elevation to the leadership, this was not surprising, but Clark sensed a real depth of hostility. After a discussion with a fellow Conservative MP he noted that in the Cabinet 'Carrington – hates her; Prior – hates her; Gilmour – hates her; Heseltine – hates her; Walker – loathes her, makes no secret of it; Willie [Whitelaw] – completely even handed, would never support her against the old gang. Geoffrey Howe – no personal loyalties – durable politburo man.'[12] Nor did reports improve. In January 1981 Clark noted that the former Labour grandee, George Brown, expected to see Thatcher removed from the party leadership by the end of the year.[13] Brown's views were shared by a key figure in Thatcher's own Policy Unit, John Hoskyns, who noted in his diary in July 1981, following a Cabinet meeting at which some of Thatcher's supporters had opposed her, that it was 'the beginning of the end – or at least a step in that direction.'[14] In the summer and autumn of 1981 such views were widespread, and understandably so. The British economy was in deep recession and, as a consequence of widespread closures and bankruptcies in the manufacturing sector, unemployment was rising to levels generally assumed to be politically unacceptable. A letter appeared in *The Times,* signed by 364 economists, to the effect that the government's economic strategy was theoretically flawed and damaging the economy, and in September Sir Ian Gilmour left the government and declared that the economy was being steered onto the rocks. In London, Liverpool and Bristol rioting had taken place in the summer, and raised the concern that Britain's social fabric had been seriously damaged by the recession. In 1981 Thatcher had the lowest prime ministerial popularity rating since such polls had first been taken. Whether or not the economy was heading for the rocks, it was difficult to see either Thatcher or the Conservative Party with her as its leader heading in any other direction.

Had Thatcher been run down by the proverbial Whitehall bus in late 1981 or early 1982 her historical reputation would not have been particularly noteworthy, except, ironically, for the fact that she had been the first female leader of a major party and the first woman prime minister. In October and November of 1981 the newly formed SDP-Liberal alliance won two by-elections, in Croydon and Crosby, with swings against the Conservatives of 24.2 per cent and 25.5 per cent. Had such results been repeated at a general election the Conservatives would have been crushingly defeated. The Conservative Party was in severe difficulty and much of the blame was placed on the leader. Yet, a little over 18 months after the trauma of the Crosby by-election defeat, the Conservative Party enjoyed a general election victory and a substantial increase in its parliamentary majority. Moreover, in a biography of Thatcher published a few months after the 1983 election the author could quote the Austrian Conservative leader, Alois Mock, describing her as 'one of the greatest politicians of our time', and the former US president, Richard Nixon, to the effect that she was 'among the best'. Perhaps most surprising, however, was a quotation from *Paris Match*, which stated in June 1983, 'If only Margaret Thatcher were French', and went on to refer to her as 'the Western World's Mother Courage'.[15] In 1980 the French president, Valéry Giscard d'Estaing, had referred to Thatcher contemptuously as 'la fille d'épicier', and Thatcher had been labelled 'Madame Non' by French negotiators and commentators during the EEC budget negotiations of 1980. Praise for her in a French journal, especially a 'popular' rather than 'serious' publication, was an important turnaround. The change in Thatcher's reputation, both national and international, between 1981 and 1983 was marked, and almost wholly attributable to the successful outcome of the Falklands conflict. The Falklands war will be discussed in detail in chapter 6 – suffice it here to say that it was a crucial turning point in terms of her own standing and her party's electoral fortunes.

In the period from the summer of 1982, which saw the victory in the Falklands, and the autumn of 1987, which saw a major fall on the stock market, Margaret Thatcher's reputation was at its peak. She was by no means untroubled – that would have been too much for any politician to expect – but both internationally and domestically she seemed to have achieved many of her stated aims. Apart from the victory in the Falklands she had presided over the closure of a long-standing issue stemming from Britain's retreat from Empire: the Rhodesian controversy, which had begun in 1964, was formally settled in 1980 through the creation of the new State of Zimbabwe. Thatcher had also secured a successful resolution of the long-running dispute over Britain's contribution to the EEC budget at the Fontainbleu conference in 1984. She had also played a major part in constructing the agreement for a single European market that was to come into being in 1992, and which was enshrined in the passage of the Single European Act in Parliament in 1985. She had developed a close personal and political relationship with the US president, Ronald Reagan, and, as a consequence of both this and the Falklands, appeared to re-establish Britain's international standing. This was reflected and confirmed by the fact that she was the first Western leader to develop links with the new Soviet leader, Mikhail Gorbachev, during and after 1984. In some respects this was unexpected. Thatcher had not held any government or Shadow Cabinet posts in the area of foreign affairs prior to becoming Conservative leader and prime minister, and one foreign policy specialist told Alan Clark that in 1977 Thatcher had asked him, "'Must I do all this international stuff?'" Clark's acquaintance then stated that she was 'a Little Englander through and through'. Clark disagreed with the latter remark, and suggested that Thatcher's initial uncertainty had been replaced with a relish for foreign policy.[16] Chapters 6 and 7 will examine Thatcher's view of international relations and her stance on Europe, and will explore the question of whether Thatcher's increasing interest in walking the world stage by no means precluded and even reinforced her essentially 'Little Englander' outlook.

If international affairs grew increasingly important for Thatcher, it was the domestic sphere, in particular the economy, that she saw as the basis for both her own and her governments' reputation for achievement. The Conservative Party's election victory in 1983 was widely attributed to a 'Falklands factor', but their triumph in 1987 was equally widely attributed to the economy. The *Conservative Manifesto* of 1979 had established strengthening Britain's defences and its relationship with its allies as one of five tasks a Conservative government would seek to achieve, but in a 32-page document this task took up only 3 pages, whereas the economy, trade union reform, home ownership and welfare took up 13.[17] Domestic tasks set out in 1979 included 'controlling inflation', providing 'incentives so that hard work pays', 'striking a fair balance between the rights and duties of the trade union movement' and 'helping people to become home-owners'.[18] By 1987 Thatcher and her party claimed that these goals, and others, had been largely achieved. First of all the inflation rate had fallen to 6 per cent. With regard to 'incentives', the first Conservative Budget of 1979 had seen the basic rate of income tax reduced from 33 to 30 per cent and the top rate cut from 83 to 60 per cent, and in 1987 the basic rate had been reduced to 25 per cent and the top rate to 40 per cent. The phased reduction of direct tax was accompanied by increases in indirect tax – VAT was raised from 8 per cent to 15 per cent in 1979 and to 17.5 per cent in 1987, while the range of goods and services liable to VAT was extended. The aim of these changes was to create a fiscal regime in which, first, government would increasingly obtain revenue from indirect rather than direct tax and, second, individual taxpayers would have more 'choice' when to pay tax, through pursuing or deferring consumption. It was also the case that by 1987, the trade union reforms of 1980–84 had changed the industrial relations environment and had helped the government to defeat the year-long miners' action of 1984–85. Furthermore, the sale of council houses that had commenced in 1981 and moved at pace thereafter had contributed to a more general housing boom, which led to 70 per cent of households becoming owner-occupied by 1987.

In addition to extending what Thatcherites, like an earlier generation of Conservatives, called property-owning democracy, the Conservative governments of the mid-1980s also sought to create a 'capital-owning democracy' through the sale of shares in privatized companies. Tentative beginnings were made by Thatcher's first administration, but, starting with the sale of British Telecom in 1984, the second and third Thatcher Governments privatized the bulk of Britain's State-owned industries and utilities, with the Government's holdings in British Airways, British Steel, British Gas, the CEGB, the regional water companies, British Petroleum and a number of smaller concerns being offered for sale on the stock market. The full impact of privatization will be examined in more detail in chapter 3, but from 1983 to 1990 the privatization campaign saw the shareholding population of Britain grow from 2 to 10 million. The series of large-scale share issues it generated not only allowed the Conservatives to claim that they had created 'popular capitalism', but also assisted the prolonged mid-1980s boom on the newly deregulated stock market. With the financial and service sector enjoying a particular boom, the British economy as a whole experienced growth from the spring of 1982 to the autumn of 1987. Unemployment remained high, but had fallen after 1983, and this fall was accompanied by a rise in real incomes for those in work. These developments, taken together, were the 'economic miracle' that Thatcher and the Conservatives claimed had banished 'the British disease' and transformed the fortunes of the country.

The general election of 1987 saw Thatcher's reputation at its apogee, and even if her post-election declaration that she would 'go on and on and on' was hubristic, it did not seem wholly unrealistic. But if the upturn of the economy had been a key to the sweeping Conservative victory in 1987, the return of economic difficulty was to play a part in Thatcher's downfall. In October 1987 the advent of a hurricane in Britain coincided with a similar gust through the stock market, and the protracted boom in Britain's financial sector came to an end. Through the 1980s the City and the financial service sector had seemed immune to recession, and their success and prosperity had seemed to symbolize the Thatcherite 'economic miracle': the manner in which the City's hubris turned to nemesis was in some ways to be a foretaste of Thatcher's own experience. In part the two events were not wholly unrelated. Lawson, the Conservative Chancellor, responded to concern about economic downturn by lowering interest rates and fostering a further surge in the housing boom and consumer spending. Largely as a consequence, the 'demon' of inflation, which Thatcher claimed to have vanquished, reappeared. This in turn led Lawson to raise interest rates, which choked off the housing boom and triggered a more general economic downturn and a rise in unemployment. All of this dented claims concerning the 'economic miracle', and a new ogre, negative equity, joined the old economic demons of inflation and unemployment.

At the same time as Thatcher's mantle of economic competence slipped, the 'little Englander' in her came to the fore in her dealings with Europe. She had, since 1986, shown some disquiet at the way in which the French president of the

European Commission, Jacques Delors, was interpreting the movement to a single market. In a speech at Bruges in September 1988, Thatcher voiced her concern that there were those who favoured a federal, centralized governance of the European Union, and that they were seeking to impose on Britain forms of social and economic intervention from Brussels which she had been at pains to remove. In addition she made clear that her view of a European single market did not include economic and monetary union, and she vigorously opposed suggestions that Britain join the European Exchange Rate Mechanism (ERM). Thatcher's position was almost certainly in accord with public opinion, but it created tensions with both her Chancellor and her Foreign Secretary, and these manifestations of intra-party disagreement were to be politically and electorally damaging.

Thatcher had experienced an uncomfortable moment in 1986, when her Minister of Defence, Michael Heseltine, had resigned and raised objections to her authoritarian approach to government. The policy issue that prompted Heseltine's resignation – whether a European or an American bid for the British helicopter company, Westland, should be favoured – was largely lost in the controversy which followed his action. Instead, debate focused on the question of how far Thatcher and her press office had coordinated a campaign to undermine Heseltine's position. One outcome of the episode was that the ministerial career of Leon Brittan was brought to an end when he was, effectively, forced to resign over his part in leaking comments from the government's legal officers to the press. Thatcher's position was briefly compromised, but poor handling of the issue by the Opposition ensured that questions with regard to her style of government were raised but not fully addressed. As a result, Heseltine's complaints, although they were not dismissed, were not pursued at length, and they did not significantly impinge on the election campaign the following year. However, such complaints were to resurface in 1988–89, in a more damaging context. The first occasion was the resignation of the Chancellor of the Exchequer, Nigel Lawson, in October 1989. Lawson resigned because he could not accept Thatcher's apparent willingness to prefer the advice of her personal economic adviser to his own. In his memoirs Lawson described this as part of Thatcher's tendency 'After seven and a half years in No 10 . . . to see loyalty as a one-way street. Something her ministers owed to her but not she to them.'[19] In his memoirs, Geoffrey Howe, who had been removed as Foreign Secretary earlier in 1989, described the situation Lawson faced in more colourful terms, when he stated that 'Margaret would quite often – more frequently as the years went by – cite advice she had received from "one of my people". It seemed sometimes as though she was Joan of Arc invoking the authority of her "voices."'[20] The issues of policy that underpinned the ruptures between Thatcher and, respectively, Lawson and Howe were more important than any personal differences, as will be made clear in chapters 6 and 7. This was crucial, for whereas Heseltine's criticisms had been viewed, in part, as a product of his personal ambition and egotism, these were difficult charges to level against either Lawson or Howe. As Howe points out in his memoirs, he and Lawson were, unlike Heseltine, 'card-carrying foundation members of Thatcherism'.[21] Whether or not one accepts Lawson's claim that he coined the term 'Thatcherism', he was, as the author of the Medium Term Financial Strategy (MTFS) of 1980, an architect of its economic policy foundations. Likewise, Howe, as Thatcher's first Chancellor, had played a vital role in constructing those foundations and building the Thatcherite economic edifice upon them. That Thatcher, Howe and Lawson, who could all assert their responsibility for Britain's economic trajectory in the 1980s, were engaged in a series of increasingly barbed disputes between 1988 and 1990 served only to weaken Thatcher's position.

That Thatcher faced a leadership challenge in the autumn of 1989 was testimony to how far the style and substance of her leadership was being questioned. Her challenger, Sir Anthony Meyer, had no chance of winning the contest, but the fact that 60 Conservative MPs, either through supporting Meyer or abstaining, registered their disapproval of Thatcher's leadership indicated how far internal party opinion had moved away from her. The issues of the economy, Europe and Thatcher's 'autocratic' style of leadership were the underlying cause of a burgeoning post-1987 disillusionment with Thatcher, which was particularly marked within the Conservative parliamentary party. In short, broad issues were in play, but one separate, particular issue had an especially important role – the poll tax. The poll tax, or community charge, was introduced in the United Kingdom as a whole on 1 April 1990, having been introduced in Scotland the previous year. The idea of the poll tax/community charge had, like most of the policy initiatives associated with Thatcherism, been part of the subculture of Conservative policy discussion for many years. However, its introduction saw this long-standing grassroots 'dream' become a nightmare. In Scotland the new tax provoked significant popular opposition, and when it was implemented in England there was an even stronger reaction, with the summer and early autumn of 1990 being marked by a number of violent anti-poll tax demonstrations. Had protest been confined to such episodes it could feasibly have been dealt with, and dismissed, as a 'law and order' question – like the inner-city riots of 1981 and 1985. But what concerned many Conservative MPs and local activists, especially in marginal seats, was that the new tax was having an adverse effect on many middle-class households and alienating voters normally considered part of the core Conservative constituency. As opposition to the poll tax developed, so too Conservative concern over its electoral impact grew in intensity. This had a damaging effect on Thatcher personally, for she was very much committed to and associated with the poll tax, and on this issue her conviction, which had seemed a political asset in the early 1980s, took on the guise of a damaging political inflexibility.

By the autumn of 1990 Thatcher's position had become fragile. The British economy was experiencing recession, the European Union was moving in a direction at odds with her conception of European unity, there was palpable unease within the Conservative parliamentary party and the Cabinet, and all of this was compounded and exacerbated by the troubles generated by the poll tax. It was against this backdrop that Geoffrey Howe resigned from his position as deputy prime minister. With Nigel Lawson sitting, and nodding, beside him in the

Commons, Howe indicated in his resignation speech that Thatcher's autocratic style of political management, and her stance with regard to Europe and the ERM in particular, were undermining Cabinet government, damaging Britain's European relations and, as a consequence, its economic prospects. In terms of its form, content and provenance, Howe's speech could only be very damaging to Thatcher. Since 1975 he had been one of her chief lieutenants, and as her first Chancellor had faced alongside her an avalanche of criticism with regard to the impact of the government's economic policy. Likewise, as Foreign Secretary from 1983 to 1989, he had dealt with her distrust of the Foreign Office and her frequent instinctive and undiplomatic forays into foreign affairs. He had quietly endured his unceremonious removal as Foreign Secretary, when Thatcher had moved him sideways to the largely meaningless post of deputy prime minister. Hence, when he engaged in major criticisms of her diplomatic faux pas with regard to Europe, and attacked her autocratic style of leadership, his comments carried weight and were not drowned out by the sound of axes being ground. It was thus not surprising that his resignation speech triggered Heseltine's decision to challenge Thatcher for the leadership. Nor was it surprising that she failed to defeat the challenge. In November 1990 the circumstances favoured a Heseltine. The downturn in the economy, the bubbling cauldron of European issues, Thatcher's 'carelessness in jettisoning her natural supporters'[22] within the Cabinet, and her close association with the introduction of the poll tax, all combined to make her seem an electoral liability. Within the Conservative parliamentary party Thatcher's reputation had shifted dramatically between 1987 and 1990, and this brought about her downfall. Conservative MPs, it seems, came to the conclusion described by the journalist Edward Pearce, that 'Mrs Thatcher was outstandingly successful for the majority of her reign, but in the last three years changed for the worse and hence had to be removed.'[23]

A political animal

Thatcher was from the outset a political animal. She was denied the classical route into the British political hierarchy by the conservative sexual politics of the mid-1940s, in that she could not, as a woman, become president of the Oxford Union, but had to be content with being president of the Oxford University Conservative Association. This still provided her with the jumping-off point into politics, for she was only 23 when, in January 1949, she was selected as Conservative candidate for Dartford, in spite of the fact that it was described as 'not a good constituency for a woman candidate.'[24] The party official who made this last remark attributed her selection to the fact that 'Her political knowledge and speaking ability are far above those of the other candidates',[25] and the CCO agent for Home Counties South-East reported that she was 'tremendously impressed with her [Miss Roberts] and think she is a winner. I only wish she had a better chance than she will have at Dartford'.[26] Party officials were unusually impressed by the young Margaret Roberts, and this impression was confirmed as she nursed the constituency. Eleven months after her selection, the Conservative Party was congratulated by one local activist for having chosen a candidate with such an intelligent grasp of affairs and whose ability to communicate was so strong.[27] CCO was also informed that 'Miss Roberts, although young and comparatively inexperienced, has made considerable progress and is putting new life into the Association. She is a good speaker, devotes a good deal of time to the Constituency, and is extremely popular.'[28] The area agent sang even louder songs of praise, for she told CCO shortly before the 1950 general election that 'I am sending you a note about Dartford because the candidate, Miss Margaret Roberts', performance is so outstanding. Every meeting she has had has been packed . . . She excels at questions, and always gives a straight and convincing answer. She is never heckled, they have too much respect for her'.[29] The agent further informed CCO that 'Her [Miss Roberts'] success is equally outstanding in her personal canvassing', that she had been the first candidate to visit factories and

> Miss Roberts has put real heart into our people in Dartford. More peo-
> ple are turning out to work for her than have ever been known in the
> Division before. It seems ridiculous to think we have a chance . . . but the
> Election Agent thinks that there is a 50–50 chance . . . I do not think
> there is a hundredth chance of winning the seat, but I am quite sure the
> majority will be down with a bump. This will be an entirely personal tri-
> umph for Miss Roberts.[30]

The Labour majority, in what was a safe seat for them, was reduced, falling by 50 per cent, and the Conservative candidate's budding reputation was secured.

Margaret Roberts enhanced her reputation through her willingness to fight Dartford again at the 1951 election. Once again the area agent spoke fulsomely about the candidate, telling CCO that

> Miss Roberts, the Prospective Candidate, contested the seat in 1950 and
> is standing again through loyalty to the Association. She is a most able
> young woman and worthy of a better seat. She is a very good speaker, has
> a flair for the right type of propaganda and publicity, and is a very hard
> worker. She is an industrial chemist, at present employed by Messrs.
> Lyons, but she is also reading for the Bar. She has taken on rather much,
> but seems to be coping.[31]

Unsurprisingly, Labour retained the seat, and a disappointed Margaret Roberts wrote to Dartford Conservative Association to inform them, 'I shall not be con-testing this division again'.[32] At the same time, she insisted that 'I have no inten-tion of leaving politics' and some party officials were equally keen that she should not be lost to Conservative politics as she was 'An excellent candidate in every way . . . She should not be lost sight of because she is quite outstanding in ability . . . a most attractive personality and appearance.'[33] Initially it seemed as if Margaret Thatcher, as she had become shortly after the general election, would continue her political career, but in 1954, as will be seen below, she stated that she wished to prioritize her legal career. This decision, however, was to be short-lived, and in 1956 she asked CCO to reactivate her politically, because she felt, as she told the party's general director, that 'I seem to have done very little in 30 years.'[34] Attached to CCO's copy of Thatcher's request were assessments of her calibre by a number of party officials and 'sponsors', all of which were very positive and one of which summed up the key reason for her desire to re-enter politics when it described her as a '1st Class candidate who cannot keep away from politics.'[35] Before her marriage and her legal career provided her with financial security, it had been the party and her political activities which had offered assistance in her employment opportunities rather than vice versa.[36] For Thatcher, politics was her vocation, and all other activities were either secondary to, or a means to achieve, that chosen path.

In terms of securing selection for her preferred type of constituency, that is, a safe Conservative seat in Kent or London, Thatcher's single-minded determination was to cause her some difficulties, but, ultimately, was to serve her well. Thatcher applied in 1958 to be considered for the North London constituency of Finchley. When the selection committee of 17 met to shortlist candidates in July 1958 they decided unanimously that the local party should interview Thatcher, with the next most favoured candidate securing only nine votes; and the deputy agent for Home Counties North told CCO that there was 'no doubt that she completely outshone everybody we interviewed.'[37] But the party adoption meeting was less unanimous. In the first round there were four candidates, and Thatcher came top by only one vote, and the deciding round saw her win by three votes.[38] In spite, or perhaps because, of her less than overwhelming selection triumph, Thatcher immediately set out to reshape aspects of the Finchley Conservative Party. One particular issue Thatcher raised was the ethnic composition of her constituency. Two months after she was selected Thatcher told CCO that

> The electorate of Finchley is nearly 25% Jewish. For reasons with which I need not bother you, the Jewish faith have allied themselves to Liberalism and at the last local elections won five seats from the Conservatives on our council. We are now finding great difficulty in making headway in these particular areas, particularly in Hampstead Garden Suburb. As Finchley has had a Liberal MP in the past we are naturally apprehensive.[39]

Throughout her time in Parliament Thatcher cultivated and enjoyed close relations with the British Jewish community, a relationship which reflected both her interest in North London local politics and her close political allegiance with people like Keith Joseph and Alfred Sherman. This ethnocentric dimension was, however, only one of Thatcher's initial concerns. She felt that activism in Finchley was generally at a low ebb, and she told CCO, 'I fear the division as a whole has not been very dynamic in the past', and thus that she was encouraging the local party membership to make 'great efforts to further the Conservative cause.'[40] To this end she wrote to the party's joint chairman, Oliver Poole, to get him to send a message to encourage the founding of new Young Conservative branches.[41] Altogether, Thatcher looked to energize Finchley with the form of activism she had displayed 10 years earlier at Dartford. She seems to have succeeded, for the Conservative vote climbed in 1959 and Finchley only became vulnerable after she retired from the Commons in 1992.[42]

Professionalism rather than personal charisma was the hallmark of Thatcher's politics at the local level, and this was later to be translated onto the national stage. Thatcher's Labour opponent at the 1959 general election described her as cold and lacking interest in the human side of politics and political issues. This could be seen as standard electoral fare, but such comments did not come from the Labour side alone. In 1962 the Conservative deputy agent, who had spoken so highly about Thatcher's professional abilities in 1958, visited the Finchley Conservatives' Annual General Meeting, and she reported to CCO that 'Mrs. Thatcher made her usual competent speech. It is a pity that with such a good endowment of brains and beauty she has so little humanity.'[43] Throughout her career Thatcher's *political* persona was always described as cool, and even the anger she expressed over certain issues has been described as chilly or frosty rather than passionate or incandescent. One of her political allies in the Conservative Party has described Thatcher as 'puritanical and committed to the work ethic',[44] and this is difficult to gainsay. Thatcher viewed politics, and her own politics in particular, as *serious* matters, and, as a consequence, humour was not her métier. Shortly after Thatcher resigned, the then US ambassador to the UK, Henry Cato, told Tony Benn that he had never heard Thatcher tell a joke,[45] and one of her main speech writers has indicated that it was difficult for Thatcher to see the value of humour unless it contained or contributed to a clear political point. Few politicians in twentieth-century British politics have been quite so exclusively or relentlessly political.

Deadlier than the male?

Margaret Thatcher's first major public appearances came in late 1949 and early 1950, when she was Conservative candidate for Dartford. At the time a great deal of attention was focused on the fact that she was a woman. The day after her adoption Marjorie Maxse described her as 'very attractive looking with a quiet efficiency',[46] which was not how she spoke about male candidates. Not all of this attention was positive. For example, the Conservative MP for Chiselhurst, Sir Waldron Smithers, wrote to Conservative Central Office (CCO) to complain about her selection, stating that 'I was at a meeting on the borders of the Dartford Division, and was asked the question why a young girl of 23, Miss Margaret Robertson [sic], had been selected as Candidate for Dartford? Could not they have got some prominent business man, etc. etc. etc. etc. etc.'[47] An attempt was made to mollify Smithers, and he was informed that 'Miss Roberts created an excellent impression when she came to this office', but given Smithers' misogyny and diehard conventionalism the attempt was unsuccessful.[48] Thatcher's opponent was equally unimpressed by her candidacy, but unlike Smithers preferred to deploy condescension as opposed to outright hostility. Hence, the *People*'s 'Man from Man', who covered Thatcher's public debates with her Labour opponent, referred to her as a 'glamour girl' and reported that 'Mr. Dodds [the Labour MP for Dartford] thinks a great deal of her beauty but not a lot of her election chances – or her brains.'[49]

Thatcher's sex was to be a recurrent issue in her early political career. She failed to win Dartford either in 1950 or 1951, but she sought to secure other candidacies in the 1950s. In the summer of 1952 CCO noted that Mrs Thatcher, as she had become, 'because of marriage ... wished to be put in cold storage', but that she also wished to remain politically active.[50] CCO was keen to encourage Thatcher to remain in politics. The Home Counties South-East area agent, who had witnessed her in action in Dartford, described Thatcher as 'The best woman candidate she has ever known.'[51] This view was shared by other members of CCO, and one official described Thatcher as 'a woman of immense personality and charm with a brain quite clearly above the average.'[52] This particular CCO officer had warned Thatcher about 'the horrors of life in the House of Commons, especially in so far as this life effects [sic] the home', but Thatcher was 'not deterred'.[53] In March 1953 she became a mother of twins, but it was not motherhood that led her to ask CCO to remove her name from the list of possible candidates, for in January 1954 she explained to John Hare of CCO that it was her being called to the Bar that had prompted her to make this request; she told him, 'I have quite made up my mind to pursue law to the exclusion of politics.'[54] She soon changed her mind, for in December 1954 she agreed to CCO sending her name to Orpington,[55] and in March 1956 she wrote to Donald Kaberry and requested that he fully reactivate her political career by placing her on the candidates' list,[56] albeit 'for safe Conservative seats only'.[57] Several constituencies shortlisted Thatcher before she secured the nomination at Finchley in 1958, and in her memoirs Thatcher argues that her failure to secure selection before this date was in no small part due to the reluctance of local party committees to adopt a mother of young children as a candidate.[58] Thatcher was certainly concerned about this at the time, for in 1958 she went to CCO specifically to discuss 'the prospects in a variety of constituencies in realtion [sic] to women candidates.'[59] This discussion seems to have resulted from Thatcher's experience on a shortlist at Maidstone, when 'She was asked about her ability to cope as a Member, having in mind the fact that she had a husband and a small family.' The local agent felt that Thatcher's reply, in which she mentioned her 'excellent nanny ... did not a lot of good,'[60] although the president of the Maidstone Division reported that 'This lady should surely be in Parliament soon.'[61] Even when she was adopted for Finchley, Thatcher's concerns about sexual prejudice in the party were not assuaged, and she told Donald Kaberry, 'I am learning the hard way that an anti-woman prejudice among certain Association members can persist even after a successful adoption meeting but I hope it will subside.'[62]

Thatcher's umbrage reflected her own, publicly stated views on working mothers. In 1952 she had written an article for the *Sunday Graphic* entitled 'Wake Up Women', in which she used examples of female public figures, such as the Queen, to argue that women could have a family and a career; and turning to politics, Thatcher asked, 'Why not a woman Chancellor or Foreign Secretary?'[63] Two years later Thatcher expanded on this theme in an article for the CCO magazine for Young Conservatives, *Onward*, in which she scorned the idea that 'a woman's place is in the home' and argued that for a woman 'it is essential both for her own satisfaction and for the happiness of her family that she should use all her talents to the full.'[64] Over the course of her political career, particularly in her first decade as an MP, Thatcher frequently restated this argument, but at the same time she never abandoned the arguments that being a housewife could be 'the most worthwhile occupation in the world',[65] and that 'The welfare of her family is the prime concern of nearly every woman.'[66] Thatcher reconciled these positions by reference to her own career, first at the Bar and then in Parliament: she stated that careful organization and time management had been crucial to her, and that she had ensured that her home had been run on her lines, even when day-to-day supervision of the children and house had been delegated to nannies and domestic help.[67]

In 1949 Thatcher's sex had been the focus of attention during her first candidacy, and when she was adopted and elected in Finchley in 1959 little had changed, for it was as a *woman* MP that Thatcher was often singled out. In 1961 Thatcher was moved to tell the Women's Citizens Association in her constituency that 'in local government and parliament women were being accepted, though they were once thought of as "rather peculiar creatures".'[68] Evidently they had not been fully accepted or deemed wholly 'non-peculiar' by the mid-1960s, for in early 1965 Thatcher told the *Daily Express* that for women, 'It appears to be more difficult to get adopted for safe seats than before.'[69] Thatcher's own seat was safe, and in 1962 she had been appointed to a junior ministerial post, but at the 1966 general election the *Daily Telegraph* found the fact that Thatcher's labour opponent was a woman to be worthy of comment.[70] Much of the comment upon and response to Thatcher as a female politician trivialized her politics. In the case of the press this was unsurprising, but others were equally guilty. For example, when Thatcher was appointed to a junior ministerial post at the Ministry of Pensions in 1962, the Permanent Secretary there, Sir Eric Bowyer, seems only to have noted that 'she would turn up looking as if she had spent the morning with the coiffeur and the whole afternoon with the couturier'.[71] Such references to Thatcher's physical appearance were commonplace. Many articles in the press commented on her 'good looks', and the instant biographies that appeared when she became Conservative leader echoed this view.[72] Shortly after her election as leader she was asked by *The Times*, 'How much of a help or hindrance has it been to be a good-looking woman?'[73] Thatcher's response indicated a degree of irritation, for she noted that, 'As soon as I came into politics people would say "brains and beauty". I thought, well, how silly.'[74] Her irritation was confirmed in 1978 by Patrick Cosgrave, for she told him that she disliked all discussion of her looks.[75] That being said, Thatcher, especially as Conservative leader, did pay a great deal of attention to her appearance,[76] and she was clearly aware that her femininity could be politically useful. In 1958, following her selection as candidate for Finchley, she wrote to Donald Kaberry, and, having mentioned her concern about a latent anti-woman prejudice in the local party, told him, 'You may be interested to know that I wore the outfit you said I was to wear the night I was finally selected.'[77] Although not openly coquettish, this remark implicitly flattered an ostensible flatterer and used a tone and an approach that Thatcher was frequently to deploy in her later career. When interviewed for the BBC documentary on Thatcher's Downing Street Years, James Prior remarked upon Thatcher's ability flirtatiously to exploit her femininity, and another colleague later stated that 'she was quite capable every now and then of – almost deliberately – turning on a feminine charm.'[78] In many respects it was understandable that Thatcher used her femininity, especially given her difficulties, as seen above, securing a candidacy in the mid-1950s. It may well have been the case that, in the late 1960s, her position as an able *woman*, one of only 7 in a Conservative parliamentary contingent of 253, did as much as anything else to recommend her to Edward Heath and the party hierarchy. But although it may have been helpful it was by no means either good for personal morale or indicative of a promising future.

British politics in the third quarter of the twentieth century was a masculine world, and Conservative politics even more so. For a woman trying to make her way in that world the issue of 'double conformity' was difficult to overcome. Thatcher's position, and the development of her career, embodied the dilemma that a woman politician, and above all a Conservative woman, faced at that time. A Conservative backbencher, Ernest Money, said in his admiring 1975 biography of Thatcher that 'she is a feminist, but not in a militant sense.'[79] In many respects this was a fair description. There were a number of times in the 1960s when Thatcher addressed issues to which feminists attached considerable significance. Perhaps the most significant of these was equal pay. At the Conservative Party Conference of 1969 a party document 'Fair Shares for the Fair Sex' was debated. Thatcher declared in the debate on this document that

> there are two factors which we must keep in mind. Many women will still make their main job in life the creation of a home. Others at some time in their life will go out to work and possibly seek a part-time job suitable to their special circumstances. Yet others – some married women and some single women – will carry out the same jobs with equal competence and under the same conditions as men. We must make provision for all of these circumstances, but let us recognise that perhaps the most important job of all is the creation of family and family life.[80]

Thatcher's position on 'the woman question' was that of a middle-class 'domestic feminist', in so far as she valorized women's domestic roles and argued that they should be as highly valued as any career. In part this helps to explain why, as one commentator noted in 1978, 'she regularly invokes, and identifies with, the image of the housewife.'[81] At one level it was a populist image, but it required a vocabulary and imagery that was directed at a particular audience and which deliberately eschewed any hint of 'women's lib'. This was the essence of an interview she gave in 1961, when a woman journalist from the *Daily Express* asked Thatcher if it was her 'view ... that all wives should, if possible, have a second career?' Thatcher replied

> I hate those kind of sweeping generalisations. I hate the division of wives into those who go out to work and those who stay at home. I believe myself the real dividing line is something quite different ... There are good wives and bad wives, good mothers and bad mothers. You can stay at home all day and every day, and still bring up your children appallingly.

As a result of this interview the *Express* journalist reported that Thatcher had 'sent me on my way, more of an ardent feminist myself than ever' as she had 'met a genuinely emancipated woman at last'.[82] This was a somewhat paradoxical outcome, for one of the last words Thatcher would have used to describe herself was 'feminist', and when she was asked by Patrick Cosgrave about her views on 'women's lib' she replied, 'what has it done for me?'[83] Indeed, Thatcher stated in her second volume of memoirs that her own experience had shown that feminist arguments were wrong, inasmuch as it had been women at selection meetings in the 1950s who had opposed the appointment of a mother of young children as a candidate.[84]

Thatcher's experience as a woman Conservative MP was, prior to becoming party leader, typical of the general experience of Tory women, and even after she became leader and prime minister the position did not change dramatically. That the latter would be the case was to some extent apparent during the 1975 leadership contest. Shortly after she had announced her candidacy she received a letter from a Conservative voter and local party member who told her that although he was 'a life-long Conservative', he would 'never accept a woman Prime Minister – not even you.'[85] Misogynistic local Conservatives were one thing, but the problem existed at higher levels in the party. One of Thatcher's backbench supporters told her, 'Don't worry about the anti-woman complex',[86] but it was clearly something she had grown used to being anxious about. Even after she had won the first ballot Thatcher was not wholly reassured, and understandably so. Her main opponent in the second ballot, William Whitelaw, did not seek to play the anti-woman card, and he was to play a central and loyal role throughout her leadership and premiership, but in 1980 he confessed to Penelope Murray that Thatcher frightened him and that in fact he was frightened of all women politicians;[87] it is, to say the least, unlikely that he was an isolated example. Just before the ballot, when she defeated the 'cowed' Whitelaw, Thatcher was asked by ITN's Julian Haviland about the prejudice of Conservative MPs against women, and she went only so far as to say, 'I think that is gradually melting.'[88] The thaw lasted for 15 years, but the chill never ended and, ultimately, was to help freeze Thatcher out.

The grocer's daughter

That John Campbell chose *The Grocer's Daughter* as the title of the first volume of his fine biography of Thatcher is understandable. As leader of the Conservative Party and prime minister, Thatcher was often identified and identified herself as the product of a relatively modest background – the child of a middle-class grocer and a family that had provided her with the opportunity for advancement on the basis of their 'Victorian values' of self-help, hard work, thrift and belief in self-improvement. As leader of the Opposition, Thatcher referred to her upbringing in Grantham on 11 occasions, and as prime minister on 28, although she rarely went into detail. Early in her ministerial career she had sought to defend the interests of small shopkeepers against the effects of the abolition of Resale Price Maintenance, and in the process pointed out that 'her father had owned two shops in the grocery trade.'[89] Six years later, shortly before she was to enter the Cabinet, the *Sun* wrote of Thatcher that she 'likes to describe herself as the daughter of a Grantham retail grocer. "[And] was an ordinary girl who went to a fairly ordinary grammar school,"'[90] and this image was to become a central feature of her political/biographical persona as her high-level career took off.

On close examination, Thatcher's image as 'Grantham woman' unravels somewhat. Campbell has noted that after she arrived at Oxford as an undergraduate, and especially after her marriage to the metropolitan Denis, Thatcher comprehensively discarded her Lincolnshire roots. Certainly she made it clear to CCO after 1951 that she was only interested in safe London, or preferably Kentish, seats and her personal and political compass was focused on the south-east. As Campbell points out, the fact that neither of her twins has any strong memories of their grandfather, who died shortly before their seventeenth birthdays, indicates that neither Grantham – nor indeed the Roberts family – loomed very large on Margaret Thatcher's post-1951 horizon. Perhaps most telling of all in this context is an interview Thatcher gave to Brian Walden at Downing Street in January 1981. She spoke about the influence of her father upon her views and Walden asked her when he had died. Thatcher was flummoxed and asked one of the staff at No 10 to check for her. She was 'reminded' by this assistant that her father had died in 1970, at which point Thatcher declared that 'He died when I was Secretary of State for Education ... and a member of the Cabinet', and she recalled his pride about this development in her career.[91] This indicated a significant lapse of memory, for Alfred Roberts had died at the end of February 1970, which was nearly four months before Thatcher entered the Cabinet. It may have been that Thatcher was feeling pressed at a difficult time in her premiership, but all the same it is difficult to grasp how she could have forgotten and then misdated the timing of the death of a man who had featured so prominently in both her own and her publicity machine's presentation of her formative years and influences. It is difficult to avoid the conclusion that Thatcher's provincial past was largely a product of image-making, perhaps to compensate for the fact that Denis Thatcher's wealth had led to their becoming an embodiment of metropolitan wealth, with a home in Chelsea and their children at expensive public schools.

Leaving aside the provincial aspect of her image, Thatcher was, from the outset of her parliamentary career, keen to identify herself with the middle classes. In 1961 Thatcher told the Finchley Conservative women that 10 years of Conservative government had produced greatly increased living standards in Britain, and that 'This was not something contemptible or sordid [and] nor was the acquiring of middle class values so bad.'[92] But if Thatcher was clear that Conservative governments benefited the middle classes, she was even more certain that Labour governments were their committed enemies. In May 1966 she attacked the Labour Government's budget for 'indulging in ... rather contemptible old-fashioned class hatred',[93] and concluded that the Wilson administration had demonstrated that 'The first lesson of Socialism is increased taxation ... and it is the middle income group who have to pay most.'[94] But it was in the six months between the Conservatives losing the electoral campaign of October 1974 and the ensuing Conservative leadership campaign that Thatcher made her strongest statements with regard to the defence and furtherance of middle-class interests. In an interview with Thatcher, the *Evening Standard* noted that 'there is a considerable air about Mrs Thatcher of "the middle class c'est moi", and she does indeed embody almost all of its virtues and weaknesses'. Thatcher's own contribution confirmed this, for she argued that Keith Joseph, who was then viewed as the most likely challenger to Heath, was 'perfectly right' when he declared that Britain was witnessing 'the twilight of the middle class'. She went on to restate her views of 1966, that the Labour Party was bent on putting Britain back to being a 'class-ridden society', and she added that in defending middle-class values she was not defending a particular income group but 'a whole attitude to life ... to take responsibility for oneself'.[95] The *Evening Standard* concluded that Thatcher 'has often claimed to dislike being branded as the apostle of the middle class. But today, when the middle class are under economic assault as never before, she is perhaps their most forceful and dedicated defender.'[96] Indeed, during the leadership campaign early the next year she made it clear that a watchword of her 'kind of Tory Party' would be that 'To stand for "middle class values" is no bad thing', and she argued that her actions as Minister of Education, notably her defence of direct grant and grammar schools, had demonstrated her commitment. Thatcher noted that as a result of these actions she had been 'attacked for fighting a rearguard action in defence of "middle class values"', but declared that she had been proud to do so on the grounds that

> if middle class values include the encouragement of variety and individual choice, the provision of fair incentives and rewards for skill and hard work, the maintenance of effective barriers against the excessive power of the State and a belief in the wide distribution of individual private property, then they are certainly what I am trying to defend.[97]

This was picked up as a major theme by the press during the leadership contest. Cummings, the *Daily Express* cartoonist, captured Thatcher's presentation in his depiction of her as 'St. Joan Margaret de Finchley. Saviour of the Middle Classes. Scourge of the Lower Orders & the Left'.[98] This was not an identity her campaign sought to play down. At her press conference after her victory in the first ballot it was pointed out that John Gorst, one of her backbench party campaigners sitting beside her, was 'one of the leading lights of the new Middle Class Association' and that his prominent role, along with Thatcher's own statements, indicated that 'The implication was that she was promoting the Conservative Party as a middle-class orientated party.'[99]

Nor was Thatcher's identification with the middle class simply a 'horse for the course' of the leadership contest – it remained a central motif throughout her leadership and her premiership. Immediately after she became leader Thatcher declared that 'my patience has been sorely tried by recent attempts to drive a wedge inside the Tory Party between those who are alleged to represent middle class values and those who – presumably – stand for something quite different'.[100] Her impatience was in part informed by her view that these values – her values – had a wide social resonance and catchment. For example, in May 1977 she wrote an article for the *Sunday Telegraph* on 'How Tories Will Face the Unions', in which she argued that the values of hard work, skill, reward for effort, law and order, self-discipline, standards in education and the idea that individuals and not institutions should care for others were all working-class values, and not an exclusive middle-class preserve,[101] and a year later she underlined this message when she told the *Sunday Times* that in her youth 'We were taught to help people in need ourselves not to stand about saying what the government should do. Personal initiative was very strong. You were actually taught to be clean and tidy ... All these ideas have got saddled as middle class values, but they are eternal ...'[102] Eternal, perhaps, but, equally important, Thatcher felt these values were widely held, and in particular by the aspirational sector of the skilled working class. It was here that Nigel Lawson came to feel there was an important difference between Thatcher and himself and other close economic policy-making colleagues, in that neither he nor Geoffrey Howe nor Leon Brittan had 'Margaret's instinctive identification with the interests of the upper working and lower middle classes as she conceived them,'[103] and by the mid-1990s Thatcher saw this as one of the main reasons why her successors had 'failed' to defend her political and social legacy, for in 1996, with the Conservative Party in a deep slump, she argued, 'We are unpopular, above all, because the middle classes – and all those who aspire to join the middle classes – feel that they no longer have the incentives and opportunities they expect from a Conservative government.'[104]

But if Thatcher saw one of her main objectives as being to expand the middle class, she was also keen to defend, and certainly not offend, the existing members of that social group. The sale of council houses was an important element of the Thatcherite goal of bringing about working-class embourgeoisement, but there were limits to the measures that were deemed acceptable. In this context, when

Peter Walker – who, as Minister of the Environment in Heath's administration, introduced the first 'Right to Buy' legislation for council-house tenants – suggested that long-term tenants simply be given their properties, Thatcher opposed the idea. Thatcher felt that such a move would upset 'our people', who had struggled to pay mortgages on their homes.[105] Thatcher's use of the phrase 'our people' was important here, for, since the 1950s, it had become commonly used Conservative shorthand for the party's core, middle-class constituency. Thatcher's colleagues were also wont to use the expression, and grasped its importance to their leader. In his memoirs Geoffrey Howe notes that whenever the topic of MIRAS came up for discussion, as it did on several occasions in the 1970s and 1980s, Thatcher always opposed any suggestion of its being reduced or abolished 'because it was of special value to "our people"'.[106] But in this specific context Howe himself had known exactly which 'people' were being referred to, for in early 1976 he had argued that the Conservatives, when they took office, should not keep the MIRAS level at the standard rate of income tax as this would be 'another blow to middle management.'[107] Moreover, there was for Thatcher a link between the idea of 'our people' and her identification of allies within the party as 'one of us'. Hence in her memoirs she explained that her Conservative opponents disliked her and her policies because

> In the eyes of the 'wet' Tory establishment I was not only a woman but 'that woman', someone not just of a different sex but of a different class, a person with an alarming conviction that the values and virtues of middle England should be brought to bear on the problems which the establishment consensus had created.[108]

Thatcher felt that the middle-class values of independence and self-help had been subjected either to attack or condescension and that their incomes had been hit by punitive taxation, as a result of their having been caught between the millstones of Socialist organized labour and/or guilt-ridden privilege.

Looking back on her own career, Thatcher described herself as 'a Conservative revolutionary',[109] and, in relation to her championing of the middle class, this was a fairly accurate description. In 1976 Keith Joseph, Thatcher's 'general spiritual and intellectual solace'[110] in the party, wrote an essay in the *New Statesman* which suggested that the absence of a true 'bourgeois revolution' in British history lay at the root of the country's modern economic 'decline'. In Joseph's view the middle-class leaders of the industrial revolution had failed to establish political ascendancy and had instead allowed the aristocracy to establish patterns of economic and social governance which had, ultimately, proved inimical to entrepreneurial success.[111] Here Joseph echoed scholars of the New Left and anticipated the work of the historian Martin Wiener,[112] but in Joseph's case, he, like Thatcher, sought to recast the socio-political mould, and, in terms of the economy and the social and political culture of the Conservative Party, bring about a belated 'bourgeois revolution'. The early Victorian Liberal, Richard Cobden, was referred to by one historian as 'the Marx of the middle classes', and Thatcher was in many ways a late twentieth-century version, with aspects of her political economy as well as her core support consciously echoing that of Cobden. In a different vein, Denis Healey once referred to Thatcher as 'la Pasionara' of the middle classes, and, although this comparison had no appeal to Thatcher, it cannot be gainsaid that she was seen, and saw herself, as the great champion of the middle classes. For a 'wet' Conservative critic like Ian Gilmour, Thatcher's 'suburban' politics and values led the Conservative Party to 'retreat behind a privet hedge', but for a left-Labour critic like Tony Benn, Thatcher's class politics had a more sinister aspect. In September 1975 Benn told the Belgian politician, Henri Spaak, that Thatcher was 'trying to build up the Conservative party on a narrow class basis', to which Spaak replied that, 'She seems to me to be a bit of a Fascist.' Benn was not prepared to go quite this far, and instead suggested, 'well, Poujadist perhaps'.[113] The suggestion that middle-class activists in the Conservative Party could be compared to Poujadistes had been made by some members of the Conservative leadership in the late 1950s, and in a wholly disparaging way. Macmillan in particular had made scathing references to the discontented middle class and had sought to prevent the party from being aligned with middle-class interests. Thatcher, however, actively sought to identify herself and her party with the middle class. In 1977 the committee set up under Thatcher to discuss small business policy stated that their work carried 'the risk of encouraging Poujadist tendencies',[114] but nonetheless they concluded that 'Concern for the small business sector and the self-employed should not be an occasional apologetic after-thought. It should take its place naturally at the heart of our economic and industrial strategy.'[115] Thatcher's frequent references to her own background as a grocer's daughter and her equally frequent pleas for small businesses encouraged the use of the Poujadist shorthand. Indeed, one of her great admirers, the Conservative political writer Russell Lewis, noted soon after she became leader that to fixed income suburban managers, clerks, professionals or small businessmen with mortgages, who felt disadvantaged and intimidated by trade unionists, Thatcher carried a reassuring message, but perhaps 'too reassuring some might say, thinking that it smacks too much of Poujadism.'[116] To call Thatcher a Poujadist was inaccurate, but the use of the term was significant. The way it was deployed in the 1950s and 1970s was as a shorthand for militant campaigners for middle-class interests, particularly those concerned with shopkeeping and small businesses. This was exactly how Thatcher wished to present herself, in contrast not only to the Labour Party but also to her own predecessors as leader of the Conservative Party, who, she contended, had neglected the interests of this section of society and, equally important, this core element of the Conservative grass roots.

The ideologist

In June 1987, during a pre-election interview on the BBC's *Panorama*, Sir Robin Day told Margaret Thatcher, 'you have stamped your image on the Tory party like no other leader ever has before. We never heard of Macmillanism; we never heard of Heathism; we never heard of Churchillism.[117] We now hear of Thatcherism.'[118] To some extent, Day was right, for in 1987 the term Thatcherism was not only used by political commentators in Britain (and indeed much of the world), but had become part of everyday language. It was also true that none of Thatcher's near predecessors had been granted an 'ism', but a common error that arose as a result of statements such as this was the notion that 'Mrs Thatcher is the only Prime Minister whose name has given rise to an "ism"'.[119] In fact, Thatcher was not unique in this respect. In the nineteenth century 'Gladstonianism' was used by both allies and enemies of the Liberal prime minister and continued to be used long after his death.[120] Similarly, Beaconsfieldism was coined as a political pejorative by Disraeli's Liberal opponents, and the terms Chamberlainite and Chamberlainism were attached, again by both friend and foe, to the various programmes Joseph Chamberlain pursued during his career. Thatcher may have been the first British politician for 70 years to have had an 'ism' conferred upon her, but she was *not* the first.

An ideology demands ideas, and it is the social and political purchase of those ideas which transforms them into an ideology. Thatcher herself played very little part in generating the ideas that were at the heart of the Thatcherite agenda. Her most extended, 'formal' contribution to contemporary political debate was her 1968 CPC lecture, 'What's Wrong With Politics?', but this paper, although it anticipated many themes that were to become associated with Thatcherism, articulated and synthesized arguments that were already circulating in Conservative circles. This was characteristic of Thatcher's political thought. She was not an original thinker, bur rather she both drew upon and drew together the work of other thinkers. This has been commented upon by a number of Thatcher's biographers, by scholars and also by some of her acolytes. In 1975 Ernest Money wrote that 'she may not be the most intellectual [politician]',[121] but shortly after her friend and admirer Patrick Cosgrave argued that Thatcher was 'more interested in matters of general policy and political philosophy than was fashionable'.[122] Nor was it only Conservatives who thought this, for Harold Wilson described Thatcher as 'much more ideological than any Conservative leader I've ever known . . . both an intellectual and moral ideology',[123] and Tony Benn argued that she was 'a serious intellectual woman.'[124] The fullest scholarly biography of Thatcher has confirmed these somewhat contradictory descriptions, and noted that 'No intellectual herself, she was nonetheless unusual among politicians in acknowledging the importance of ideas,'[125] which in turn confirms the notion that Thatcher 'was a consumer of ideas produced by others.'[126]

Thatcher herself never claimed that the ideology that took her name was original. In fact she frequently stated that it was not: in 1988 she told *The Age* that Thatcherism would live on after her 'because it started before me', and only a month before her resignation she told her constituents, 'Thatcherism is much older than I am . . . I have only recreated it'.[127] Exactly what Thatcher thought she was recreating in terms of 'much older' ideas will be examined in chapter 1. Here this book will briefly introduce how Thatcher sought to 'consume' and also propagate ideas with which she agreed. At an institutional level Thatcher drew upon a number of think tanks, most notably the Institute of Economic Affairs (IEA) and the Centre for Policy Studies (CPS).[128] The latter had been founded by Keith Joseph in the spring of 1974 to generate social and economic ideas different to those which Joseph and Thatcher deemed the governing orthodoxies of post-war Britain. Moreover, the CPS was consciously designed as a source of alternative ideas to those offered by the Conservative Research Department (CRD), which was perceived by Joseph and Thatcher as having absorbed and assimilated those ortho-doxies. Indeed, it was only when Thatcher became Conservative leader and appointed Angus Maude as Chairman of CRD that she began to draw on the party's own think tank for advice. With regard to individuals, Keith Joseph was the single most important direct influence on Thatcher, as she herself was to acknowledge. As to other close colleagues, Thatcher once remarked that in her Cabinets she had thought it essential to have 'six good men and true', which indicated to some that she felt Jesus Christ had been overmanned. But there were many of 'Thatcher's people', as John Ranelagh called them, who were not high-level Conservative politicians. Ranelagh, who was himself one of the 'people' he later wrote about, numbered them at about 30, ranging from veteran politicians like Enoch Powell to political thinkers like Alfred Sherman and Shirley Letwin and successful busi-nessmen like John Hoskyns and Norman Strauss.[129] Thatcher could not be called an intellectual herself, and she rarely sought to present herself as one. But although Thatcher's pretensions did not stretch quite that far, she did like to have close contact with intellectuals, both collectively and individually, as if, as another of her 'people' noted, she was 'working on her image in history as a great stateswoman surrounded and respected by the leading brains of the time.'[130]

There may have been something to George Urban's rather jaundiced, even cyn-ical, view, but to focus on this narrow biographical point is to miss the political importance Thatcher attached to ideas. A few weeks after she became Conservative leader, Thatcher told the Federation of Conservative Students (FCS) that 'we find ourselves . . . as we were in 1945, faced with a situation in which far too many of the influential opinion-formers are left-wing in outlook.'[131] In this situation Thatcher argued that the only way forward was to promulgate Conservative ideas and arguments and to offer a forceful, wide-ranging alternative to Socialist thought, and she stated that 'The intellectual counter-attack is as important as the counter-attack in Parliament and in the constituencies.'[132] Thatcher felt it was particularly important to 'influence the whole climate of *edu-cated* public opinion',[133] and hence she told the FCS that they could help provide the party with a cadre of informed proselytes in the constituencies. But a question remained as to who would educate and proselytize the proselytes, and here the role of university teachers and researchers was deemed crucial. A few months after the leadership election Thatcher told Joseph, 'I am anxious that we should devel-op closer links with the Universities',[134] and shortly after she informed Baroness Young, 'I have appointed Leon Brittan to be the official link between the acade-mic world and the Parliamentary Party . . . As you know, I am very anxious to improve the Party's relationship with academics and I am hoping that we can get results soon.'[135] In early July Joseph was told that there was a vein of support here that could be tapped, in that

> A small number of academics are known to be willing to help the Party ... but nowhere is there an effort to co-ordinate their efforts and assess the Party's requirement of them ... The Party wishes to establish firm links with Academics and their Departments, to utilise the research facilities they can provide and to 'aright' the left swing balance whenever possible in the media especially through television interview/discussion programmes and in the specialist journals/articles and weeklies.[136]

Thatcher felt that it was important to garner ideas and support from the academic community and that this would doubly benefit the party. To begin with, academics could provide the party with a reservoir of ideas, and at the same time they could, both directly and indirectly, influence their students. Both of these were deemed crucial by Thatcher, for her view was that 'If we can win the battle of ideas, then the war will already be half-won'.[137] To Thatcher, ideas, and especially political ideas, were an essential part of demonstrating that she was not the leader of 'the stupidest party', and, equally important, that the Conservatives were headed by someone who could offer leadership in this battle.

Legacy

When Thatcher stated that she did not invent Thatcherism, her principal aim, as will be seen in chapter 1, was to position her ideas within a heritage of intellectual weight. However, this analysis will show that the formal intellectual base of Thatcherism is of less importance to contextualizing and understanding the roots of Thatcherism than long-standing arguments and trends in the Conservative Party's subculture since 1945. Thatcherism was not only a part of a 'battle of ideas' between Thatcher and her opponents on the Left, but also between her, her supporters and their opponents within their own party. Thatcherism was a product of a 'struggle for the soul of the Tory Party',[138] and this was a struggle which, in spite of the unceremonious way in which the party forced her resignation, Thatcher won comprehensively. It is essential to separate Thatcher from Thatcherism, and this study will show that if she herself did not go 'on and on and on' her eponymous ideology did.

This book's desire to 'depersonalize' Thatcherism will be in keeping with its general approach to Thatcher's career. It will not examine her ideas and policies in terms of her personal beliefs, but rather will look at the way she constructed responses to a range of issues on the domestic and foreign policy fronts and sought to adopt strategies to maintain political and electoral support both within and behind the Conservative Party. That she was able successfully to achieve this for 15 years was in part attributable to her political determination and skill, but it was also due to good fortune. Thatcher's opponents both on the Left and within her own party made life easier for her. The split in the Labour Party in 1981 and the subsequent formation of the SDP-Liberal alliance meant that for two of her three election victories Thatcher faced a divided opposition. As a consequence it mattered not that the Conservative share of the vote fell over the 1980s and that Thatcher's party gained its highest share of the vote in 1979. In turn, the Conservatives' successive electoral triumphs marginalized internal party opposition to Thatcher, for in politics little succeeds like success, and it was the fear of electoral defeat that was to crystallize internal party opposition to Thatcher. But it was to be Thatcher and not Thatcherism that the Conservative Party jettisoned in 1990. Moreover, after her resignation, Thatcher sought to ensure that the Conservative Party remained on what she deemed to be a true Thatcherite course, often to the discomfort of her successors. In 2001 John Major, who had himself been damaged by the fact that Thatcher had hovered over and occasionally swooped upon his leadership, was asked whether he felt that his own successor had been hampered at the general election of that year 'by an excessive emphasis on Thatcherism in the Tory party'.[139] Nor was it simply Conservatives who were troubled by Thatcher's legacy, for, from the mid-1990s on, voices were raised on the Left that Thatcher and Thatcherism had had a profound political impact on the Labour Party. On both the Right and Left, with regard to both domestic and foreign policy, Thatcher's legacy is as profound in the early twenty-first century as it was in the late twentieth.

1

Thatcher, Thatcherism
and Conservatism

In 1987 Sir Robin Day asked Thatcher if she could define the doctrine that had taken her name, enquiring, 'What is it that Thatcherism means?'[1] Even in 1987 this was a vexed question. Nigel Lawson, who has claimed to have coined the term Thatcherism, has defined it as 'a mixture of free markets, financial discipline, firm control over public expenditure, tax cuts, nationalism, "Victorian values" (of the Samuel Smiles self-help variety), privatisation and a dash of populism.'[2] The journal *Marxism Today* also has strong claims to having been the source of the term, but the editors and authors who popularized its use in that periodical in the early 1980s defined it along the same lines as Lawson.[3] Political and scholarly interpretations of the origin and meaning of Thatcherism burgeoned in the course of the 1980s and 1990s, and some are discussed below. This study will begin, however, with Thatcher's own views about what Thatcherism was, what it was seeking to achieve and where it came from.

The first time Thatcher used the term Thatcherism was only a few weeks after her election as party leader. She told the Conservative Central Council that her opponents were trying to label her and her supporters as 'extremist Right-Wingers', but she declared that she was pleased to know that 'To stand up for liberty is now called Thatcherism.'[4] At this point Thatcher did not discuss the meaning of Thatcherism, and it was over 10 years later that she produced her first definition of the term in an interview with *Der Spiegel* in April 1985. There she stated that 'my own definition . . . is really sound financial policies and sound industrial policies against a background of limitation of the power of the State in order to give freer rein to the talents and abilities of the individuals and companies to make the most of the available opportunities.'[5] She expanded on this in her 1987 election interview with Sir Robin Day. When he asked her, 'What is it that Thatcherism means?' Thatcher's reply again stressed the centrality of an approach to the economy, but she also argued that broader social objectives were part of the Thatcherite programme. Thatcherism, she stated, stands for sound finance and Government running the affairs of the nation in a sound financial way. It stands for honest money – not inflation. It stands for living within our means. It stands for incentives . . . It stands for the wider and wider spread of ownership of property, of houses, of shares, of savings. It stands for being strong in defence – a reliable ally and a trusted friend.[6]

Later that year she presented a variation on this theme when she argued, again in *Der Spiegel*, that 'The management of property, whether it is a home, whether it is your shares or savings, building up your own security for the future, brings a sense of responsibility . . . that is what Thatcherism is'.[7] Freeing the economy from the 'dead hand of the State' was to provide individuals with the opportunity to exercise their talents to the full and thereby enable them to take responsibility for their own fate. Indeed, 'rolling back the frontiers of the State' was to force people to be free, in so far as they would have to rely on their own actions to obtain security rather than depend on others in the form of taxpayer-subsidized industries or benefits. Reducing the scale of State activity and giving more scope to the individual, providing incentives for effort through cutting the level of personal taxation, encouraging people to acquire and pass on property in the form of houses and equities, all established a link between economic freedom and the ability to exercise and fulfil personal choice.[8] What Thatcherism provided, according to Thatcher, was 'the politics of liberty and justice backed up by the economics'.[9]

In order to achieve these ends the chief aim of Thatcherism was to 'roll back the frontiers of the State' in the economic and social spheres. The State was to remain strong with regard to defence – in order to be a 'reliable ally' – and 'law and order'. This was to provide the essence of what one political scientist has termed the Thatcherite 'strong State'. But, as the same scholar has argued, the other side of the Thatcherite coin was the 'free economy'.[10] This last was to be achieved by replacing the mixed economy with a private-sector-dominated market economy. This was to be complemented by a reform and reduction of the welfare state, a lowering of direct personal taxation and the encouragement of wider property ownership. Institutions which hampered the operation of the market, notably trade unions, were to be curbed. Finally, low inflation – sound money – rather than full employment was to be the main goal of economic policy. In short, Thatcherism sought to dismantle the policy structures that had come to be defined as the 'post-war settlement' or the 'post-war consensus'.

For Thatcher personally these were long-standing goals. When she had first stood for Parliament in 1950 her election address had emphasized eight key points, and five of them – a call for cuts in personal taxation, hostility to nationalization, praise for private enterprise, extending home ownership and the maintenance of strong defence – were to be central to her later career.[11] Nor were these the only elements of her early political position that were to echo down the years. At the 1949 Annual General Meeting of Dartford Conservative Association it was recorded that 'Miss Roberts stressed that the security a family could have by saving its own money, buying its own house and investing, was far better than the ordinary security one would get from any national scheme.'[12] A few months later she underlined her message and declared that 'personal responsibility is the keynote to the future of the country.'[13] Twenty years later she made almost the identical point, telling an audience in Sweden that there were limits to what governments could and should do in the realm of welfare: 'They can', Thatcher argued, 'ensure that state welfare, although adequate, does not either prevent people from making their own provision for themselves and their families, from taking an interest in their children's education or from helping each other.'[14] A leitmotif of Thatcher's leadership of the Conservative Party and her premiership was her 'conviction that the welfare state creates a culture of dependency.'[15] Her goal was to change this culture, for, as Thatcher's press officer noted, she and her close colleagues felt that 'Britain needed to accept some good old fashioned personal responsibility'[16] – exactly the vocabulary the young Margaret Roberts had used.

The corollary of Thatcher's emphasis on personal responsibility was hostility to State intervention. In the run-up to the 1975 Conservative leadership election Thatcher declared that 'the Government was intervening far too much'. She contrasted this with her own position in which 'the whole philosophy is to keep power in the hands of the people and to limit the power of the State.'[17] For Thatcher and the Thatcherites the main culprits in the growth of the State had been Socialists. In a paper he produced for the 'Policy Group Exercise' he and Thatcher set up in the spring of 1975, Keith Joseph, Thatcher's intellectual mentor, argued that

> In Socialist thinking the State is dominant . . . The Conservative view is more subtle and more complex. We have, if anything, an even greater sense of patriotism and public service but we do not see this as exclusively expressed through the elected public authorities. We recognise rights, responsibilities and freedoms of the individual, of the family, of voluntary bodies and other institutions such as companies as valuable in themselves and needing to be strengthened rather than weakened in a healthy society.[18]

After Joseph's death Thatcher summed up what she thought was one of his main contributions to their political project, namely that he had seen that 'What marks out our Conservative vision is the insight that the State – Government – only underpins the conditions for a prosperous and fulfilling life. It does not generate them'.[19] But Thatcher and her followers felt that Conservative governments had also fallen into the Statist trap. Two months after Thatcher became Conservative leader Joseph produced a lengthy analysis of the party's past mistakes and possible future strategies. In this paper, which was circulated to the Shadow Cabinet, Joseph noted that a key error of post-war Conservative administrations was that they had 'competed with the Socialists in offering to perform what is in fact beyond the power of government.'[20] Thatcher and her colleagues argued that their

party should seek to reduce the scale of State activities and allow individuals maximum liberty under the law to develop their abilities and sense of enterprise. This
objective lay at the heart of Thatcher's political philosophy. In the summer of
1988 she told *Svenske Dagblat* that the goal of Thatcherism had been to give free
play to the British character, which had been constrained by the 'shackles of
Socialism', and that this had demanded that the role of government be mini-
mized.[21] Thatcher's hostility to State intervention also informed her increasingly
critical view of the European project. Thatcher saw European enthusiasts, whether
politicians or officials, whether Left or Right, as having a predisposition to think
in collectivist or corporatist categories, both of which she saw as subsets of
Socialist thought – hence her denunciations of the 'centralising', 'federalist' – that
is, Statist – drift of the EU.

In an article she published in the *Daily Telegraph* in late January 1975, which
was essentially her 'manifesto' for the leadership election, Thatcher argued that

> people believe too many Conservatives have become socialists already.
> Britain's progress towards socialism has been an alternation of two steps
> forward with half a step back ... If every Labour Government is pre-
> pared to reverse every Tory measure, while Conservative Governments
> accept nearly all socialist measures as being 'the will of the people' the
> end result is only too plain. And why should anyone support a party that
> seems to have the courage of no convictions?[22]

That Conservatives could have come to be regarded as Socialists was a result of
what Thatcher and her followers saw as their ongoing failure since 1950 to reverse
Labour's Statist legislation. Here Thatcher was openly critical of the idea of 'consensus', or the notion that there had come to be key policy areas where the ideas
of the main political parties had converged. On this point Thatcher's view was
perhaps unsurprisingly close to Joseph's; in 1974 he had used the idea of a 'ratchet effect' to explain the progress of Socialism in Britain. Joseph's argument was
that whereas Socialist governments had enthusiastically turned the ratchet of the
Statist cogs, Conservative governments had supinely failed to turn them back,
with the result that they had become 'stranded on the middle ground'. But
Thatcher was not simply echoing Joseph. In October 1968, in a CPC lecture on
'What's Wrong With Politics', she had stated that

> There are dangers in consensus; it could be an attempt to satisfy people
> holding no particular views about anything. It seems more important to
> have a philosophy and policy which because they are good appeal to suf-
> ficient people to secure a majority. No great party can survive except on
> the basis of firm beliefs about what it wants to do.[23]

A few months later she made it clear that consensus was precisely what was
'wrong with politics', for she told *Daily Telegraph* readers that 'In politics,

certain words suddenly become fashionable. Sometimes they are just words. Sometimes they reveal a whole attitude of mind and influence the development of thought. Then they can be dangerous and set us on a false trail. Consensus is one of these.'[24] In October that year she went further, and told the magazine *Time and Tide* that 'The main weakness in opposition . . . is the failure to make the difference between the two parties more distinct – "this has not been got across"'.[25] Thatcher was critical of the idea that there could be any meaningful convergence between what she saw as the irreconcilable philosophies of the Labour and Conservative Parties; and during and after 1975 she made it clear that 'her' Tory Party would offer the electorate a real choice. Thatcher and Thatcherism rejected consensus as 'the process of abandoning all beliefs, principles, values and policies in search of something in which no-one believes, but to which no-one objects'[26] and instead offered the politics of 'conviction'. In the context of the mid- to late 1970s, when academics as well as political commentators had begun to chart the history of an apparently extended 'post-war consensus',[27] Thatcher's position seemed radically new. But she had been openly critical of the idea of consensus in the late 1960s, and, as will be shown below, her views were shared and had been equally long held by many in her party. As was the case with a number of the positions that came to be regarded as Thatcherite, Thatcher articulated rather than created anti-consensus sentiment[28] in the Conservative Party.

But if at one level the roots of Thatcherism can be traced to intra-party debates over Conservative policy in the 1950s and 1960s, it also had more 'formal' roots. Thatcher herself identified three thinkers as key influences on her ideas – Adam Smith, J.S. Mill and F.A. Hayek. At a press conference in Edinburgh in September 1987 she expressed surprise when it was suggested that Thatcherism was less popular in Scotland than in England, and argued that Thatcherism could be described as 'Adam Smithism',[29] given that Smith and his Scottish Enlightenment contemporaries had been trailblazers for the idea of the free market.[30] Smith was particularly important for Thatcher because he was, as she was keen to point out, a 'moral philosopher' and not simply an economist. She felt that Smith's pattern of thought anticipated her own in so far as he had indicated that free market economics were necessarily linked to broader social and cultural principles. Likewise, she praised J.S. Mill's defence of individual liberty, which, she felt, supported her view that liberty gained its fullest expression within the framework of the law. Friedrich Hayek was, however, the thinker she felt closest to. She underlined Hayek's importance in her 1996 Keith Joseph Memorial Lecture, in which she argued that

> The view which became an orthodoxy in the early part of this century – and a dogma by the middle of it – was that the story of human progress in the modern world was the story of increasing State power . . . progressive legislation and political movements were assumed to be the ones which extended the intervention of the government.

It was here that Thatcher felt Hayek played a vital role, in that 'It was in revolt against this trend and the policies it bred that Hayek wrote *The Road to Serfdom*, which had such a great effect upon me when I first read it – and a greater effect still when Keith [Joseph] suggested I go deeper into Hayek's other writings.'[31] Smith, Mill and Hayek, because of what she saw as their commitment to the economic, social and moral benefits of free enterprise, individual liberty under the law and hostility towards the extension of the State, were, in Thatcher's view, forerunners of her own philosophy and policy agenda.

Of the three thinkers Thatcher picked out, Hayek was the figure that she and Thatcherite politicians and thinkers referred to most frequently.[32] As well as her remarks in her Joseph Memorial Lecture there is also the story of Thatcher banging the table at a meeting, with a copy of Hayek's *The Constitution of Liberty*, and declaring, 'this is what we believe'.[33] Thatcher also claimed in 1985 that Hayek 'has been one of my staunchest supporters', and was clear that 'the conservatism which I follow does have some things in common with what Professor Hayek was preaching'.[34] The more formal statements of her political beliefs appear to confirm that this was the case, for they were redolent with Hayekian language and precepts, particularly those relating to liberty, markets and the rule of law.[35] It was in this last context that Thatcher's position was close to *The Road to Serfdom*, the political text she cited most often, for in that work Hayek identified individual freedom with political freedom, and political freedom with market freedom under the civil equality of the rule of law.[36] Whether or not Thatcher was an avid reader of Hayek's work is not really relevant. What is important is that she, and many of her supporters, chose to identify Hayek and his work as a major influence.

The emphasis Thatcher placed on Hayek is important in terms of identifying the nature and meaning of Thatcherism. If Hayek's *The Constitution of Liberty* was the embodiment of what Thatcher felt she and her party 'believed', it was somewhat problematic that the last chapter of that book was entitled 'Why I Am Not a Conservative', and also that, late in life, Hayek said, 'I am becoming a Burkean Whig'.[37] Thatcher's intellectual heroes, Hayek, Smith and Mill, pose a problem in terms of positioning Thatcherism as a political ideology, for they are all figures who occupy, in different ways, positions in the pantheon. At the time of the 1975 leadership contest Thatcher declared that what she stood for was 'true Conservatism',[38] and in 1977 she stated very firmly, 'I am not a Liberal.'[39] This was not a view that was shared by one member of her first administration, who told a newspaper in 1982, 'I am a nineteenth-century Liberal. So is Mrs Thatcher. That's what this Government is all about'.[40] More important still, Thatcher herself proved willing to accept publicly that her political philosophy 'has some things in common with ... old-fashioned Liberals,'[41] and in 1996 she stated in her Joseph Memorial Lecture that 'The kind of Conservatism which he [Joseph] and I ... favoured would be best described as "Liberal". And I mean the Liberalism of Mr. Gladstone not of the latter day Collectivists'.[42] In spite of her insistence that Thatcherism was 'traditional Conservatism',[43] Thatcher herself accepted that at the heart of her doctrine was a blend of Liberalisms, with classical nineteenth-century Liberalism melded with neoliberal ideas.[44]

Revolution

Thatcher once described herself as 'a Conservative revolutionary,'[45] and some of her close colleagues echoed this by referring to themselves as 'radical Conservatives.'[46] The problem for some Conservatives was that Thatcher and Thatcherism were too revolutionary and radical, in that their political ideas and goals, as evinced by their proximity to Liberal and neoliberal thought, were at odds with what they deemed 'true' Conservatism. At the 1975 Conservative Party Conference Edward Heath informed journalists that Thatcher and Joseph were not Conservatives but 'fanatics', whose ideas would ruin the Conservative Party.[47] Given its provenance this remark was hardly unbiased, but if Heath's bitterness made him one of the first to voice this opinion he was by no means the last. That the former Conservative prime minister, Harold Macmillan, chose to republish his book *The Middle Way* in 1978 was not simply because it was the fortieth anniversary of the first edition. Macmillan, who had initially welcomed Thatcher's election as leader, was concerned that Thatcher and her associates were taking the Conservative Party in the wrong direction, and his celebrated critique of liberal market economics was offered as a corrective. Moreover, it was a corrective Macmillan continued to advocate until his death in 1986.[48] Nor was it only former Conservative leaders that voiced such concern. Within Thatcher's Shadow Cabinet from 1975 to 1979, and also her first Cabinet in government, there were many who shared Heath and Macmillan's views. Those who came to be known as the 'wets', notably Ian Gilmour, Francis Pym, James Prior, Peter Walker and Christopher Soames, had strong reservations about Thatcher's policy agenda. To an extent personal politics played a part here, in that most of the 'wets' felt an ongoing loyalty to and sympathy for Heath, but this should not obscure the importance of the fact that they expressed their antipathy towards Thatcher in ideological terms.

Ian Gilmour was perhaps the most eloquent of these critics of Thatcherism. He was dismissed from the Cabinet in the autumn of 1981, but he had voiced concerns long before. In February 1980 his lecture 'On Conservatism' to the Cambridge University Conservative Association made clear that Thatcher's emphasis on liberal market economics was at odds with Conservatism's traditional social concerns, an argument he reiterated that summer and consistently pressed throughout the 1980s and 1990s.[49] When Gilmour was dismissed from the Cabinet he told journalists that the Government was heading for political disaster – 'steering full speed ahead for the rocks' – but his antagonism to Thatcher was rooted in his unwillingness to accept her desire to unify the party around her vision of Conservatism. For Gilmour and other 'wets', Thatcherism was not Conservatism but a bastardized form of nineteenth-century Liberalism. Francis Pym's 1984 publication, *The Politics of Consent*, portrayed Thatcherism as the child of nineteenth-century Liberalism, and the short-lived movement he led within the party, Centre Forward, was presented as a home for adherents of 'traditional' Conservatism on the basis that it sought a middle ground between Socialist Statism and laissez-faire Liberalism.[50] In a similar vein, the longest-serving of Thatcher's 'wet' ministers, Peter Walker, remarked in his memoirs that he found Thatcherism to be at odds with Conservatism because 'We fought the Liberals in the nineteenth century because we disagreed with laissez faire. We [Conservatives] believed in intervention'.[51] For anti-Thatcherite Conservatives, Thatcher's 'revolution' simply sought to replace Conservatism with Liberalism.

Thatcher's open admiration of 'old-fashioned Liberals' only served to confirm her opponents' case. In 1983 she told the Conservative Party Conference, 'I would not mind betting that if Mr. Gladstone were alive today he would apply to join the Conservative Party.'[52] This echoed a speech made by Thatcher's father at the meeting in February 1949 when his daughter was adopted as prospective Conservative candidate for Dartford. Alfred Roberts had said that 'by tradition his family were Liberal, but the Conservative Party . . . stood for very much the same things as the Liberal Party did in his young days.'[53] Two years before Alfred Roberts made this statement the Conservatives had cemented their alliance with the National Liberals and, following a 'pact' negotiated by Lord Woolton and Lord Teviot, the two parties had announced a 'United Front Against Socialism'. Between 1947 and the general election of 1950 a large number of local Conservative associations added 'Liberal' to their title, and when the Liberal Party effectively failed to contest the 1951 general election, former Liberals over-whelmingly transferred their allegiance and their votes to the Conservatives. One interesting individual example of this late 1940s trend is Thatcher's first Chancellor, Geoffrey Howe. Howe's father, like Thatcher's, had been a Liberal, and his Welsh family's Liberal tradition was even stronger. In his memoirs Howe recalls that when he was a student at Cambridge in the late 1940s the university Liberals were in decline, and he had come to the conclusion, *because* rather than in spite of his Liberal upbringing, 'that the post-war Conservative party should inherit the Liberal mantle'.[54] The notion that Thatcherism's Liberal inflections were at odds with Conservatism can be contested on the grounds that the post-1945 Conservative Party had consciously set out to assimilate Liberal nostrums as part of the process whereby it attracted and absorbed former Liberals. Indeed this process had arguably been under way since the 1880s, when the Liberal Unionist defectors from Gladstone's Liberal Party, especially the Whig element, brought their ideas as well as their support and votes into the Conservative camp. It was thus possible for Thatcher's admiration of Liberal thinkers and ideas, and for their influence upon her ideological stance, to be seen in relation to long-term trends in the Conservative Party's development.

Certainly Thatcher was by no means the first Conservative politician to accept and indeed welcome the influence of Liberal ideas on the party. In the interwar years Stanley Baldwin had consciously sought to make his party a congenial political home for old Liberals, and Thatcher's father was but one testimony to his success. Writing in 1949, Nigel Birch had noted that although Conservatives had opposed Liberalism in the nineteenth century, it was right that, after 1945, they should espouse laissez-faire ideas because 'to-day they are seeking to preserve what was of lasting value in nineteenth-century Liberalism against the ever-increasing aggression of an authoritarian State'.[55] Ten years later Lord Hailsham echoed this point when he argued that 'Laissez-faire economics were never orthodox Conservative teaching and Conservatives have only begun to defend them when there appears to be a danger of society swinging too far to the other extreme'.[56] The essential argument was that nineteenth-century Conservatives had supported State intervention in order to rectify the social, economic and political imbalances caused by extreme laissez-faire Liberalism. However, in the twentieth century, and especially after 1945, the threat of imbalance was coming from the other direction in the shape of Socialist Statism, and hence laissez-faire Liberalism was acceptable as a counterbalancing philosophy. The notion that a dose of anti-Statism was needed to rectify the imbalance caused by 30 years of doctrinaire Socialist and misguided Conservative Statism lay at the heart of Thatcher's political, economic and social agenda. Hence, when Lord Home was asked, in 1979, whether Thatcher had, as she had told Patrick Cosgrave in 1978, 'changed everything' in the Conservative Party since becoming leader, his response was:

> I don't think she's changed the traditional Conservative approach. I think what she has done is to change the economic direction – the direction of economic policy – and by and large this fits in with a good many Conservative interpretations, that the State should interfere in the mini-mum way – that the intervention of the State in industry should be kept to a minimum ... We have always aimed to tread that path, but in post-war years it's been extremely difficult to keep the State out of it.[57]

Myth, betrayal and 'true' Conservatism

Home's early defence of Thatcher's Conservative credentials can in part be attrib-uted to his own ideological predisposition, for he had been the candidate favoured by the Right of the party in 1963, at a time when Conservative backbenchers – and even more so the grass-roots membership – were beginning seriously to ques-tion the party's post-war policies. But if Home was not a wholly disinterested observer, his view that Thatcher was seeking to redress an imbalance that had developed since the war with regard to the role of the State was widely shared within the Conservative Party. Had this not been the case it would have been more difficult for Thatcher and her followers to defend themselves against the charge that Thatcherism was a departure from the party's traditional precepts.

From the beginning of her leadership, Thatcher enjoyed strong support in the middle and lower ranks of the parliamentary party and quickly established a devoted following in the constituency associations. Here, the primary short-term factor that worked for Thatcher was widespread disappointment in the Conservative Party with regard to the Heath Government, the failings of which were deemed responsible for the party's two election defeats in 1974. In his memoirs William Whitelaw noted that 'The period following the second 1974 Election was an unhappy one inside the Conservative Party'.[58] This was a piece of characteristic understatement by Whitelaw, who also remarked that, as Chairman of the Conservative Party at the time, he 'observed from one particular vantage point the bitterness, dissension and general bad feeling in the Parliamentary Party'.[59] Among the Conservatives who felt most bitter, both within and outside the parliamentary party, were those who were to become Thatcher's strongest supporters in the leadership election of February 1975, in her Cabinets from 1979 to 1990 and, in some cases, after her resignation. Norman Tebbitt, Nicholas Ridley, Cecil Parkinson, Lord Young and Keith Joseph were unhappy with the way the Tory Party had been led off course from 1970 to 1974, and felt that the Conservative Party during Edward Heath's premiership had lost touch with its principles, its sense of political direction and, as a consequence, the electorate.

The main cause of unhappiness in the Conservative ranks was the Heath Government's 'betrayal' of its supposed promises of 1970 to pursue a radical policy agenda. The term most frequently used as a shorthand to describe what had been betrayed was 'Selsdon'. For Conservative critics of the Heath Government, the Conservative Shadow Cabinet Conference at the Selsdon Park hotel in Croydon in February 1970 had taken on mythical status. The term 'Selsdon Man' was coined by the then Labour Prime Minister, Harold Wilson, in an attempt to ridicule and condemn the outcome of the Conservatives' policy deliberations. In effect he suggested that the Conservatives had embraced Stone Age economics and were bent on clubbing the British economy and dragging it back to a liberal-market cave. This was typical Wilsonian knockabout, but the combination of his remarks and the press coverage of both them and the Selsdon Conference created a climate of expectation, especially among the Conservative rank and file, that the Conservatives, if elected, would pursue a liberal-market strategy. In fact, 'Selsdon Man' was the political equivalent of Piltdown Man. The Selsdon Park Conference, as minutes of its discussions reveal, did not see the development of a clear policy programme, and there was very little discussion and certainly no adoption of a liberal-market economic strategy.[60] However, neither Edward Heath nor any of his Shadow Cabinet sought vigorously to counter the representation of Selsdon Park, and the Selsdon myth began to take hold. Heath himself spoke before the general election of June 1970 of his desire to bring about a 'quiet revolution', and in his speech to the Conservative Party Conference in October that year, which was both a celebration of election victory and a statement of intent, Heath declared that his government's aim was 'to change the course of history of this nation'. This modest task was to be achieved, Heath argued, through policies to

> reorganize the function of government, to leave more to individual or corporate effort, to make savings in government expenditure, to provide room for greater incentives for men and women and to firms and businesses . . . to encourage them more and more to take their own decisions,

to stand firm on their own feet, to accept responsibility for themselves and their families.[61]

Furthermore, in its first year of office the Heath administration appeared to confirm that it had embraced a new approach to governing the economy. The Industrial Reorganization Corporation was abolished, the Industrial Expansion Act was repealed, seven of the regional Economic Development Councils ('little Neddies') were scrapped, the Mersey Docks and Harbour Board was allowed to go into liquidation, the Land Commission was abolished and the Prices and Incomes Board was wound up. All of these were regarded as key elements of 'Socialist' corporatism, and their removal was greeted with enthusiasm by the Conservative Party rank and file. On taxation the government also seemed to make all the right moves. The first Budget saw the basic rate of income tax reduced by 6d (2.5p), a 25 per cent cut in corporation tax, and the phasing out of the Regional Employment Premium and Selective Employment Tax.[62] The government also promised a tough stance on trade unions, and December 1970 saw the publication of the Industrial Relations Bill. In its first year the Heath Government seemed to be marching to the beat of a liberal-market drum, and this rhythm clearly appealed to many in the Conservative middle and lower ranks.

In 1972–73, however, the government engaged in what famously became known as an economic policy U-turn. The notion that there was any such dramatic reversal of policy has been played down in some studies of the Heath Government.[63] There is a logic to this argument if one accepts that 'Selsdon Man' was a myth and that the government was not committed to a coherent liberal-market strategy to begin with. If such was the case then there could of course have been no U-turn, and the argument that there was a change of direction becomes another piece of historical-political mythology. But here the resonance of the 'myths' of Selsdon and the U-turn is precisely what makes them important. Without exception, the memoirs of Thatcher's close political allies highlight the experiences of 1970–74 as formative. For example, Lord Young comments that 'when Ted Heath paraded Selsdon Man I perked up. Here at long last was the realization that the wealth of the nation has to be created by its citizens and not by the government . . . [and that] the 1970 election seemed to bring a ray of hope to us all.'[64] Likewise, Norman Tebbitt notes that the 'Selsdon declaration . . . marked the Tory Party's first repudiation of the post-war Butskellite consensus' and that 'the 1970 manifesto . . . was music to the ears of radical Conservatives like myself'.[65] In the same vein the Heath government's deployment of State intervention in industry, particularly the 1972 Industry Act, has been depicted by these men as a clear break with the 'promises' of 1970, even an adoption of 'Socialist' strategies,[66] and a demonstration that 'the conversion of both Ted Heath and the Party to the Selsdon programme' was only skin-deep.[67] It may have been that Tebbit, Young, Ridley and others were deceived by the Selsdon 'myth' and in turn created their own 'myth' of a U-turn, but even before the fall of the Heath

Government these myths had become some of those 'myths we live by' – just as 'real' as any 'objective' assessment of the events of 1970–73. Why else should those Conservatives who dissented from the government's policies have formed themselves in 1973 into the 'Selsdon Group' if the name in itself did not conjure up a particular political message? Why also should Edward Heath have been so keen to tell the party conference in 1973 that the promises of Selsdon Park had been fulfilled, unless he too understood its resonance?

The intensity of the disappointment in the Conservative Party over Heath's 'betrayal' of Selsdon stemmed from the feeling that 1970–74 had witnessed an opportunity to rectify long-term problems in British social and economic development in general, and Conservative policy in particular. Following the Conservative defeat at the general election in February that year, Keith Joseph delivered a series of speeches in which he argued that the root of Britain's problems lay not in the short-term policy failures of 1970–74, but in the mistaken strategies adopted by all governments since 1945.[68] At Upminster in June 1974 he stated that 'our industry, economic life and society have been . . . debilitated by 30 years of socialistic fashions', and he was equally clear that 'for half of that 30 years Conservative governments did not consider it practicable to reverse the vast bulk of the accumulating detritus of Socialism' and had failed to present an alternative vision.[69] For Joseph the key thing was for Conservatives to abandon 'bi-partisanship . . . [and] middle of the road policies' and adopt 'a distinctive Conservative approach'.[70] Joseph's views were echoed by others. Nicholas Ridley noted in his memoirs that he had first entered politics to reverse the Attlee Government's reforms,[71] and Cecil Parkinson argued that 'the failure of the Conservative governments of 1951–64 to reverse the Attlee experiment was deplorable'.[72] Conservative critics of the Heath Government depicted it as the last in a line of post-1945 Conservative governments which had accommodated themselves to Socialism and failed to implement truly Conservative policies. The most succinct statement of this position was produced by Joseph, who declared in 1975 that 'It was only in April 1974 that I became converted to Conservatism'. This was a remarkable statement by someone who had been a member of the Conservative Party for over 30 years and a minister in three Conservative administrations. What Joseph meant was that after the fall of the Heath Government in February 1974 he had embraced a policy approach underpinned by liberal-market economic policy, and that this represented true Conservatism. This view was shared by many other Conservatives, who, in the late summer of 1974, saw Joseph as the champion of 'true Conservatism' most likely to offer a challenge to Heath's leadership. But by early 1975 Joseph had ruled himself out as a contender for the party leadership and the devotees of 'true Conservatism' looked instead to Margaret Thatcher.

The sense of betrayal and disappointment that surrounded the fall of the Heath Government was pervasive within the Conservative Party. However, the strength of this feeling cannot be fully understood unless one acknowledges that the election victory of 1970 was seen by a powerful body of Conservative opinion as the climax of a 25-year battle against not only the Labour Party's Socialism but also the 'quasi-Socialism' of their own party's failure to dismantle what, by the 1970s, many scholars and commentators had come to refer to as the 'post-war settlement'. However, from the outset, many in the Conservative Party felt that nothing had been settled.

As early as 1950 there were calls from within the Conservative ranks for the party to develop and embrace a distinctive, radical alternative to the Attlee Government's reforms, particularly in the realms of social and economic policy. These demands were to grow in intensity during the 1950s and 1960s, and were to take a variety of forms. At one level they appeared in the guise of 'popular' rank-and-file protests. In 1950 the Conservative Party Conference unanimously passed a modernized version of Dunning's motion, and declared that 'Government expenditure has increased, is increasing and ought to be diminished.' This was to be the first of many such declarations, but whereas in 1950 it was directed at the Attlee Government, thereafter Conservative conferences produced a constant flow of motions critical of the Churchill, Eden and Macmillan Governments for failing to repeal the reforms introduced between 1945 and 1951. Through the 1950s the Conservative grass roots voiced almost constant hostility to nationalization, State intervention, the welfare state, high personal taxation, trade unions and inflation. Nor were party conferences the only medium through which the grass roots expressed their resentment. Independent protest movements appeared, notably the Middle Class Alliance (MCA, founded in 1956) and the People's League for the Defence of Freedom (PLDF, also founded in 1956). The MCA campaigned on all of the issues that represented the recurring complaints at Conservative conferences, whereas the PLDF was a single issue, anti-trade union movement. Both caused the party hierarchy concern, for although neither organization challenged the Conservatives at by-elections, the CCO committee that investigated their activities and membership concluded that they were – the MCA, in particular – made up of disgruntled former members of the Conservative Party and ex-Conservative voters.[73] Such leakages of support saw the Conservatives experience some very uncomfortable by-election results between 1955 and 1959, often in seats they would normally have regarded as filled with their core constituency. As a consequence, several internal party policy committees were established to examine ways to appease backbench and grass-roots opinion on the nationalized industries, inflation, taxation and trade unions – and all of these committees saw much criticism of the existing status quo. That the Conservatives won the 1959 general election without having acted on these criticisms was in no small part due to the impact of the one response they did make, in that the Budget of 1959 introduced the then largest ever single reduction in the basic rate of income tax. Nevertheless, shortly after the election a Conservative Party Committee was set up to examine the future of the social services, with a remit to find ways of reducing the size of the welfare state and its budget. The ghost of grass-roots criticism of the 'post-war settlement' could not be easily laid to rest.

The 1960s saw liberal-market views enjoy continued and indeed extended popular prominence within the Conservative Party. Studies of local Conservative opinion in this decade have shown that there was widespread and growing insistence that the party establish a more distinctive approach to the economy. Hence the London Area Conference of 1965 insisted on 'an assurance that the next Conservative Government will govern by true Conservative principles, not seeking electoral popularity by the adoption of quasi-Socialist measures', while the North Cornwall Conservative Association demanded in February 1966 that there should be 'a return to Conservative principles with greater emphasis on individual freedom and less control from government.'[74] The language and the underlying message of these statements was strikingly similar to the arguments that had been frequently voiced at party conferences in the 1950s. The only difference was that in the 1960s the party hierarchy was more in harmony with, or at least more responsive to, grass-roots opinion.

On the issue of trade union reform the pressure from local Conservative associations continued unabated. In 1963 the former leader of the PLDF, Edward Martell, reappeared as chairman of Hastings Conservative Association, and the Conservatives began the long march to the 1971 Industrial Relations Act. A similar journey began in relation to the mixed economy, in that, after Heath's election to the leadership in 1965, arguments for the denationalization of State-owned industries burgeoned at the centre as well as the periphery of Conservative politics.[75] It was also after 1965 that the general Conservative approach to the governance of the economy veered towards 'Powellism', in terms of its original meaning as a statement of faith in liberal-market economics. Across a broad front of policy options and arguments the critics of the 'post-war settlement' were gaining strength through the 1960s. Thatcher's position, as expressed in her articles on 'What's Wrong With Politics?' and 'Consensus or Choice', reflected this. In this respect, if Thatcherism existed *avant la lettre* at a popular level within the Conservative Party, Thatcher had shown herself to be in tune with its essential precepts long before she became Conservative leader and the term Thatcherism became part of the British political vocabulary.

The rise of Thatcher and Thatcherism in the Conservative Party reflected a change in the dynamics of the relationship between the party leadership and the Conservative constituency. Thatcher's self-presentation as a 'conviction politician' was to lead her to demand that the Conservative Party establish a clear, distinctive policy identity that reflected the beliefs and desires of the Conservative grass roots. Arguments like this had been common currency at Conservative Party Conferences in the 1950s and 1960s, but Thatcher was the first leader to accept and articulate these positions. In his memoirs Nigel Lawson has commented that 'Harold Macmillan had a contempt for the party, Alec Home tolerated it, [and] Ted Heath loathed it. Margaret genuinely liked it. She felt a communion with it'.[76] Harold Macmillan, albeit from a different perspective, expressed a similar view. After seeing Thatcher at a party conference he remarked on the contrast to his own period as leader, noting that we [his Cabinet] used to sit there listening to these extraordinary speeches urging us to birch or hang them all or other such strange things. We used to sit quietly nodding our heads and when we came to make our speeches we did not refer to what had been said at all . . . But watching her . . . I think she agrees with them.[77]

From 1975 to 1990 (and beyond) Thatcher had a unique hold over the party rank and file, which was in part a product of the electoral success the party enjoyed under her leadership, but also due to the fact that, for the first time, the Conservative middle and lower ranks felt they had a leader who shared their preferences and prejudices. This had been clear at the time she was elected as leader. The response to both her decision to stand for the leadership and her victory, as expressed in the letters she received from members of the public, indicated that she had struck a chord. One of her assistants examined the 245 letters and telegrams Thatcher received in the run-up to the leadership election[78] and noted that all but two were strongly supportive. It was probably reassuring for her to learn that 'A remarkable thing about these letters is that there is not one which is from anyone who is clearly mad. Unique in my experience of letters to public figures.'[79] To learn of the sanity of her public support was doubtless welcome, but equally welcome was the fact that some old parliamentary colleagues signalled their recognition, and approval, of Thatcher's intentions for precisely the same reasons she had given for standing. The former Conservative Cabinet minister, Lord Boyle, wrote to congratulate Thatcher on her election, and noted that

> Your decision to stand did not surprise me, remembering what you had said the last occasion we met, and the need (as you felt) for the admission of past errors in relation – not so much to this specific policy or that – as to the lack of rapport between the Conservative front bench and its supporters in the constituencies.[80]

In terms of contextualizing Thatcherism, the ideas, arguments and prejudices of the middle and lower ranks of the Conservative Party provide a route to understanding the 'popular' origins. Thatcher herself recognized this and constructed her appeal in these terms. Speaking at Finchley in January 1975 she explained and defended her decision to stand for the leadership and declared, 'I am trying to represent the deep feelings of those many thousands of rank-and-file Tories in the country – and potential Conservative voters too – who feel let down by our party and find themselves unrepresented in a political vacuum.'[81] To address the concerns of these people, Thatcher argued that the party need only raise the banners of what she and the party rank and file deemed 'true' Conservative values, for then, she argued, 'we shall not have to convert people to our principles. They will simply rally to those that are truly their own'.[82]

One nation and 'society'

Thatcher successfully constructed herself and her ideas as the expression of grass-roots Conservatism and the embodiment of a 'true' Conservatism forsaken by her predecessors, but there were links between the 'popular' origins of Thatcherism and its more 'formal' ideological roots. At the time of her election as leader, the veteran backbench MP Richard Thompson told Thatcher, 'The opposition had just ceased to be credible . . . People wanted a clean break, a new start, something to go for, a redefinition of policy and objectives, an end to the numbing me-too-ism which seems to have suffocated us for so long.'[83] Thompson's reference to 'me-tooism' chimed with statements made by Thatcher in her article, 'My Kind of Tory Party', but also echoed the sentiments expressed by some Conservatives in the immediate post-war period. Indeed, one group of Conservative MPs, which was formed in 1950, was particularly exercised by this issue, and their work was to play an important part in framing Thatcherism – they were the One Nation group.

In 1950 Iain Macleod had written to R.A. Butler to inform his former chief at CRD that the party's main aim should be to construct an approach to economic and social reform which was not 'me-tooing Socialist policies'.[84] Macleod himself was shortly to help produce a document which sought to do just this. As a founder-member of the One Nation group, Macleod was one of the authors of *One Nation*, which was published in 1950. The subtitle of *One Nation* was *A Tory Approach to Social Problems*, and its aim was to draw a clear distinction between the Conservative and Socialist positions on issues of social reform. Likewise, the second One Nation pamphlet, *The Social Services: Needs and Means*, written by Macleod and Enoch Powell and published in 1952, criticized the universalism of the welfare state and called for greater means-testing of benefits – all positions directly opposed to Labour's stance. In 1954, One Nation published *Change Is Our Ally*, the subtitle of which was *A Tory Approach to Industrial Problems*, and which called for a reduction in the scale and scope of State intervention in the economy and eulogized the role of the private sector and small business. The final One Nation publication of the 1950s, which was produced in 1959, was *The Responsible Society*, which argued that the creation of such a society required not government action but that individuals and groups acknowledge their responsibility for themselves and towards others.[85]

The work of the One Nation group and its members over time enables one to contextualize Thatcherism more fully within the development of the Conservative Party's political thought. When Sir Robin Day interviewed Thatcher on the eve of the 1987 general election he pointed out that many of the Cabinet ministers she had sacked since 1981 were identified as 'One Nation' Conservatives, and that they had accused her of pursuing socially divisive policies at odds with traditional Conservatism. Thatcher denied this and aligned herself with earlier 'One Nation' Conservatives. 'All my predecessors', she argued, yes, I agree Disraeli; yes, Harold Macmillan – I would say I am right in their tradition. It was Disraeli's one nation. We have had an increase in home ownership – the heart of the family under this Government . . . far more share ownership; far more savings in building society accounts. This is what is building one nation – as every earner becomes a share-holder as more and more people own their own homes . . . We are build-ing one nation through wider property-owning democracy.[86]

For Thatcher there was no difficulty in reconciling Thatcherism either with the Conservative tradition in general or with the more particular strand of 'One Nation' Conservatism. Her use of the phrase 'property-owning democracy', which had been popularized by Anthony Eden in the immediate post-war years, enabled her to link Thatcherism's objectives to one of the most important leitmotifs of post-war Conservatism.[87] In the 1950s, successive Conservative governments had sought to extend owner-occuppiership, with the Macmillan administration's aboli-tion of Schedule A taxation on homes in 1962 being the last in a series of fiscal and regulatory fillips to promote and benefit homeowners. Likewise Peter Walker, Secretary of State for the Environment in the Heath Government, had introduced the first 'right to buy' legislation to enable council tenants to purchase the prop-erties they were renting – a scheme which the Thatcher Governments extended and accelerated. Moreover, the notion of a 'property-owning democracy' had itself evolved out of the late nineteenth- and early twentieth-century Conservative idea of spreading property ownership to strengthen the 'ramparts of property' against Socialist assault.[88] Thatcher could thus plausibly claim that the growth of owner-occuppiership under her governments, fostered by the sale of council houses and the wider availability of mortgages as a consequence of financial deregulation, was in keeping with long-established Conservative goals. Thatcher could further claim that Thatcherism had not only built upon the particular tradition of encouraging home ownership, but had also, through the privatization of State-owned indus-tries and utilities, created a complementary 'capital owning democracy'.[89] The Conservative Party's evolution in the period from the interwar years to the 1970s has been described as one which can be understood in terms of the complex rela-tionship between its being a 'Party of owners or a Party of earners'.[90] Thatcherism can be seen in these terms, in that it sought to construct an environment in which 'earners' could become 'owners', both of real property and equities. This is what underpinned Thatcher's claim to be fulfilling the ideal of 'one nation', in that her goal was to facilitate the removal of institutional and social obstacles to, and pro-vide the opportunities for, the acquisition by all individuals of homes, capital and savings.

Thatcher's Conservative critics tended to describe themselves as the true inher-itors of 'one nation' ideals, and that is one reason why her claim to be part of this particular Conservative tradition has been viewed with scepticism. But here Thatcher's reputation has been ill served by historical misreadings of 'one nation' Conservatism. The phrase itself, as Thatcher acknowledged, originated with

Disraeli and the title (and theme) of his novel, *Sybil or The Two Nations*. Disraeli's two nations were, of course, the rich and the poor, and his supposed ideal was for the latter to realize its obligations to the former and thereby ensure that social inequality did not result in social conflict. But although Disraeli talked, and especially wrote, a good game of social amelioration, he had shown very little enthusiasm for the sport in terms of political practice.[91] This in itself is of only marginal importance, except in so far as it provides a fitting preamble to a consideration of the post-1950 One Nation group. In discussions of Thatcherism the One Nation group has often appeared as a precursor of 'wet' Conservatism, but this is a travesty in terms of the group's personnel and their ideas. Three of the leading figures in One Nation in the 1950s were Enoch Powell, Angus Maude and Keith Joseph, all of whom played an important part in the development of Thatcherism. Powell, of course, had left the Conservative Party before Thatcher became leader, but his economic ideas have been acknowledged as having influenced Thatcherite discussion groups through the 1970s and 1980s.[92] Angus Maude was appointed by Thatcher to be head of the Conservative Research Department and served in her first Cabinet, where he was singled out as one of the minority of 'true believers' in the administration. Joseph's contribution to Thatcherism is well known. An important point about all three of these individuals is that their ideas did not alter dramatically from the 1950s to the 1980s. One might assume that as Joseph underwent a 'conversion' in 1974, he must have renounced earlier 'heresies', but in fact his views remained consistent, as is very clear if one examines his contribution to *The Responsible Society*. Likewise, Powell was the co-author, with Ian Macleod, of *The Social Services*, which had argued, as did *The Responsible Society* seven years later, that greater private provision of pensions and health care would be both economically and socially beneficial in terms of reducing costs and taxes and creating a wider sense of personal responsibility. Powell was also joint author/editor, with Angus Maude, of *Change Is Our Ally*,[93] which had called for reduced State intervention in the economy and the promotion of free enterprise. One Nation may have taken a Disraelian moniker, but its 1950s publications had a strong liberal market flavour, and it was quite accurate for Thatcher to argue that her position was congruent with many of the original objectives of One Nation Conservatism.[94]

The overlap between One Nation and Thatcherism is made very clear if one examines at length the full background to and meaning of one of Margaret Thatcher's best-known, and also most misquoted and misunderstood, statements as prime minister. In 1987 she told the magazine *Woman's Own* that people had developed a tendency to cast 'their problems on society and who is society? There is no such thing.'[95] In the same interview she argued that instead of society there were 'individual men and women and there are families and ... It is our duty to look after ourselves and then also to help look after our neighbours ... life is a reciprocal business.'[96] Thatcher did not deny the existence of society as such, but objected to the use of the term as an abstract concept. For Thatcher the abstract concept of 'society' both informed, and was often coterminus with, an overemphasis on the 'social' role of the State, in so far as she contended that:

> Only if the State's role in our society is kept to modest dimensions will respect for it be combined with respect for the large number of private associations which contributes so much to the stability and richness of society. Associations ranging from business to charity, and from voluntary organisation to the family.[97]

Thatcher's position here was confirmed by an exchange she had with George Urban at a meeting of the Centre for Policy Studies (CPS) shortly after her resignation as prime minister and party leader. Urban suggested that a major problem of Central and Eastern Europe under Communist rule had been the collapse of civil society, which prompted Thatcher to demand, 'What on earth is civil society?' Urban explained that he meant 'all those customs and assumptions among individuals which are not regulated by law but upon which civilized living depends. They are distinct from the State; they are spontaneous', and having provided examples, such as the assumption that policemen help children cross roads, employees of charities do not embezzle contributions, and voluntary associations were indeed voluntary and did good works, he noted that Thatcher was 'mollified'.[98] K McFarlane

Urban's description of civil society as made up of spontaneously generated associational activity separate from the State expressed an important, long-running theme in Conservative thought which had been particularly pronounced in the post-1945 period. In 1947 David Clarke of CRD wrote that Conservatives, unlike Socialists, looked to 'intermediate organisations' rather than the State as the key facilitators of individual and social self-expression, by which he meant: 'Families, villages, towns and cities, churches, trade unions, provident societies, learned societies, charitable organisations, sports clubs and a thousand and one groups for this and that interest [which] compose the richness of our national life and add their voices to "this grand chorus of national harmony"'.[99] Here Clarke echoed, perhaps consciously, Quentin Hogg's hymn to civic associational life in his work *The Case For Conservatism*, which was published in the same year.[100] Nor were Clarke and Hogg alone in this. In 1949 R.A. Butler praised the 'vast array of voluntary associations for sport, for social activities, for material protection, catering for every class'[101] that existed in Britain, and the following year R.J. White stated that society was 'the product of a system of real relationships between individuals, classes, groups and interests', and he restated Burke's call for reverence towards the 'little platoons' of civic life that were the best expressions of spontaneous social interaction.[102] Enoch Powell presented an eloquent expression of this position when he stated in 1954 that 'the social services to the needs and standard of life of all members of the community is . . . something which ought to flow from the nature and organisation of the community itself'.[103] Given Powell's membership of One Nation, his statement has particular resonance in the context of this book's suggestion that even in the 1950s One Nation thought was, in important ways, anticipating an emphasis that was to be central to Thatcherite Conservatism and Margaret Thatcher's own view of the meaning of 'society'; but it was Angus Maude who was to provide the most important intellectual precursor to Thatcherite ideas on 'society'. In October 1966, in a paper on 'Modern Conservative Philosophy', Maude argued that Burke's

> conception of the 'spiritual unity of society' . . . has been swallowed up by the modern conception of 'society', which ought to be anathema to Tories. 'Society' . . . is now our real enemy. First, it has become the repository of all the primary responsibilities of individuals and families; all the claptrap about 'social security', the 'social conscience', 'social needs' and 'social action' . . . is an elaborate conspiracy of self-deception. Talking about 'social needs' absolves us from thinking about real people in distress and who could do with some help from other real people like us. 'Society' does not provide 'social security' which is State officials doling out the taxpayers money. 'Society' has no 'social conscience' only a vague and woolly benevolence anxious to absolve itself from personal action and difficult decisions about priorities. Secondly, and worse still, 'society' has become the ghastly statistical average of mediocrity to which everyone is now urged (or forced) to conform. It is incapable of action (it expects the State to do that for it), it only 'behaves', and its behaviour is statistically aggregated and averaged until the average becomes the 'norm' and finally the 'norm' becomes the morally right standard from which it is wrong (i.e. 'anti-social') to deviate . . . I think we have to destroy 'society' . . . First, because it is steadily eroding the notion of individual and family responsibility; and secondly because its 'conformity' is a sign of a sterile pessimism . . . in the individual's ability to live by standards of his own. Our main task is . . . to give people back some standards by which they can live individual lives.[104]

Maude's conception of 'society', as indicated by his constant placing of the term in inverted commas, is wholly consistent with the way in which Thatcher was to speak of 'society' in 1987. 'Society' was presented by Maude as an abstract and ultimately chimerical entity which had no relation to 'real' people and their relationships with one another. Furthermore, the barely concealed contempt Maude displayed when he wrote about 'norms', statistical aggregates and 'anti-social' deviance carried a clear implication that these terms were the work of abstract modellers and social theorists. For Maude, like Thatcher, 'society', as an abstract concept, was the enemy, and this was what needed to be destroyed.[105]

For Maude and his One Nation colleagues a priority from the outset was to develop and articulate 'A Tory Approach to Social Problems'. But this required not only a set of policy objectives, but also, as a necessary prerequisite, a Tory conception of the social. The conception that they developed, both individually and as a group, was of society as a network of spontaneous, associational relationships. In June 1962 the Young Conservatives' Policy Group, making specific reference to One Nation influence, stated that society was 'the whole sum of voluntary bodies and associations contained in the nation ... with all their various purposes and with all their institutions', from sports clubs to trade unions.[106] This, as noted above, was neither original nor unique, but the context and, equally important, the context of refutation, and the breadth and coherence of the One Nation group position, were indeed novel. Apart from their desire to valorize the 'little platoons', British Conservatives after 1945 – especially One Nation – placed increasing importance on the role of civic associations in deliberate contrast to what they saw as the Socialist attempt to undervalue such organizations in relation to the role of the State. *One Nation, The Social Services, Change Is Our Ally* and *The Responsible Society* all contrasted the 'Tory Approach' with that of State interventionist Socialism, which explains One Nation's emphasis on constructing 'a proper balance between the power of the State and the rights and initiative of the individual.'[107] But their idea of a 'proper balance' was informed by their view that Britain had 'swung away from laissez faire toward the opposite extreme of centralized planning and control', and thus had swung too far away from 'the general principle that freely-operating competition is the most effective means of promoting economic advantage.'[108] The notion of a 'proper balance' was at the heart of a fundamental aspect of Conservative thought throughout the twentieth century, namely that of reconciling the role of the State with agencies of civil society, with the latter always regarded as having the primary constructive role in the social and economic life of the nation.[109]

Thatcherism and the State

The input of One Nation members and One Nation ideas into Thatcherism at first glance strengthens the case made by Thatcher that her eponymous ideology was, if not 'true' Conservatism, then at least consistent with Conservative thought. Thatcher's trenchant anti-consensualist stance echoed the way One Nation had sought to construct social and economic policies that did not 'me too' Socialist positions. Furthermore, both One Nation and Thatcherism were, it seems, looking to strike a balance between the role of the State and the role of the private individual and private civic and business enterprise – an 'imbalance' having been caused by the advance of Socialism and by mistaken, or craven, Conservative 'appeasement' of that advance.

However, if the critique of Statism by Thatcher and the Thatcherites can be presented as part of the Conservative tradition, the emphasis on the individual and individualism, and the adoption of the neoliberal ideas of thinkers like Hayek, is more difficult to present in these terms, for historically Conservatives had been hostile to individualism. Party critics of the introduction of free trade in 1846 had depicted that policy as the expression of a broader, individualist social philosophy, and in contrast portrayed Conservatism as an organicist credo that rejected the Liberal/individualist notion that society was the sum of its individual parts. This criticism was restated by Edwardian Conservative social and tariff reformers, with the Unionist Social Reform Committee stating in 1914 that

> We have in this country now outlived that curious philosophic conception of the relations between the State and the individual which finds its origin in Rousseau and its most powerful exponents on this side of the channel in Bentham, the two Mills, Herbert Spencer and Cobden . . . [and that] the old Cobdenite and laissez faire view that the conditions of wages, health, housing and labour among the vast majority of the population of this country was the concern of private individuals and of private contract has long since been abandoned.[110]

During the Second World War this argument was pressed home with great vigour by Viscount Hinchingbrooke of the Tory Reform Group, who declared that

> True Conservative opinion is horrified at the damage done to this country since the last war by 'individualist' business men, financiers, and speculators ranging freely in a laissez faire economy and creeping unnoticed into the fold of Conservatism to insult the Party with their votes at elections, to cast a slur over responsible Government through influence exerted on Parliament, and to injure the character of our people . . . these men should collect their baggage and depart. True Conservatism has nothing whatever to do with them and their obnoxious policies.[111]

Likewise, Lord Beaverbrook described a head-on collision within the party when he told one correspondent in the autumn of 1945 that 'The battle within the party is a fight between the Tory individualists who follow ironically enough the creed of nineteenth century Liberalism, and the Tory Reformers who raise the banner . . . of Disraeli's Young England.'[112]

This was to be a refrain of Conservative critics of the individualist position throughout the last half of the twentieth century, and reached, as noted above, a peak of intensity in the 1980s. Conservative critics of Thatcherism, like Gilmour, Pym and Walker, had no hesitation in describing it as wholly alien to the Conservative credo and as a derivative of nineteenth-century Liberal individualism. It has been suggested that it is wrong to describe Thatcherism as a derivative of Liberalism, because, unlike Liberalism and neoliberalism, individualism was 'an adjacent concept' rather than a core element in Thatcherite ideology.[113] However, in her Nicholas Ridley Memorial Lecture of November 1996, Margaret Thatcher praised her late colleague as 'one of a long line of British individualists', and noted that individualist was 'a term which is often used disparagingly, but which should be rehabilitated'.[114] When she was challenged about her individualism she was forthright in defence of her philosophy. She demanded of the BBC's James Naughtie, 'How can you make up a community except of individuals?' and when asked to comment on her supposed 'ruthless individualism' she replied, 'it is the

State's job to serve the freedom of the individual'. Likewise, she told the Annual Meeting of the Centre for Policy Studies that those who described individualism as 'selfish' were talking 'nonsense', because wishing to do well for oneself and one's family was admirable and that she wished 'more people would in fact take responsibility for looking after their own families instead of expecting others to look after them'.[115] These comments were not made by a politician who saw individualism as an 'adjacent concept'. Rather they imply a philosophy that emphasized a polity that was an aggregate of individual citizens and in which individual rights and duties were the fulcrum of social and political life.

That individualism was central to Thatcher and Thatcherism raises a major problem in terms of placing them in the Conservative tradition. In his study *The Politics of Imperfection*, Anthony Quinton argues that four closely related principles make up the fundamental elements of Conservatism.[116] The first is the notion of *intellectual imperfection*. Related to but distinct from the idea of original sin, the concept of intellectual imperfection rests on the premise that human rational faculties are necessarily inadequate to the task of comprehending the complexities of social development, and that abstract reasoning cannot be trusted as a guide for social and political behaviour.[117] Quinton derives from this three other fundamental tenets of Conservatism. The first of these is *political scepticism*, or 'the belief that political wisdom ... is not to be found in the theoretical speculations of isolated thinkers, but in the historically accumulated social experience of the community as a whole'.[118] The second is *traditionalism*, by which is meant that Conservatives have an attachment to established customs and institutions and a hostility to 'sudden, precipitate and revolutionary change'.[119] The third is *organicism*, that is to say, Conservatives regard society as 'a unitary, natural growth, an organized living whole not a mechanical aggregate', composed of 'social beings, related to one another within a texture of inherited customs and institutions which endow them with their specific social nature'.[120]

This last notion, of society as a living whole rather than a 'mechanical aggregate', was specifically held up in antagonism to, on the one hand, individualist philosophies and, on the other hand, Socialism with its class-based precepts. This did not mean that Conservatives denied the existence or importance of either the individual or class, but rather they argued that neither could or should be abstracted from their existence within a larger whole. This had been an aspect of Conservative thought since the early nineteenth century, but, in the context of this book, it is important to note that it had been particularly prominent in post-1945 Conservative ideas. David Clarke's statement in 1947 that 'society is an organic whole in which the social atoms react in all their movements upon one another'[121] was reiterated in July 1952 by his colleague at CRD, Michael Fraser, who stressed that 'It is a feature of Conservatism ... not to consider society as merely a haphazard aggregation of individuals in isolation ... We believe man to be a social animal, happiest when he is free to take part in the life of a variety of groups and communities within the nation'.[122] Ten years later the Young Conservatives' pamphlet on *Society and the Individual* denounced the notion of society as an aggregate of individuals as one of the most misleading and damaging ideas promulgated by the French Revolution,[123] and in 1965 Enoch Powell argued that

> society is much more than a collection of individuals acting together, even through the complex and subtle mechanisms of the free economy, for material advantage. It has an existence of its own; it thinks and feels; it looks inward, as a community, to its members; it looks outward as a nation.[124]

For Conservatives the relationship between individuals and society was necessarily symbiotic and the notion that one had primacy over the other was a misconception, in that it was only as a consequence of rules and customs regulated and enforced by laws and social norms that individuality could be expressed.[125]

It is in relation to organicism that the question arises most clearly as to whether Thatcherism departed from Conservatism. For some, notably the 'wets', the Thatcherites' desire to roll back the State in the economic and social spheres saw them embrace a liberal-market antagonism to State intervention that was characteristic of either classical nineteenth-century Liberalism or late twentieth-century neoliberalism. There are, however, problems with seeing the adoption of liberal market economics as indicative of a *simple* Conservative 'conversion' to Liberalism or neoliberalism. To begin with, although Thatcherites engaged with neoliberalism they did not fully embrace, and on occasion explicitly rejected, neoliberal economics in their purest form.[126] Furthermore, the period after 1975 was not the first occasion when the Conservative Party adopted aspects of liberal market economics, and these doctrines have been and can be defended on Conservative rather than neoliberal grounds. Hugh Cecil was clear in *Conservatism* that 'a policy of State interference is not, as such, alien from Conservatism',[127] but he supported free trade and wished to limit State action in the sphere of social policy. His grounds for this were that the decisions of the market were wholly impersonal, free of ethical content, and thus that the State, as an ethical entity, had no part to play in them.[128] In Cecil's schema State action to deal with the social ills that market outcomes produced, such as poverty or hardship in old age, could only be deemed acts of national philanthropy rather than acts of social justice.[129] For Cecil and later Conservative advocates of the free market, notably Powell, liberal market economics were also justifiable in terms of intellectual imperfectionism and political scepticism, in that market transactions and outcomes were natural, spontaneous products of the 'invisible hand' and attempts to regulate them through State intervention were necessarily based on the (erroneous) assumption that those who implemented them had a complete grasp of human material wants and needs and how to satisfy them.

But if a case for liberal market economics can be made on Conservative grounds it is not unproblematic. To begin with, liberal market economics can be deemed guilty of intellectual perfectionism, in so far as attempts to establish models of supply, demand, propensity to save, invest or consume in terms of rational expectation can be and have been criticized as dependent upon abstract, deductive reasoning, which makes assumptions that are as flawed as those made by advocates of State intervention and regulation of the market.[130] In addition, market relations may be deemed spontaneous, but they are different from other actions of social association, such as friendship, in that a *result* is expected from them. This in turn raises two further problems for Conservatism. The first is that if market relations assume a result – an outcome that will see a distribution of gains and losses – it is difficult to sustain the notion that market relations are free of ethical content. Gunnar Myrdal argued that in the study of economic theory the perpetual game of hide-and-seek was to find the norm hidden in the concept,[131] and this underlines the problem of harmonizing liberal market economics with the political scepticism of Conservative thought. The second is that those of a conservative disposition wish to defend and preserve the freedom of activities which bring enjoyment without producing 'a reward, a prize or a result in addition to the experience itself',[132] and market relations and activities are difficult to describe in these terms. Indeed this last point leads to the most difficult aspect of reconciling Thatcherism with Conservatism.

The problems that liberal market economics produce for Conservatism stem from their broad socio-political implications as much as from their political-economic logic. Thatcher and the Thatcherites had sought to roll back the State in part to allow room for spontaneous, voluntary, civic associations to flourish. But whether as a consequence of a mismatch between intention and outcome, or as a result of a failure to anticipate where a liberal-market strategy could lead, Thatcherism stretched organicism to breaking point. In a study published in 1997, *Is Conservatism Dead?*, John Gray noted that the emphasis in late twentieth-century Conservatism on market relations as a basis for social relations had acted as a solvent of social bonds, which had existed in the shape of varied and complex webs of associational activity.[133] The *individualist* logic of the liberal market, explicitly embraced by Thatcher and her party, carried the intrinsic possibility of a tendency not only to *political* individualism, but also to social *individuation*, both of which placed question marks, in terms of theory and practice, against the importance of social action and social capital. That the emphasis on market relations, which had informed much of the political, economic and social agenda of the 1980s and 1990s, appeared to have brought about the possibility of such a fracturing of social cohesion was a matter of concern across the political spectrum, and it was a concern that was not confined to Britain.[134] But it presented particular problems for British Conservatives,[135] in that its implications were wholly at odds with the organicist emphasis on social association that had been such a marked feature of Conservative thought.

One way of understanding the trajectory of Conservatism in Britain in the twentieth century is through its complex relationship with classical Liberalism and its neoliberal derivatives. Thatcher and Thatcherism accepted individualist assumptions that were central to these political positions and, as a result, departed from the Conservative emphasis on the organic nature of society. The marked and acknowledged influence of such ideas reinforces the argument that Thatcher embraced a libertarian philosophy that was not part of, and could not be reconciled with, the Conservative tradition. Thatcher did not begin this intellectual and ideological transition, but rather she and her ideological adherents embodied and articulated the moment of a shift that had been in process since the late nineteenth century.

Thatcherism and Conservatism

Thatcher oversaw the transformation of not only Conservative ideology but also the make-up and membership of the Conservative Party hierarchy and the parliamentary party. Her election to the party leadership was in itself both a symptom and a cause of these processes. The notion that in 1975 the Conservatives simply elected someone who was 'not Edward Heath' and that the choice of Thatcher was ideologically innocent has long ceased to have any credibility.[136] Equally important, her accession to the leadership confirmed and accelerated changes in the Conservative Party's make-up. The veteran 'wet' Conservative backbencher, Julian Critchley, memorably termed Thatcher's election as 'the peasants' revolt'. This remark was a light-hearted aside, but it carried some weightier implications. Critchley implied that Thatcher's election was a crucial moment when, to paraphrase Tennyson, 'the old order changed, giving way to new' within the Conservative Party, and, generationally and socially, he was right.

The social composition of the Conservative hierarchy and parliamentary party changed markedly in the last quarter of the twentieth century. Thatcher's first Cabinet, as many commentators noted in 1979, looked very traditional. It contained only three members (including Thatcher) who had not been educated at public school, and included six Old Etonians and three Wykehamists. Furthermore, of those with a university degree all but one had been to Oxford or Cambridge. In contrast, when Thatcher resigned there was only one Old Etonian in the Cabinet, Douglas Hurd, and this was seen as a handicap when he stood in the leadership election to succeed her. In important ways John Major, both ideologically and socially, embodied the Thatcherite legacy. He had humble social origins and his educational background was vocational rather than formal. Here the fact that he had worked in the financial sector was significant, for the Conservative Parliamentary Party had become dominated by private-sector professionals, and the law and financial services had emerged as the most common occupational route to the Conservative benches. Furthermore, a new occupational category appeared that played an increasingly prominent part in the late twentieth-century party hierarchy, namely the professional politician. Figures such as Michael Portillo, John Redwood, William Hague and David Willetts – one of whom became leader while two others stood – were all representatives of this new phenomenon; these individuals in particular, and professional politicians in general, were products of the Thatcher years.[137]

With regard to its generational make-up, Thatcher's Party at Westminster was also a new breed. After the 1966 election only 60 per cent of Conservative MPs had sat continuously since 1959, and only 11 MPs had been in Parliament before 1945. This generational change understandably continued, and by February 1974 only 50 per cent of MPs had been in Parliament before 1964, and the bulk of them were of the 1959 vintage. For historians of Conservative politics in the 1950s and early 1960s, the 'class of 1950' has had particular significance in terms of its contribution to Cabinet personnel and the influence it exercised. Arguably, the 'class of 1959' should have equal importance for scholars of Thatcherism.[138] The 'class of 1950' had come into politics with the memory of the 1945 defeat still strong and with the 'myth' of the 'hungry thirties' seen as the explanation. The 'class of 1959' came into politics in a climate dominated by the questions of 'slow growth', the grumblings of grass-roots discontent and a querying of the social and economic achievements of the 'post-war settlement'. At the same time the social and geographical base of the 'class of 1959' was markedly different from that of their predecessors. The presence of the 'knights of the shires', military and other public servants had declined, and they had been replaced by representatives of the salaried, professional middle classes. In short, the new generation of Conservative MPs was closer socially to the kind of people who had expressed discontent with the 'post-war settlement'.

Furthermore, members of this new generation of MPs were increasingly returned from constituencies south of Birmingham. The changing, and narrowing, base of the Conservative Parliamentary Party reflected general economic and demographic shifts in the country, as employment and population trends followed the decline of Britain's old industrial heartlands. From 1951 to the 1970s, and accelerating through the 1980s, demographic and economic change saw the population and, through redistribution, the representation of the south and south-east of Britain grow markedly. This growth was fuelled, in particular, by a massive surge in service-sector activity, or what would once have been termed white-collar and black-coated employment. Many of these occupations were non-unionized, and, even if they were unionized, employees showed a greater degree of 'economic instrumentalism' in their voting allegiance than workers in the older industrial communities.[139] The possibility that a Conservative, liberal-market appeal could be made to this social and regional constituency had been mooted in the late 1950s when the idea of the 'opportunity state' had been in vogue. Although this concept had been designed to meet the needs of the 'beleaguered middle class', it was also seen as appealing to the aspirational lower-middle and working-class voter, on the basis that, as one Conservative minister put it, 'potentially the foreman class is ours'.[140] Likewise the Conservative Lord Chancellor of the late 1950s hinted at a potential regional appeal of the 'opportunity state', noting that tax cuts, wider property ownership and lower inflation were 'an acute political problem from the standpoint of Conservative workers 'South of the Trent, in the north they are much more concerned with their council houses, factories, schools and hospitals'.[141] Essentially the same regional point was made about Thatcher on the eve of her election as leader, when David Watt wrote in the *Financial Times* that

'To anyone north of the Trent she might as well come from Mars'.[142] In the 1980s this constituency was to be labelled 'Essex Man', and was seen, rightly, as an electoral vanguard of Thatcherism. 'Essex man' was, of course, a comic and journalistic shorthand, and it was too regionally specific. A more accurate term would be 'English man' or perhaps 'South English man'. The late nineteenth-century Conservative Party has been referred to as 'the English nationalist Party', but this is a label that fits Thatcher's party still better. Conservative support and representation in Scotland and Wales declined sharply in the period after 1979, and the breach with the Ulster Unionists, which had opened in 1972, not only went unrepaired, but was deepened by the Downing Street declaration of 1986. Furthermore, within England the Conservatives' geographical base narrowed, for the party grew increasingly dependent on constituencies south of the line from the Bristol Channel to the Wash.

Thatcherism was as much a symptom as a cause of changes in Conservatism and the Conservative Party. From the very outset Conservative voices had been raised against the 'post-war settlement', and through the 1950s and 1960s some elements of the Conservative party leadership, a substantial section of the backbenches and probably a majority of the party membership were predisposed to accept a liberal-market diagnosis of and prescription for their own and the nation's economic troubles. The Churchill, Eden and Macmillan Governments chose not to respond positively to liberal-market opinion for two reasons. First, the generation of Conservative leaders dominant into the 1960s was heavily influenced by the trauma of the 1945 defeat and accepted the view that it was a 'delayed punishment' for the 'hungry thirties'. As a consequence they were reluctant to take risks, particularly in the realm of unemployment. Equally important, the post-war boom that began in 1952 meant that, for the most part, Conservative governments were able to square the circle of high public expenditure and full employment with occasional tax cuts and relatively stable prices. Indeed, in the context of the 1950s, when inflation was reasonably low (albeit historically high), the economy was growing and living standards rising, the remarkable thing is the amount of discontent there was in the Conservative ranks. In this sense there was an indication in the disgruntled voices of the 1950s of how powerful the reaction might be if the post-war boom came to an end, inflation became more pressing and the dilemma of the power of organized labour in a fully employed economy was more graphically exposed. In short, there was almost a ready-made Conservative audience for the Thatcherite agenda when Britain was hit by the economic troubles of the 1970s, as the end of the long post-war boom and the onset of 'stagflation' combined to create space for Thatcherite political economy.

Thatcherism can be seen as simply an historical-institutional phenomenon in so far as it was a product of the changed nature of the Conservative Party and, equally, a change in the relationship between the party's centre and its periphery. But it was also a complex product of how the party shaped its response to the social, economic and political environment created by the long post-war boom and, more particularly, its termination. The assumptions that had informed much of the political economy of Britain between 1945 and 1973 were that mass unemployment was electorally unacceptable and the mixed economy and comprehensive health and welfare provision were fait accompli. Many Conservatives had questioned these assumptions, and had wished to replace them with an alternative range of both questions and answers as to how British society and the economy should be governed. In this respect Thatcherism was a 'hegemonic project', in that it questioned and, in some critical areas, overturned assumptions with regard to the accepted norms of governance, and thereby replaced certain presumed priorities with an alternative range. Most notably, inflation replaced full employment, low personal taxation was accorded equal if not higher priority than State health and welfare provision, the State sector was deemed unwanted, inefficient and inferior to private enterprise, and individual, personal responsibility was valorized and State social assistance deemed the root of 'dependency'. Although Thatcherism may not have changed 'the soul', it was in large part successful in redefining key norms.

2

Thatcher and the economy

Three months before the 1979 general election Nigel Lawson told Margaret Thatcher that a Conservative general election victory was essential, as it would provide the party with 'our last chance to rescue the British economy from the depressing spiral of decline.'[1] Such a remark was characteristic, not only of Lawson and Thatcher's views, but of British political economy in the last quarter of the twentieth century. In the 1970s, and on through the 1980s and 1990s, much of British political debate revolved around conflicting diagnoses of and prescriptions for the 'British disease' of economic decline. This was very apparent in the years between Thatcher's accession to the Conservative leadership and her becoming prime minister. In late 1975 Harold Wilson spoke in Parliament about a meeting at Chequers, of the Cabinet, industrialists and trade union leaders, where, he stated, 'The objective accepted by all of us . . . Government, unions and management . . . was to reverse the postwar economic decline.'[2] Shortly afterwards, Thatcher declared herself unimpressed with Labour's record on this issue, and stated that the decline of Britain's 'relative power in the world was partly inevitable – with the rise of the super powers with their vast reserves of manpower and resources. But it was partly avoidable too – the result of our economic decline accelerated by Socialism. We must reverse that decline when we are returned to Government.'[3] Nor was Thatcher any more impressed by the efforts of Wilson's successor, for in October 1976 she declared that James Callaghan's administration had 'presided over the worst economic decline we have seen in the post-war period,'[4] and two years later she argued that the Labour Government's failings had been demonstrated 'Most conspicuously of all . . . in the country's economic decline.'[5] Small wonder Thatcher told the voters on the eve of the 1979 election that Labour's return would mean 'carrying on with the present decline'.[6]

Thatcher was clear that 'if we are to halt and then to reverse the long years of our country's economic decline, fundamental changes of policy and of attitude are required at almost every level.'[7] To begin with, she argued that it was essential to reverse Labour's 'philosophy of an increasing share of the national income going to the state and more state control over people's lives, over housing, over

55

companies big and small, over pension funds, and insurance.'[8] This was the essence of Thatcher's anti-interventionist philosophy, as summed up in the phrase 'rolling back the frontiers of the State'. This encompassed a wide range of anti-Statist policy positions, from calls for a reduction of public expenditure to dismantling the mixed economy through the sale of nationalized industries.[9] But anti-Statism was the simplest element of Thatcherite political economy, and, as Thatcher said to the Ulster Unionist Council in June 1978, her aim was to change the whole approach to the way the British economy was governed. For Thatcher and her close colleagues this required jettisoning the theoretical policy assumptions and practices that had underpinned what she and many others by the 1970s had come to term the economics of consensus.

The key features of the consensual approach to the economy were seen to be that the government's primary responsibility was to maintain full employment, and that this could be achieved through 'demand management', that is, by the government's active use of fiscal and monetary policy either to boost or reduce aggregate demand, depending on the phase of the economic cycle: in the language of the Conservative prime minister of the late 1950s, Harold Macmillan, governments had to drive the economy through judicious use of both the accelerator and the brake. From the 1950s on, a particular problem came to be associated with this approach to economic governance, namely that the pursuit of full employment led to inflation. In 1956 a Treasury paper on 'The Economic Implications of Full Employment' stressed the dangers of inflation, and in 1957 Harold Macmillan stated that 'the problem of our time ... [is] can prices be steadied while at the same time we maintain full employment in an expanding economy?'[10] Macmillan's observation was politically understandable, for in 1957–58 inflation was the main cause of the 'middle-class revolt' that caused his government problems at a number of by-elections, and led to some uncomfortable debates at the Conservative Party Conference. In 1958 A.W. Phillips sought to demonstrate and define this problem theoretically, and concluded, in the shape of his soon-to-be-celebrated eponymous 'curve', that there was an inverse relationship and, in effect, a trade-off between the levels of employment and inflation. In both theoretical and political terms the issue of the link between and the relative priorities of employment and inflation was prominent in the lead-up to Thatcher's entry into Parliament. Furthermore, in the 1960s and early 1970s the issue of inflation became increasingly central, not only in Britain but throughout the industrialized world. Thatcher's pre-1975 career was, both in government and opposition, shaped by the political economy of inflation, but during her time as opposition leader the terms of economic debate in Britain, notably on the issue of inflation, shifted markedly, in part as a consequence of the contributions of Thatcher and her economic advisers.

In the 1970s Britain's economic experience under the Heath Government of 1970–74, and the Labour governments of Wilson and Callaghan in 1974–79, seemed to indicate that the prevailing assumptions of post-war economic theory and governance were flawed. In particular, the phenomenon of 'stagflation' appeared to give the lie to Phillips' idea of a trade-off between the levels of unemployment and inflation.[11] As a consequence, politicians and economists reassessed the approaches and policy options that would enable them to address and meet the economic, social and political problems attendant upon the end of the long 'post-war boom'. In the spring of 1976, the Labour administration faced rising unemployment, inflation and a sterling crisis. In response they opted for a £1 billion reduction in public expenditure for 1977–78 and set a target for the growth of the money supply of 12 per cent for 1976–77. But the economic situation continued to deteriorate – sterling's value fell, the government's currency reserves haemorrhaged as it sought to halt the fall of sterling and in early September the government opened negotiations with the IMF in order to secure a US$3.9 billion medium-term loan. As a condition of granting this loan the IMF demanded cuts in British public expenditure and tighter UK monetary policy, and the government accepted these deflationary terms. Shortly before accepting the IMF loan, James Callaghan told the Labour Party Conference that his government had abandoned the goal of maintaining full employment through expansionary demand management. He declared that 'we used to think that you could just spend your way out of a recession and increase employment by cutting taxes and boosting government spending. I tell you in all candour that option no longer exists': such a strategy, he stated, had resulted and could only result in ongoing rounds of inflation.[12] Callaghan's administration thus reduced public expenditure and introduced a scheme of tight cash limits for public services, on the grounds that these measures would reduce monetary aggregates and, as a result, have a deflationary effect. After the first round of cuts in the spring of 1976, the Minister for the Environment, Anthony Crosland, declared that, with regard to public spending, 'the party is over', but the party was over for all of the once seemingly established norms of post-war economic governance.

The Conservatives' response to the policy options chosen by the Labour administrations in and after 1975 was unwontedly positive. To begin with, they welcomed the fact that the government had prioritized inflation. In July 1975 the government published a White Paper on 'The Attack on Inflation', and at a meeting of the Shadow Cabinet it was agreed that it would appear 'inconsistent' and 'unpatriotic' if the Conservatives did not support the government's basic aim.[13] But in addition to pointing out, 'patriotically', the weaknesses and omissions of Labour's anti-inflation strategy, the Conservatives also claimed that the government had adopted Conservative policy. The new system of cash limits was particularly important to this last argument. At a meeting of the Conservative Finance Committee, held soon after Denis Healey had introduced cash limits in his 1976 Budget, John Biffen argued that the Labour Chancellor's action had been 'Very advantageous for Conservatives as [the] government have adopted cash limits, which we have been calling for', and Douglas Hurd suggested that the Conservatives should 'Hail' this policy 'as a triumph for Tories'.[14] This stance was understandable, for in July 1975, the Shadow Chancellor had sent a circular to his colleagues, which had outlined his own plans for cash limits in the public sector and demanded that any policy proposals that required increased expenditure be cleared by both himself and the Shadow Cabinet collectively.[15] Howe and the Shadow Cabinet further anticipated Healey's initiative when, at a meeting in February 1976, they concluded that 'we should above all give attention to the fiscal and monetary aspects of controlling inflation, and the use of *cash limits*.'[16]

Thatcher's Shadow Cabinet, and Thatcher herself, presented their approach to inflation and economic policy as offering a radical break with post-war theory and practice. A few months after she was elected to the party leadership Thatcher told her Shadow Cabinet 'that the opposition would be attacked for not having a clear economic policy,'[17] and in order to pre-empt this attack the Conservatives established an Economic Reconstruction Group (ERG), chaired by Geoffrey Howe. The ERG's task was 'to establish an economic strategy for the Party both for the present and the future',[18] but an important part of this strategy was jettisoning the past. One of the ERG's immediate targets was 'fine-tuning' of the economy by government. 'Fine-tuning' referred to State manipulation of fiscal policy at the macro-economic level, and represented, for Thatcher and her colleagues, the worst example of constant government tinkering with the economy that had been a feature of economic policy since the war. In December 1975 an ERG discussion saw strong criticism of 'fine-tuning', and a month later the group heard a paper by an academic economist, Alan Budd, which denounced 'fine-tuning' for its short-term thinking.[19] Thereafter, all references to 'fine-tuning' in Conservative intra-party discussion invariably disparaged its 'short-termism'. In contrast, Thatcher, her colleagues and their economic advisers described their own thinking as based on either medium- or, more generally, long-term considerations. Hence Geoffrey Howe spoke in his 1976 paper, 'Liberating Free Enterprise', of the need to construct a policy strategy for a government that would be in office for the 'two or three terms necessary to restore the health of the economy.'[20]

The Conservatives planned to achieve some basic goals in this extended period in office. In early 1979 Nigel Lawson, who was already beginning to emerge as one of Thatcher's closest economic counsellors, summed up these goals in a paper for his leader. 'The Conservative Party's economic policy', Lawson wrote, 'has two overriding aims. The first is to release the frustrated energies of the British people ... the second is to bring down the rate of inflation.'[21] Since the 'middle-class revolt' of the late 1950s, and certainly since Edward Heath had famously promised to 'cut prices at a stroke' in 1970, inflation had been a central concern of all political parties – the galloping inflation of the mid- to late 1970s simply served to make it the chief priority. After the first meeting of the ERG in 1975 Geoffrey Howe had concluded that there were four dominant problems that needed to be addressed, and the first of these was inflation.[22] In early 1978, as the Conservatives made their preparations for an election they expected that year, George Cardona, a senior research assistant at CRD, argued that 'The mastery of inflation is the most important single task which must be fulfilled if our society and economy are to be restored to health and economic growth resumed.'[23] The question was how these goals were to be achieved. Cardona argued that in the battle against inflation, and more generally, 'monetary policy must now play a wider and even more central role in economic strategy.'[24] Here Cardona stated a position that had first been voiced in Conservative politics in the 1950s, had grown in strength in the 1960s and had blossomed in the 1970s, namely that the key to controlling the rate of inflation, and the most important instrument of economic policy, was control of the money supply. In this respect the resurgence of monetarist economic thought was to be central to the construction of Thatcherite political economy.

The first time monetarism had made an appearance in post-war political argument was in 1958, when Harold Macmillan's Treasury team – Peter Thorneycroft, Enoch Powell and Nigel Birch – resigned because they could not secure Cabinet agreement to the reductions in public expenditure they had proposed. That these reductions were part of an anti-inflation strategy gave rise to the idea that the 1958 resignees were Thatcherites *avant la lettre*, a point that was reinforced by the fact that one of Thatcher's first actions as Conservative leader was to appoint Thorneycroft as party chairman. The link was apparently confirmed by another of the resignees, Enoch Powell, who, in 1989, stated that 31 years earlier he had been 'led to conclude that inflation was being generated by the level of government expenditure and the increase in the money supply which government borrowing to cover the excess of expenditure over the receipts was causing. This assertion . . . was later to be known as monetarism.'[25] Whether it is theoretically accurate to describe as unequivocally monetarist either what the Treasury team of 1958 demanded or the Thatcher Governments' economic policies is open to doubt. What is not open to doubt is that Thatcher and her governments themselves described their economic strategy, at any rate until 1984, as monetarist.

Thatcher herself first used the term 'monetarism' in public debate in 1978, when she was content to be labelled a monetarist and declared in Parliament that

> Whenever money supply or monetarism was mentioned in this House the Chancellor of the Exchequer would accuse us of monetarism, or 'Josephitism'. At the next moment, the Chancellor would say that he was far better at holding the money supply than we were. I am glad that the Chancellor says that he has been wholly and utterly converted to the necessity of holding the money supply very firmly. We agree with him wholeheartedly, for reasons that he knows. That is the only final way in which inflation can be held and reduced. He knows it and we know it.[26]

Thatcher had, however, been identified as an adherent of monetarist economics early in her leadership. In the summer of 1975, in a debate on unemployment, Harold Wilson had made dismissive references to monetarist ideas, and had argued that although she had not used the term monetarism in the debate, he knew that Thatcher's views were informed by 'the right hon. Member for Leeds, North-East — the right hon. Lady's Rasputin', that is to say, Keith Joseph.[27] Joseph, since his 'conversion' to Conservatism in the wake of the February 1974 general election, had also announced his conversion to monetarism in a series of speeches that were published in 1975, but although Joseph was the best-known Conservative proselyte of the monetarist cause, he was by no means alone. Indeed, nearly all of Thatcher's Shadow Cabinet with an economic brief – Geoffrey Howe, Keith Joseph, John Biffen, John Nott and David Howell – were monetarists or inclined to monetarism, and of the shadow 'economic' ministers, only James Prior stood out as someone outside the monetarist camp.

The economic beliefs of individual members of the Shadow Cabinet, especially those close to Thatcher, were important, but more important still was the overall direction of Conservative economic policy after February 1975. In summer that year, Geoffrey Howe outlined what he saw as the policy options available with regard to inflation. The first options he discussed were '*A "gradualist" monetary approach*' and '*A "dramatic" monetary approach*'.[28] He went on to argue that both of these carried significant difficulties, but also contended that an '*Ideal Programme*', which would bring indirect market pressure to bear on inflation, required tighter monetary policy, zero growth of money wages and a reduction in public expenditure and of public sector borrowing.[29] Howe further underscored his arguments in a paper circulated to the Shadow Cabinet in late 1975, in which he argued that curbing inflation demanded 'proper management of the money supply' and, as a necessary complement, 'greater restraint and economy in public spending'.[30] Howe's position was in turn echoed and extended by Keith Joseph, who told Thatcher that a Conservative government should aim to reduce the government's share of GNP to 40 per cent in two Parliaments, in order to slash inflation, borrowing and taxation and work towards a balanced Budget.[31] That Howe and Joseph's positions, and the general development of Conservative policy, were wholly in line with monetarist thinking was further reflected in, and reinforced by, the economic advice Thatcher and her party chose to draw upon. For example, when Alan Budd presented his critique of 'fine-tuning' to the ERG, he not only emphasized its 'short-termism' but also its inadequate grasp of monetary policy.[32] The summer after Budd's presentation the ERG 'agreed that it would be sensible to get together a small group of academic monetarists in order to promote further thinking on this and to work out ways of influencing informed opinion in the right direction'.[33] The 'right direction', as was to become clear in the late 1970s and 1980s, was monetarist thinking, and economists such as Budd, Patrick Minford,[34] Alan Walters[35] and Tim Congdon were drawn into the Conservative policy discussion circuit, while non-monetarists such as the Department of Applied Economics (DAE) at Cambridge, under Wynne Godley, were cast into outer darkness.[36]

One attraction of monetarism to the Conservatives was that it provided both a simple explanation of and a solution to the problem of inflation. The classical monetary equation – $mv = pq$ – provided ready answers, in so far as it indicated that if the supply of money increased then so would prices, and if it decreased, then prices would fall. But there were further important dimensions to the monetarist argument. One dimension, which had crucial policy and political implications, was that the key determinant of the money supply was government expenditure and, in particular, government borrowing. The Labour governments of 1975–79 faced a constant barrage of Conservative criticism for their 'profligate' borrowing,[37] but this was accompanied by consistent assertions that the Conservatives would demonstrate financial probity. Hence, when Geoffrey Howe told his Shadow Cabinet colleagues in July 1975 that any proposals for future expenditure would be vetted, he argued that 'It is only if we impose this kind of discipline upon ourselves that we can reasonably criticise the Government. We should be able to make a significant public relations impact if we can show to the world that we are practising, within the Tory Party, what we are preaching.'[38] Soon after, the Conservatives began to explore how this could be institutionally guaranteed by a future Conservative government. One suggestion was that a new 'Budget Ministry' could be established to ensure fiscal probity, as it had become clear that to ensure such discipline 'the departmental balance between spending ministers and Ministers committed departmentally to reduce public spending must be changed substantially in favour of the latter.'[39]

Ultimately, Thatcher's party, neither in opposition nor in government produced proposals for administrative action. Rather they relied upon policy initiatives to produce the changes deemed necessary. In this context a key departure was the first Thatcher administration's adoption of the Medium Term Financial Strategy (MTFS). The main architect of this policy, which was announced in the 1980 Budget, was Nigel Lawson, who was then Financial Secretary to the Treasury. Lawson had underlined the central importance of government finance and borrowing in the policy 'module' he had prepared at Thatcher's request in February 1979,[40] and he placed the MTFS at the economic heart of what he termed the 'New Conservatism'. In a pamphlet which described this political creed, which he published shortly after the 1980 Budget, Lawson argued that the Conservative government was 'committed to a steady reduction in the rate of growth in the money supply for the foreseeable future',[41] and it was in this context that the MTFS was central. Lawson proudly described his brainchild, and wrote: 'we have published – for the first time ever – a quantified medium-term financial strategy setting out a gradualist path to a monetary growth target of around 6 per cent in 1983–4 and committing us to a fiscal policy compatible with this path.'[42] The MTFS marked an important policy departure. Whereas the Callaghan administration had set monetary targets, the Thatcher Government narrowed the goals of economic policy to the spheres of money and borrowing alone, and they had no concern with regard to output.[43] In his first Budget speech as Chancellor in 1984, Lawson described the MTFS as having been and remaining the 'cornerstone' of the Thatcher Governments' economic policy,[44] and the following year he indicated how the Conservatives' adherence to the MTFS differentiated their approach from that of their predecessors: 'The great mistake of post-war demand management', Lawson argued, '. . . was to react to rising unemployment by injecting more money into the system, whether through the Budget or through the banks. So far from halting the upward trend of unemployment, this simply generated runaway inflation.[45] Demand management in general, like its particular instrument, 'fine-tuning', was, in the Thatcherite schema, guilty of mistakenly prioritizing employment, considering only the short term and ignoring the importance of money-supply control, whereas the MTFS prioritized inflation and was designed, as its title implied, to ensure that government took a longer-term view of its monetary and fiscal responsibilities.

The centrality of monetary policy and the MTFS to the first two Thatcher administrations illustrated how the monetarist position had strengthened its hold on Conservative political economy and, in particular, counter-inflation strategy after Thatcher had become leader. In mid-1975 Geoffrey Howe had written that 'The current inflation has many causes – unions, their monopoly, power and militancy, excess demand, monetary policy, expectations, and the size and growth of the public sector.'[46] One might have thought that this multi-causal analysis would have led to the development of a complex variety of anti-inflation strategies, but Howe and the bulk of the Conservative economic policy-making hierarchy, including Thatcher, focused their attention on monetary policy. This was not, however, because they ignored all the other factors Howe had referred to in 1975, but because they felt that the correct monetary policy would address them either directly or indirectly.

One of the most important ways in which monetarist thinking shifted Conservative thinking was in the realm of 'wage inflation' and the related issue of the role of the trade union movement in economic policy. Since 1945, and in particular after the 'pay pause' of 1961, all governments had seen pay restraint as an integral part of containing inflationary pressure. But Thatcher and her economic compadres jettisoned both the theory and practice of this approach. The only member of Thatcher's economic team who consistently advocated an incomes policy was the non-monetarist James Prior, but even he did not argue that it was an alternative to a monetary approach. In the summer of 1975 Prior presented a paper to the Shadow Cabinet on 'Counter Inflation Policy', in which he argued that Labour's 'social contract has failed to bring about wage restraint . . . [and] The public sector deficit has been allowed to grow unchecked as the quid pro quo for non-existent wage restraint.'[47] This argument, with its emphasis on the public sector deficit, was one which Thatcher and the monetarist critics of the social contract were wont to use, and Prior was clear that 'We can all agree that to master inflation a tight monetary policy is essential', but he also argued that 'it [monetary policy] will not be enough and there is not sufficient time. We need some form of wage restraint too.'[48] Hence Prior's case for an incomes policy was as a supportive adjunct to monetary policy and not, as in the 1960s and early 1970s, the main strategy. It may have been that Prior thought that this was the best way of 'selling' his preferred policy option to his colleagues, but if so this only confirms the point that, early in Thatcher's leadership, the economic agenda was being defined in increasingly monetarist terms.

Underlying the opposition of Thatcher, her party and her governments to incomes policies was, as will be shown elsewhere,[49] hostility to the trade union movement. A primary reason for this was political, in so far as Thatcher and her supporters felt that 'Major wage negotiations must be depoliticized.'[50] Incomes policies, however, were seen, necessarily, to politicize wage bargaining. Indeed, Keith Joseph argued that it was precisely for this reason that trade unions liked these policies. 'Trade Union leaders', Joseph contended, favoured incomes policies

> for a combination of reasons. First, the negotiation of an incomes policy gives them political power – extra power ... the pursuit of a voluntary incomes policy leads to bargaining on a far wider than incomes basis or economic policy generally. It becomes political and the resulting package invades the sphere of many other interests and of Parliament.[51]

In Joseph's view, if it was accepted, or even suggested, 'that inflation can be abated to the slightest extent by wages or price control ... then Mr Jones [the leader of the TGWU] and his colleagues must unquestionably rule the roost'.[52]

What made incomes policies even more objectionable to Thatcherite Conservatives was that they saw them as economically unnecessary and ineffective as well as politically damaging.[53] For Thatcherites the only economic area that the trade unions could significantly affect was the labour market, where, so Joseph told Thatcher, 'trades unions can abate unemployment – by wage restraint: by less overmanning and restrictive practices so as to make us more competitive'.[54] By the same dint, trade unions could have an adverse effect on employment. In an article for the *CBI Review* in the autumn of 1975, Thatcher argued that the unreasonable wage demands by unions were a prime example of the problem of 'paying ourselves more money' without expanding productivity,[55] but she was also clear that the solution to this problem was 'not pay restraint imposed by Government interference' as the labour market could not 'work properly with rigid pay controls'. Rather, she wished to see 'responsible realistic collective bargaining: according to the prospects and circumstances of the company, and within the overall constraints of the money supply.'[56] In this context the money supply, as Thatcher implied, was to provide the key disciplinary framework. Tight control of the money supply would mean that labour costs could not simply rise, whether in the shape of an expanded labour force or increased wages and benefits for those in work. If they did, for example as a consequence of trade union wage claims, then employers and firms would run into the barrier of the non-availability of funds or the prohibitive cost of borrowing. In these circumstances economic activity would be reined back and workers would be laid off, and hence trade union activity, and especially militancy, would be directly responsible for unemployment as – in an expression that was to become a Thatcherite catchphrase in the 1970s and 1980s – trade unionists 'priced themselves out of a job.' One of Thatcher's economic gurus, Ralph Harris of the IEA, advised her that this provided the Conservatives with both a political and an economic bullet point to deploy against Labour. 'On unemployment', Harris argued, you can surely gain most telling hits against the trade unions. Given that some increase is an inevitable side effect of checking inflation it cannot be denied that the phoney 'social contract' pushed wages to a level that was bound to price more labour out of jobs as monetary demand was checked.[57]

It was this aspect of the Labour Government's wages policy that led Joseph to describe the social contract as 'a devil's bargain' for both the government, which failed to control inflation, and union members, whose job security was undermined.[58] In contrast the Conservatives offered an economic regime in which employers and employees in both the private and public sectors would be, as had been said of the return to the Gold Standard in 1925, 'shackled to the reality' of a strict and stable monetary policy. In the case of the private sector, the monetary regime was to impose limits which, if overstepped, would force economic activity to be reined back as borrowing became too costly, workers who 'priced themselves out of jobs' became unemployed, and other indirect market pressures were produced. In the public sector the direct operation of cash limits to bear down on government expenditure and borrowing was to have equally deflationary and then stabilizing effects.[59]

Thatcherite Conservatives were, in the late 1970s, keen to disavow incomes policies and instead place monetary policy at the heart of their economic strategy, but this was not, in spite of the growing strength of monetarist opinion, a wholly straightforward political process. One problem was public opinion. In the summer of 1975 one long-serving CRD officer noted that: 'We know from other research (notably the ORC research for ITN) that the vast majority of the electorate (about 70 per cent) believe the government should have legal control over the size of pay increases. Their doubt is whether the actual policy will be either effective or fair.'[60] But if the electorate at large had to be persuaded that incomes policy was not the way ahead, this was also true of economic interest groups that the Conservatives looked to as 'natural' allies, notably the CBI. In early 1976 Thatcher and her chief economic Shadow ministers had a meeting with the CBI hierarchy and learned that, 'In regard to pay policy the CBI were keen on a continuing tougher policy', that 'CBI members would be "horrified" if the Conservatives did not support the Government's incomes policy' and 'They were committed to supporting a second and possibly a third year of incomes policy.'[61] Thus although Thatcher and her close colleagues were wholly against incomes policies, they felt that it was politically difficult to voice their scepticism and/or antagonism openly. Even Joseph, who was perhaps the most intellectually committed opponent of incomes policies, noted that many influential groups, including former Conservative and then current Labour ministers, the CBI, 'the great and the good', overseas financiers and, it seemed, the general public felt that incomes policies could solve inflation, and in these circumstances it was 'useful for an unfashionable opinion to be expressed.'[62]

That there was widespread support for and interest in wage restraint was not the only reason Thatcherite Conservatives fought shy of publicly rejecting incomes policies. To begin with they were also concerned that, ineffective as they felt such policies were, there were no readily available, proven alternatives. In early 1976 the Shadow Cabinet concluded that

> We would be unwise to oppose an incomes policy until we have found a method (if there was one) of reducing the monopoly power of the unions. However much recession and high unemployment were moderating pay claims, the problem remained of what we would do when the recession came to an end.[63]

But in addition some were willing to accept that monetary policy could, de facto, act as a restraint on wages, especially in the public sector, and, again, the Shadow Cabinet declared that 'We needed an incomes policy of sorts in the public sector enforced through cash limits.'[64] The central argument for cash limits was that they would reduce public expenditure, but a further result was intended to be that public sector wage costs would be reduced as either pay settlements or the number of employees fell in order to conform to the cash limits. To some extent there was an inconsistency here, but the circle was squared by the argument that trade unions and excessive wage claims and/or settlements were only responsible for job losses and not inflation.[65]

The essential Thatcherite claim was that 'trades unions do not cause and cannot cure inflation',[66] and that their only causal role was indirect. Joseph argued that the inflationary surge of the early 1970s had come about because 'the monetary expansion under Mr Heath was pushed too far at the prompting of the TUC, CBI, NEDC and of none more than Michael Foot and his friends'.[67] In short, trade unions and other interest groups could tempt or seek to pressurize governments to cause inflation by advocating policies that demanded monetary indiscipline, but it was the case that governments could and should resist such temptations and pressure. The Thatcherite position was that as government controlled the money supply it followed that 'Government and government only can abate inflation.'[68]

The attention devoted to inflation raises the question as to why this was given quite such priority over all other economic issues. A simple answer would be that a high and rapidly increasing level of inflation was the most novel and pressing problem of the 1970s. This was true, but provides only part of the answer. Large-scale unemployment had, for the first time since the 1930s, made a reappearance in Britain in the 1970s, and yet, in spite of the post-war notion that high unemployment spelt electoral disaster, inflation was prioritized by the Conservatives. This was a conscious political choice. The first indications that this choice would be made were apparent before Thatcher became leader. Shortly after the February general election of 1974, Anthony Barber, the Chancellor in the Heath administration whose 'boom' was seen as having triggered the inflationary surge, stated that 'with the benefit of hindsight, it would appear that when we had decided to reflate with unemployment at one million, we had in fact done so too quickly.'[69] This somewhat sotto voce mea culpa by Barber was accompanied by a general reappraisal of economic priorities by what had become the Shadow Cabinet. Keith Joseph, who had already emerged as the strongest internal party critic of the Heath administration, wrote a paper on inflation in May of 1974, which began with the statement that 'We all agree that inflation is our most urgent preoccupation', and went on to say that 'if this country is to return to sound money by gradual steps then consistent policies – involving some unemployment, some bankruptcies and very tight control on public spending – will be needed for at least five years . . . [and] some increase in unemployment will be unavoidable if inflation is to be mastered'.[70] Joseph's analysis was confirmed in late 1976 by one of CRD's economic specialists, who noted that combating inflation would probably require 'the likelihood of a prolonged period of high unemployment' and that it could be 'necessary to attempt a redefinition of what is the highest sustainable level of unemployment.'[71] There were parallels here with the situation in the late 1950s, when, faced with rising inflation, Harold Macmillan and his Treasury team had briefly considered redefining what constituted 'full employment', on the grounds that controlling inflation might demand an increase in unemployment.[72] But in 1958 Macmillan and his party had concluded that the political and electoral costs of higher unemployment were too great, whereas Thatcher's Conservatives clearly viewed inflation as more threatening.

The danger posed by inflation was, as noted above, not seen in purely economic terms. Speaking at Preston in September 1974 Keith Joseph, who was increasingly Cassandraesque on the subject, contended, 'Inflation is threatening to destroy our society.'[73] Joseph's argument was to be a Thatcherite leitmotif, and just over a year before she won power, one of Thatcher's favourite CRD advisers expanded upon the theme, noting that:

> Inflation threatens to an equal degree the confidence of the individual both in the strength and virtues of the mixed economy and a free society as a whole; and his confidence in the security of his position in it, whether of his job, his earnings, his savings, or the future of his family.[74]

In her first months as Conservative leader, Thatcher herself warmed to this theme. She told the Conservative Central Council that 'one of the greatest threats to liberty – to all our freedoms – is inflation', and she further informed the Conservative National Union that 'Inflation is a threat to our political and economic systems', and then, almost directly echoing Joseph's sentiments, declared to the Tory Reform Group that 'inflation . . . will destroy the basis of our society.'[75] In Opposition Thatcher spoke on the subject of inflation on average once every four days, and often addressed what she saw as the wide-ranging, socio-political ramifications of rapidly rising prices. But Thatcher was also, and arguably primarily, concerned with inflation's narrower effects. In her first major news interview after winning the Conservative leadership, Thatcher stated:

inflation affects different groups in very different ways – some people have benefited from it – their wage and salary increases have exceeded price increases by quite a large amount. Others have suffered by it enormously. Not everyone's had wage and salary increases to keep up with price increases, and those who saved or have taken out insurance policies have suffered a lot, and it's destroyed the faith of many people in some of our traditional ways of life, in being independent, in being thrifty and saving for a rainy day.[76]

Thatcher was asked if this meant that she had 'more sympathy with people who are competent at being thrifty, at saving for a rainy day than you have with people who don't find it so easy to manage.' Her initial reply to this was, 'I believe that if people do save you should not let their savings down', and when challenged 'about people who find it pretty hard to put anything by from a very small wage', she remarked, 'Well, they're entirely free to spend all they earn or to save it. But you mustn't in fact let down those who put something by and then in fact find that it won't buy what they thought it would when they saved the money up in the first place.'[77] Thatcher's interviewer was clearly implying that she saw the interests of the middle classes as especially threatened by inflation. He was right, for both Thatcher and her compadres had a particular interest in the middle class, or 'our people', and the problems inflation caused for them. Joseph had argued in 1974 that 'Inflation at the present rate let alone worse spells disaster for us as a country, as a society and as a party. It is cruel beyond words for the poor and the thrifty, and it destroys the *middle class*.'[78] It was precisely because of this that the Labour governments of Wilson and Callaghan had, in the view of Thatcher and the Thatcherites, neglected or delayed the battle against inflation, for the redistributive effects of inflation were a thinly disguised means of pursuing class war. Hence, when inflation had risen and 'When the masses of middle Britain were calling in desperation for real leadership',[79] Labour had failed to respond. Thatcher was determined that her party would respond, in order 'to alleviate the redistributive injustice of inflation',[80] and because she understood 'that the Tory party's natural constituency is the social group which is most threatened by rapid inflation'.[81]

Thatcher's admirer and early biographer, Russell Lewis, argued that Thatcher's interest in inflation was not 'sectional',[82] but the prioritization of inflation carried often explicit and always implicit social politics. In the early 1960s Ian Macleod had described the defection of suburban voters from the Conservative Party at by-elections such as Orpington as a protest of the 'unorganized', and, as Thatcher made clear immediately after her election as party leader, it was those who lacked the ability to secure 'salary and wage increases' that kept pace with inflation that she sought most avidly to defend. But the social politics of the prioritization of inflation were matched by the social politics of the deprioritization of employment. At one level, Thatcherites were keen to deny that their economic policies would create problems in this area, and Nigel Lawson argued in the summer of 1978 that he was a little disturbed, at the meeting of junior front-bench spokesmen . . . to discover how many of our colleagues appear to have swallowed the Labour line that our economic policies, especially on the public expenditure front, would cause increased unemployment. There is of course no reason whatever why they should do so, quite the reverse . . . I do hope our doubting colleagues can be straightened out before the campaign.[83]

At the time Lawson wrote, a general election was expected, and he was keen that no electoral passes should be sold on unemployment. Thatcher was also keen that Labour should not be allowed any space on this front. With unemployment having risen to then record post-war levels under Callaghan, Thatcher had told the Engineering Employers' Federation (EEF) in February 1978 that 'Our opponents will claim that our policies of disengagement will increase unemployment', and she described this as 'truly Socialist effrontery.'[84] In comments such as these by Lawson and Thatcher lay the roots of what was to be the Conservatives' most famous election poster of the 1979 campaign, that of a dole queue under the caption, 'Labour Isn't Working'.

However, although Thatcher and her colleagues were keen to avoid their party being labelled the party of unemployment, and sought to use Labour's record on this issue against them, they were also more than willing to contemplate a steep rise in joblessness. In early 1975 Thatcher stated that 'No government deliberately creates unemployment. But equally, politicians should not be hypnotised by dubious statistics into subsidising the wrong things . . . We can't go on for ever propping up inefficient firms and dying industries.'[85] This position, reminiscent of Heath's 1970 declaration about not rescuing 'lame-duck' industries, was confirmed by the Shadow Cabinet's decision of April 1975 to oppose the government's plan to subsidize selected industries, on the grounds that 'This would amount to the Government subsidising over-manning in British industry: redeployment of labour would be more difficult, the private sector further enfeebled and a significant step taken towards a seige [sic] economy.'[86] The Shadow Cabinet's discussion of the implications of this stance was very revealing. It was recorded that

> Sir Keith Joseph, whilst agreeing with the dangers inherent in any scheme for labour subsidies, said that opposition to them could invite the charge that Conservatives favoured high unemployment . . . Mr Maude said that there was no doubt that labour subsidies would further diminish the incentive for firms to reorganise and become more efficient. What was needed was redeployment of labour now to those sectors which were most likely to benefit from an improvement in world economic conditions. Mrs Thatcher said that in this case the correct policy was to encourage the retraining of labour and pay redundant workers higher allowances for this purpose rather than keep them in their present jobs.[87]

But it was not only the unemployment that would result from the elimination of subsidized 'over-manning' that the Thatcherites were ready to consider. At a meeting of the ERG in the summer of 1975,

> There was discussion of the feasibility of a policy of high unemployment, if this were required in order to end inflation. It was pointed out that unemployment and bankruptcies would be unpopular with both workers and our industrial supporters; on the other hand it was thought possible that unemployment in the 1970s would be (or could be made) less unpalatable than unemployment in the past.[88]

At another high-level meeting shortly afterwards, the ERG's chairman, Geoffrey Howe, concluded by

> inviting those present to think about two questions: First, how could the effects of unemployment be made harsher, for example for those elements of the labour force which were insufficiently mobile; and second, how could the effects of unemployment be made less harsh so that either frictional or disinflationary unemployment could be less unpalatable and likely to cause less social strain.[89]

It would overstate the case to argue that Thatcher and her close colleagues *planned* for mass unemployment, for it beggars belief that any politician or any government could have embraced the idea of the economic losses and social hardship that accompanied the joblessness of the 1980s. But it is no overstatement to say that, from the outset of Thatcher's leadership, the Conservative Party's approach to high unemployment was radically different to that of any of their predecessors. In 1978, as noted above, Adam Ridley of CRD called for a 'redefinition' of the acceptable level of unemployment, and in 1975 Geoffrey Howe argued that one result of a large, rapid reduction of the public-sector borrowing requirement (PSBR) 'can be unacceptable unemployment',[90] but neither defined specifically what they meant by 'acceptable' or 'unacceptable'. That no specific figure, or any other measure, was put on these terms was largely irrelevant. The main economic priority – a constant Thatcherite refrain – was to cut inflation, and, if high unemployment was attendant upon the measures required to achieve this, the end was to justify the means.

In addition to inflation, another factor militated in favour of accepting what had once been deemed an unacceptable level of unemployment, namely humbling the trade unions. In February 1976, when they discussed the issue of whether to endorse the Labour Government's Social Contract or to construct their own incomes policy, the Shadow Cabinet noted that in the future such a policy might be rendered unnecessary if 'much recession and high unemployment were moderating pay claims.'[91] Such thinking informed what at the time was deemed by many to be the 'perversely contractionary' Budget of 1981, when, faced with recession and rapidly rising unemployment, the Chancellor implemented a severely deflationary package. Given that in 1980 and early 1981 many industrialists and industrial leaders had expressed scepticism about or hostility towards the Thatcher Government's economic policy, it seems at first glance surprising that the 1981 Budget did not elicit more business opposition, but the fact that it did not was in large part a result of the broader aspects of its deflationary political economy. Business and industry in Britain had seen a previous Conservative government, that of Heath, come into office 'talking tough' about inflation and industrial relations, and had witnessed it U-turn and reflate the economy when unemployment began to rise and trade union protests about both wages and job security had escalated. In 1981 the Conservative Government and prime minister indicated they were 'not for turning', by both word and deed. That Thatcher's government stood by its deflationary strategy, in spite of large-scale, rising unemployment, and in tandem with its first Employment Act reforming trade union law, sent a clear message that it was prepared to confront the protests and actions of the trade union movement over the economy. Hence the 'bare-knuckle fight' the head of the CBI had promised the government over interest rates never materialized.

Thatcher judged rightly that Britain's businessmen and their leaders would accept the prioritization of controlling inflation, even if it meant rising bankruptcies and unemployment, as long as it also meant a direct and indirect weakening of the trade union movement. Likewise, she judged rightly the attitude of many trade unionists. When visiting unemployment-stricken Tyneside in 1985 Thatcher (in?)famously told local journalists they should not be 'moaning minnies' about the situation, but she made a more serious point when asked about the 20 per cent unemployed on Tyneside, replying, 'look, eighty per cent are in work', and trumpeting their job security and success.[92] It was a simple point that 80 per cent was larger than 20, but very telling in the political circumstances. On Tyneside, and in Britain as a whole, the number in work during the 1980s outweighed those unemployed, and those in work enjoyed rising real wages. Leaving aside the fact that joblessness was regionalized, the majority of the working population in the 1980s enjoyed rising living standards. Here there were parallels with the 1930s. It had been the political mythologizing of the experience of the 'hungry thirties' that had led many Conservatives, notably the party leadership, to assume from 1945 to the 1970s that mass unemployment was politically and electorally unacceptable. Yet the Conservatives had been dominant in the 1930s, in spite of the fact that unemployment remained high between the elections of 1931 and 1935, and there was no indication that Labour would have made substantial gains had an election been held in 1940. In short, there were no historical indications that high unemployment worked against a government that presided over that phenomenon, especially if, as in both the 1930s and 1980s, the working population enjoyed increased prosperity. The Thatcherite downgrading of employment and prioritization of inflation thus worked at both a general as well as a particular level for the Conservative Party.

At the time of the 1987 general election Thatcher and the Conservatives claimed that they had brought about an 'economic miracle'. The proximity of an election encouraged hyperbole, but references to what Thatcher's personal economic adviser Alan Walters termed Britain's Economic Renaissance were widespread, and not confined solely to the Conservative Party. In the two years immediately prior to her resignation neither Thatcher's own rhetoric nor that of other commentators was quite so hubristic, but nonetheless, both then and subsequently, few have questioned her claim to have presided over a major change in the British economy.

At the beginning of this chapter it was noted that the aim of Thatcher and her colleagues was to reverse what was seen as the long-term, ongoing and, in the eyes of some observers, potentially terminal decline of the British economy. 'Declineology' was a long-established part of British public and academic debate. Discussion of decline had begun in earnest in the late nineteenth century and had continued in various guises and degrees of intensity thereafter. What exactly British economic decline meant was not always clear. Indeed, as Peter Clarke and Clive Trebilcock have pointed out, Britain's decline was 'Like Elgar's Enigma', in that it possessed 'a haunting resonance which . . . inspired many variations.'[93] But among these many variations two were particularly recurrent, namely the ideas of *relative* and *manufacturing* decline. The notion of relative decline was simply that Britain had been and was being surpassed by other nations in terms of its economic performance and standing. In the late nineteenth and early twentieth centuries this took the form of the 'made in Germany' and 'American invader' scares, and the related concerns of the Edwardian tariff reform campaign that British industry was being driven out of foreign markets and challenged in its home market by foreign manufacturers.[94] After the late 1950s this concern took a more 'modern' form. The post-1945 creation of the OECD saw the emergence of comparative studies of, for example, national growth rates, and Britain was seen to be performing poorly when compared to all major and some minor competitor nations.[95] This relative decline was central to Conservative conceptions of Britain's economic slippage from the 1880s onwards, and was very much part of the Thatcherite appraisal of Britain's economic situation in the 1970s.

Alongside relative decline, the other common variation on the 'enigma' of Britain's decline was the idea of its slippage as a leading industrial and manufacturing nation. Again, this had been a focus of attention when decline was first raised as an issue, and throughout the twentieth century many of those who spoke about decline, academics as well as politicians, often saw it as synonymous with the decay of British manufacturing industry.[96] This was also a long-standing part of the subculture of the Conservative Party's economic thought, and was certainly prominent in the late 1970s. Thatcher and the Conservatives were clear that one (of many!) of the Labour Government's major failings was that its economic policies had not only been unsuccessful in arresting but had accelerated industrial decline, and the Conservative manifesto of 1979 set out the revival of British industry as a major objective. Furthermore, the Conservatives sought, in the late 1970s, to trump the Labour Party's idea of using the revenue windfall from North Sea oil to regenerate industry. One Conservative document argued that, with regard to North Sea oil, 'Realism demands . . . that the wealth from this freshly discovered patrimony is applied to produce income and benefits long after the sources of oil have failed – and that means industry.'[97] Likewise, Thatcher herself wrote in the *CBI Review* that 'we should now determine every penny of the revenue accruing to the Government from North Sea Oil will be devoted to investment in industry and commerce. Otherwise we shall squander a valuable national asset in supporting current living standards and shall fail to guarantee future economic strength.'[98] That Thatcher wrote this in the CBI's 'in-house' journal reflected the attempts that she and her party made in Opposition to develop closer relations with Britain's industrial leadership. To help achieve this, Thatcher and her Shadow economic ministers had frequent meetings with the CBI hierarchy. At one such meeting in January 1976 some potential tensions emerged, in that the CBI voiced their interest in incomes policy, but at the same time there was complete agreement that the regional committees of the NEDC should investigate overmanning and that the Labour Government's legislation with regard to planning agreements should be repealed.[99] In the summer of that year Thatcher underlined her desire for a close relationship with the CBI to its then general director, Harold Watkinson.[100] It might be assumed that this could have been taken for granted, especially because Watkinson himself was a former Conservative Cabinet minister, but the CBI chief told Thatcher, 'I have been meeting a good deal of criticism from some of our members that contacts between the Conservative Party and industry are not as close as they would wish.' Watkinson went on to add that many of the CBI's regional chairmen were impatiently waiting for the Conservatives to offer 'clearer industrial alternatives to the policies put forward by the present Government . . . [and wanted] the opportunity of learning what future Conservative policy on industry and economic affairs is likely to be.'[101] The CBI then set out to make clear exactly what alternatives it wanted, for the following summer the man who was to succeed Watkinson told Thatcher and other leading Conservatives that he would inform them what the CBI's membership wanted a Conservative government to deliver, immediately on taking office.[102]

No itemized list of CBI demands has survived in the Thatcher papers, but even if one was drawn up it is difficult to believe that any positive demands or requests that were made were met. In Opposition the Conservatives called for the regeneration of British industry, but under Thatcher's governments British manufacturing industry experienced its worst recession – worse even than the interwar slump – and lost 15 per cent of its capacity. Furthermore, in 1983 Britain experienced its first trade deficit in manufactured goods since the early nineteenth century. Thatcher often spoke proudly of Britain's history as the pioneer of the industrial revolution, but her premiership saw the country establish itself at the forefront of what could be termed the 'deindustrial revolution'. Thatcher's period in office and Thatcherite economic policies were not the cause of the deindustrialization process. This had been underway for a considerable period of time, and the fact it affected Britain sooner and faster than other industrialized countries may in itself have been a result of it having been the first industrial nation, for all the countries that followed and overtook Britain as major industrial, manufacturing nations had experienced significant deindustrialization by the turn of the twenty-first century. Thatcher and Thatcherism accelerated rather than inaugurated what seems to have been an evolutionary path that was common to all maturing industrial capitalist states.[103]

If Thatcher's Conservatives proclaimed their commitment to industry and business as a whole, they expressed particular interest in small business. It was this interest which led some Conservatives to become concerned that their party would be labelled 'Poujadist', but nonetheless the party and Thatcher herself advanced strongly pro-small business positions. Hence, in the summer of 1977 the ERG discussed a policy document on small businesses, which argued that they were the seedbed of future invention and growth, provided one-third of all jobs and concluded that 'Smaller businesses are vitally important to Britain.'[104] The same document also stated that small businesses had been hampered by Labour's regulatory and tax policies, and the following summer Keith Joseph explained that to comprehend the contrasting Conservative and Labour approaches, one needed to appreciate that 'The difference between the two main Parties is that the Conservatives are, in principle, intensely concerned with the health of small businesses – on social and political grounds (that is, freedom) – while the Labour Party is, in general, antagonistic to free enterprise in all its forms.'[105] Joseph went on to argue that 'despite this philosophic difference . . . Conservative governments have not always taken the interests of small businesses enough into account', and he demanded a more positive, committed Conservative policy stance.[106] Thatcher evidently responded to Joseph's prompting, for he was able to note, at the end of August 1978, that 'The intention of Mrs Thatcher . . . is to instruct all our ministers to take the interests of small businesses, especially, into account in all their work.'[107] Doubtless as a consequence, Conservative Party general election preparations and its 1979 manifesto emphasized the importance of small businesses and the need to provide them with support.[108] But in spite of their avowed intention to foster the interests and growth of small business, the policies of the administrations of the 1980s did not wholly favour small enterprises. During the depression of the early 1980s bankruptcies reached a record level of 11,131 in 1982, dropped in the mid-1980s and then rose again in the post-1987 recession – during Thatcher's premiership more small businesses went bankrupt each year than were created and survived.

As a consequence of the deep recession of 1979–83 and the chequered economic recovery of 1984–90, British manufacturing industry, large and small, suffered significant decline in the scale and scope of its operations in the Thatcher years. But if Britain's deindustrialization accelerated in the 1980s, so too did its passage along a particular avenue of that evolutionary path. When politicians and commentators first sounded alarms about British industrial decline in the late nineteenth and early twentieth centuries, they argued that Britain's problems were sectorally specific, for they contended that while the manufacturing sector was suffering acute economic difficulties, the financial sector was prospering. Joseph Chamberlain, who led the Edwardian tariff reform campaign, was very concerned that Britain was shifting by region and by sector, as London and its banking operations waxed while the industrial north and Midlands waned. One of the chief tariff reform economists summed up what he saw as the tale of the future, when he told the then Conservative prime minister that Britain would 'become more and more a creditor country – a banking country rather than an industrial country.'[109] This concern was to be a leitmotif of twentieth-century discussion of 'decline'. Through the interwar debates on the Gold Standard and the post-1929 slump, and the discussions of the 1950s and 1960s of Britain's 'slow growth', and the related question of the quantity and quality of investment provided by the City for industry, a large number of Conservatives aligned themselves with critics of the City and valorized the economic and social role of the industrial, manufacturing sector.[110] This, however, changed completely in the Thatcher era, for then the Conservative Party's tone and policy approach became markedly positive towards the financial sector. In 1978, speaking to overseas bankers based in London, Thatcher praised the City's contribution to Britain's overseas earnings, and noted that 'invisible earning . . . shipping, banking, insurance and other services provided for the world community by the City of London – brought in $4.5 billion: more than all the savings in foreign currency which we hope to enjoy from North Sea Oil'. She also celebrated the fact that 'this was not the achievement of politicians [because] the services provided by the City attract no subsidies, no hidden subventions from Government'.[111] In Thatcher's view the only thing that government did for the City was to place 'barriers . . . in the way of its improvement',[112] and hence her governments, after 1979, moved to dismantle all such barriers. One of the first things the first Thatcher administration did was to abolish exchange controls, and this was followed between 1983 and 1986 by the wholesale deregulation of the London financial markets, known as 'Big Bang'. In the Thatcher era the City boomed, at any rate until 'Black Monday' in October 1987, and the prime minister's admiration of and support for the City was reciprocated. Whereas Conservatives earlier in the century had tended to be suspicious of or hostile towards the City, Thatcherite Conservatives had no such prejudices. Thatcher again expressed the position well, when she stated at the Lord Mayor's banquet in 1981 that 'the City of London is a precious national asset' and that 'any government which fails to recognise this, fails to understand our national interest.'[113] Thatcher was clear that she and her government grasped both the importance of the City and how best to ensure its continued growth and prosperity, in that they understood how and why the City had become 'perhaps the greatest banking centre in the world.'[114] The Thatcher years witnessed, and Thatcher's own views embodied, a new departure in the political economy of Conservatism, in that the period after 1975 saw the Conservative Party embrace the structural shift in the British economy from the secondary to the tertiary sector, which they had opposed and inveighed against so strongly over the previous 90 years.

While the City prospered and grew under Thatcher it also underwent important institutional change, which resulted in a somewhat paradoxical outcome. The nature and structure of Britain's financial sector had changed noticeably over the course of the second half of the twentieth century, and after 'Big Bang' the process of change accelerated. Furthermore, the elite at the heart of the City changed as noticeably as its structure as a whole. For the greater part of the twentieth century, and indeed before, the financial sector's elite were the 'gentlemanly capitalists' of London's accepting, discount and merchant-banking houses, whose origins pre-dated the industrial revolution; alongside them there had emerged the 'big five' clearing banks that dominated the domestic capital and high-street banking markets until the 1970s.[115] But the City and its long-established institutions were the hub of Britain's financial system. Yet the creation of the Eurodollar market in the early 1960s, and the increased international banking presence in London, had, by the 1970s, begun to alter the socio-economic and functional make-up of the City. These changes accelerated in the 1980s, with the increased pace of globalization of the London capital market and the shifts that resulted from comprehensive deregulation in and after 1983. Large-scale, British-owned investment banks disappeared, all but one of the old stockbroking houses merged with or were taken over by international concerns and the 'big five' clearing banks were also transformed[116] and were no longer dominant on the high-street market. At the close of the twentieth century, largely as a result of the market-led expansion of the City's activities which Thatcher and her governments had embraced, London had witnessed 'the death of gentlemanly capitalism'.

If the structure of the British economy changed markedly under Thatcher, so too did the governance of the economy. At first glance, the story of this change may seem simple, namely that Keynesianism was replaced or supplanted by monetarism. Given that Thatcherite Conservatives denounced the economics of the 'post-war consensus', and that John Maynard Keynes was regarded as having been the basis of those economics, one might assume that Thatcherites would have dismissed Keynes as the root of all post-war economic policy evil, but this was not the case. In June 1974 Keith Joseph stated that the period since the war had been dominated by '30 years of Socialistic fashions,'[117] and in January 1978 Margaret Thatcher denounced 'The Socialist creed . . . whether the methods used owe more to Keynes or to Marx.'[118] The implications here were that Keynes was at least partly responsible for 'socialistic fashions', but still more common were arguments that Keynes' ideas had been misrepresented, distorted or hijacked. In 1976 Joseph declared that Keynes had not been a 'Keynesian',[119] and in 1980 Lawson spoke of 'the excesses of the Keynesian delusion,' and added that he 'did not attribute this delusion to Keynes himself.'[120] Thatcher herself was also equivocal. During her first year as leader she told the students of Roosevelt University in the United States that, 'Since the late 1930s, we in the Western World have relied on one great economist – Lord Keynes . . . what would Keynes have advised concerning the control of inflation . . . I venture to suggest the answer is not what some of his latter day disciples are advising.'[121] Likewise, Thatcher declared in December

1979 that 'Keynesianism has gone mad and it wasn't in the least little bit what Keynes thought.'[122] On occasion, these arguments were taken a stage further. In 1976 Joseph claimed that Keynes was not only not a Keynesian, but that he was a monetarist,[123] and in the same year Thatcher stated that 'Keynesian conventional wisdom – monetary expansion, indifference to inflation, the indifference to deficits – is dead. But Keynes himself had an insight, almost an obsession, that money was important,' and had acknowledged the relationship between money and inflation.[124] Far from subjecting Keynes to a barrage of criticism for providing the intellectual base for the 'unsound' post-war economic consensus, Thatcherite Conservatives sought to present Keynes' ideas as having been distorted and, when properly understood, supportive of their own position.

That she and her supporters were the 'true' interpreters of Keynes ran parallel to Thatcher's claim that the policies of her government represented the best interpretation of the route to the goal laid out in the famous 1944 White Paper on employment. This document had gained an almost mythopoeic status in post-war political economy, particularly on the Left, for it was generally, and erroneously, described as an embodiment of a 'Keynesian' commitment to full employment. Thatcher's first major reference to the document was in an interview with the *Sunday Times* in 1983. There she noted that:

> If you look back in that Full Employment White Paper – It was not called Full Employment, it was called Employment for the 1944 White Paper . . . It foresees structural unemployment. It foresees what would happen if industry had become obsolete, or the goods they produced no longer in fashion. It says 'Look, no amount of demand can overcome that'. It foresees the need for mobility of labour.[125]

Thatcher reiterated her claim to be this White Paper's true interpreter shortly before the 1983 general election. When asked about it by *The Times*, she declared that she was carrying a copy of the document, and she added at length that

> I know almost every word of it. So much of it is thoroughly true and sound still. Let me read you the last sentence of that foreword. 'The success of the policy outlined in this paper will ultimately depend on the understanding and support of the community as a whole, especially on the efforts of employers and workers in industry'. This is the important part: 'for without a rising standard of industrial efficiency we cannot achieve a high level of employment combined with a rising standard of living.' It goes on, it deals with obsolete products, it deals with mobility of labour, it deals with the importance of having balanced budgets, taking one year with another. It goes on to say things like this – 'Workers must examine,' paragraph 54, 'their trade practices and customs to ensure that they do not constitute a serious impediment to an expansionist economy and so defeat the object of full employment

programmes.' And then it says, paragraph 56, 'If an expansion of total expenditure were applied to cure unemployment of a type due not to absence of jobs but a failure of workers to move to places and occupations where they were needed, the policy of the government is frustrated and a dangerous rise in prices might follow.' There's far more in this White Paper that's on the side of my philosophy and my economic practice than anyone else's. And I can read you out sentence after sentence which says there's no substitute for industrial efficiency, industrial cooperation and for sound money.[126]

At her pre-election adoption meeting, and at a press conference during the election campaign, Thatcher quoted the interview referred to above and underlined her commitment to the 1944 document's goals and ideals, which, at a time when unemployment was at a post-1945 peak, might seem somewhat paradoxical. Certainly it is difficult to see the official figure of 3.1 million unemployed and the unofficial figure of close to 4 million as a 'high and stable' level of employment.

Whether Thatcher's governments caused or failed adequately to respond to mass unemployment is not fundamental in this particular context. What is important here is the intellectual framework which underpinned her approach to the issue. In this context the 1944 White Paper is important, not only because of its historical importance but also because of the way Thatcher interpreted its meaning. When she quoted it, and particularly when she brandished at a Conservative Conference what she claimed to be a copy she had bought as an undergraduate, there were many who questioned whether this was either historically or, more important, doctrinally accurate. With regard to the first, there is a battered copy of the 1944 White Paper, with 'M. Roberts' written on the front cover, in the Thatcher Archive.[127] The interpretative schema is more complex. Thatcher selected, in both her quotations from the White Paper and her annotations on her copy, the sections that related to 'supply-side' issues. Furthermore, she was fond of quoting the opening paragraph of the document, which stated that employment could not be created by Act of Parliament or government. Thatcher insisted:

> That White Paper accepted that a partnership was required if one was to defeat the problem of unemployment. It set out many factors which have been totally ignored. Had they been accepted it would have been easier to keep jobs, easier to be competitive and easier to create jobs in the future. As I said at my own party conference, I accept most parts of this Paper – pretty nearly all of it except those aspects which over time have changed.[128]

This reading of the 1944 White Paper was selective, but then so were readings that interpreted it as a simple 'Keynesian' blueprint for demand-side-led full employment. Indeed, Thatcher was correct when she insisted on pointing out that the document's title did not refer to 'full employment'; but cautious as the 1944

White Paper had been,[129] it had attached importance to the government's role in helping to stimulate demand, and Thatcher edited out, or at any rate downplayed, this dimension of its analysis.

Thatcher's interpretation of the 1944 document was in harmony with the more general Thatcherite argument that Keynes was, in effect, 'one of us'. This somewhat surprising argument raises questions not only as to how Thatcherites read Keynes, but also how they defined their own position. Thatcherites described themselves as monetarists, that is to say that they saw the money supply as the key implement of economic governance, particularly with regard to the control of inflation. But what exactly they meant by monetarism was not always unambiguous. One of Thatcher's personal economic advisers, Gordon Pepper, has suggested that there were three different kinds of monetarist working with Thatcher as ministerial colleagues and within the civil service – 'genuine', 'political' and 'pragmatic' monetarists. In Pepper's view the genuine monetarists believed in controlling the money supply as part of controlling money GDP; the political monetarists sought to reduce inflationary expectations and to stabilize the financial markets; and the pragmatic monetarists accepted monetary theory but felt that it was unrealizable in practice. With regard to the Thatcherite hierarchy, Pepper argues that only Thatcher was a genuine monetarist, while Howe and Lawson were political monetarists. In practical terms, the crucial difference between genuine and political monetarists was that the former wished, above all, to control the money supply, whereas the latter focused more attention on regulating the demand for money. For Pepper, a genuine monetarist was necessarily interested in Monetary Base Control (MBC), which demanded that the government regulate not only public expenditure and borrowing, but also those of the private sector. This required proper controls over banks and other elements of the financial sector as instruments of credit, including their provision of credit to one another. In contrast, political monetarists saw public finance and interest rates as the essential policy instruments.

In terms of Pepper's strict definition of the term, the Thatcherite governments of the 1980s were never genuinely monetarist. Pepper underlined his case by pointing out that the most celebrated monetarist economist, Milton Friedman, had criticized the first Thatcher administration's 1980 Green Paper for its assertion that fiscal policy and interest rates were adequate for controlling the money supply. It was mainly because Geoffrey Howe and Nigel Lawson had, for the most part, relied upon these instruments that Pepper considered them political monetarists. Furthermore, neither Howe nor Lawson saw MBC as a viable option, and in his 1984 Mais Lecture and his 1985 Mansion House speech, Lawson expressed scepticism as to the value of monetary targets as an economic indicator, and looked to what he saw as a wider disciplinary framework, in particular the exchange rate, as the basis of his macro-economic, anti-inflation strategy. Not even Thatcher *fully* met Pepper's criteria. That he described her as a genuine monetarist was largely due to the fact that she had ordered an investigation of MBC one month after she had become prime minister, and periodically voiced her interest in this approach over the 1980s,[130] but Pepper was critical of her statement that interest rates were 'the only effective way to control inflation', and he concluded that 'She was a monetarist more by conviction than scientific argument.'

Even taking account of the jaundiced nature of Pepper's judgement, it is difficult to sustain the Thatcherites' claim that their economic credo was pure monetarism, and the question remains how best to describe the economics of Thatcherism. In addition to their claim to be monetarist, Thatcherites also argued that they sought to recover what Lawson referred to as the 'pre-Keynesian consensus'.[131] One aspect of this was the monetarist priority of maintaining 'sound currency', but the idea of pre-Keynesian principles carried other policy implications. Keynes had been clear in his *General Theory* that his primary goal was to establish what came to be termed the macro-economic dimension as the basis of economic analysis and policy. Aggregate behaviour, rather than the behaviour of individuals, firms or particular industries, was Keynes' chief interest. This is not to say that he was uninterested in the micro-economic dimension,[132] but his emphasis was fundamentally macro-economic. In contrast, the core of the Thatcherite approach to the economy was micro-economic, with Thatcher herself speaking out against 'The basic fallacy . . . that decisions in industry are taken at the level of the sector', and arguing, 'They are not; they are taken at the level of the firm.'[133] As well as this micro-economic emphasis, Thatcherites, again in contrast to Keynes, focused on the supply rather than the demand side of the economic equation. Lawson stated the rationale of this approach very succinctly in his 1985 Budget, when he argued that 'The supply side policy is rooted in a profound conviction, born of practical experience both at home and overseas, that the way to improve economic performance and create more jobs is to encourage enterprise, efficiency and flexibility; to promote competition, deregulation and free markets.'[134] But Lawson argued that the Thatcherite strategy had '*two* key components', one of which was 'supply side policy designed to improve the competitive performance of the economy.' This was the micro-economic priority, but there was also a macro-economic goal, a 'monetary policy designed to bring down inflation.'[135] Here the Thatcherites constructed, in many ways, a new version of the 1944 White Paper, namely to maintain 'a high and stable level of competitiveness and a low and stable level of inflation'.

The replacement of employment by inflation as the focus of macro-economic policy was not, however, accompanied by a wholesale shift in the policy instruments deployed. In spite of all the talk of monetarism as the basis of Thatcherite strategy, the basic policies used by the Thatcher administrations, with the partial exception of the MTFS, were similar to those used by their predecessors. When the Conservatives had taken office in 1951, their adoption of 'demand management' had foregrounded the role of monetary policy through the active use of interest rates. The 'Bank Rate' was used, in Macmillan's terms, as both the main brake and accelerator of the economy, with the Budget and fiscal policy playing an important secondary role.[136] After 1979, the Thatcher Governments embraced a form of contractionary Keynesianism, as embodied by the MTFS. The first Thatcherite Chancellor, Geoffrey Howe, stamped on the monetary policy brake and in 1981 added fiscal policy weight to the pedal in an attempt to purge an inflationary culture. Howe's successor, Nigel Lawson, also used the macro-economic blend of fiscal and, above all, monetary instruments in his attempts to keep the 'judge and jury' of economic policy – the inflation rate – at a low level, even after he abandoned targets for monetary growth.[137] At the same time, internal party critics of Lawson, including Thatcher, blamed his insufficiently firm pressure on the monetary and fiscal brake for the rise in inflation in the late 1980s. Whether Thatcherites came to praise Lawson on inflation or to bury him, it was, ironically, through practising what he had once termed 'a bastard form of Keynesianism'[138] that he received both credit and blame.

The impact of Thatcher and Thatcherism on the performance and governance of the British economy was mixed. During Thatcher's premiership the structure of the economy underwent major change; most obviously the 'mixed economy' disappeared with the privatization of the majority of State-owned industries, and the industrial, manufacturing sector shrank markedly, while the service sector – personal services, retailing and financial – grew equally dramatically. The economy moved along a pre-existing path, and if its course did not change, neither did many of its key performance indicators. The growth rate fluctuated and never consistently reached the levels of the 1950s and, on average, only matched that of the oft-derided 1970s. During the recession of the early 1980s Thatcher commented that the economy was becoming 'leaner and fitter', but as measured by productivity this was not the case. Between 1979 and 1990 British productivity grew by 11 per cent, but in the same period that of France and Germany rose by 25 per cent and that of the USA by 65 per cent. Furthermore, the growth in British manufacturing productivity can in part be attributed to mass unemployment rather than any change in the culture and practice of work, in that output was being produced by fewer workers and thus productivity per man necessarily rose.

In many ways the productivity 'miracle' of the 1980s was similar to the Thatcherite 'economic miracle' as a whole. Had mass unemployment not brought about a rise in productivity that would indeed have been miraculous. Thatcher frequently argued that there were no simple answers to Britain's economic problems, but to deploy unemployment to achieve the end of raised productivity was to do so by the simplest means. A more difficult, complex route would have required the negotiation of a genuinely corporatist relationship between government, industrial leaders and trade unions, similar, perhaps, to German 'concerted action'. This option was considered by some senior Thatcherites, but for Thatcher the notion that trade unions could take any part in shaping economic policy was anathema, and the concept of corporatism – and the very word itself – was unacceptable. It may be that it was considered impossible to negotiate a constructive relationship with the trade unions, as this had been unsuccessfully attempted in the past, but it may also have been, as George Bernard Shaw once said of

Christianity, not that it had been tried and found difficult, but that it had been found difficult and not tried. The so-called 'governing institutions' of the British economy, the CBI and the TUC, in fact had very little governing authority over their membership. The CBI had no agreed, positive policy agenda and tended to share negative goals, such as hostility to trade unions and high taxation. Furthermore, the financial sector had deliberately excluded itself from both the CBI and the NEDC. Similarly, the TUC, as the winter of 1978–79 had demonstrated, had limited control over its membership, which at any rate had peaked at only 58 per cent of the workforce. When she denounced corporatism, Thatcher, as is the wont of politicians, assaulted a straw man. Since the failure of the first attempt, under Harold Macmillan, to introduce a British variant of French indicative planning, there had been much discussion and publication of corporatist thought, but little corporatist action. Corporatism was Thatcherite shorthand for State intervention in the economy that deployed and favoured the interests of organized labour. It was possible, as Howe suggested, that had the government sought to engage positively with broadened NEDC membership, a more effective tripartite structure could have been built. Thatcher, however, preferred to choose the path of confrontation, for, ultimately, it was politically far easier in terms of holding her party and its constituency together.

The issue of the institutional structure of British industrial relations necessarily carried a broader, very different question, namely that of the institutional structure of British business as a whole. Although Thatcher and the Thatcherites ostensibly sought to look at economic decline, the question of whether there was a division of interest between the financial sector and industry was never acknowledged by Thatcherites. As a consequence they never addressed one of the longest-running issues raised by the debate over British economic decline. In part this may have been because they did not accept the argument that there was such a structural divide, but equally important was that they could not accept the key underpinning of the argument, namely the idea of market failure. For Thatcher and her colleagues the market simply could not have had anything to do with decline, because the essential failure had been State interference with the market, and other factors, such as the actions of organized labour, which had hampered the market's operation. Once again the Thatcherite strategy was straightforward, that is, simply to accept the decisions of the market. In parallel with the Thatcherite refusal to accept the idea of market failure ran their lack of interest in the institutional structures of the marketplace. In the Thatcherite schema institutions were merely registers of market information, and the idea that they could have a significant input into and effect upon the market did not figure in their economic calculations. There were aspects of the analysis of decline which, for a combination of political and theoretical reasons, did not interest Thatcherites.

The politics and economics of Thatcherism were inseparable, in terms of both intra- and inter-party politics. When Thatcher became leader of the Conservative Party Lord Boyle wrote to congratulate her and remarked, 'I remember how, in the autumn of 1952, you used to appraise – a bit critically – the policies of RAB and the Churchill government.'[139] In 1952 criticism of RAB could only have meant, in the year the word 'Butskellism' was coined, criticism of his economic policies and their similarity to those of his Labour predecessor. Thatcher's critique continued through her description of what was 'wrong with politics', her offering of 'choice' rather than 'consensus', her vision of her 'kind of Tory Party' and her constant attacks on Socialist economics. Thatcher, throughout her career, singled out State intervention as her primary economic enemy and equated Statism and Socialism. Whereas many Conservatives in the first half or two-thirds of the twentieth century accepted the argument that Socialism and State intervention could be, as Arthur Balfour stated, as opposed as 'bane and antidote', Thatcher and the Thatcherites regarded them as bane and more bane. Thatcher effectively accepted what was essentially an 'old Liberal', individualist definition of 'Socialism', and this foreclosed the possibility of there being any consensual meeting point between Labour and Conservative economic policy. On these grounds the Conservative administrations of the 1950s and early 1970s had misunderstood the economic essence of both Socialism and Conservatism. As a consequence, Thatcher had a ready response to a question raised at a Shadow Cabinet discussion in the summer of 1975, when 'Mr. Maude said that it was important to get a clear idea of how much could be sacrificed of Conservative principles and policy in an endeavour to gain additional support from outside the ranks of the Party.'[140] For Thatcher, the 'clear idea' was none at all, but, in the first place, this was to require a clear definition or redefinition of the nature of Conservatism.

The political economy of Thatcherism is perhaps best understood in terms of the perspective offered by a group of French scholars, namely the 'Regulation School'. The work of these theorists, notably that of Michel Aglietta and Alain Lipietz, suggests that global capitalism as a whole, and, necessarily, British capitalism, changed markedly in the late twentieth century.[141] The mass manufacturing structure characterized by strongly regulated labour markets – termed 'Fordism' by the 'Regulationists' – shifted towards a 'regime of accumulation', which favoured deregulated labour and capital markets, and a move to what came to be known as the 'globalization' of productive and financial markets. Thatcherism's trade union legislation and its comprehensive, complementary deregulation of financial markets both reflected and anticipated developments in the nature of international capitalism. In this respect, Thatcher was the first world leader to embrace the new economic order that emerged in the wake of the end of the long 'post-war boom' and the impact of the first and second OPEC oil price crises of 1973 and 1979. Whether Thatcher herself, either fully or consistently, grasped the political and policy implications of the new order is open to question. Thatcher's attitude to European economic and monetary union indicated that she saw the new 'regime of accumulation' through a glass darkly and, furthermore, wished fully to embrace only certain aspects of its structure. One could argue Thatcher was an apostle of globalization, but one could also contend that the outcome of her economic policy was only partly her intention. Thatcherite political economy was, in terms of both theory and practice, complex and often contradictory.

3

Thatcher and privatization

Ownership by the State is not the same as ownership by the people. It is the very opposite.[1]

One month after she became prime minister, Margaret Thatcher told the Ulster Unionist Council, 'We will create a capital-owning democracy, in which all our people will have the chance to save for themselves.'[2] The most direct way for her government to encourage capital owning was through the sale of public assets, namely the industries and concerns that made up the State sector. Yet the *Conservative Party Manifesto* of 1979 only contained one paragraph on the nationalized industries, which focused on criticism of the principles and effects of nationalization and the Labour Party's plans to extend State ownership. The manifesto announced that a Conservative government would 'sell back to private ownership the recently nationalized aerospace and ship building concerns, giving their employees the opportunity to purchase shares', and further stated that it would 'sell shares in the National Freight Corporation to the general public'.[3] But the words 'denationalization' or 'privatization' did not appear in the manifesto, and there was no indication of any ambitious plan to reduce public ownership.[4] Margaret Thatcher's own statements on the subject in the 1970s seem to confirm this caution. Shortly before the general election of October 1974, Thatcher declared on Radio 2 that 'I do not think we have any wholesale plans for denationalisation,'[5] and only a year before she became prime minister she told the *Sun*, 'I am not going to go rushing into mass denationalisation.'[6]

The first Thatcher administration sold British Aerospace and Associated British Ports, and it also sold the government's holdings in the British National Oil Corporation, Cable and Wireless and Amersham International. The 1983 manifesto was more robust than its predecessor in this sphere, and it echoed Thatcher's 1979 remark when it declared that 'our goal is a capital-owning democracy'. This was to be achieved by the Conservative Government 'returning nationalised industries to the people . . .[to] encourage the widest possible spread of ownership; [and] by making it easier to buy shares in British industry through employee share schemes and Personal Equity Plans.'[7] The following year, the first move in what came to be known as the 'privatization campaign' took place, with the public flotation of shares in British Telecom. In 1986 British Gas followed, and then in 1987 British Airways, the British Airports Authority, Rolls Royce and BP; in 1988 the water companies and British Steel were privatized and in 1989 the electricity generating and supply companies. Altogether 40 State-owned concerns were privatized during Margaret Thatcher's premiership, and by the time she left office the railways and coal mines were the only major concerns that remained State-owned. The Conservative manifesto of 1987 had laid out the rationale of this campaign. Under the heading 'A Capital-Owning Democracy', it noted that in 1979 'only seven per cent of the population held shares' and that the Conservatives had set out 'to make share-ownership available to the whole nation'. This, the manifesto argued, had been done by introducing 'major tax incentives for employee share-ownership', by extending 'Personal Equity Plans, which enable people to invest in British industry entirely free of tax', and, above all, through 'a major programme of privatisation, [and] insisting that small investors and employees of the privatised companies should have a fair chance to join in the buying.' The result, it was claimed, had been the advent of 'a profound and progressive social transformation – popular capitalism,' which the Conservatives planned to extend with further moves to 'privatise more state industries in ways that increase share-ownership, both for the employees and for the public at large.'[8]

In so far as it had not featured in the Conservative manifesto of 1979, the privatization campaign could be, and has been, portrayed as a product of the 'pure', 'mature' Thatcherism of the mid- to late 1980s. The implication of this portrayal and these statements is that privatization had, at best, a very limited pre-history, but this was not the case.

Tentative debate

The twentieth-century Conservative Party's view of nationalization was, at best, one of grudging acceptance, and, at worst, complete hostility. This was hardly surprising. Nationalization was a logical corollary of Clause IV of the Labour Party's 1918 Constitution, and hence both the principles and practice of State ownership could only be 'Socialist'. The interwar Conservative Party regarded State intervention as acceptable in extremis, but sought to keep government at arm's length from the economy. Its response to the Sankey Commission's recommendation of the nationalization of the coal industry was wholly negative, and even on a local rather than national issue 140 Conservative MPs voted against the creation of the London Passenger Transport Board, which 'municipalized' the London underground and bus services in 1933. Nor did the party's position alter dramatically after 1945. Between 1945 and 1951 the Attlee Governments nationalized 20 per cent of Britain's industrial and utility concerns, but the Conservatives did not welcome this creation of a 'mixed economy'. The Conservative Party's *Industrial Charter* of 1947, often regarded as a milestone in the construction of a 'post-war settlement' or 'consensus', expressed hostility to State ownership. 'We are opposed to nationalisation as a principle', the Charter declared, and it went on to state that: 'If all industries were nationalised Britain would become a totalitarian country. If only a few industries are nationalised, they become islands of monopoly and privilege in a diminishing sea of free enterprise . . . Moreover . . . the bureaucratic method is highly inefficient when applied to business matters.'[9] One of the team that wrote the *Industrial Charter* was Harold Macmillan, who, in the interwar years, had spoken of his desire to see the British economy as a 'mixed system', but who was nonetheless critical of Labour's programme. Macmillan accepted the nationalization of coal and the Bank of England,[10] and he saw electricity, gas, water and the railways as effectively in public ownership already. However, Macmillan opposed further State ownership, and he argued in late 1946 that the Labour government's ongoing nationalization schemes indicated 'the totalitarian tendencies of modern Socialism'.[11] In the same vein, Anthony Eden declared in 1949 that when the Conservatives returned to office, 'Where they cannot denationalise, they will decentralise.'[12]

In the immediate post-war period the Conservative Party, for the most part, accepted that the utility industries had been publicly owned even before nationalization, and that the problems of the coal industry and railways were beyond the capacity of the private sector to rectify. But iron and steel and road haulage were seen as different matters. Here the Conservatives fought strongly against nationalization, and they also backed the sugar industry's successful 'Tate not State' campaign against public ownership in 1950.[13] On returning to government in 1951, they moved swiftly to denationalize iron and steel and road haulage and ended State control of development rights in land. The Conservative Government's stance, according to the One Nation group's 1954 pamphlet, *Change Is Our Ally*, 'marked a reaction in opinion against the trend not merely of the years of Socialism since 1945 but in many respects of the whole period since the first World War.'[14] For One Nation, and many other Conservatives, nationalization was an unwanted extension of the 'rationalization' movement of the interwar years: both developments were seen as expressions of faith in economies of scale, but with nationalization having an added faith in the State as opposed to private enterprise.

The Conservative Party, especially the parliamentary backbenchers and the party grass roots, demonstrated very little faith in economies of scale and none whatsoever in State enterprise – indeed they considered the latter phrase to be an oxymoron. Here, *Change Is Our Ally* provided support for the grass roots when it noted that firms employing under 500 workers, rather than big corporations, were more numerous and responsible for most industrial and other economic output in Britain.[15] One Nation did not denounce large-scale enterprise as such, but wished to see its development as the 'right response to economic environment',[16] rather than the product of artificially engineered conditions, and there was nothing more artificial than nationalization. Furthermore, *Change Is Our Ally* saw small-scale businesses as having intrinsic value as the seedcorn of innovation and future development, and they were clear that 'freely-operating competition is the most effective means of promoting economic advantage.'[17]

Through the 1950s the Conservative rank and file was consistently and persistently critical of the nationalized industries. A good example of a commonly held position was voiced by the young Margaret Roberts in her election address to the voters of Dartford in February 1950, in which she stressed that nationalization resulted in inefficiency and that private enterprise was the best guarantor of economic prosperity.[18] Here she was developing a theme she had raised a few months before. Speaking at Erith she had declared that a key difference between the State and the private sector was that 'private enterprise might make mistakes but if it did the cost was borne by the people making the mistake and not the taxpayer.'[19] This remark was typical of Conservative rank-and-file opinion, and was to be a feature of frequent criticisms of the public sector at Conservative Party conferences. The Conservative hierarchy was anxious to calm these criticisms, and at the party conference at Llandudno in 1956, which had seen strong expressions of anti-nationalization sentiment, a party Policy Committee on the Nationalized Industries (PCNI) was established.[20] The PCNI's terms of reference were:

> To examine and make recommendations regarding the position in our economy of the nationalized industries, both collectively and individually with particular reference to: the possibility of introducing any element of competitive enterprise; their administrative organisation and structure; relationship to responsible minister and accountability to parliament; statutory machinery for the protection of the consumer.[21]

Over the course of 1957 the PCNI examined a range of policy options for the State sector and provided a forum for leading backbench critics of the nationalized industries.

In March 1957 one of the senior members of the PCNI, Reginald Maudling, wrote, 'I understand it to be the view of the Committee that our general policy should be to denationalize and restore competition where this is practicable, but where it is not practicable, to make the nationalized industries as efficient as possible.'[22] For the most part, the PCNI concentrated on the latter question, but here they argued that it was difficult for the nationalized industries to 'secure a standard of efficiency comparable with the best in private enterprise in the absence of any incentives and bench marks which the competitive system provides.'[23] Keith Joseph produced two suggestions designed to address this issue. The first was to subject all the nationalized industries to an 'efficiency audit', that is to say, to use the then developing techniques of private sector management consultancy to assess the State sector's functions and performance.[24] The second was for the nationalized industries to raise investment capital from the private sector rather than receive government money. This, Joseph argued, would serve two purposes, namely, 'Government finances would be relieved and the relevant industries disciplined if they were required to raise the capital they need on the market.'[25]

The function and operation of the State sector occupied a great deal of the PCNI's time, but they also addressed questions of ownership and control. Some individuals on the committee, such as Gerald Nabarro and Ian Horobin, were 'denationalizers', but the Committee as a whole were not, and in March 1957 Maudling noted that 'The Committee felt that there is no case for complete denationalization of any of the nationalized industries.'[26] Nonetheless, the options considered by the PCNI indicated a desire to dilute the State's role. At a PCNI meeting in February 1957, it was suggested that the national airlines were 'the most likely candidates for some form of commercialization and denationalization,'[27] and it was noted that the Minister of Transport, Harold Watkinson, had suggested a move to a 'BP model'.[28] The following month Watkinson outlined his scheme, which was to make the national airlines, BOAC and BEA, into holding companies, which would then rent equipment and staff from operating companies, which would provide flights.[29] The idea was that State ownership would remain, but that operation would be quasi-autonomous and commercially driven. The PCNI welcomed Watkinson's idea,[30] and the idea of the 'BP model' was frequently to recur in its discussions, and continued to have adherents through the 1960s and 1970s.

The 'BP model' represented a form of halfway house between State ownership and private enterprise, and the PCNI explored variations on this theme in the form of 'hiving off' aspects of the nationalized industries' activities. Gerald Nabarro was particularly keen on this idea, and wanted to see the sale of the National Freight Corporation, the national and municipal bus companies, the railway hotels and coal retailing. This he saw as a way of 'testing' public attitudes to denationalization, with more ambitious schemes to follow if results were positive.[31] Nabarro's ideas, like Watkinson's, were greeted quite warmly by the PCNI, which rather troubled the committee's chairman, R.A. Butler, who told Harold Macmillan that it would be wrong to pursue such a policy as 'we should not give the impression we are nibbling at the nationalised industries before the public has a clear idea of our general policy towards them.'[32]

After a year of deliberation the PCNI produced no major policy proposals, but its work was nonetheless revealing. To begin with it showed that there was a substantial gap between the Conservative backbenches and the ministerial and party hierarchy. Indeed, one CRD official felt that although PCNI had produced no clear policy proposals it had served to help defuse tensions between backbenchers and ministers.[33] With regard to party opinion in the round the situation was more problematic. James Douglas, a senior research officer at CRD, told a colleague that it was difficult to convince the rank and file that industries like rail and electricity, 'which underpin the development of the whole economy are . . . matters which are best thought of in national terms.' He felt that the government should stress good Conservative stewardship of the industries rather than slip into 'the temptation to blackguard all forms of nationalization,' but added that 'this is something which it will not be easy to get accepted by the Party.'[34] Douglas also expressed concern that one of the

PCNI's papers gave 'one in the eye to the anti-nationalization boys' and that this was 'definitely asking for trouble.'[35] Within the parliamentary party opinion was, at best, divided on the nationalized industries, but rank-and-file Conservative opinion was, as the party conferences had consistently shown, decidedly hostile. The tensions and confusion within the party were summed up by a member of the PCNI, Ian Horobin. Horobin was himself a 'denational-izer', but when he told the second meeting of the PCNI that they should explore whether the government could 'denationalize' parts of the State sector, he added that it would be 'undesirable' to use the term.[36] It was as if 'denational-ization' carried an unpatriotic or anti-public interest taint that had to be approached with caution.

One way of defusing possible public suspicion of denationalization was to give the public a sense of their own material interest in the issue, and hence the debate on the nationalized industries fuelled a discussion on share ownership, although the two were not explicitly connected. In November 1958, a year after the PCNI was wound up, the Chancellor of the Exchequer, Deryk Heathcoat-Amory, stat-ed that 'The Conservative concept of a property-owning democracy may be said to include the widest possible ownership of shares in industry.'[37] Lord Hailsham, the party chairman, rapidly picked up the theme, expressed concern that the Liberals were developing policies on the subject and suggested that the Conservatives should do so as 'there is a very strong pressure inside the Party for adoption of proposals of this kind.'[38] As a consequence, two committees were set up, one in the Treasury and one in CRD, to investigate the question of wider ownership of shares in industry, and by the spring of 1959 both committees had produced reports. The Treasury welcomed the idea and indicated that removing obstacles, such as tax levels on unit trusts, would be the best way forward.[39] The Treasury also suggested that the Government should not 'propagandize' on the question, but this advice evidently did not reach CRD, for only a month after the Treasury report the CRD document was published, and bore the anodyne title, *Everyman a Capitalist*![40] In terms of future developments, the title in itself is of some interest, as is the fact that two later Thatcherites, Arthur Cockfield and William van Straubenzee, were part of the team that produced the pamphlet. At the same time, 'denationalization' was not seen as the obvious route to creating a share portfolio for 'Everyman'. Furthermore, Heathcoat-Amory, who had spoken so positively about widening share-ownership, stated that there would be a prob-lem justifying the tax concessions for small investors called for in *Everyman a Capitalist*. In the late 1950s it seems that the Conservative Party was wary of the public response to the issues that both share-ownership and the sale of national-ized concerns might raise.

In the 1960s, Conservative suspicion of and antagonism towards the national-ized industries continued to develop, but the party's caution diminished. A Policy Group on the Nationalized Industries (PGNI), chaired by Nicholas Ridley, was set up, and in 1968 produced some ambitious proposals. The PGNI's final report argued that 'the public sector is a millstone round our necks', that 'we have a built-in system of misallocation of capital in our economy', and that there was 'a very strong case for embarking on a course of gradually dismantling the public sector'.[41] The benefits of this course of action were to be increased efficiency, lower government costs and wider share-owner-ship.[42] Candidate industries for denationalization were steel, BEA, BOAC, BAA and Thomas Cook, and it was suggested that, at some stage, other sectors could be put on a sound financial basis and then sold off, notably coal, buses, elec-tricity, gas, telephones and Cable and Wireless.[43] As an interim measure, the 'BP model', as in the late 1950s, was put forward as a first step.

As a follow-up to the PGNI paper, Ridley produced what he referred to as a 'purely personal'[44] examination of policy options with regard to the State sector. This paper, in terms of both its authorship and the issues it raised, is of great importance to the history of privatization. Ridley began by lamenting the fact that the objectives of the nationalized industries were not defined, the commercial role of their management was obscure and it was not even clear whether they were sup-posed to seek profits. As a result, Ridley suggested that the nationalized industries 'should be given the objective of behaving in an entirely commercial fashion', sub-ject only to some restraints that could be set out in an annual directive.[45] Beyond complying with this directive, each of the industries, Ridley argued, 'should be left alone to maximize its profits', and their 'Management ... left free to manage', with the result that they 'should ... have the freedom to charge according to what the market will bear.'[46] He also raised the issue of denationalization, and his com-ments on this subject, especially given the conclusions of the PGNI that he had recently chaired, are worth dwelling upon. 'Denationalization', Ridley stated,

> is an unpopular word. The electorate think that it is 'playing party politics'. To talk about it is said to be bad for the 'morale' of those who work in Public Industry. Nevertheless, a substantial number of people, particularly Tories, (as evidenced by our public opinion poll) believe that we should do some denationalising. The politics of the matter appear to suggest that we should denationalise some industries but avoid using that word.[47]

In spite of the unpopularity of the word, Ridley was clear that there were impor-tant economic reasons for pursuing denationalization. To begin with, Ridley argued that if the industries were self- rather than public-financed this would cre-ate space for tax cuts as public subsidies were reduced. Furthermore, the nation-alized industries, he stated, took 21 per cent of national investment, while they employed 8 per cent of workers and produced 11 per cent of goods, which meant that they absorbed much more than they produced. On top of this, their losses were paid for by the taxpayer and they competed unfairly with the private sector. Finally, Ridley felt that decisions about the State sector were not taken on com-mercial grounds and that 'Political interference is probably the worst feature of Nationalised Industry,' which private shareholders would put an end to.[48] 'These together', Ridley concluded, add up to a very strong case for embarking on a course of gradually dismantling the public sector *as a whole*. It is a way of obtaining large savings in Government expenditure, and will provide more equity shares for the public to own. Moreover, we can avoid the cumbersome and unpopular method of denationalising individual industries which we used with steel last time.[49]

For Ridley, nationalization had to become a thing of the past, but the Conservative leader, Edward Heath, was unenthusiastic about Ridley's ideas, and Keith Joseph, who had been one of the more forthright members of the PCNI, baulked at their radicalism.[50] The 1970 Conservative manifesto was to reflect Heath and Joseph's caution rather than PGNI or Ridley's ambition, but, as the chief of CRD noted, the wording of the manifesto's industrial section was 'sufficiently broad to give a mandate for as much of the Ridley-Eden[51] policy as a Conservative government might wish to implement'.[52]

The 'Ridley-Eden' denationalization tendency in the Conservative hierarchy was given some rein in the first year of Edward Heath's administration. Nicholas Ridley and John Eden were appointed as ministerial deputies to John Davies at the newly created Department of Trade and Industry, and industrial policy seemed to move in accordance with their thinking. To begin with, Thomas Cook, the State-owned travel company, and the Carslisle breweries were sold to the private sector. In addition, the Industrial Reorganization Corporation was abolished, the Industrial Expansion Act was repealed, seven of the regional Economic Development Councils were scrapped and the Mersey Docks and Harbour Board was allowed to go into liquidation. These last actions were not denationalizations as such, but they indicated a desire to withdraw the State from industrial activity that seemed the shape of things to come. However, developments such as the State takeover of the bankrupt Rolls-Royce corporation and the interventionist 1972 Industry Act, which led Ridley to resign from the Government, brought an end to the prospect of large-scale denationalization. The Heath Government was an intense disappointment to denationalizers, who had thought, briefly, that their time had come, but the experience served only to reinforce their determination. In turn, Margaret Thatcher's rise provided them with an opportunity to develop their ideas still further under the aegis of a leader who had, from the beginning of her career, shared their views.

When and how?

In the year she became Conservative leader, Thatcher, like Heath, established a PGNI to advise the Shadow Cabinet, and, again like Heath, appointed Nicholas Ridley as its chairman. As well as examining the structure and performance of the nationalized industries the PGNI addressed the question of public attitudes to the State sector, and possible popular responses to reform and/or denationalization. Two major themes emerged from PGNI discussions. To begin with, there was the question raised by the PCNI in 1957 and underscored by Ridley in 1969 with regard to the commercial purpose of the nationalized sector. The management of the nationalized industries indicated to the PGNI that the relationship between the State and State-owned industries needed fundamental reassessment. In April 1976 a subcommittee of the PGNI reported that

> There is obvious and intense public dissatisfaction with the services provided by the nationalised industries, their prices, and the lack of public accountability. There is no genuine protection for the consumer in his dealings with the nationalised industries, and there would be great political advantage in implementing a positive and effective policy in this field ... our proposals are founded on the self-evident truth that the Consumer and taxpayer are the same person, and that in neither capacity are they getting value for their money, or good service.[53]

The Conservatives saw a political opportunity here. The PGNI subcommittee on consumer interests argued that Conservatives should propose the creation of three things – a Nationalized Industries Consumers and Taxpayers Audit Board, a Nationalized Industries Consumer Protection and Competition Council and a Nationalized Industries Ombudsman.[54] Together these would, it was contended, reassure consumers and taxpayers that the public sector was in every sense accountable. The subcommittee also argued that these proposals should be made public, as they felt that the Labour government was beginning to appreciate the unpopularity of the State sector and was 'likely to announce before long some half-baked scheme for consumer protection against the nationalized industries which our policy could pre-empt.'[55]

Consumer and taxpayer grievances were one thing, but they were seen as a symptom of the nationalized sector's broader problems. Here, the major concern was that the State sector had no clearly defined commercial role. As a consequence, the PGNI argued that, as a first step, the nationalized sector should be managed in a fashion as close to that of the private sector as possible. In the summer of 1975 the Shadow Cabinet's main economic policy committee, the Economic Reconstruction Group (ERG), noted that one objective with regard to the State sector was to improve public confidence in the nationalized industries. Here the PGNI suggested a number of reforms, notably phasing out subsidies to the nationalized industries, strict cash limits on their expenditure and curtailing ministerial intervention in their management. These reforms were to persuade the taxpayers that costs were falling and that they were getting value for money. The ERG noted that the regulation of prices had been discussed, but had been 'discarded at an early stage as impractical and too interventionist.'[56] That a government could be 'too interventionist' in a nationalized industry may seem a somewhat paradoxical notion, but it illustrates that the PGNI wished to alter the relationship between government and the nationalized industries. Michael Heseltine produced a paper in July 1976 which argued that the monopoly position of the nationalized industries should be ended and their operations fragmented to create small-scale units which could be sold to the private sector.[57] Heseltine was a member of both the PGNI and the party's Small Business Group, and his position here bridged the two. The Small Business Group had heard many complaints that small companies faced unfair competition from the State sector, and Conservatives were keen to address these grievances. But it was pointed out that 'The reference to preventing nationalised industries from competing unfairly while admirable in principle, raised serious questions as to how we would do it, unless a very hard policy of hiving off were imposed.'[58] Good intentions towards the small business sector thus opened and paved the road to denationalization.

The PGNI looked to create a more commercial 'culture' in the State sector and a climate of popular anticipation and expectation of greater commercialization. The ERG, having examined the PGNI's position, concluded that there were 'fundamental differences between the private and public sector,' and that whereas the former had the incentive of profits and the carrot of bankruptcy, the latter had neither.[59] The PGNI's assessment was that 'The Government's attitude to the public sector is not commercially orientated . . . [but] determined by a mixture of . . . political pressures and . . . union pressures . . . Striving after efficiency has . . . tended to be fruitless – because both the financial inputs and the financial outputs are the result of political determination.'[60] It was further contended that, as a result of their activities being shaped by 'political' rather than commercial priorities, a situation had arisen where 'the nationalised industries are run for the benefit of those who work in them . . .[and] The need to satisfy the customer is less and less apparent.'[61] In the view of both the ERG and PGNI this culture had to change. The nationalized industries were to be given clear goals, and investment was to be confined to their specialist business realm. Management was to be given powers to act commercially and to have full control over the setting of prices and wages, although on prices, the interests of consumers – as the PGNI's subcommittee had stated – were to be safeguarded.[62] Finally, the chairmen of the industries were to be paid salaries commensurate with their new commercial responsibilities. The purpose of these proposals was to create a structure in which the State sector was 'exposed as far as possible and appropriate to the disciplines of the market place.'[63] The essential logic was clear, namely that the public sector should be made to behave like the private sector.

Nicholas Ridley's personal summary of the PGNI's work, written for the ERG in the summer of 1977, stated that

> members of the Group represented a wide range of opinion within the party on nationalization. They had come under pressure from those who wanted substantial denationalization – which was impractical except in a few cases – and from those who wanted to maintain the status quo but to have far less ministerial intervention. There was an unresolved conflict between these two views.[64]

In effect, Ridley suggested that there was a division between those who wished to make the public sector look and behave like the private sector and those who felt the public sector should *become* the private sector through denationalization. This was an overdrawn demarcation. The PGNI argued that in an ideal world the nationalized industries would have clear commercial goals, well-defined financial targets and controls, and more independent management, but this was regarded as an unobtainable objective. Hence, in July 1976, the PGNI's Interim Report stated, 'Our discussions have brought us to the conclusion that there are defects in Nationalized Industries which exist because they are nationalized ... The only solution which would have dramatic effect would be to return the industries to the private sector.'[65] For Thatcher's PGNI the questions were not *whether* or *if* the State sector should be jettisoned, but *when* and *how*. With regard to timing, they felt that this 'will depend on the political climate at the time, but we should make such preparations as we can so that we are at least ready to take advantage of a favourable mood if there is one.'[66] Moreover, they were keen to help create such a climate.

Michael Heseltine consistently pressed the PGNI to voice and publicize Conservative plans for denationalization. In June 1976 he wrote, 'I recommend that we declare our intention of winding up the N[ational] E[nterprise] B[oard] in its present form ... [and that] its shareholdings ... [will] be sold back to the private sector.'[67] He accepted that 'some of the shareholdings we inherit are today unsaleable to the private sector (e.g. Rolls Royce 1971, British Leyland as a whole, Alfred Herbert)', but to meet this problem he suggested that 'a holding company will have to be retained unless we transfer the holdings back to government departments ... [and that] there are arguments for using commercial managers to scrutinise and monitor state holdings thus keeping those entities at one remove from political and bureaucratic interference.'[68] He went on to suggest that the NEB's name should be changed, that it should be prevented from acquiring new holdings and that it should act simply as a government agency and not initiate policy. Heseltine added that if the Labour Government's planned nationalization of British Shipbuilding and British Aerospace came to fruition, then the Conservative election manifesto should state the party's intention to return them to private ownership.[69] The following month, Heseltine underscored his position and declared that 'as an earnest of our intentions we should denationalize at least one industry at an earliest date, probably the National Bus Company.'[70] All of Heseltine's proposals were endorsed by the PGNI, and the ERG noted in July 1977 that the implication of their work was that 'It will be very much easier to attempt a permanent form of denationalisation after we have achieved a certain degree of fragmentation, for most of the industries, rather than to try and dena-tionalize whole corporations.'[71] Indeed, the ERG felt that there were good politi-cal reasons for adopting this approach. It noted that

> The process of returning nationalised industries to the private sector is more difficult than ever. Not only are the industries firmly institution-alised as part of our way of economic life, but there is a very large union

and political lobby wanting to keep them so. A frontal attack on this situation is not recommended. Instead the group suggest a policy of preparing the industries for partial return to the private sector, more or less by
stealth. First we should destroy the statutory monopolies; second, we
should break them into smaller units; and third we should apply a whole
series of different techniques to try and edge them back into the private
sector.[72]

This was very much the PGNI's preferred approach, for they tempered their
enthusiasm for denationalization with notes of caution. With regard to ending
State-sector monopolies and fragmentation, Heseltine felt that 'We should . . . be
cautious of applying these policies at an early stage in very sensitive industries.'[73]
He did not list the 'sensitive' industries, but the PGNI as a group suggested that
gas, electricity, the postal services and the railways should not be early candidates
for action. This was partly because their functions were difficult to fracture, but
also because public response was more difficult to measure and predict as there
would be concern over prices, for example. Hence the ERG concluded that 'The
utilities are clearly the least likely candidates – partly because they are big and
unlikely to be saleable, and partly because they need "regulating"'.[74] Caution was
also advised in the case of the British Steel Corporation, on the grounds that 'we
need to bear in mind that the steel industry is already very decentralised, and any
purely structural change would cause considerable upheaval in an industry that
feels it has already been interfered with over-much by politicians'.[75]

The administrative complexity of altering the structure of the State-owned
industries was not the only problem the denationalizers confronted. The PGNI
noted that the sale of the public corporation would face difficulties such as 'the
shortage of buyers, particularly under the threat of "renationalization"'.[76] This last
point was a particular concern, for in 1977 the ERG stressed that the 'danger lim-
iting our options was that a Labour government would threaten to renationalise
without compensation. [Hence] It was agreed that gradual fragmentation of the
industries, and step-by-step decentralisation of decision making, were the best
ways to proceed.'[77] A slow dismembering of the State sector was deemed the best
route to reducing the 'difficulty of legislating, and the possibility of bitter industrial action to frustrate us.'[78] With regard to legislation, the PGNI felt their
approach would require 'The minimum of legislation. Perhaps one enabling Bill
might be necessary to end the monopolies and to take power to dispose of assets.
But even this could perhaps be done administratively.'[79] The avoidance of large-
scale legislation would, it was thought, lower the chances of set-piece confrontations with the public-sector unions. The PGNI was clear that 'we should avoid
invoking [provoking?] major political battles', but they also stressed that 'we needed to have a clear idea which strikes it was possible to withstand and to win. [and
that] Successful resistance required preparation beforehand.'[80] Ways of avoiding
and dealing with strikes in the State sector were discussed at length by both the
PGNI and ERG. It was suggested that strikes in industries vulnerable to such

actions could be avoided through generous pay awards, and that it was particularly important to placate workers in the electricity and gas industries. If a strike was to be provoked, a non-vulnerable sector – such as the postal industry – needed to be selected. However, it was thought to be crucial to anticipate trouble in the docks and, more particularly, the coal industry.[81] Both the ERG and the PGNI felt that any move in the direction of denationalization would arouse strong trade union opposition. But it was also clear that they felt that this could, with planning and determination, be faced and defeated.

The PGNI moved to construct 'plans for . . . organic and automatic erosion of the public sector of industry.'[82] The State sector's inefficiency and cost were the prime concern, but it was also felt that the nationalized industries caused problems for the private sector and contributed to Britain's general economic problems. In the summer of 1975 the ERG emphasized 'the need to make an immediate start in shifting resources from the public to the private sector.' This was vital, they argued, because of the 'so-called "crowding out" argument, namely that the growth of the public sector was making it difficult to achieve expansion in the private sector of industry.'[83] Whether or not one accepted the 'crowding out' argument, and of course Thatcherites did, the costs, and especially the losses, incurred by the State sector had significant fiscal implications. Reducing these was important to the Conservatives for two reasons. First, there was the contribution they made to the public-sector borrowing requirement (PSBR), the reduction of which was a primary Thatcherite goal. Second, lowering public expenditure was to provide room for cuts in personal taxation, which was another priority. In this respect, saving taxpayers' money by reducing public sector costs was to be 'an example of our general policy of transferring resources from public to private sectors'.[84]

The PGNI, having decided that 'the party should make clear our dislike of the size of the public sector', concluded that 'We do not . . . favour a policy of wholesale denationalization by legislation in the old-fashioned way.'[85] The reference to 'old-fashioned' denationalization was a reference to the return of the steel industry and road haulage to the private sector in the early 1950s, which had been achieved through their sale to private corporations. The PGNI, however, wished to proceed in a different way. In July 1976 both Heseltine's paper and the PGNI's Interim Report stated that a Conservative government's first steps should be 'the issuing by nationalised industries of various types of shares as a means to denationalisation, including the issue of equity shares to workers.'[86] Exactly what kind of capital issue to deploy was not wholly decided upon. The PGNI discussed a number of options, namely Treasury loan stock, convertible shares, partially guaranteed equity shares for the workforce and equity shares on the open market. Treasury loan stock was deemed inappropriate as it would simply represent a form of second-class gilt, and convertible shares and partially guaranteed equities for the workforce were deemed 'delayed action denationalization'. Open-market equity sales were deemed full denationalization, 'since equity means ownership', and equity capital issues would be 'only meaningful as a means of denationalization.'[87]

Nicholas Ridley's paper of June 1978 closed by noting, 'The objective must be pursued cautiously and flexibly, recognising that major changes may be out of the question in some industries such as the utilities. [And that] Different methods should be used for different industries.'[88] He went on to list four ways of bringing about denationalization. The first was selling equity shares to workers. The second was selling equity shares to workers in proportion to their years in the company. The third was selling equities on the open market, and ensuring that any government holding was less than 50 per cent. The fourth was the direct sale of various assets directly to private-sector companies.[89] Denationalization by the sale of equity, with preferential share options for workers in the individual industries, was the option favoured by Ridley and his committee.

As the PGNI pieced together its plans it became apparent that its members regarded denationalization as the primary policy route for dealing with the problems of the State sector. Moreover, unlike the PCNI in the 1950s, the PGNI had a major input into party policy, for the party's 1977 policy document, 'The Right Approach', accepted all of the PGNI's conclusions. It also endorsed Michael Heseltine's argument that 'The National Enterprise Board must be abolished', although it added the rider that 'we shall have to retain some sort of administrative mechanism for selling off NEB shareholdings'. In terms of administering the State sector, 'The Right Approach' accepted that the nationalized industries had, in the first place, to be granted quasi-autonomy. It stated that 'The first requirement [was] to re-establish and to adhere to clear financial objectives for each corporation . . . [which] will be irrelevant unless management is granted the degree of freedom needed to set prices and meet each industry's statutory obligations without outside interference.' Mindful of the PGNI's subcommittee on consumer interests, it noted that 'Total freedom to set monopoly prices can . . . encourage management to tolerate inefficiency and pay too little regard to the consumer interest. There is, therefore, need for effective monitoring of each corporation's performance.'[90] These measures were deemed a necessary prerequisite for fragmentation and denationalization, and here a draft for 'The Right Approach' was clearer still, for it stated that 'The long-term aim must be to reduce the preponderance of State ownership and to widen the base of ownership.'[91]

In the 1950s the PCNI had argued that the introduction of private-sector managerial techniques was essential if the State sector's deficiencies were to be addressed, but in the 1970s the PGNI and 'The Right Approach' saw this not as an end in itself but as a means to the end of denationalization, which was seen as bound to other concerns. Foremost of these was whether denationalization could be used to create wider share-ownership, which in turn would help generate what came to be termed an 'enterprise culture'. Michael Heseltine argued in 1976 that 'denationalization . . . through the issue of shares and the sale of small units should appeal to work forces who should see consequent increases in productivity and earnings.'[92] The PGNI agreed and stated that the fragmented sale of the industries with shares for employees could produce 'a genuine experiment in co-ownership or worker control . . . [and] There might be demands for its extension by workers in other nationalised industries.'[93] Since the Edwardian period, co-partnership and profit-sharing had recurrently featured in Conservative attempts to foster a sense of employee involvement with their employers, especially among trade unionists. After 1975 share-ownership emerged as a new, central variant on this theme. Thatcher's shadow Employment Ministry picked up on this, and in the summer of 1976 argued that

> Encouragement should be given to schemes which would encourage wider share ownership among those working in industry and tax incentives should be given to the acquisition and retention of shares by all employees on a medium to long term basis . . . Only 3 per cent of Britons over 21 own shares in their own right. It must be in the interests of the Conservative Party to increase this number, both because it will lead to a greater understanding of industry and greater identity with the success of the enterprises.[94]

Furthermore, the Conservatives' target audience broadened to the population at large and not only industrial employees. Hence the Shadow Cabinet demanded that the party move to provide 'an explanation that our general economic policy was designed to create an atmosphere in which people would think it worthwhile to invest in equities.'[95] Thatcherite Conservatives wished to pursue Heathcoat-Amory's link between 'property-owning and 'capital-owning' democracy,[96] and, echoing the CRD pamphlet of 1959, the Shadow Cabinet agreed in January 1978 that 'our capital tax proposals should be presented in a high-key manner as part of our major strategy to encourage and enable every man to become a capitalist.'[97] This was viewed as particularly important in the context of a popular battle of ideas against Socialism. There was concern among Conservative thinkers and politicians that Socialist ideas had established a degree of ascendancy and that, in the public perception, '"Capitalism" is not a good word, and we do not think even "Free Enterprise" rings many bells'.[98] The spread of capital ownership was seen as a crucial complement to property ownership in this battle.

Popular capitalism

When the Conservatives came to power in May 1979, plans for denationalization had been fully discussed, and the idea of creating a 'capital-owning democracy' was more than just a slogan. The first Thatcher administration, as the PGNI had suggested, moved cautiously. It sold a block of government shares in BP in 1979, and over the next four years sold shares in British Aerospace, Cable and Wireless, Amersham International, Britoil (the former British National Oil Corporation) and Associated British Ports. These sales were not given a great amount of publicity – Aerospace and Ports were the only ones that had figured in the 1979 manifesto, and Cable and Wireless and Amersham were not household names – nor were they targeted at a mass share market. Indeed, in the first phase of denationalization the Government only once, in the case of Britoil, floated the shares without setting a price, and the issue was undersubscribed. In other cases, notably Amersham, an initial share price was set at a level considerably below what was considered to be the market rate, and, as a result, the issues were heavily oversubscribed. It seemed as if the Government was on a denationalization learning curve, both in terms of techniques of disposal and public response. In this respect the first, cautious, phase in denationalization was important in terms of evolving changes of emphasis in the public and political rationale of denationalization.

Margaret Thatcher made her first use of the term 'privatization' in July 1981, when she stated in Parliament, in the context of commenting on the sale of the British National Oil Corporation and the National Bus Company, that the policy was aimed at 'de-monopolising the powers of the nationalised industries and introducing competition.'[99] She emphasized the same point a few months later when, again in Parliament, she explained that privatization would end the monopoly of the nationalized industries, which was crucial because 'monopolies tend to be bad for the public . . . there is no competition, and therefore they lack the spur to efficiency.'[100] This argument about monopoly and the greater efficiency of competition was at the heart of the first wave of what had been termed denationalization, but what soon came to be known as privatization.[101] Geoffrey Howe underlined this point in his 1981 Budget speech. The nationalized industries, he argued,

> are not subject to the same market disciplines as the private sector. They have often been slow to adapt. And when eventually they do adjust, the financial and social costs can be very heavy. But the cost of delaying change has often been even greater, in terms of markets lost and jobs destroyed. It is the need to make nationalised industries more responsive to market disciplines which lies behind the Government's vigorous programme to increase competition in, for example, transport and telecommunications, and wherever possible to return parts of the State-owned sector to private enterprise.[102]

Linked to the question of the State sector's 'inefficiency' was the issue of its cost. Speaking at Georgetown University in 1981, Thatcher lamented that 'Nationalisation was supposed to make these great industries financially self sufficient . . . Alas, the reality has been very different . . . the publicly owned industries . . . have . . . massive deficits which are now being borne by the long suffering taxpayer.'[103] The cost of the loss-making nationalized industries, in terms of their cumulative deficits, had been an important issue for the PGNI. They had insisted that 'any policy adopted should entail an overall saving in public expenditure,'[104] and this had underpinned their commitment to denationalization. In 1976 Michael Heseltine had stated that, as a first step, State-sector reform would mean 'public expenditure must be reduced through the gradual elimination of subsidy and the movement towards commercial pricing.' At the same time he was clear that the level of saving 'will depend on the extent of denationalisation . . .

[but the] Amounts saved may eventually be quite substantial.'[105] The rising costs of the nationalized industries had led the Shadow Cabinet Finance Committee to welcome the Labour Government's introduction, in July 1976, of cash limits for the State sector. They had argued that this policy was a 'triumph for Tories', as they had been calling for such 'discipline',[106] and in January 1978 one PGNI adviser asserted that the money absorbed by the British Steel Corporation alone amounted to 10 per cent of the PSBR.[107] The public expenditure rationale for denationalization as a way of jettisoning a cumulative drain on government funds was set in train long before privatization began, and it remained a central part of its public raison d'être.

In terms of the income they brought into the Exchequer, the privatizations of the 1980s made a substantial contribution to the public finances and seemed to fulfil all hopes and expectations – in total the sales generated £4,394.7 billion. This brought about a significant year-on-year reduction in the PSBR and also provided a financial cushion that helped the government to lower the basic rate of income tax. But the gross receipts only provide part of the financial history of privatization. To begin with there were substantial government outlays in the form of underwriters' fees, advertising campaigns and other transaction costs, which totalled £2,408.6 million. In addition to this, the Government, following the sale of Amersham International, followed a policy of setting an initial share flotation price at a point significantly below what was regarded by analysts as the market price. As a consequence of, in effect, undervaluing its assets, the Government lost, or forewent, £5,804.6 million. Total government costs thus amounted to £8,213.2 million, or 17.72 per cent of the proceeds of privatization,[108] and, in purely financial terms, it is difficult to avoid the conclusion that 'the privatization exercise represented a net loss to the British public.'[109] The Thatcher administrations could have pursued less costly routes to privatization, either by simply selling the industries piecemeal to private-sector operators or, if encouraging small investors was crucial, by offering tax concessions. The former 'old-fashioned' approach had been rejected by the PGNI, while the latter was deployed, in Nigel Lawson's Budgets of 1984–85, as a complement, rather than an alternative to, public equity flotation. This raises the question of why governments so publicly committed to public 'economy' should have chosen such a costly approach.

The answer to this question lies with the growing emphasis that was placed on the ideas of a 'capital-owning democracy' and/or 'popular capitalism.' Margaret Thatcher herself first used the term 'popular capitalism' in February 1986,[110] although the previous year she told the US Congress how the response to the privatization of British Telecom had demonstrated capitalism's popularity.[111] If efficiency was the watchword in 1981, the second wave of denationalizations, during Thatcher's second term, saw a change of emphasis. During and after the large-scale public flotations of shares in British Telecom and British Gas, the theme that was given pre-eminence was that of the 'capital-owning democracy' or 'popular capitalism'. At the 1986 Conservative Party Conference Thatcher declared:

The great political reform of the last century was to enable more and more people to have the vote. Now the great Tory reform of this century is to enable more and more people to own property. Popular capitalism is nothing less than a crusade to enfranchise the many in the economic life of the nation.[112]

A few weeks later she reiterated exactly the same historical parallel, but added new twists when she said:

The response to the offers for sale of British Telecom and others has been spectacular. It's called privatisation. Not a word I'm particularly fond of. In fact a dreadful bit of jargon to inflict on the language of Shakespeare. But how much hope it offers, and how great the benefits it brings. Private ownership – of companies, of homes, of property of every kind – goes far deeper than mere efficiency . . . Our aim is to consign to the dustbin that most damaging of phrases 'the two sides of industry'.[113]

Efficiency, having been foregrounded in the early 1980s, now had a secondary role behind broader socio-political objectives. In his 1986 Budget speech, Nigel Lawson explained that

Just as we have made Britain a nation of home owners so it is the long-term ambition of this Government to make the British people a nation of share owners, too; to create a popular capitalism in which more and more men and women have a direct personal stake in British business and industry.[114]

The route to ending 'the two sides of industry' was, in effect, to make 'everyman a capitalist'.[115] Whereas the supposedly greater efficiency of the private sector and the related ending of monopoly had been foregrounded in 1980–83, 'popular capitalism' was the key motif thereafter. In this context Nigel Lawson made an interesting remark, albeit in retrospect, about the sale of Amersham International, noting that 'The serious underpricing of Amersham . . . may have been no bad thing. The enormous publicity given to the profits enjoyed by subscribers conveyed the clear message that investing in privatization was a good thing.'

The privatization campaign of the 1980s had its roots deep in the Conservative Party's subculture. From the time that nationalization was introduced by the Attlee Government there was strong hostility to the State sector, particularly among the Conservative rank and file. This hostility increased rather than diminished over time, and on this issue, as with many others, the party grass roots found in Thatcher a leader who shared their prejudices. Equally important, Thatcher's Shadow Cabinet and her governments contained personnel who also shared these prejudices, and who constructed a detailed strategy for dismantling the State sector. But although privatization was not, in terms of its underlying principles, a product of the 1980s, the political dynamics of the privatization campaign were. For the Thatcherite Conservative Party privatization had multiple and related political roles, but two were particularly important. To begin with, privatization was used as a defence against the charge, constantly made against Thatcher and her governments from the time they took office, that they were socially divisive. The creation of a 'capital-owning democracy' meant, Thatcher argued, that 'we have earners and owners both in management and on the shop floor',[116] as a consequence of her governments having made it 'possible for ordinary people with an ordinary wage or salary to build up their own capital.'[117] That employees in the privatized firms as well as the traditional investing class were given shares as an employee bonus, and options to buy additional equity, was presented as clear evidence of share-owning democracy. Thatcherites also deployed 'popular capitalism' to confront internal party critics. Here, the argument that genuine popular 'ownership' required members of the public to have a tangible sense of *personal* ownership allowed Thatcher to turn Harold Macmillan's critique of privatization around, and hence she told a Conservative rally in 1987 that privatization was 'selling the family silver back to the family.'[118] She took this argument deeper into the territory of her Conservative critics when she declared that 'The spread of ownership of housing and shares under this government is creating a new society ... fulfilling the Tory dream of One Nation.'[119] Indeed, the Conservative manifesto in 1987 stated that 'we are building One Nation', and, when challenged about divisions between North and South and employed and unemployed, Thatcher stated that 'where there were few shareholders, there are now eight and a half million', and that 'one nation' was being created by giving 'power and ... property to the people.'[120]

In 1980 there were 3 million shareholders whereas in 1990 there were 11 million. In this respect, the privatization campaigns, as Thatcher and her colleagues claimed, had a dramatic effect on the number of small shareholders. At the same time, 54 per cent of these 'capital owners' held shares in only one company, and a further 20 per cent owned shares in just two. Moreover, institutional ownership of British companies increased over the 1980s, from 72 to 79 per cent. The limitations of 'popular capitalism' and the 'capital-owning democracy', in terms of ownership and control, were thus as significant as the extension of the number of individual shareholders. Thatcher's claim to have distributed 'power' as well as 'property' was thus difficult to sustain. At no time was this more apparent than at shareholders' meetings of the privatized utilities, when motions critical of the boards of directors were tabled. On these occasions critical small shareholders were very numerous and, as individual voters, were always in the majority, but they were outweighed by the votes cast by institutions. Somewhat ironically, 'capital-owning democracy' faced the same bloc vote issue as had so often been the basis of Thatcherite criticism of the TUC.

4

Thatcher and trade unions

Margaret Thatcher was always suspicious of the trade union movement. She made her first public statement on unions during the general election campaign of February 1950, when she argued that they had come under Communist influence because their membership was too apathetic.[1] After her defeat she continued to nurse the constituency and voiced further criticism of unions, declaring at a local Young Conservatives' 'Brains Trust' meeting that 'general strikes should be made illegal.'[2] At the same time she sought to avoid being labelled 'anti-union', and when she spoke to an audience of local Conservative trade unionists in November 1950 she stressed that she herself was a member of a trade union.[3] During the 1951 campaign she stated in her election address that 'Free and independent Trade Unions are an essential part of industry',[4] and that a Conservative government would 'confer with the leaders of the Trade Union movement on economic and labour problems.'[5] But she also emphasized that trade unions should concentrate on their 'proper function', which was to safeguard their members' interests at work, and she called upon them to 'leave the problems of Government to the Government.'[6] Thatcher felt that the demarcation between industrial and political activity had broken down as trade unions had 'of recent years . . . become strongly pink.'[7] She wished to see this divide re-established, and this was to be a recurrent theme in her career and a central goal of her premiership.

Between 1952 and 1958, with her political career on hold, Thatcher made no public statements on trade unions. She remained a member of the party, and through the 1950s the party's grass roots became very restive on the issue of trade union activity.[8] Every Conservative Party conference saw numerous motions hostile to unions and calls for trade union law reform. Thatcher's suggestion of 1950, that apathetic members had allowed their unions to become dominated by Communist activists, was frequently repeated,[9] and it was suggested with equal regularity that legislation that required unions to hold secret ballots before strikes would reduce militant industrial action. This last point was presented very strongly at the 1956 Llandudno Conference, and the Minister of Labour, Iain Macleod, was given a cool reception when he stated that legislation for strike ballots would serve no useful purpose.[10] Apart from the difficulties faced by Macleod at the party conference, the Conservative hierarchy was also exercised in 1956 by the founding and activities of the People's League for the Defence of Freedom (PLDF), a single-issue lobby group which campaigned for the reform of trade union law. CCO thought that the PLDF could be useful in so far as it might help create a climate of opinion that would press trade unions to reform themselves, but they were also concerned that it offered a home to Conservatives frustrated by the government's reluctance to take direct action against the unions.

Nor were calls for legislation on trade unions confined to the party's grass roots. In 1958 the Inns of Court Society, a group of Conservative barristers, published *A Giant's Strength*, a pamphlet which examined the legal position of the trade unions and suggested radical reform of their legal immunities. This pamphlet was read by Macleod, and it was a focal point of discussions that he and the party's Steering Committee held in the latter half of 1958. Macleod's view of *A Giant's Strength* was that 'the Conservative lawyers are much too legalistic and radical in their approach to trade union legislation and, in particular, to the 1906 [Trade Disputes] Act.'[11] Macleod underlined this point when he told the Steering Committee that 'we can't go back and should not go back . . . [to] Taff Vale,'[12] but he also stated that 'he believed trade union legislation would be extremely popular with the Party . . . more than almost anything else.'[13] The Conservative dilemma here was summed up by Lord Hailsham, who noted that 'there was an important body of public opinion eager for action about victimization, the exclusion of workers from closed shop unions, sympathetic strikes and political strikes', and yet the party also had 'to avoid antagonizing trade unionists, of whom we had many in our Party.'[14] Many senior Conservatives, including Harold Macmillan, agreed with Hailsham's analysis, and felt that satisfying the demands of the Conservative rank and file in Parliament and the country at large would cost the party the support of Conservative-voting trade unionists who were critical to Conservative electoral success.[15] The Conservative leadership, and Macleod in particular,[16] sought to tread very carefully on trade union issues, and by September 1958 the Minister of Labour had concluded that 'there is no case at all for legislation aimed at strikes or restrictive labour practices.'[17] But although Macleod was against wide-ranging union legislation, he argued that action on sympathy strikes and on the closed shop and its 'petty tyrannies' could be considered,[18] especially the last, because 'the greatest public disquiet is felt on the issue of the liberty of the individual . . . [and] steps to give them greater protection would certainly be warmly welcomed by our supporters, and also by an important sector of middle of the road opinion.'[19] The Steering Committee accepted Macleod's cautious approach,[20] but the groundswell of constituency and back-bench hostility to trade unions was difficult to ignore. As a consequence, Macleod, who had no desire to confront the unions, felt obliged to propose that a commitment to trade union law reform be placed in the Conservatives' 1959 manifesto, only for the prime minister to veto the suggestion.[21]

Hostility to trade unions was an important part of the context within which

Thatcher relaunched her political career in the late 1950s, and she was very much in the 'reform' camp as a critic of the unions. From 1952 to 1958 she had not been politically active, but no party member could have been unaware of the tide of anti-union sentiment that flowed through the Conservative camp. More important still, Thatcher had joined the Inns of Court Society and was thus a member of one of the most important groups within the party campaigning for trade union law reform. Thatcher was not one of the authors of *A Giant's Strength*, but she was in accord with the Society's position.[22] At her adoption meeting in Finchley she spoke of the threat from a new 'despotism' that was being promulgated by trade unions, and argued that 'A man should have the right not to strike . . . We must regulate trade unions and protect the individual worker.'[23] Later that year, she spoke to Finchley Young Conservatives about the troubles of a number of Britain's older industries, but stressed that 'the shipbuilding industry had largely itself to blame for its troubles. There had been so much inter-union strife over demarcation that ships in British yards were taking 18 months to build. Orders therefore went to German yards.'[24] This argument – that unions were a root cause of Britain's industrial difficulties – flourished in the Conservative grass roots in the 1950s and was to remain a constant refrain of intra-party debate through the 1960s. It was accompanied by an equally persistent call for the reform of trade union law, and Thatcher was in complete harmony with the Conservative grass roots. When she spoke to the Finchley Chamber of Commerce a few months before the 1964 general election, she highlighted the case of *Rookes* versus *Barnard*, a crucial test case concerning the closed shop. Thatcher argued that the case 'opened up the whole question of the rights of trade unions under the present law, which was last reviewed sixty years ago.'[25] 'Sixty years' took the issue back to the Taff Vale dispute and the origins of the Trade Disputes Act, with Thatcher seeming to disagree with Macleod's stricture that a return to the former was neither viable nor desirable. Many Conservatives, ranging from Thatcher's fellow members of the Inns of Court Society to adherents of the PLDF, agreed with her view of the implications of *Rookes*, and looked forward to the removal of trade union legal immunities.

In 1963–64 Conservative grass-roots hostility towards trade unions reached new peaks. In March 1963 CPC groups pressed the case for legislation on compulsory strike ballots, and by November that year 279 constituency discussion groups had endorsed the Monday Club's call for trade unions to be made liable to actions of tort for losses incurred by employers during strikes.[26] Thatcher herself banged the drum for trade union reform through the 1960s. She was not a member of the Conservative working party on trade unions that was created in 1965, but as the party readied itself for the 1966 election she clearly shared Angus Maude's view that Conservatives needed to 'stop pussy-footing on the trade unions.'[27] At her adoption meeting for the 1966 election she assailed the intrusiveness of trade unions in the realm of individual rights,[28] and told another audience in Finchley that 'It is now the individual who needs protection against the power of the Unions and the public who needs protecting against unofficial strikes.'[29] By the time of the lead-up to the 1970 general election she was still more critical, calling for a drastic change in trade union law to bring an end to what she referred to as 'near industrial anarchy.'[30] With regard to trade unions and their legal status, Thatcher's position contained nothing original. On these issues, as on many others, she consistently echoed views emanating from the middle and lower ranks of the Conservative Party.

After their 1966 election defeat, and in the wake of the industrial disputes that racked the Labour government in and after 1967, the Conservative Party hierarchy embraced the cause of trade union reform. The party's 1968 document, *Fair Deal At Work*, outlined a case for legal changes which would reduce trade union legal immunities and lay the foundations for an ambitious reform of industrial relations law. By the summer of 1969 Thatcher was telling her constituency association that 'collective agreements should be enforceable in law',[31] which reflected the direction in which the party was moving on industrial relations. Thatcher also participated in the Selsdon Park Conference, at which 'comprehensive' industrial relations reform[32] was presented as a priority for the next Conservative government.[33] The aim of such reform, according to Heath's contribution to discussions at Selsdon, would be to shift the balance of power in industry which, since 1945, had swung decisively in the unions' favour.[34]

The Conservative victory at the 1970 general election saw the rapid introduction of the Industrial Relations Act, and Thatcher extolled the virtues of this 'essential' legislation to her constituency association when it became law in the spring of 1971.[35] Thatcher, like her Cabinet colleagues and the rest of the Conservative Party in Parliament and the constituencies, hoped that the Industrial Relations Act would transform both the workplace and the political environment. However, these hopes were to be disappointed, and industrial relations worsened. In the year that the Act was introduced the number of working days lost due to strikes – 13,551,000 – was almost double the number lost in the last year of 'industrial anarchy' under the previous, Labour government.[36] Furthermore, the Act proved to be not only complex and difficult to administer but also politically embarrassing to enforce. It placed individual union members in breach of its provisions under the jurisdiction of the criminal law, which resulted in the imprisonment and 'political martyrdom' of a number of trade unionists. As a consequence of these multiple problems, the Act was rarely used by either the government or employers, and in many respects the Heath administration's deployment of a sequence of statutory incomes policies after 1972 was a mark of the failure of the Industrial Relations Act in terms of both principle and practice: it had failed effectively to restructure the legal position of trade unions, and had failed to end – and indeed had exacerbated – the confrontational aspects of British industrial relations.

The failure of the Industrial Relations Act was an important factor in the fall of the Heath administration; had it been possible for the government to deal successfully with the industrial unrest of 1972–73, and, most notably, the miners' strikes of 1972 and 1973–74, there would have been no need to pose the question, 'who governs Britain?' Opinion polls taken when the Heath Government was in office indicated that the majority of voters supported the Industrial Relations Act,[37] which confirmed the views of those Conservatives who had been most deeply committed to trade union law reform. On this issue, and on more general questions of economic and industrial governance, the Heath administration was viewed by both voters and many Conservatives as having missed an opportunity, but it was also clear that the government had failed fully to define and articulate its goals. The Government had sought to curb or remove restrictive practices and regulate industrial action, but at the same time to strengthen the authority of the TUC over its membership. The reasoning here had been that 'official' strikes could be regulated and that union leaders had an interest in curbing 'unofficial' strikes that, in effect, questioned their own authority. This point had been made by Keith Joseph on the trade union working party in 1965, when he had spoken of the need to build 'constructive trade unionism',[38] but it had not been made clear exactly how this balance was to be achieved.[39]

The Heath Government's experience provided the Conservatives with a steep learning curve on the pitfalls of trade union law reform. At one level it seemed that the economic and political strength of organized labour was insurmountable, but this was not the only conclusion that was drawn. Public support for the Industrial Relations Act had been strong, which indicated that the difficulties which had stemmed from its implementation, such as the three-day week and power cuts, were the main cause of public grievance. This in turn indicated that it might be possible to construct a strategy that would enable trade union law reform to be achieved without alienating public support. Most Conservatives, both at Westminster and in the constituencies, blamed militant trade unionism for their party's electoral defeats in 1974, and the desire for further action, and indeed revenge, was strong. But the assumption that the trade unions were both powerful and anti-Conservative ensured that the Conservative leadership was predisposed to caution on the regulation of industrial relations. This became apparent shortly after the Conservative defeat in February 1974. A Shadow Cabinet Steering Committee met in March to discuss the new Labour government's repeal of the Industrial Relations Act and its introduction of new industrial relations legislation. Here James Prior expressed concern 'about the monopoly power of the unions' and pointed out that they 'had now effectively brought down two governments.' At the same meeting Anthony Barber stressed 'that we should try to avoid getting into an anti-union posture', and yet he also agreed with Robert Carr when the latter suggested, with regard to Labour's proposed legislation, that 'the clauses on picketing and the closed shop should be opposed.'[40] The implication of these exchanges was that the Conservatives should not pursue comprehensive reform, but should instead address particular areas of union activity that had been identified as unpopular by opinion surveys. Thatcher's campaign for the Conservative leadership reflected this cautious approach, and she declared before the second ballot that she regretted that 'it has been too easy to mistake us as a party of confrontation and divisiveness.'[41]

Planning for the future

During Thatcher's period as leader of the Opposition, the issue of how to deal with the trade unions was a constant theme of Conservative debate.[42] In December 1975 the Shadow Cabinet considered how 'to develop and communicate our answer to the frequently asked question, "how would the Conservatives deal with militant unions?"'[43] Nor was this question raised solely within the domestic political context, for in 1977 Geoffrey Howe reported that when he had visited the American Enterprise Institute he had found its members hoping for a Conservative electoral victory in Britain, but voicing concern: '"How can you be confident that a Conservative Government will be able to deal with your dreadful unions?"'[44] To some extent the Conservatives produced a simple answer to this question, which was that they would *not* attempt to repeat the approach adopted in 1971. In the summer of 1975 the Shadow Cabinet's Economic Reconstruction Group (ERG) held 'a discussion about the extent of the work that could be done in order to be in a position to resist strike pressure as effectively as possible.' At this meeting 'It was agreed that reforms should be unobtrusive and piecemeal, and should as far as possible be indirect approaches to the problem.'[45] Senior Conservatives presented the case for such an approach to both sides of industry. In May 1975 the Shadow Employment spokesman, James Prior, told the Industrial Society that

> The troubled field of industrial relations does not lend itself well to specifics. The detailed legislative approach has been tried it may have deserved to have succeeded but we have to operate now in the knowledge that it failed [sic] ... I promise you no legislative field day when the Conservatives are returned ...[do] not expect wholesale repeal of the Trade Unions and Labour Relations and the Employment Protection Bill.[46]

Prior had a reputation as a 'conciliator', but his message to an audience of employers was echoed by Thatcher when she addressed Conservative trade unionists in early 1976, for she told her audience, 'We don't intend ... any major legislation, like the Industrial Relations Act, to regulate the affairs of Unions.'[47] In spite of the deep-seated resentment of trade unions in the party's grass roots, the cautious line taken by Prior and Thatcher was regarded as an appropriate one by their colleagues. For example, Nigel Lawson, who was himself very critical of the unions, accepted the logic of the 'softly-softly' approach when he wrote to congratulate Thatcher on her speech to the Conservative trade unionists. 'I note', Lawson declared,

> that you said in your speech over the weekend that we do not intend any major legislation like the IRA [Industrial Relations Act], to regulate the affairs of Unions. The Labour Government of 1966–70 and ours of 1970–74 learned that such major changes can lead to 'more disharmony

than they are worth.' I am sure that this is right for the immediate future as for your first administration, although the day well may come when major legislation (although very different from the IRA!) is required.[48]

Lawson's closing remark carried the implication that the political climate after the fall of the Heath Government demanded that the Conservatives play a waiting game on industrial relations. Thatcher was clearly aware of this, and stated, in her reply to Lawson, that 'If we can't assure ourselves of the support of the Unions we must at least guard ourselves against their positive antagonism – the fate of the IRA [Industrial Relations Act] and Phase III proves as much.'[49]

The conclusion Thatcher, Lawson and the Conservative leadership drew from the Heath Government's experience was that they had to perform a balancing act on questions concerning industrial relations and the trade unions. This was, in itself, informed by their somewhat contradictory interpretation of the events of 1970–74. James Prior, who chaired the Shadow Cabinet committee on employment policy, noted in the summer of 1976 that 'we must bear closely in mind that we are *seen to have interfered too much* by legislative means in industrial relations in the past (however justified that legislation may have been, and unresolved though many of the problems remain).'[50] Prior's remark implied that there had been nothing wrong, *in principle*, with the Industrial Relations Act, that the Heath Government had sought the right ends and that the Conservatives needed to find new means of reaching them. Hence Prior argued that

a major task must be to convince the public (and as far as possible the unions themselves) that we are not antipathetic towards trade unions and do not seek a major confrontation. But this objective must be balanced against the need to ensure that people know we share their concern about the growth of union power and influence and have no intention of allowing it too much scope. We must appear neither unduly provocative nor unduly timid.[51]

This balance was not always easy to achieve. In November 1977 Geoffrey Howe made a speech that was greeted by the media as critical of unions. The following month he prepared another speech which sought to raise questions about the role of unions. He began his outline notes with references to the reception of his November speech. He asked, 'What is "union-bashing"? And have I been guilty of this grave offence?' He then went on to note that he hoped to raise 'questions worth asking while the reaction to my recent "outburst" is still fresh in people's minds.'[52] Howe sent his outline to Thatcher, and by the first remark she wrote, 'No. Why put it into people's minds?' and by the second she wrote, '*Too defensive* – if you can only be defensive – leave it alone'.[53] In contrast to James Prior, who was regarded as having a conciliatory approach to unions, Howe, the architect of the Industrial Relations Act, was seen as quite 'hawkish', but for Thatcher even he was too timid.

The social contract

Framing a general approach or attitude to trade unions was in itself important, but defining their role in the economy and their legal position demanded specific policy commitments, and in the context of the 1970s incomes policy had particular importance. Thatcher and her closest colleagues were, from the outset of her leadership, hostile to incomes policies for a variety of reasons. In April 1975 Keith Joseph and Angus Maude outlined some of them in a paper for the Shadow Cabinet, in which they argued that

> Our policy is bound to come under attack from the militants. We must make up our minds from the start on which grounds to fight. By not trying 'incomes policy' we avoid mass confrontation. But there are likely to be political strikes particularly in the state sector to try to force the government to subsidize them indefinitely. By withdrawing subsidies, and making it clear that wage increases will go onto the price we shall be able to apprise the public of what the battle is over.[54]

For Joseph and Maude, incomes policies turned the micro-economics of wage settlements into a macro-economics of the governance of the economy, with the result that governments which implemented them took on unnecessary and politically onerous responsibilities. The experience of the Heath Government was instructive here, in that the failure of its statutory incomes policies was seen as the proximate cause of the conflicts between the government and the trade unions that had led to the Conservative electoral defeats in 1974.

Thatcher and her close colleagues and advisers regarded incomes policies as not only politically dangerous, but also intellectually flawed. Since the Second World War incomes policies had been discussed and introduced by governments and their economic advisers as anti-inflation strategies, on the basis that inflation was a 'wage-push' phenomenon. The revival of interest in monetarist economics in the late 1960s and early 1970s led to a questioning of the anti-inflationary potential of incomes policies, and Thatcher's chief strategists accepted the monetarist critique. In the summer and autumn of 1974 the minority Labour Government reached an accord with the TUC which established a commitment to voluntary wage restraint on the part of the trade unions. The promise of this 'social contract' was an important part of the election campaign in October 1974, as Labour presented itself as the party of industrial peace and the Conservatives as the party of 'confrontation'. Initially, the Conservatives were unsure how to respond to the Labour initiative. Given that nearly all the Shadow Cabinet had been members of a government that had pursued an incomes policy it was difficult for them simply to reject the social contract. The Conservative leadership discussed the Labour Government's policies in the summer of 1975, and Thatcher stated that 'the City appeared to want the Conservative party to support the Government', but she was sceptical about both the effect and the popularity of wages policies. Likewise, two of her personal economic advisers, Brian Griffiths and Gordon Pepper, felt that such policies could only have a short-term impact and were invariably followed by a wages explosion. James Prior argued that 'it was necessary to redress the balance of power within society against the trade unions before the economy could be put right,' that an incomes policy of some form was necessary and the social contract should be supported. In contrast, Geoffrey Howe felt that the Government could only be backed if its fiscal and monetary policies were correct, as they, rather than wages, were the key to controlling inflation.[55] This debate continued, and at a meeting of the ERG in late 1975 Prior stated that it 'was not certain whether a Conservative Government could abandon incomes policy if one had existed for the previous 2 or 3 years.'[56] In contrast, Sir Keith Joseph and David Howell echoed Howe's argument that monetary and fiscal policy, and not wages, were the priorities. Indeed, Howell stated that the Heath Government's monetary policy in 1970–72 had worked, but had been abandoned mistakenly in the pursuit of incomes policy. Prior countered the monetarist position, and noted that in the early 1970s it 'had been hoped that the Industrial Relations Act might restrict the power of the unions.' He went on to argue that, even if one accepted that early 1970s monetary policy had been correct, the chances of 'effectively repeating this would be much reduced when we faced a more antagonistic union movement.' Prior concluded that 'If a reduction in public expenditure was enforced without co-operation from the unions on pay, the use of their monopoly power could rapidly negate the achievement. So fragile was the state of the economy that some form of pay controls was likely.'[57] Howe, the chairman of the ERG, papered over the disagreements by stating that 'the differences in opinion within the Group on the possible uses of incomes policy should be seen as a reflection of the views of the intellectual community,' but he also accepted that 'political industrial pressure by trade unions could persuade Governments to abandon monetary continence.'[58]

In 1976 the Conservatives were still unsure of how to approach the social contract. In February Geoffrey Howe told the Shadow Cabinet that they should resist the idea of a long-term pay policy; but he also declared that 'We needed an incomes policy of a sort in the public sector enforced through cash limits,' and suggested that the way the West German Government worked with their trade unions might provide a model.[59] In the summer of 1976 matters had not been clarified. CRD was clear that divisions within the party prevented a definitive statement of policy, and noted that 'The party is believed to be in a profound state of disagreement and to be making occasional, half-hearted equivocal noises in order to conceal that situation.'[60] Howe told the Bow Group's economic committee that there was a tendency to see the wages question in 'theological' terms, and that disputes were prevalent between those for whom 'incomes policy is "vital" on the one hand or "disastrous" on the other.'[61] In October he suggested that a solution might be found in a change of vocabulary. He told Keith Joseph that

> there persists an understandable hesitation in saying outright that we are
> against the social contract. This is because we all equally recognise the

need for pervasive understanding between government and people . . . If we call this, as I do, 'concerted action' it is difficult not to recognise that that is simply German for the kind of social contract that is essential in a complicated modern economy.[62]

Howe pursued the idea of 'concerted action', but ran into strong opposition, notably in the shape of Margaret Thatcher.

Thatcher was wholly opposed to incomes policies on political grounds.[63] When Nigel Lawson wrote to Thatcher after she had spoken to the Conservative trade unionists' conference, he stated, 'We need to treat the union leaders with benign neglect – and with an incomes policy, that is not possible.'[64] Thatcher was in complete accord with her future Chancellor and argued that 'the lesson of 1966–74 is that an incomes policy can only have a chance of succeeding with the consent of the Unions [but]. . . As I mentioned in my speech "we are not in the business of handing over the Government of this country to any group, however important, which has not been elected to govern".'[65] It was this attitude that underpinned Thatcher's criticism of Howe's interest in 'concerted action'. In late 1976 and early 1977 Howe, influenced by the example of West German economic management, worked with the ERG on the idea of setting goals for the economy, publicizing them and attempting to secure the cooperation of all sectors and interests of the economy in a concerted effort to achieve them. But when the ERG produced a document that outlined the conceptual and administrative structure necessary for 'concerted action' in Britain Thatcher was appalled, and she wrote on the paper, 'Please tell Geoffrey and Adam Ridley that I disagree most strongly with this paper. We are trying to cut down advisory bodies and requests for statistics – not multiply them.'[66] Howe sought to mollify Thatcher. He told her, 'I was not at all surprised to see your reaction to the Economic Reconstruction Group paper on "concerted action"', and he explained that he envisaged using a remodelled NEDC as a means of 'getting away from social contract-type deals with the unions while nevertheless seeking general understanding of our policies in such a way as to place on the shoulders of Union leaders a responsibility for hostility from their side.'[67] But Thatcher would not be mollified, and 'concerted action' quietly slipped off the Conservatives' policy radar screen.

Howe was frustrated by Thatcher's hostility to the work he and the ERG had put into 'concerted action', and understandably so. In a paper on pay policy that he had written earlier in 1977, Howe had indicated that there was a link between the party's emphasis on monetary and fiscal policy and the wages question. He argued that 'Money supply targets for the economy as a whole and cash limits for the public sector, imply clear limits to the growth of wages which can be reconciled with our other economic objectives. Thus we clearly mean to influence the level of pay settlements, even if not directly.'[68] Howe contended that there was an important difference between this indirect influence and an incomes policy, for the latter required that the government negotiate directly, largely exclusively and often secretly with the trade unions, whereas the former would 'not be part of a policy of political appeasement or of a willingness to appease if necessary.' Howe felt it was clear that 'We are not seeking to continue to sell the nation's birth-right for ever more dubious messes of pottage.'[69] For Howe, and others in the Conservative leadership, one of the beauties of a firm monetary policy in general, and the imposition of strict cash limits on the public sector, was that together they obviated the necessity for an incomes policy. In 'The Right Approach to the Economy', a document produced in August 1977, Howe, Joseph, Prior and Howell stated that pay bargaining was a matter for the workplace and should be the preserve of management and workers, not government.[70] They also contended that the tensions produced between the Labour Government and the trade unions by the social contract had created a situation in which 'union leaders may well find it both convenient and refreshing to deal at arm's length with a Government which knows both its place and theirs.'[71]

The Conservative Party's position on incomes policy, like the policies themselves, moved through a number of stages. In the wake of the experience of 1972–74 the party leadership, and certainly the backbenches and the grass roots, were predisposed to reject any statutory or institutionalized bargaining process between government and the trade unions. For Conservatives to have rejected the social contract tout court would have been politically difficult, as it would have left them open to the charge that they inveighed against inflation and yet rejected an anti-inflation strategy that they had pursued themselves. The Labour Government's introduction of cash limits on public sector expenditure in 1976, following its application for an IMF loan, was a godsend for the Conservatives. To begin with it enabled them to trumpet the Government's 'incompetence', and at the same time allowed them to argue that the Government was being forced to adopt Conservative policies to compensate for its own failings. But it was also helpful in terms of intra-party politics. Cash limits were an integral part of the argument for an emphasis on monetary policy and against government management of the real economy, and incomes policy in particular.

By the end of 1977 the Conservative position on incomes policy had been clarified, and at the beginning of 1978 it was possible for the party to construct a statement which defined its position. A meeting on pay policy in February 1978 concluded that a future Conservative government would supervise 'a return to free collective bargaining in the private sector, pay bargaining for the public corporations ... governed by the amounts which could be afforded and ... no subventions from the Government to finance excessive pay deals and bargaining within cash limits throughout the remainder of the public sector.'[72] This was to be 'free collective bargaining' within a disciplined framework, with the key being the Government's commitment to tight monetary and fiscal control. It was contended that in such a situation there would be no need for a direct pay policy, because

> With tight monetary control companies awarding large pay rises would find their customers unwilling to pay higher prices and therefore negotiators would have to choose between more responsible pay bargaining or

higher unemployment . . . It was erroneous to argue that any Government had to have an incomes policy simply because more than 7 million people were employed in the public sector. The vast majority of these were not employed directly by the Government but by public corporations, local authorities and only a minority by the Government itself.[73]

The lengthy and often tense intra-party debate over incomes policy revealed a great deal about Conservative thinking on trade unions. The goal of Thatcher and her colleagues, especially those on the Right of the party, was to remove trade unions from the realm of economic decision making. For Thatcher herself this was fundamental, and it explains why she was critical of Howe, one of her closest allies, when he expressed admiration for West German 'concerted action'. Although Thatcher acknowledged West Germany's post-war economic achievements, she was no admirer of that country's political economy. She saw West Germany as the prime example of 'corporatism', which she regarded with almost as much hostility as she did Socialism – indeed she saw corporatism as a derivative of Socialism.[74] Over the course of her career Thatcher made 25 public references to corporatism and the corporate state – all of them deeply critical.[75] This helps to explain her scathing, handwritten marginalia on Howe's outline notes for a speech on trade unions in 1977. Thatcher was not impressed by her Shadow Chancellor's overall approach, and wrote at the top of the first page, 'This is *not* your subject . . . the press will crucify you for this.'[76] But she was particularly exercised by his remark that if trade unions did not exist they would have to be invented as they were needed 'to represent the individual and group interests of those who earn their living in the corporate world of an industrial society.' Here Thatcher circled the word 'corporate' and told Howe that he 'should not use this word – it is too close to corporatism.'[77] Thatcher saw the role that trade unions had been granted in economic policy as leading Britain down the path of corporatist/Socialist economic governance, and in her view incomes policies embodied this trend. Hence, in 1985, when she told an American journalist about how she had arrested and reversed the corporatist trend in Britain, Thatcher described incomes policies as a dominant and damaging feature of the pre-1979 situation. 'We started [in the 1960s]', she declared, 'to have incomes policies which gave the trade unions far more power . . . the powers given to them by incomes policies . . . was a true collectivisation – government, trade union and industry.'[78]

Thatcher's goal was to disentangle, as far as was possible, the economic and political spheres, and this demanded that government withdraw from any direct involvement in questions related to pay. In her view, wage levels – and most other aspects of working life – were a matter for negotiation between management and unions/workers, and were not a concern of government. Thatcher and her ministers made this objective very clear during the industrial disputes that hit the nationalized industries in the first half of the 1980s. The first was the clash between the British Steel Corporation (BSC) and the Iron and Steel Trades Confederation (ISTC). In February 1980 Thatcher was asked in the Commons whether the Government had fixed the wage offer BSC had presented, and she replied, 'of course we have not fixed a wage increase ... the cash limit applies to three matters – investment, working capital and redundancy – The wage increase will depend upon the level of productivity';[79] and the following month she underlined that BSC and the ISTC 'must reach a settlement themselves ... because it is the management and those who work in the industry who must run it in the future.'[80] After BSC and the ISTC had reached a settlement Thatcher explained the rationale of the Government's approach, and told the Birmingham Chamber of Commerce that the goal was 'to move responsibility back where it belongs, and to where it can best be exercised – namely, to each firm. We are working to restore this principle to state-owned industries ... That is why we refused to intervene in the steel dispute.'[81] The Government took the same stance during the rail strike of 1982, with Thatcher telling the Labour leader that the dispute was 'a matter for the management and the board and not for the government';[82] and at the start of the miners' strike of 1984–85, Thatcher again stressed that 'The Government leave the National Coal Board to get on with the management of the industry within the objectives that it has been given within the financial arrangements that have been made.'[83] Although the miners' strike was about pit closures rather than pay, in Thatcher's schema both were the responsibility of the industry's management, and the Government's only role was to set the financial framework within which the management's decisions were taken.

In her memoirs Thatcher stated that 'Because our analysis of what was wrong with Britain's industrial performance centred on low productivity and its causes – rather than on levels of pay – incomes policy had no place in our economic strategy'.[84] This was only partly true. Thatcher and her administrations did indeed de-emphasize incomes policy, for in the Thatcherite analysis of British industrial 'decline', the 'wages problem' was seen as a symptom rather than a cause of Britain's general economic problems. But the economic analysis went hand in hand with a political aversion to incomes policies. The framing of an incomes policy demanded the close involvement of trade unions in policy making, and this was anathema to Thatcher and her close colleagues. Fourteen months before the Conservative victory at the 1979 election, one of the few Thatcherite members of CRD wrote a lengthy critique of government use of incomes policy, whether statutory or voluntary. He argued that it was

> the price which normally has to be paid to obtain the acquiescence of the union movement to the imposition of controls. For this bargaining between Government and unions engenders the feeling that responsible wage negotiations bring no rewards of their own but are a painful sacrifice which must be 'rewarded'. It has tended to involve the Government ceding radical, lasting and normally harmful social, economic and political changes in the structure of the economy in exchange for, at most a year of transient restraint at a time. The analogy of selling one's birthright for a mess of pottage cannot be denied.[85]

There was a dual 'birthright' in this case. To begin with, management's 'right to manage' was lost as government action replaced 'the resolve of employers to fight their own battles.'[86] At the same time, the Government sold its independence and became a broker between interest groups. In terms of pay, the result was a 'growing politicisation of major wage negotiations,'[87] but on a larger scale, questions that should have remained economic or business matters had, in the view of Thatcher and the Thatcherites, become issues of government policy and political controversy. Thatcher sought to 'depoliticize' the economy, and this required if not the complete depoliticization of the trade unions (their relationship with the Labour Party excluded that option), then the removal of their interests and activities from the centre of the political stage.

'Stepping Stones'

With regard to defining the Conservative Party's position on the social contract and incomes policy, 1977 was a crucial year, but the question of how to approach the unions more generally was still a matter of debate and no clear strategy had been defined. According to John Hoskyns this was the case when, in the spring of 1977, he and Norman Strauss began work on a strategy document, 'Stepping Stones', that focused on the trade union issue, which they presented to Thatcher in October that year.[88] Thatcher's response was enthusiastic, and she appointed a committee, chaired by William Whitelaw, to examine the document to see if others shared her enthusiasm. The committee was equally positive, and in January 1978 the Shadow Cabinet had a special meeting to discuss the document. Hoskyns' paper for this meeting, 'The Stepping Stones Programme', outlined the Conservative dilemma when it stated:

> Anti-Union hysteria gets us nowhere, but the unions do pose a real dilemma ... the Tories can either challenge the trades union status quo – and risk losing the election in the subsequent rumpus; or they can promise to govern on the unions' terms ... knowing that they are then almost certain to fail the country in office. Any move to break out of this trap has, so far, been successfully halted by the unions' shouting 'confrontation'.[89]

Hoskyns, like Angus Maude in 1966, felt that the Conservatives should not pussy-foot on the union question, but strongly assert that the unions were causing economic and political damage. Hence Hoskyns wrote that 'The Stepping Stones programme concentrates on linking socialism and Labour with the union leadership ... the link is widely perceived', and he urged the Conservatives to seek 'to create a feeling of exasperation and disillusionment among union members ... [and] bring out into the open ... the extent of communist domination of the unions.'[90] In short, 'Stepping Stones' stated the case for a radical, aggressive approach to the union issue.

The Shadow Cabinet was not wholly persuaded. John Davies, who had been

Secretary of State for Trade and Industry under Heath, felt that the paper side-lined the unions and did not acknowledge the mediatory role that the TUC, in NEDC, had played in 1972–73. The party chairman, Thorneycroft, agreed with Davies, and argued that the authors of 'Stepping Stones' took a position of 'extreme antagonism to the unions', and that while he accepted that 'criticism of the unions was generally well founded', he felt 'we should be careful about our tactics.' In contrast, Francis Pym, John Peyton and Whitelaw were all very positive about the paper, as was Thatcher. These differences were not reconciled, and all that was agreed upon was the matter of presentation, with Davies stating that 'if we told the truth about the unions we should certainly lose the election,' and Thatcher agreeing that the union issue 'could not be the centrepiece of our [election] strategy.' In the light of this last conclusion it was agreed that Prior, the conciliatory face of the Shadow Cabinet, should have sole responsibility for presenting the Conservative position on unions, and that care should be taken that there were no leaks to the press of 'Stepping Stones'.[91]

The minutes of the Shadow Cabinet discussion on 'Stepping Stones' confirm Hoskyns' view that there were divisions in the party hierarchy over how to deal with the unions. But they also confirm that the tensions did not foreshadow the 'wet–dry' divisions of the 1980s. Hoskyns clearly felt that Prior was too conciliatory, and in May 1978 he sought to persuade Thatcher that he should be replaced as Employment spokesman,[92] but Pym supported 'Stepping Stones' and Whitelaw, when chairing the committee that initially examined the paper, told Hoskyns that there was 'no option but to tackle the union issue head on.'[93] There was no disagreement that curbing the unions was a *political* priority, and here the points of tension simply concerned the nature and the timing of trade union reform. Equally important, however, was the question of whether the unions were an *economic* priority. For Prior, Thorneycroft, Davies and Gilmour, the unions were a cause of Britain's economic problems, and they were predisposed to use incomes policy as a means of halting wage-push inflation. For Howe, Lawson, Joseph, Hoskyns and Thatcher, wage-push inflation was a chimera, and the unions were a symptom rather than a cause. In the burgeoning monetarist schema unions responded to the fiscal and monetary conditions set by government, and if their wage claims could not be met by their employers in those conditions, or if union productivity did not match their wage claims, the result would be unemployment. For the monetarists the only link between wages and inflation was the public sector wage bill, in that, as it represented one-third of public expenditure, it contributed to the public-sector borrowing requirement (PSBR) and thus the growth of the money supply.[94] This helps to explain the importance the Conservatives, both in Opposition and in government, attached to cash limits for the public sector. Once the Medium Term Financial Strategy (MTFS) had been established as the basis for the contribution of government expenditure to monetary growth, public-sector pay and employment levels had to be tightly controlled. Without such control the MTFS simply would not work,[95] and hence Hoskyns, for one, railed against the first Thatcher administration's decision in 1980 to honour the Clegg Report on public-sector pay[96] and grant a 20 per cent pay rise to the miners.[97] Although the Thatcher Government consciously avoided any talk of a pay 'norm', it did, in effect, operate a wages policy for the public sector. The rationale was that the public-sector wage bill could have an *indirect* inflationary effect by pushing public finances askew – it was not 'wage push', but PSBR-led monetary inflation that public-sector pay was deemed to produce.

Strike action

The main objective of Thatcher and her administrations with regard to the trade unions was to remove them from the realm of economic governance, and although this entailed treating unions with what Lawson termed 'benign neglect', it also demanded legislative action. In Opposition, the Conservatives were clear that there would be 'no attempt by a future Conservative Government at a sudden overhaul of industrial relations law',[98] but this did not mean that they abandoned all thought of legal reform. Instead of a rapid and comprehensive alteration of trade union law, the Conservatives looked to pursue a set of detailed, incremental reforms. A first target was the closed shop, which, since the 1950s, had been identified by Conservatives as an issue which provoked much popular criticism on the grounds of individual liberty. In the 1970s the Conservatives regarded the closed shop as an area where the unions could be placed on the defensive, and soon after Thatcher became party leader, a Shadow Cabinet subcommittee examined issues relating to 'Individual Rights and Freedoms', with a particular focus on the closed shop.[99] The work of this committee was extended by the Employment Policy Committee, chaired by Prior, but its interim conclusions were cautious. Prior's team ruled out making the closed shop illegal, on the basis that 5 million workers were covered by such agreements and that it would be 'extremely disruptive' to abolish them. Instead, the committee accepted the arguments presented by Prior and Thatcher at the Conservative Trade Unionists Conference in February 1976, namely that all closed-shop agreements had to be negotiated with employers and subject to a ballot of the workforce, that a 'conscience clause' should allow individual workers to 'opt out' and that individuals who lost their job by refusing to join a union could claim compensation. The Employment Policy Committee suggested that closed-shop agreements should be regulated by a code of practice drawn up by the Arbitration and Conciliation Advisory Service (ACAS).[100] Prior described the conclusions of the committee as 'neither final nor comprehensive',[101] but they were confirmed a year later by 'The Right Approach to the Economy', which declared that 'The Conservative party is *not* in favour of the closed shop ... [but] We recognise ... that outlawing closed shops can sometimes not only be ineffective, but positively damaging to the individuals concerned.'[102] These conclusions formed the basis for action taken in the 1980 and 1982 Employment Acts, which legalized closed shops only after a ballot of 80 per cent of the workforce had been taken,[103] and made it compulsory to offer compensation to employees dismissed as a result of closed-shop agreements. However, closed-shop legislation went further in the fourth and sixth

Employment Acts under Thatcher: in 1988 post-entry closed shops were made unlawful, and in 1990 pre-entry closed shops were further restricted and it was made unlawful to refuse employment to a non-union member. Thatcher's third administration thus moved from the cautious, pragmatic approach to the closed shop taken by her first government, to the point where the creation and functioning of closed shops was rendered legally and administratively very difficult.

Since the 1950s a leitmotif of Conservative discussion of trade unions had been that political militants exercised an undue influence over their activities because of apathy on the part of 'moderates'. This had been the basis of Thatcher's first public statement about trade unions, and her views had not changed by the 1970s. From the 1950s on there were constant Conservative demands that union officials be elected by secret ballot – the assumption being that this would allow 'moderate' voices to dominate. Likewise it was assumed that pre-strike ballots would have the same, moderating effect. The 1976 Employment Policy Committee concluded, 'We . . . consider that a Conservative Government should not seek to compel postal ballots in trade union elections . . . [but] provide free postal ballots . . . on an optional basis,'[104] and this was the option that Prior took when he introduced the Thatcher Government's first Employment Act in 1980. This Act offered public funds for ballots for *all* union activities, including industrial action, and was informed by two assumptions: first, that unions would be obliged to make use of the legislation or risk being labelled 'undemocratic'; second, that ballots would reduce union militancy by giving 'moderates' more of a voice, because, as Thatcher argued, 'The militants will oppose the provision for secret ballots. They do not wish the silent majority to be heard.'[105] By 1984 the Government felt in a position to ensure that 'moderate' voices would be heard, for the Employment Act of that year stipulated that secret ballots had to be called before any strike action could be taken.

The way in which strikes were conducted was as important to Thatcher and her governments as the process of their being called. During the miners' strikes of 1972 and 1973–74, and the strike wave of the winter of 1978–79, the issue of secondary action and the behaviour of pickets had emerged as major issues. At a Shadow Cabinet meeting held at the height of the 'Winter of Discontent', Thatcher stated that 'She would suggest to the Government that they could count on Conservative support if they took a firmer line on picketing, and, in particular, if they were to introduce legislation to outlaw secondary picketing.'[106] The 1979 Conservative manifesto contained a commitment to provide 'the protection of the law . . . to those not concerned with . . . [a] dispute',[107] and the 1980 Act defined lawful picketing as restricted to the place of work of those involved in a dispute. The Act also restricted secondary action, such as sympathetic strikes, and laid down a code of conduct for lawful picketing, with particular emphasis on curbing violence and obstruction. The Act also enabled employers who sought to restrain union activity to seek an injunction against the leader of a union involved in a dispute. If an injunction were breached it was the individual leader who was deemed responsible and held liable for a damages suit – the Government assumed that unions would back their leaders and that an injunction against the leader would, in effect, be an injunction against the union.[108]

Thatcher described the 1980 Act as 'modest' and a 'first step',[109] with the clear implication being that further steps would be taken. In 1982 Thatcher's government passed a second Employment Act, which enabled employers to take injunctions against unions, narrowed the legal definition of a trade dispute and further restricted secondary action. Then, in 1984, the third major Employment Act of the Thatcher era made it compulsory for unions to hold secret ballots before industrial action, and also required that they ballot their membership every 10 years on maintaining their political levy. Thus, five years after taking office, the Conservatives under Thatcher had, in stages, carried out a comprehensive reform of trade union law. The approach they had adopted and the nature of the reforms were wholly different to those implemented by the Heath Government. To begin with the pace of change was gradual and the main areas of reform – closed shops, secondary action, picketing and ballots for the election of union officers and strikes – were areas where opinion surveys had shown there was significant public disquiet. However, there was no attempt to repeat the 1971 legal experiment of creating a National Industrial Relations Court (NIRC). In some respects the reforms of 1980–84 were similar to powers that had been granted to the NIRC, inasmuch as it had been granted the power to limit the lifetime of and compel ballots for the existence of closed shops, and, if requested by an employer or an employee in a dispute, to compel a ballot on strike action. In addition, the NIRC, having been granted a legal status equivalent to that of the High Court, had possessed the powers to imprison those in breach of its judgments for contempt of court. The crucial difference in the 1980s was that injunctions and actions for breaches of injunctions were civil matters, and they carried not the threat of imprisonment but punitive damages. Only violent or obstructive action by pickets was subject to criminal law, for the political risks were deemed to be low as the public and the media were overwhelmingly critical of such actions.

The 'right to strike' was not questioned by the Thatcher administrations,[110] but industrial action was ring-fenced by the employment legislation of 1984. Her governments also took administrative action to constrain trade union activity. Here, one important measure concerned the receipt of welfare benefits by strikers' families. In December 1975 the Shadow Cabinet had deemed it a priority to find 'how best to put our case on social security benefit to strikers' families',[111] and the following July the Employment Policy Committee had argued that, legally and morally, strikers' dependants were their responsibility, and not the taxpayers', and that they should not receive supplementary benefit. The committee contended that such a course of action would have 'a very wide measure of support both in the Party and in the country as a whole.'[112] The Conservative Government acted on this advice 10 months after taking office. Having decided that trade unions supported, or should support, strikers' families to the tune of £12 per week, the Government, in March 1980, reduced social security payments to strikers' families by the same amount.[113] It was not the stated ministerial intention to deter strikes through hardship, although party conference debates indicated that the Conservative grass roots hoped this would be the case. Thatcher presented the aim in somewhat prosaic terms, in that she argued that if unions 'have any thought or care for the people they are calling out on strike, they should use some of their enormous funds to help support those families . . . That is if the trade unions really care.'[114] Her theme of 'responsibility' was again to the fore.

Reducing the ability of strikers to engage in lengthy action was one strategy, but another was contingency planning to withstand major disputes. In July 1977 the Final Report of the PGNI contained a 'Confidential Annex', which examined how to deal with extra-parliamentary political opposition to what was then still referred to as 'denationalization'. Here strikes were seen as the most likely threat. Cutting off strikers' financial support through reducing social security and freezing union funds was discussed, as was making generous pay settlements to reduce the likelihood of strikes in sensitive industries, such as gas and electricity supply. In the light of the Heath Government's experience, it was thought that the coal mines were the 'most likely area' for a major confrontation, and it was suggested that 'we should seek to operate with the maximum quantity of stocks possible, particularly at the power stations . . . [and] make such contingent plans as we can to import coal at short notice.' In addition it was suggested that non-union drivers should be found to transport coal, and that power stations should as far as possible be fitted with dual oil and coal-firing capabilities.[115] These suggestions were made in the specific context of combatting opposition to 'denationalization', but when the Conservatives took office they were to take on a more general significance.

Scargill stand-off

Thatcher and her government faced sporadic bursts of industrial unrest during their first term, but nothing that threatened disruption on the scale experienced by the Heath Government. The lurking concern of Thatcher and her Government was that they would face a confrontation with the Conservatives' 'old enemy', the miners. The first Thatcher administration worked hard to avoid such an event, but also prepared very thoroughly to face such a confrontation, should it occur.[116] In February 1981, faced with the possibility of a miners' strike, the Government put pressure on the National Coal Board (NCB) to abandon its plans to close 23 collieries,[117] thereby contradicting its claim that such decisions were the sole responsibility of the industry's management. Later that year Thatcher told her new Energy Minister, 'Nigel [Lawson], we mustn't have a coal strike',[118] and in 1982 the government again pressed the NCB to reach an accommodation with the National Union of Mineworkers (NUM), while the 'moderate' Joe Gormley was still the union's president.[119] At the same time, the Government encouraged the NCB to increase output. This could have served an economic purpose, but in spite of the Government's emphasis on profitability in its 1980 Coal Industry Bill, the NCB was not allowed to raise the price of coal sold to the Central Electricity Generating Board (CEGB),[120] and thereby take advantage of the market opportunity offered by the doubling of oil prices. The primary purpose of increasing output was to build up reserves of coal for Britain's power stations. The economic recession led to a build up of colliery stocks which Lawson accelerated, and in 1982 Thatcher personally instructed the sale and transfer of stocks to the CEGB and the power stations.[121] By the time of its re-election in 1983, the government's logistical preparations for a miners' strike were largely complete.

That the Government was willing to face a showdown with the miners was confirmed in September 1983, when Iain Macgregor was appointed chairman of the NCB. As chairman of BSC, Macgregor had carried through a rationalization programme which had reduced the steel industry's capacity and workforce, and the expectation was that he would do the same with coal. Macgregor's predecessors, Derek Ezra and Norman Siddall, had concluded that the industry needed to reduce productive capacity by 4 million tonnes and that this demanded the closure of 20 collieries. Siddall's strategy for achieving this goal had been 'rationalization by stealth', in that the initial assessment of the possible closure of a colliery was delegated to management in the NCB regions. This, it was hoped, would prevent closures from becoming a national issue and, with the support of a relatively generous redundancy package, would reduce the possibility of a confrontation with the NUM.[122] In his first months at the NCB Macgregor continued Siddall's policy, but in March 1984 the poorly handled announcement of the planned closure of Cortonwood colliery triggered strike action by Yorkshire miners.[123] This presented the NUM leader, Arthur Scargill, with an opportunity. He had been seeking a confrontation with the government since he had been elected president of the union in the spring of 1982. In his first two years as leader, Scargill called for a national miners' strike on three occasions, but each time a ballot of the NUM had rejected the call. In March 1984 he decided upon a different course of action and called a strike without a ballot, on the basis that most regions would follow Yorkshire's example, and that mass picketing would either persuade other regions to join or prevent their working fully.

Scargill was determined to confront the Government, but the Government was equally determined to confront and defeat Scargill and the NUM. Scargill's 'flying pickets' and mass pickets, which he had first deployed as Yorkshire NUM leader in 1972 and 1974, were met with a mass police presence. The changes in the law controlling the conduct of pickets in the 1980 and 1982 Employment Acts gave the police the power to halt the movement of 'flying pickets', and to arrest those in breach of the picketing code of conduct for public order offences. Furthermore, the police deployed in the mining areas were usually drawn from regions outside those localities to ensure that 'community solidarity' did not obstruct rigorous policing of the picket lines. Nor were the laws on picketing the only elements of the new employment laws used against the miners. Because the strike had been called without a ballot it was in breach of the 1984 Act, and an injunction was taken out against the NUM which allowed the seizure of NUM funds in October 1984, thereby cutting off union strike pay to miners. The government also played a major role in shaping the conduct of the dispute. Although

Thatcher claimed that Macgregor and the coal industry's management were in charge of the dispute, the Energy Minister, Peter Walker, was in daily contact with Macgregor to discuss tactics;[124] the outcome of the miners' strike was far too important for the Government to play a hands-off role. The Government's strategy was simple, namely that Scargill and the NUM were to be beaten and the miners were to return to work unconditionally.

One measure of the importance of the miners' strike to Thatcher's administration was its cost. Lawson calculated that the direct cost was £2.8 billion and its overall cost was £3.5 billion,[125] which was a major outlay given the Government's ostensible commitment to economic and financial prudence. No company in the private sector could or would have endured this, but the Government felt that the benefits of defeating the miners outweighed the cost. In her memoirs Thatcher stated that 'By the 1970s the coal-mining industry had come to symbolize everything that was wrong with Britain.'[126] As an industry, coal-mining had all the economic flaws Thatcher associated with the State sector – it was 'inefficient' and 'over-manned' and, as a result, was a loss-making burden to the Exchequer and the taxpayer. Also, the industry's workforce represented in her eyes the worst aspects of trade unionism. In Thatcher's view the miner was not the 'archetypal proletarian', but the 'archetypal overmighty subject', as had been demonstrated in 1974. For Thatcher it was essential that the NUM, the vanguard of militant trade unionism, be humbled in order to establish that trade union power had been broken. Once it had begun, the miners' strike took on the guise of a war, and Thatcher's language, like that of the self-professed class warrior, Scargill, reflected this. Hence Thatcher compared the NUM to the recently vanquished Argentinians, and told the 1922 Committee that whereas in the Falklands she had confronted 'the enemy without', she was now engaged with 'the enemy within . . . more difficult to fight . . . [but] just as dangerous to liberty.'[127] This tendency to deploy the vocabulary of war was reinforced by the fact that confrontations between police and pickets were often violent; that at Orgreave, in June 1984, was termed 'the Battle of Orgreave' by the press. If the conduct of the dispute was described in these terms, so too was its outcome. In his memoirs, Lawson states that the result of the 1984–85 strike compared to that of 1973–74 was similar to the result of the Falklands compared to Suez; and Thatcher speaks in her memoirs of the defeat of the 'Fascist Left' in 1985 in similar terms to those of the victory 40 years earlier.[128] For the losers, the outcome was as decisive as for the victors. When Thatcher took office there were 253,000 members of the NUM, but by the time of her resignation the number had fallen to 53,000 and the decline continued through the 1990s. If the NUM had been the proximate cause of Heath's political downfall, Thatcher's premiership was the NUM's political and occupational nemesis.

The defeat of the miners was the apogee of Thatcher's campaign against organized labour and, as Lawson suggested, laid to rest the ghost of Heath's downfall. The comprehensive 'triumph' over the NUM was not, however, due simply to the government's strategy and policies. The trade union legislation of 1980–84 played a part in defeating the NUM by depriving the union of funds six months into the strike, as did pre-strike preparation, rigorous policing and the Government's willingness to bear the huge economic cost. But the Government was fortunate in that its opponents fought a tactically poor campaign and, partly as a consequence, received little support from the rest of the labour movement. Scargill was determined to confront the Government and chose to do so over the issue of pit closures rather than pay, which had been the issue in 1973–74.[129] This opened divisions within the NUM, for whereas pay was an issue which affected all regions, pit closures were perceived, and presented by the NCB, as regionally selective in their impact. This, combined with Scargill's refusal to hold a strike ballot, divided the mining workforce, with the result that some regions, notably the Midlands, did not support strike action, and approximately one-third of the industry remained at work. The absence of a strike ballot also contributed to the reluctance of other trade unions and the Labour Party to offer their unequivocal support. In 1973–74 the miners' action had received the backing of the TUC and the Labour Opposition, and even the Pay Board established by the Heath Government had concluded that the miners' desire to be treated as a 'special case' was justified. In short, Scargill attempted to repeat the miners' success of the early 1970s in an economic and political climate that was utterly different and wholly unfavourable. In 1984 the recession and rising unemployment inclined the TUC and the labour movement to caution – a common effect of economic recession – and with the Thatcher Government having won a landslide election victory in 1983, the political environment was equally inauspicious. From the outset the NUM faced an uphill and uneven struggle.

No more 'beer and sandwiches'

In 1978 opinion polls showed that 78 per cent of the British electorate felt that trade unions had too much power and that trade union leaders were the most powerful figures in the country, but by the time Thatcher left office only 17 per cent thought this was the case. Nor was it simply the image of power that trade unions lost, it was also membership, which fell from 13,289,000 in 1979 (51.9 per cent of the labour force) to 10,158,000 (37 per cent of the labour force). The changes in trade union law introduced under Thatcher placed constraints on industrial action, but the decline in membership was equally important in weakening the trade unions' position. Thatcher's period in office contributed to the latter development. Between 1979 and 1990, and especially during the economic recession of 1980–83, Britain's deindustrialization accelerated and the percentage of the working population employed in the manufacturing sector declined markedly. Manufacturing industry had been highly unionized and hence its decline led to a sharp fall in union membership, which was further underscored by a growth in the less unionized service sector and in non-unionized part-time employment. But although manufacturing decline made an important contribution to the fall in union membership, other factors were also important. To begin with there was an increase in decentralized wage bargaining, a trend which had been under way since the 1960s, but which accelerated in the 1980s. There was also an increase in the number of employers who engaged in collective agreements with their employees even if they were non-unionized, which reduced the incentive for workers to join a union. The decline in union membership continued through the 1990s and did not revive significantly when Labour took office in 1997. When viewed in the light of this trend, Thatcher's impact on the trade unions is placed in perspective, in that the success of her anti-union campaign appears as a symptom as well as a cause of changes in the nature of British trade unionism that resulted from structural changes in the British economy.

Thatcher's governments introduced comprehensive, and almost constant, trade union law reform, passing new legislation once every two years that produced 'the most radical package of changes to the law at work ever seen in the English law.'[130] This coincided with a marked drop in the number of working days lost as a result of industrial action, which fell from a yearly average of 12,870 during the 1970s to 7,213 in the 1980s.[131] For Thatcher and her supporters these two things were self-evidently related – the legislation having fulfilled the purpose of cowing the trade unions and curbing strike action. To some extent this was the case, for the legislation that outlawed secondary action and controlled intensive picketing did curb the scope of union action. In addition, the removal of civil, legal immunities meant that the use of injunctions and sequestration orders, and interlocutory injunctions, could either cripple unions financially or delay industrial action. Yet the union legislation of the 1980s was on occasions double-edged, for 90 per cent of the ballots required for industrial action by the 1984 Act resulted in strikes, which somewhat qualified the idea that strikes had been due to the 'moderate majority' having been kept silent. Indeed, as a consequence of this the Government sought, in its 1988 and 1990 Employment Acts, to amend ballot legislation to limit the constituency balloted and to reduce local strike initiatives – democracy, it seems, was only acceptable if it produced the right answer to a question. Equally important, other forms of non-official action, such as unofficial strikes and non-strike action, like working-to-rule, became alternatives to litigation-prone strikes. The new legislative framework did have an effect, but it could be circumvented, and although industrial action in the 1980s was much lower than in the 1970s, the level was higher than during the 'industrial anarchy' of the 1960s. What appears to have contributed most to the fall in both militant union action and union membership was not the new labour laws, but mass unemployment and the sense of insecurity which it engendered among the trade union rank and file.

It is difficult to assess with certainty the impact of the Thatcherite labour laws on the industrial relations environment, for it is difficult to separate their effect from those caused by longer-term structural changes in the economy and the culture of the workplace. Their political importance is, however, more readily discernible. In terms of intra-party politics, the trade union reforms provided an area of common ground where individuals and groups who were suspicious of or hostile to Thatcher and Thatcherism found a point of contact with their leader's policies. One example of this is the position of Ian Gilmour. In Thatcher's first

Cabinet Gilmour was one of the most forthright critics of the Government's economic policy, famously declaring after he was sacked by Thatcher that the economy was being steered onto the rocks. Through the 1980s and 1990s Gilmour voiced ongoing criticism of Thatcher and the political and economic strategies of her administrations, and in 1993 he published a comprehensive critical survey of Thatcher's premiership, the title of which, *Dancing with Dogma*, summed up his general disdain for her and her governments. Yet in a book that was essentially a sustained philippic against Thatcher and her works, one chapter was very positive, namely that which dealt with the reform of trade union law. Nor was Gilmour the only 'wet' critic of Thatcher who accepted and indeed endorsed the substance, if not the style, of her governments' trade union legislation. Internal party critics of Thatcher were numerous and vocal, especially in the period before the Falklands and the 1983 election, but they never formed a coordinated bloc. There were many reasons for this, but one that should not be underestimated is that antagonism to the 'common enemy' overrode internal party tensions. Indeed, the senior figure in the party who was generally viewed as occupying a mediatory position between the Thatcherites and the 'wets', William Whitelaw, was, as noted above, in favour of an aggressive union policy. After the experience of the Heath Government, the desire at all levels of the party was to curb the trade unions, which had become 'entrenched . . . as part of the demonology of the Conservative Party.'[132]

The trade union legislation of the Thatcher Governments could easily be presented as the product of a visceral loathing of organized labour, but to see the legislation solely in these terms would be to ignore other dimensions. Political revenge may have been an important motive for the employment legislation of the 1980s, but the underlying goal of Thatcher's trade union reforms was to confine the trade unions to what she and her close colleagues saw as their legitimate role, that is, as representatives of their memberships' industrial and workplace interests. Thatcher saw trade unions as, in terms of their origins, apolitical, voluntary, civic associations that had been hijacked by political militants – initially by the Labour Party, but later by activists of the far Left. The Conservative Party was not only united in the face of a common enemy, but also in terms of a common perception of the proper role of trade unions as an agency of civil society. In the late 1950s Lord Hailsham, who was to become Lord Chancellor in the early 1980s, had expressed scepticism about both the need for and the possibility of introducing trade union reform, but by the early 1980s he had come to the conclusion that trade union behaviour had become characterized by 'selfishness and . . . repeated attempts at domination'.[133] This view was widely shared in the Conservative Party, and State action was deemed necessary to address the problem. In 1980 Thatcher outlined the case for trade union legislation, stating, 'We don't want to stop proper Trade Unionism from operating, we need it. We need it to operate well, we need it to operate in the interest of its members'.[134] The basic problem, she contended, was that trade unions had been acting for political not economic ends and had placed themselves above the rule of law.[135] In short, they were breaching all the norms for the behaviour of a civic agency – ignoring the rule of law, failing to stay outside the political sphere and not acting in accord with their membership's interests or even their wishes. Legislation was essential to force trade unions into fulfilling their proper functions, which required that their actions be disengaged from the political sphere and limited to the area of economic interest in which individual unions were involved.

By the time Thatcher left office, her goal of removing the trade unions from the political stage had largely been achieved. Here, the fact that her governments refused to pursue an incomes policy marked an important turning point in the governance of the economy. Starting with the 1961 'Pay Pause' of the Macmillan Government, incomes policies had, with one exception, been deployed by every administration. As a result, as Thatcher argued, trade unions had necessarily been given a central role in economic policy. Under Thatcher, cash limits for the public sector may have acted an indirect incomes policy, but wage negotiations were left to management and the private sector was not even addressed indirectly. Those areas where the trade unions had an institutionalized place in the discussion of economic policy, notably in the shape of the TUC's membership of the NEDC, were downgraded to the point where, for example, Lawson wished simply to abolish the NEDC, which he saw as a relic of a bygone, corporatist age.[136] The Thatcher Governments' 'benign neglect' of the trade unions removed them from public centre stage and relegated them to the role of bit-part, or perhaps character actors. In response, the unions adopted a position which was referred to as the 'new realism', which meant occupying what Thatcher defined as their primary, non-political role. Thatcher brought an end to 'beer and sandwiches' at No. 10 or, as Harold Wilson once referred to it, the arrival of trade union tanks on the prime minister's lawn.

5

Thatcher and the electorate

Margaret Thatcher is the only party political leader to have enjoyed three successive twentieth-century general election victories. It was also a point of pride for Thatcher that she did not suffer an election defeat and was forced to resign as a result of the 'treachery' of her colleagues and not electoral reversal. But in spite of her general election triumphs, Thatcher's electoral record was not as impressive as it might seem. In terms of the Conservative Party's parliamentary situation, the 1983 victory was Thatcher's finest hour, in that the result gave them an overall majority of 144; the 1987 victory was almost as impressive, for although the Conservatives suffered some losses, the party retained an overall majority of 102. However, in terms of the Conservative share of the popular vote, Thatcher's party did best in 1979, when it took 43.9 per cent of the electorate and yet gained an overall majority of only 43. In 1983, when the Conservatives' majority rose by 101, their share of the vote fell to 42.4 per cent, and in 1987 fell again to 42.2 per cent. Thatcher's Conservatives were not a success as a 'popular' party, and Thatcher never gained anything near the electoral support enjoyed by her predecessors as Conservative leader, with even the much-disparaged Heathite party gaining 2.5 per cent more of the electorate than Thatcher's party gained when it secured its best result.[1] The election results of the 1980s demonstrate that the British electorate never became Thatcherite. The broad limits to Thatcherism's appeal have been fully surveyed in definitive studies of the general elections of 1979, 1983 and 1987, and this book does not seek to duplicate their work. Rather it looks at a few particular issues on which Thatcher and her party approached the electorate and sought to construct a popular and also populist appeal.

The period from when Thatcher first became politically active to her election as Conservative leader was the time in British political history which saw the closest correlation between class and voting allegiance. In that time the Conservatives were generally identified as the party of the middle class, and Thatcher did not hesitate to identify herself and her social and political values as such. But the general elections of 1974 caused concern for the Conservatives, in that their share of the vote not only fell below 40 per cent but was also socially and regionally concentrated. In the summer of 1976 Geoffrey Howe caught the party's anxieties when he wrote that 'some people compare our situation to that which Crosland and others described as facing the Labour Party in 1960: with the Party's support resting upon a narrowing class base.'[2] Given that Labour's concerns in 1960 had been summed up in an influential study entitled 'Must Labour Lose?' Howe's implication was that the Conservatives were having to ask whether they were ever going to win.

In order to overcome the problem of the shrinking party constituency, Howe argued that the Conservatives needed to target particular groups. To begin with he felt that they had to reassure party workers and 'natural supporters'. He also felt that 'opinion formers' in the universities and the media had to be won over,[3] and that the business community had a crucial role to play in persuading voters that the Conservative approach to the economy was correct. Howe thought that young voters needed a great deal of cultivation as they were a group with whom the party fared poorly, but he also emphasized that 'the great mass of the skilled working class' offered the Conservatives an electoral opportunity.[4] This last point was underlined by CRD when they carried out a similar survey of target voting groups in 1978, for they argued that 'skilled manual workers whose differentials have been severely squeezed by Labour policies must be regarded as potential Conservative supporters.'[5] By the late 1970s the Conservative hierarchy argued that 'traditional Labour voters in the urban areas . . . had seen their material and other standards decline so significantly in recent years' that they were open to a carefully constructed Conservative appeal. Hence, in the spring of 1978, the shadow Cabinet surveyed their party's electoral appeal and declared that 'We had a marvellous opportunity to "jump the class barrier"'.[6] The question was *how* this barrier was to be jumped.

There were several areas that the Conservatives felt had particular resonance with the skilled working class. One was the power of trade unions and their leadership. As noted in chapter 4, the fact that nearly 80 per cent of people considered the trade unions were too powerful indicated that a significant section of the skilled working class – many of whom were members of trade unions – thought this was the case. Thatcher constantly drew a distinction between the trade unions' leadership and their membership, arguing, for example, at the 1976 Conservative Trade Unionists Conference, that 'We are worried about the apparent unrepresentative nature of some Trade Union officials, and the fact that the power of some Union leaders seems on occasion to be used more for furthering political ends than for the benefit of their members.'[7] The Conservatives generally avoided drawing this distinction explicitly for fear of seeming to blackguard all union leaders, but it was an implicit leitmotif of the Thatcherite party's approach to the unions. At the same time the issue of personal taxation, in particular the 'headline' basic rate of income tax, was seen as an essential mode of appeal. In this context it is arguable that the 1970s and 1980s represented the culmination of a trend that had in some respects been set in motion during the First World War, but which had come fully to maturity in and after the 1950s, namely the extension of taxpaying households and the overlap for many of them between the cost of the mixed economy and the welfare state and personal taxation. Finally, there was the idea of the extension of 'property-owning democracy'.

The concept of property-owning democracy stretched back to the interwar period, and Thatcher had espoused the idea since her entry into politics. Nevertheless, she by no means led the campaign to find ways of extending property ownership. In the 1970s she was briefly an advocate of the policy of fixed interest rates for mortgages, but this was an issue connected to private-sector housing, and not concerned with widespread extension of home ownership. Furthermore, Thatcher opposed Peter Walker's 'right-to-buy' policy in the early 1970s, and it was only after she became Conservative leader that she and the party became more ambitious. It was in the context of the post-1974 election defeats and the anxiety they helped to create that the Conservatives and Thatcher seized on finding a way of rapidly extending the property-owning democracy, which demanded an extension of Walker's early 1970s strategy. CRD and the Shadow Cabinet concluded in 1978 that 'The sale of council houses and flats remains popular, the idea being thought a good one by at least 80% of every group, including Labour supporters.'[8] In the early 1960s studies of the affluent worker had shown that homeowners tended to be Conservatives and/or Conservatives tended to be homeowners, and there was thus a psephological logic to the Conservative goal of extending home ownership. But here Thatcher's electoral and her broader political goals worked in tandem. Speaking shortly before the election that brought her to power, Thatcher set out her socio-political stall, and, having signalled her goal of reducing personal tax levels, declared that

> As well as tax reductions, we've got the policy to try to get more and more people to become property owners. You know, if you've got some property of your own, you're likely to look after it and you're more likely to respect the property of others. And bringing up children that way should, in the end, mean less vandalism on your council estates too. But it means, too, that people become property owners, first house owners, then their own insurance schemes, then their own savings, because if they've got something of their own, they have a degree of independence and they have a stake in Britain that we wish them to have.[9]

In 1980 the Housing Act extended greatly the right of tenants to purchase the council houses they rented, and the uptake of this was rapid and extensive. In February 1981 Thatcher was already declaring her pride in the fact that 'last year, home ownership in Great Britain went up to 55 per cent for the first time', and in 1982, with 370,000 council tenants having bought their accommodation, Thatcher told the party conference that her government had presided over 'the largest transfer of assets from the State to the family in British history.'[10]

The extension of property ownership was in itself seen as a route to extending the Conservative constituency, but there was a further dimension to the social politics of the sale of council houses. Thatcher, as her leading biographer has pointed out, opposed the idea of public housing on principle and wished to reduce its share of the market. In 1981 she told the Young Conservatives:

> The perpetuation of large Council-owned fiefdoms means that millions of families are not master in their own home; have no chance to acquire a capital asset for themselves or their children; and that millions are unable to move, unless they can find a suitable exchange – and that happens all too rarely. This is discrimination at its worst. To keep this division in Britain would be to perpetuate a system which makes whole areas dependent upon the whims of officials and politicians. The sale of Council houses has struck one of the biggest blows for freedom for many, many years.[11]

In Thatcher's view, municipal housing was both a symptom and a cause of the 'dependency culture' in which Socialist ideas and Labour voters thrived. The sale of council houses, coupled with her governments' refusal to allow local authorities to use the receipts from sales to finance new municipal housing, was designed to reduce the socio-geographical environment of Labourism, and to reconstruct the nature of important sections of the urban working-class constituency in order to render it more receptive to Thatcherite Conservative values. Thatcher sought not merely to reflect the wishes of the electorate, but to *shape* that electorate and its wishes.

That the Conservative vote fell in the 1980s indicates that the programme of council house sales did not generate a new phalanx of support for the party. What it may have done was to consolidate gains the party had already made among the skilled working class in 1979. What there can be no doubt about, however, is that Thatcher presided over the creation of a nation of property owners. As she pointed out, the percentage of homeowners in Britain in 1981 was 55 per cent, and by the time Thatcher left office it was 78 per cent. But this jump in the gross number of owners had a strong regional dimension. In Scotland the aspiration to become a homeowner was much lower than in England, and in England the aspiration and the fulfilment was highest in the south and south-east. Property prices and, hence, the opportunity for speculative gains were highest in those regions, and engagement in the housing market, especially within the London commuter belt, was a good example of Thatcherite, rational market choice. Furthermore, it was also those regions that were the 'spiritual home' of Thatcherism, whether in the shape of the 'Big Bang babies' of the City, the booming Thames Valley economy or the representatives of 'Essex Man' like 'Loadsamoney'. In this respect the housing market was akin to an electoral barometer – it was weakest where Thatcherism's appeal was weakest and strongest where the Thatcherite constituency flourished. 'Property-owning democracy' may have been conceived as a policy and a concept which possessed 'national' appeal, but its social and political resonance was much more specific, and this helps to explain why the problem of a narrowing Conservative electoral base that so concerned the post-1974 party was exacerbated in the Thatcher years.

Immigration and the populist politics of race

The programme of council house sales was one route the Conservatives took in an attempt to broaden their appeal, but it was not the only route, nor was it the most controversial. In early 1978 Nigel Lawson discussed populist themes that the Conservatives should consider in addition to economic issues. To begin with, he suggested that 'the property-owning-democracy (especially in the sale-of-council-homes aspect) is probably still the most important single area', but he went on to state, '*we must not shirk the immigration issue*, which is almost the acid test of whether a political party is in tune with the ordinary people.'[12] In raising the question of immigration, Lawson raised the question of race, for in the British political vocabulary of the late 1970s and 1980s the two were inseparable.

The questions of immigration and race necessarily flowed into the issue of whether Thatcher and her party engaged with and courted a British, and more particularly English, populist xenophobia. During her premiership Thatcher's xenophobia was most apparent in her increasing Euroscepticism, but it was also manifest in her approach to the question of the definition of British nationality. The Nationality Acts introduced under Thatcher were designed to halt, or severely limit, the entry of immigrants to Britain from the 'New Commonwealth', and in particular to withdraw their right of abode in the United Kingdom. The redefinition of the relationship between Britain and its former (and indeed remaining) imperial possessions and their inhabitants was, on occasion, a cause of some embarrassment – most notably when the Falkland islanders, whose wishes were famously 'paramount', lost their right of abode under the 1981 Nationality Act. That such a situation arose might be seen as an anomaly, for the Falklanders' rights were rapidly restored. But to see this simply as an anomaly would fail to contextualize the withdrawal of their rights, which was bound in with a more general approach to immigration and nationality taken by Thatcher and her party after 1975.

The issues of immigration and nationality were recurrent themes in intra-party discussions in the 1970s, and a clear division of approach emerged as the Conservatives sought to reconcile strands of opinion within the party and the electorate, which were, ultimately, irreconcilable. Since the 1950s, popular hostility to New Commonwealth immigration had frequently been manifest and had found strong expression in the Conservative grass roots, notably in the lead-up to the passage of the first Commonwealth Immigration Act of 1962, which was designed to reduce immigration. The popular response to Enoch Powell's statements on immigration in 1968 demonstrated that the Macmillan Government's legislation had failed to assuage concern, and this presented the Conservatives with problems. Powell's position was critical not simply of the impact of and response to immigration, but also of the behaviour of immigrants, and he was deemed to have expressed implicit sympathy for racist opinions and as a result was dismissed from the Shadow Cabinet. But Powell received a great deal of popular support, and both the Labour Government and the Conservative Opposition responded to this by adopting positions that promised greater restrictions on immigration. In 1971 the Heath Government introduced legislation to reduce immigration, but then faced an immigration 'crisis' in the shape of a large number of Ugandan Asians, who sought refuge in the UK after the expulsion of their community by the Ugandan dictator Idi Amin. As had been the case with the Kenyan Asian community in 1968, the British Government reacted positively to a situation which, in effect, challenged them to meet historically established obligations, and they decided to accept those obligations in the face of public disquiet.

When the Conservatives left office in 1974 the party was no longer directly responsible for the control of immigration, but the issue continued to bubble beneath the surface of Conservative politics. At the Conservative conference in 1976, William Whitelaw, the party's spokesman on Home Affairs, announced that a future Conservative government would curb immigration, and the following year he extended his argument in a speech to Conservatives in Leicester. Whitelaw argued that

> It is essential that a concept of nationality is created which agrees with the commonsense understanding of what nationality is. Our present nationality law is an historical jumble bequeathed to us by our imperial past. Our duties to that past are now almost all honourably discharged. We must ensure that the obligations we acquire in the future reflect Britain's drastically changed role in the world and raise no expectations amongst anyone in the world about his or her status which a British Government, answering to the wishes of the British people, cannot fulfil.[13]

In the context of the mid-1970s the mention of duties 'honourably discharged' was clearly a reference to the acceptance of the Ugandan Asians, but Whitelaw's speech carried a broader message. In the 1950s Enoch Powell had stated that the British people as a whole, and the Conservative Party in particular, needed to be weaned away from the idea and the legacy of Empire. His focus at that point was geopolitical, for he felt that Britain should abandon any pretension that it retained global status and, having 'lost an Empire', should seek another role. In the late 1960s Powell still sought to wean the British away from Empire, but the focus of his attention had shifted to the domestic legacy of Empire in the shape of immigration. After 1968, Powell was persona non grata in terms of public debate on immigration, but his views were by no means ignored. In his speech at Leicester Whitelaw echoed Powell in so far as he accepted that the imperial past was history and a redefinition of British nationality was required. British citizenship had first been legally defined in 1948 and, in spite of significant amendments in the 1960s and 1970s, offered a construction of 'Britishness' that was inclusive of members of the Commonwealth. It was this definition of British citizenship that

Powell and then Thatcher's party sought to reconstruct, largely for the purpose of reducing the scale of New Commonwealth immigration.

At the root of the immigration 'problem' were the questions of race and its electoral resonance. In February 1978 one of CRD's researchers wrote to Thatcher and enclosed a speech by Powell in which, in characteristic fashion, he blamed himself for the election result that had led to the 'disastrous' Conservative Government of 1970–74. Powell 'confessed' that he had mistakenly advised the electorate to vote Conservative because he had believed, wrongly, that the Conservatives would halt immigration.[14] Powell was not alone in claiming that his influence, particularly on the issue of immigration, had been crucial in 1970. Conservative thinkers on the Right of the party who admired Powell certainly thought this was the case, but it was a view that was quite widely held in the party in general. In June 1976 Airey Neave told Thatcher that at a meeting of the party chairman's management committee there had been 'very strong comments about the absence of a Party policy on immigration', and that Whitelaw's statements on the question were not firm enough.[15] Neave argued that the party was

> adopting an 'elitist' attitude which ignored the opinions of reasonable residents of the reception areas ... who found their neighbourhoods literally taken over ... We should publish a firm line before the Party Conference, advocating a moratorium on all immigration ... There was bound to be some fierce criticism at the Party Conference, and our spokesmen would get a rough time, unless we had a quite firm line published in advance.[16]

Neave's views were supported by one of Thatcher's parliamentary secretaries, Edward Leigh, who told Thatcher in July that 25 per cent of letters to her from the public either focused upon or mentioned immigration. Leigh attributed this, in part, to the fact that the then recent cause célèbre of Robert Relf had 'inflamed people's passions', but he was also clear that other issues had contributed to his having to send 3,000 letters for her on the question. Here, Leigh felt that 'The recent events in Rhodesia seem to have touched some chord in people's subconscious to give them an impression that we are selling our "kith and kin" down the river in Rhodesia whilst being "taken over by the blacks" in this country.'[17] Leigh noted that the bulk of the correspondents were working class, claimed that they were 'not racist', but expressed 'frustration and anger at what is considered to be the refusal of the Parties (apart from the national front) to deal with this issue.'[18] Leigh noted with concern that few of the correspondents seemed to know about, let alone appreciate, the Heath Government's 1971 Immigration Act, which indicated to him that the Conservatives were vulnerable on the immigration question.

Concern that the party's immigration flank could be turned, and that the grass roots were restive on the issue, led a core of the Conservative leadership to conclude that a firm public stance on curbing or even halting immigration was required. It was clearly difficult, however, to persuade backbenchers and the constituencies of the leadership's commitment. In January 1978 Douglas Smith, the Conservative backbencher who was chairman of the Parliamentary Select Committee on Immigration, told Thatcher that the party was awash with 'rumours of back-pedalling in some quarters on immigration', and that

> There are still too many people even among our fairly dependable sup-
> porters who believe that we are not really serious over tackling the immi-
> gration problem and that at the end of the day we shall try and ignore
> the problem, as successive governments have done in the past with such
> lamentable results.

Smith sought reassurances from Thatcher that the official Conservative position was that 'all primary immigration should be stopped', and he concluded his letter with a plea that 'the Party will maintain a robust position'.[19] Thatcher responded by referring Smith to Whitelaw's statement at the 1976 party conference, but she could not realistically have thought that this would calm backbench anxiety. To begin with, if the 1976 statement had been 'robust' enough, anxiety over immigration would not have remained so pronounced. There was the further problem that Whitelaw, although he was generally respected, was not regarded as instinctively in tune with the party grass roots on any issue, let alone immigration. Since Thatcher's accession to the leadership the Conservative Party had sought to define its position on immigration, but by early 1978 it had clearly failed to do so in a way that satisfied the party's middle and lower ranks, and the relatively strong showing of the National Front at the local level, especially in London, indicated that immigration was a potentially damaging electoral issue.

At first glance there seemed to be a simple answer to the Conservatives' immigration problem, namely to announce that the party's policy was to halt immigration. There were some Conservatives who, as noted above, would have been more than happy for the party to take this stance, but there were others who felt such an approach would be morally questionable and could in itself have damaging electoral consequences. In October 1975, when Geoffrey Howe wrote to Thatcher about the electoral impact of immigration, his main concern was the advantage the Labour Party had established in appealing to the immigrant vote.[20] After examining detailed studies of the 1974 elections, Howe expressed anxiety about 'the party's weakness in this field and the considerable effect which immigrant voters have on the outcome of the general election.'[21] To counter Labour's advantage, Howe advocated that 'we should be seeking opportunities of identifying ourselves with minority racial groups', and he himself began to hold meetings with and parties for members of the Asian business community.[22] Howe's efforts to build bridges to immigrant groups were extended by the Conservative Community Relations Committee (CRC), but its work was to highlight the tensions and contradictions of the Conservative position. Shortly after Howe had written to Thatcher about Labour's electoral advantage in the immigrant communities, the chairman of CRC, Andrew Rowe, told the Conservative chairman that building links to immigrant groups was difficult as it demanded that the party act as a pioneer on the race relations front. Rowe noted that 'Discrimination on grounds of colour is forced by legislation to be more subtle than before but of course it exists. Trade Unions, working men's clubs, Conservative clubs and many other outwardly non-discriminating institutions actually practise discernible discrimination.'[23] Given this extensive, albeit veiled, level of prejudice, the Conservatives' dilemma, in Rowe's view, was how to attract 'coloured' voters without alienating whites. Rowe argued that 'coloured' Conservative candidates would drive away numerous white voters, and that Conservatives had 'to face the uncomfortable truth that there is racial prejudice in Britain and that although in most areas it is lessening in the most affected areas it is growing worse.'[24]

In January 1978, with the Conservative leadership planning for a possible general election in the summer of that year, Andrew Rowe produced an ambitious paper on 'The Way Ahead' on immigration policy. He suggested that there were two threats to democracy in the UK, the first being Socialism, and the second, a 'feeling prevalent . . . in the minds of many in this country – that liberal traditions of asylum were . . . getting a little out of hand with Britain being taken as a "soft touch" by a flood of immigrants from the New Commonwealth, who take our jobs and strain our social services.'[25] Rowe characterized this as the 'rational' aspect of the threat to the democratic tradition posed by the response to immigration, but he argued that it was accompanied by a

> less rational, but wholly understandable fear of 'strangers in our midst' with a colour of skin, mode of dress and customs quite different to our own. Regrettably it is a fear that can be, and often is, easily exploited by the unscrupulous with emotive phrases such as 'racial balance', 'alien wedge' and 'flood of immigrants'.[26]

Rowe suggested that one way of dealing with the problem was through a change of vocabulary. 'Race', he argued, was a 'meaningless concept' and it was better to use 'ethnicity'. Likewise he felt that 'settler' was a less emotive term than 'immigrant' and would arouse a less negative response. But although Rowe thought that these changes of terminology would ease the situation, he did not think that they would solve the underlying problem. For Rowe, 'The danger to democracy of the "immigration issue" is that it is all too easy and highly tempting for the aspiring politician or the cheap vote catcher, to capitalise on . . . fears and misunderstanding with talk of "stemming the flood".'[27]

The alternative approach canvassed by Rowe was for Conservatives to engage proactively and positively with the 'settlers'. In his view, this was the only way to secure electoral support from ethnic minority communities. 'We can choose,' Rowe argued,

> whether we accept the US Republican Party's fate and permanently attract about 8% of the coloured vote or win a proper share of it. If we

fail we shall also lose many floating voters who rate courage and decency high among reasons for supporting parties. I doubt if we can win an election without more coloured support.[28]

Attracting that support, however, was something that in Rowe's view demanded genuine commitment from all sections of the party. He stated that

> unless most of our MPs, many more of our councillors, agents and Conservative associations take more trouble to meet, talk with and join in the activities of ethnic minorities so that they become real people with names and hopes and fears, we can whistle for their support at an election.[29]

Rowe felt, however, that to get the constituency parties to take these initiatives required Thatcher and the Conservative leadership to give direction and offer encouragement, not least by their own example.[30]

In terms of both the time and the context in which it was produced, Rowe's work is of particular interest. To begin with, it acknowledged that racism was widespread in Britain and it emphasized the role of language in both generating and countering racist assumptions. But it also helped to throw Thatcher's own position into relief, in so far as Rowe's desire to challenge many of the norms that surrounded the discussion and criticism of immigration was not wholly welcome. Rowe sent his work of early 1978 to Thatcher, and soon after received a note from her Parliamentary Private Secretary to the effect that 'Mrs Thatcher is not too happy about the prospect of publishing the document.'[31] In many respects this was hardly surprising. Shortly after she received Rowe's paper, Thatcher appeared on *World in Action* and spoke of the concern that many British people felt about being 'swamped' by immigrants and their alien culture and customs. This was precisely the kind of language that Rowe had described as the vocabulary of the 'unscrupulous' 'aspiring politician' and the 'cheap vote catcher', and Thatcher was unlikely to respond positively to a document which, even implicitly, cast her in such a role. It is not clear whether Thatcher's 'swamping' statement about immigration was intended as a 'cheap vote catcher', although the fact that it was made when the Conservatives were planning for an election which, at the time, they thought might take place in the summer of 1978, indicates that 'vote catching' was very much on the agenda. Also, whether or not it was the intention, the *outcome* of Thatcher's statement, in terms of media and popular response, was that she gave the impression of being in sympathy with the people described by Airey Neave and Edward Leigh as feeling 'overwhelmed' by immigrants and ignored by 'elitist' politicians. According to opinion research commissioned by the party, the response to Thatcher's *World in Action* statement was very positive, with 20 per cent of those surveyed stating that they were more likely to vote Conservative 'if the party promised to stop all immigration.'[32]

On a number of occasions during her premiership Thatcher denounced racism

followed this up three years later when she told the women Conservatives of Bath that majority rule in Rhodesia was not desirable, except in the long term.[7] Thatcher's initial reaction to the issue of Rhodesia bore many of the hallmarks of an old Empire loyalist whose heart lay with the white settler community, a position that she shared with her husband.

Rhodesia did not figure again on Thatcher's agenda until she became Conservative leader, and did not loom large until 1978. In the mid-1970s the shuttle diplomatist par excellence, Henry Kissinger, led a US initiative on the question, which Thatcher praised warmly:[8] her only other declaration was to criticize the Labour Foreign Secretary, Anthony Crosland, for calling for a reduction in Rhodesian security forces.[9] In the autumn of 1978, however, the pace of the issue picked up. The Labour Government sought to renew sanctions on trade with Rhodesia in the wake of the Bingham Report on British companies that had been involved in 'sanctions busting'. This issue posed some problems for the Conservatives. The fact that Ian Smith had accepted, under pressure from Kissinger in 1976, that majority rule was feasible, indicated to the government and the bulk of the Conservative Party that sanctions had helped produce positive effects. However, a large number of Conservatives – some on the Parliamentary front bench, but, above all, the party's constituency grass roots – took the view that sanctions should be removed. The Shadow Cabinet decided to support the renewal of sanctions, but were very sensitive over the possibility of a party split on this issue. On the one hand there was concern that 'It should not appear that the Party's policy had been changed by activists at the Conference,'[10] but equally it was thought essential that backbenchers and activists be 'educated' about the arguments 'we were using against the view that the party should officially oppose the renewal of the Sanctions Order.'[11] An attempt was made to bridge the gulf through Thatcher seeking for renewal of sanctions while, at the same time, criticizing the government for selling arms to the 'front-line' State of Zambia.[12] But the strategy did not succeed, and 116 Conservatives voted against a one-line whip and opposed the renewal of sanctions. Furthermore, two junior Shadow Ministers, Winston Churchill and John Biggs-Davison, were dismissed and resigned as a result of voting against the whip. This was a significant party revolt and caused Thatcher some political discomfort, but it was noted at the time that her public letter to Churchill showed 'where Mrs Thatcher's heart lay on the issue',[13] which was with the opponents of sanctions.

When Thatcher became prime minister the pressure for a decisive initiative in Rhodesia had mounted. A referendum in Rhodesia in late 1978 had seen the introduction of a new constitution, which had enfranchised the black population, although it had also given the white minority members of the Rhodesian Parliament special blocking powers and reserved a privileged role for whites in the country's civil service. Nevertheless, only three weeks before Thatcher became prime minister, Bishop Abel Muzorewa had been elected as Rhodesia's first black prime minister under the new Rhodesian constitution. The question Thatcher faced was whether her government should recognize the Muzorewa Government and lift sanctions, in the face of the opposition of the 'front-line' States and a general international scepticism towards the new regime. Thatcher's initial response was to buy time. In April a team of Conservatives, led by Lord Boyd,[14] had been sent to observe the Rhodesian elections and to report as to whether they had been 'fair and free'. Thatcher stated that she needed the verdict of the Boyd Report before she took any policy decisions. When the report was presented in mid-May its verdict on the elections was positive, which led many to assume that this would bring an end to sanctions. This would have been consistent with statements in the Conservative manifesto and those of the Shadow Foreign Secretary, Francis Pym, before the general election; and, at a press conference in Canberra at the beginning of July, Thatcher seemed to imply that Britain would pursue such a course of action.

On her return to London, however, Thatcher's Foreign Secretary, Lord Carrington, persuaded her that lifting sanctions and recognizing the Muzorewa Government would be counterproductive. To begin with, it would, he argued, simply prolong the war between the Patriotic Front, led by Robert Mugabe and Joshua Nkomo, and the Rhodesian authorities. At the same time, it would alienate the Patriotic Front and make them susceptible to Soviet overtures. Here Carrington's argument was buttressed by President Carter's decision to maintain US sanctions, which meant that any British relaxation would be unilateral and, as well as the East–West ramifications, would in all likelihood provoke a reaction against British commercial interests in black Africa. Thatcher was evidently convinced by the Foreign Office case, for in Parliament, towards the end of July, she spoke of the need 'to achieve a settlement', to secure a government in Rhodesia that would gain 'international recognition', and that Britain would bring forward 'proposals' at the forthcoming Commonwealth Conference in Lusaka to foster wider consultation on how to achieve those ends.[15] Her tone and her emphasis had shifted markedly since Canberra. With regard to the April election as a 'test of acceptability' of Rhodesia's new constitution, she announced that 'we have not yet determined . . . whether that . . . has been fulfilled by the elections which took place', which effectively downgraded the Boyd Report. Moreover, although she praised the 'advance without parallel' that had taken place for bringing Rhodesia 'closer to a solution than ever before',[16] her position earlier in the month had been more positive.[17] Thus when Thatcher arrived in Lusaka her position on Rhodesia had moved to the point where she was willing to accept the inclusion of the Patriotic Front's Nkomo and Mugabe in talks to bring about a final settlement of the Rhodesia question, which was no small shift given that she had described Mugabe as a Marxist terrorist, 'no better than the IRA', only a year before. As a consequence, the Commonwealth Conference saw plans drawn up for an inclusive conference in London, which was to take place in the autumn of 1979.

The Lancaster House conference successfully brought the Rhodesian imbroglio to a settlement. A new constitution was drawn up, which removed the privileged positions enjoyed by the white minority under the 1978 structure; sovereign legal authority was temporarily restored to Britain and, as the 'imperial power', it granted independence to its former colony. Apart from the irreconcilables among the white settlers in what was to become the new State of Zimbabwe, the strongest voices of protest raised against the talks at Lancaster House came from within the Conservative Party. Carrington notes in his memoirs that the Conservative Party Conference took place while the Lancaster House talks were under way, and that when he went to address the party the right-wing Monday Club organized protests festooned with 'Hang Carrington' banners. Carrington recalls that he seldom took 'more trouble with any speech composition', in a determined effort to convince the 'main body' of the party that the right wing was wrong to continue its support for a politically obsolete and morally wrong regime tinged with white supremacism.[18] Carrington felt that he was successful in this venture, and that the right wing was isolated in the party.[19]

If isolating the backbench and grass-roots right wing was a significant achievement for Carrington, his role in persuading Thatcher to accept the arguments that led to Lancaster House was equally signal. Carrington himself notes that when the Rhodesia issue loomed, 'Margaret Thatcher had not particularly bent her mind to Africa', and that 'Her instincts were in line with those of the right wing of the party.'[20] His perception is confirmed by her sympathy for the anti-sanctions lobby before she became prime minister, and by her initial response to the Boyd Report soon after she took office. On Rhodesia, as on all issues, Thatcher was in tune with the right of her party, and Carrington and the Foreign Office modulated and moderated her position. It is open to question as to whether she was fully content with the outcome of the Rhodesian settlement. In her first volume of memoirs she notes that Mugabe's sweeping victory in the first elections in the new Zimbabwe came as a surprise to her and to most observers.[21] This is a puzzling remark, in so far as 'most observers' were fully aware of both the tribal and political strength of Mugabe's support, and his victory was expected. There can be no doubt that Carrington and the Foreign Office briefed Thatcher fully on how powerful Mugabe's position would be, and if she was genuinely surprised one can only conclude that either her basic unfamiliarity with African politics or, perhaps, wishful thinking led her to misjudge the situation.

There are some interesting parallels between developments in Zimbabwe and those in Northern Ireland. When Thatcher became Conservative leader, her position on Northern Ireland – as was the case with most issues not directly related to economic or domestic socio-political matters – was not well informed. This was reflected in the fact that in her pre-Cabinet career she spoke on the subject of Ireland on only 10 occasions; in Heath's Cabinet she had no ministerial involvement with the troubles in Northern Ireland and, in keeping with traditional practice, did not venture into a colleague's territory. When she became Conservative leader, still Thatcher rarely spoke on matters related to Ireland, and she reserved her strongest statements for the 13 occasions on which she denounced the IRA.

Thatcher's position on the 'Irish Question' was in many respects akin to that of a late nineteenth-century Conservative Unionist, in that she felt that an end to violence and disorder was a prerequisite before there could be any discussion of or attempt at finding a political solution. Thatcher's initial stance as prime minister was hard-line Unionist. This may well have been an instinctive part of her political outlook – many of her commonly held hard-line views were – but some of her closest friends and colleagues in the party were equally hard line on Ireland, notably Airey Neave, who was one of the organizers of her leadership campaign, and Ian Gow, who became her Parliamentary Private Secretary. Both men were killed by the IRA, which hardly served to weaken Thatcher's pro-Unionist views, and the fact that Gow was killed five years after he had resigned from Thatcher's second administration in protest over the 1985 Anglo-Irish agreement only underpinned her Unionist sympathies. More important than her Unionist leanings, however, was her passionate loathing of the IRA. The behaviour of Unionist militants and 'Paisleyite' Unionist politicians at Westminster was to irritate Thatcher, but on the basis that 'my enemy's enemy is my friend', she remained essentially Unionist.

It was somewhat of an unexpected turn of events that Thatcher's second term saw a major Anglo-Irish accord in the shape of the Downing Street Declaration of 1985, which opened a doorway onto the path that was to lead to the Good Friday Agreement of 1998. Thatcher thus inaugurated a process of dialogue and cooperation between the British and Irish Governments, something that had been absent since the troubles had begun in the late 1960s. As a consequence John Campbell suggests that 'this should stand among her diplomatic achievements alongside ... Zimbabwe'.[22] The analogy with Zimbabwe can, though, be taken a stage further, for there was again a marked difference between intention and outcome. Thatcher herself did not view the accord with anything like unequivocal satisfaction and enthusiasm. Since the imposition of direct rule from Westminster, and, in particular, since it became associated by Republicans and many Catholics with measures such as internment, the suspension of trial by jury, exclusion orders preventing travel to the rest of the UK and the generally authoritarian role and behaviour of the RUC and the army, the reintroduction of some form of devolved government was seen as essential to quietening the troubles. This had been the goal of the 1973 Sunningdale power-sharing initiative, which in some important ways was to provide a model for the Northern Ireland Assembly created in 1998. The fact that the Sunningdale Agreement was ended in the summer of 1974 by Unionist opposition in the form of mass strike action indicated that devolution was regarded in Unionist circles as favouring the Republican movement. Thatcher largely shared this view, and was suspicious of anything that was even remotely favoured by Sinn Fein and its leadership. In 1980–81 tentative suggestions for closer cooperation between the British and Irish Governments emerged from exchanges between the respective civil services, and a meeting between Thatcher and Charles Haughey was designed to cement a new accord and joint approach to the troubles. But the Maze hunger strikes cooled the possibility of a positive response to this initiative by Thatcher. Likewise, James Prior's attempt to set in train a process of 'rolling devolution' in

1982 foundered on the rocks of Unionist and Thatcher's opposition to any hint of concession to Republican views in the wake of events at the Maze.

In 1983–84 the New Irish Forum, actively sponsored by the new Irish prime minister, Garret Fitzgerald, brought together Republican and Unionist groups under the aegis of both governments. This grouping provided a sounding board for the ideas that came to full fruition in the Downing Street Declaration, but this declaration was, according to Fitzgerald, constructed *in spite of* rather than because of Thatcher's views. Certainly, Thatcher and Fitzgerald described the declaration in very different terms at a press conference after the 'agreement' had been reached. Thatcher's emphasis was on the rejection of extremism and violence, but Fitzgerald, while he echoed this sentiment, added that 'the agreement . . . recognises also on the part of the British as well as Irish Government, the legitimacy of the aspiration to Irish unity in a sovereign Irish state.'[23] Statements such as Fitzgerald's underscored Unionist fears that the declaration was a Republican stalking horse. That Thatcher's friend and colleague, Ian Gow, resigned over the Anglo-Irish accord and then proceeded to establish an organization called the Friends of the Union, underlined the concerns of Unionist supporters in England and can only have served to confirm Thatcher's ambivalence. She made no further major effort to pursue the devolutionist logic implicit in the declaration.

Thatcher's determination to stand firm against terrorism was both politically and personally understandable. But whereas her intransigence on that issue was supported on all political sides, her intransigence on moves towards devolution in general, and on the position of the hunger strikers, led to political developments on the ground in Northern Ireland which were wholly unwelcome to her. In effect, an important political legacy of the Thatcher years was the emergence of Sinn Fein as a central force in the electoral politics of Northern Ireland. In the 1970s Sinn Fein took no part in elections, and they were known simply as the 'political wing of the provisional IRA', but this changed in 1981. The key to the shift was the hunger-strike campaign of IRA prisoners at the Maze prison. The hunger strikers' demand for recognition as 'political' prisoners attracted international attention, and Sinn Fein, as part of their new strategy of using the ballot box as well as the bullet, took advantage of this. In Parliamentary elections Sinn Fein moved from not contesting in 1979 to taking 13 per cent of the vote and having a single MP elected in 1983. At the local level they went from non-contestants to taking 12 per cent of the vote and securing 59 councillors in 1985. The Sinn Fein vote fell slightly in the later 1980s, but their breakthrough in 1981–83 proved irreversible, and the Republican movement was never to lose its seat at the top table thereafter. In this respect, Gerry Adams and Martin MacGuiness were the Robert Mugabe and Joshua Nkomo of Northern Ireland.

Thatcher's position on Rhodesia/Zimbabwe was carried over into her stance on South Africa. Thatcher consistently and publicly declared her 'abhorrence of apartheid.'[24] She described apartheid to one South African newspaper as 'contrary to my whole philosophy,'[25] and told the *Sowetan* that 'all racially discriminatory legislation . . . is profoundly repugnant.'[26] Yet at the same time, hers was the first

British government for 23 years to host a visit by the South African head of state; she supported the idea of 'constructive engagement' by British companies in South Africa;[27] and she consistently and vigorously opposed sanctions, which were the measure the South African anti-apartheid movement felt would do most to assist their cause. This last stance, in particular, left Thatcher and Britain isolated, not only in the Commonwealth, but also in Europe and internationally.

The reasons Thatcher gave for her opposition to economic sanctions fell into two main categories, which concerned their political justification and their practical effect. With regard to the politics of sanctions, Thatcher objected to what she saw as the 'singling out' of the South African regime. The Commonwealth summit at Nassau, in 1985, agreed to impose some financial and trade restrictions, but Thatcher dismissed their importance, described them as 'tiny' and announced that 'I do not think they will affect our [UK] trade with South Africa.'[28] Her then Foreign Secretary, Sir Geoffrey Howe, was mortified by her remarks, which, in his view, offended the other 36 heads of Commonwealth governments in attendance and lessened the impact of the agreement they had reached.[29] Thatcher, however, was not concerned by the offence she gave to the Commonwealth leaders, for in her view she was simply demanding consistency. At the 1987 Commonwealth summit she pointed out that other member States had had oppressive regimes, notably Uganda, but they had not been expelled from the Commonwealth or subjected to sanctions, and that South Africa was being treated unjustly.[30] Likewise, at a press conference in Brisbane in the summer of 1988, she noted, 'The Commonwealth contains many different kinds of countries, not all of them famed for human rights,'[31] while in Parliament she referred to the 'naked racialism on the part of some African countries, throwing out the Indians.'[32] But she presented her most forceful underscoring of this point in an interview with Hugo Young of the *Guardian*. She told Young that one could ask the Commonwealth heads of government, 'how many of you have states of emergency? How long have you had them? How many of you have detained people without trial? How many from time to time had censorship? How many of you have excluded people on racial grounds from some of your countries?'[33] Young suggested that this could be interpreted as a patronizing stance, but Thatcher dismissed the idea and was equally insistent that it was 'not for us to be patronising to South Africa.'[34] In the same interview she extended the scope of this demand for 'equality' of action when she demanded to know why 'people who say it is moral to isolate ... do not take the same view, human rights, that it is right to isolate the Soviet Union?'[35] Shortly after her meeting with Young, Thatcher underlined her last point in another newspaper, and stated that if sanctions were imposed on some South African mineral exports, 'the only other source ... is the Soviet Union ... where there are no human rights.'[36] In the same vein, she rounded on the Labour Party's criticism of the official visit of the South African leader, P.W. Botha, declaring, 'I do not see how they can urge me to have a dialogue with the Soviet Union and not with South Africa. It is characteristic of double standards.'[37] As an exercise in parliamentary point-scoring this was standard fare, but the following year she reiterated the Soviet Union/South Africa analogy to her own constituents, and again spoke of the '"double standards" when trade and discussions with the Soviet Union were encouraged – another country with a bad human rights record – and yet there were calls to cut South Africa off.'[38] The analogy between the Soviet Union and South Africa was simplistic, but also characteristic of the Conservative grass-roots Right and Thatcher's instinctive accord with their position. Through the 1980s this basic harmony was constant and underpinned her political opposition to sanctions.

On occasions, Thatcher's political objections to sanctions overlapped with her criticisms of their practicality. When she was asked whether her stance on sanctions meant that she rejected the call for such action by the African National Congress (ANC) and black South African leaders such as Desmond Tutu and the imprisoned Nelson Mandela, she simply replied, 'I totally reject it.'[39] To some extent this was not surprising, for she referred to the ANC as a 'terrorist' organization akin to the IRA, and therefore their views were necessarily unacceptable.[40] Her preference was to cite the views of Chief Buthelezi, the head of the Transkei, who opposed sanctions.[41] Buthelezi's point, which Thatcher endorsed,[42] was that sanctions would have a damaging effect on black employment and living standards in South Africa. This was an argument Thatcher put to Nelson Mandela when they first met, namely that 'sanctions . . . is a word . . . what it is on the ground . . . is unemployment, poverty, starvation.'[43] Furthermore, Thatcher argued that sanctions would have a damaging effect on the British economy, in that firms that either depended upon or were engaged in trade with South Africa would lose business and reduce their workforce. Thus, when she discussed the issue with her constituents, the *Finchley Press* reported the event under the heading, 'Sanctions? I'd rather put Britain first'.[44] As well as arguing that sanctions would damage both the supposed beneficiaries and the countries that imposed them, Thatcher also contended that they would not work, and cited the example of their lack of impact on Rhodesia, a point she was particularly keen to press in the wake of the Commonwealth's imposition of 'tiny' sanctions at the Bahamas Summit.[45]

For the most part, Thatcher's stance on South Africa and sanctions left her and Britain relatively isolated, in the Commonwealth especially, but also in Europe and internationally. She did, however, have one important ally on this question, Ronald Reagan. Writing to Thatcher in the summer of 1986, Reagan stated, 'As you . . . I remain opposed to punitive sanctions which will only polarize the situation there and do the most harm to blacks.' Reagan told her that he was 'not considering any limited measures against South Africa', but he added, 'You noted you may be forced to accept some modest steps within the European and Commonwealth contexts to signal your opposition to apartheid,' and expressed sympathy as action in Congress meant that 'we may be faced with the same situation summer or fall'.[46] This last remark sheds light on Thatcher's thinking when she accepted the 'tiny' sanctions at the Commonwealth summit the previous year. The term that comes most readily to mind here is 'window dressing' or, perhaps, a 'fig leaf' to cover what was, in effect, empathy for South Africa.

Thatcher's position with regard to both Rhodesia and South Africa placed her well on the right of the Conservative spectrum. Indeed, the pace and timing of change on the ground in Rhodesia/Zimbabwe was perhaps propitious. It was in the weeks immediately before and after she became prime minister that developments there took a decisive turn, and her diplomatic inexperience and lack of knowledge of the situation combined to make her uncharacteristically willing to defer to Carrington and the Foreign Office African specialists. But her ongoing displeasure at the outcome was evident, and this appears to have informed her reluctance to abandon her instinctive sympathy for white South Africa. Certainly, she is clear in her memoirs that she rapidly decided that she had no desire to heed the advice of the Foreign Office on African and especially South African questions.[47] Thatcher's frequent public denunciations of apartheid show that that she was not simply a 'fifth columnist for apartheid,'[48] but at the same time it cannot be gainsaid that she consistently obstructed international efforts to force the pace of change in South Africa. Given the outcome in that country, it could be, as in Rhodesia, that developments on the ground were more important than international pressure in bringing about change, and that Thatcher might have been right to argue that sanctions could have strengthened the hand of the South African right and/or slowed the pace of change. Yet international action helped to support the South African anti-apartheid movement, which in itself was crucial to the dynamics of internal change. Ultimately, it is impossible to answer with certainty the question of whether or not sanctions would have speeded the end of apartheid, but this is largely irrelevant here. What matters are the insights it offers in terms of Thatcher's political outlook. Here, the reasons she gave for her stance against sanctions placed her alongside committed supporters of the apartheid regime. When she drew parallels between human rights violations in South Africa and those in certain Commonwealth countries, she echoed the views of, for example, the Conservative MP John Carlisle, who, because of his pro-South African views, earned the nickname 'the member for Pretoria' in the 1980s.[49]

Unlike Carlisle and members of the Monday Club, Thatcher did not ground her defence, and indeed admiration, of South Africa on its racial politics. It was the political economy of South Africa which she eulogized. Whenever Thatcher discussed South Africa at length she always spoke of its prosperity and contended that it had 'the highest standard of living throughout the whole of Africa'.[50] This, she argued, was demonstrated by its attractiveness to economic migrants from neighbouring States. She declared at the Commonwealth summit in 1987 that

> People from other black African countries where the economy is not so good, chose to go to South Africa – over one million of them . . . because they can get better paid jobs, better paid and they can make remittances home to keep their families. Now that is what some of those other leaders of black countries in Africa cannot, will not accept.[51]

She was also concerned that black nationalism, in the shape of the Patriotic Front in Zimbabwe and the ANC in South Africa, was not only 'terrorist', but also Socialist. When she was asked if an ANC government would need time to reconstruct the South African economy, she declared, 'Reconstruction? What Reconstruction? It is a free enterprise economy'; and at her first meeting with the recently released Nelson Mandela, she was 'quite clear to Mr. Mandela "If you want prosperity, you drop your nationalisation"'.[52] This view of South Africa as a haven of free enterprise in Africa was Thatcher's most oft-played card in the hand against sanctions, in so far as she felt that sanctions threatened South Africa's economic achievements and that ANC 'Socialism' was a logical corollary of this. Thatcher's simplistic, right-wing Conservative view of post-colonial African history identified South Africa as a free-enterprise island in a rising socialist and black-nationalist tide. To cushion South Africa was, for her, to cushion free enterprise, and the racial politics were of secondary importance. It was as if, in Thatcher's construction of the country, apartheid was incidental rather than intrinsic to South Africa.

Britain's imperial legacy in Southern Africa presented Thatcher and her governments with troubling and, in the case of South Africa, ongoing problems, but it was a still existing imperial possession that saw Thatcher confront her most dramatic and, in terms of her own career, decisive overseas challenge – the Falkland Islands. The first time Thatcher mentioned the Falklands in public was in February 1977 when, on a visit to Portsmouth as leader of the Opposition, she talked briefly to a woman who had recently moved to Britain from the islands. This was the only time Thatcher mentioned the Falklands before 1982, and she stated that 'we must look after the people still there the same as we look after British subjects anywhere in the world.'[53] Thatcher's premiership was to see the Falkland islanders looked after somewhat differently, with the result that her party and her premiership were rescued from a deep political trough.

The Falklands and, more particularly, the tensions which the islands created in Anglo-Argentinian relations, had bubbled beneath the surface of British diplomatic affairs since the mid-1960s – as Lord Carrington recalls, 'every British Government had needed to face it in some degree.'[54] The history of discussions between the British and Argentine governments from 1965 to 1982 is dealt with in the *Falkland Islands Review*, generally known as the Franks Report, which was published six months after the war of 1982. The report notes that Argentinian territorial claims to the Falklands, both governmental and popular, became increasingly assertive over time; that the Wilson, Callaghan and Thatcher Governments were willing to concede much of the Argentinian case for a transfer of sovereignty; and that the main obstacle to an agreement was the opposition of the Falkland Islanders.[55] In 1980 and 1981 the Thatcher administration engaged in lengthy negotiations with the Argentinian Military Government and also with the islanders. These negotiations led to the emergence of the idea of 'leaseback' as a solution. Under a leaseback agreement sovereignty would be transferred to Argentina, which would then 'lease' the Falklands to the British, who would administer the islands. It was hoped that Britain's concession on sovereignty would meet Argentinian demands, and that a leaseback of, perhaps, 30 years would allow the islanders to become reconciled to the situation. The British Cabinet minister who handled the negotiations of 1980–81, Nicholas Ridley, concluded in the summer of 1981 that 'there was no alternative to the leaseback idea which stood any chance of solving the dispute,' and that a strong public education campaign was necessary to persuade the islanders and British public and parliamentary opinion that this was the optimal solution.[56] However, elections on the Falklands in the late summer of 1981 indicated that the islanders were opposed to any transfer of sovereignty, while at the same time there were indications that the Argentinian regime was becoming impatient.

Faced with a diplomatic impasse, the Thatcher administration had limited room for manoeuvre, and the contradictions of its own attitude to the Falklands and its domestic policy priorities only added to the problems. With regard to the Falklands and its inhabitants, successive British governments had shown very little interest, and the Thatcher administration was no exception. The islands had some scientific value in so far as their minor appendage, South Georgia, provided a base for the British Antarctic Survey, but the main islands were of no strategic or economic value. The administration of the islands was unproblematic, except for the fact that they were dependent on Argentina for supplies and communication, and this served only to strengthen the Argentinian position in the dispute over sovereignty. By endorsing the leaseback proposals, Ridley had indicated that the British Government was willing to cede sovereignty, but he had also noted that any move in this direction was 'conditional on the agreement of the Islanders'.[57] That the islanders had, in effect, veto power on the sovereignty question had been the position of every British government since discussion of the question had begun in the 1960s, and the Thatcher Government followed suit. To some extent they were keen to show sensitivity to the wishes of the Falklanders, but they were also concerned that not to do so would leave the government open to criticism by the Opposition. The Conservatives had fired warning shots on this point when the Callaghan administration had examined the Falklands' position in 1977–79, and they were thus understandably wary. This display of deference to the islanders was somewhat ironic, for the British Nationality Act of 1981 reclassified the Falklanders and removed their right of abode in the United Kingdom. They may have been keen to remain under British sovereignty, but the British Government was less keen to acknowledge them as full British citizens.

In 1981 the Falklands and their inhabitants were a mixture of embarrassment and inconvenience to the British Government. Since the late 1960s it had been clear that successive British governments, including Thatcher's, would have preferred to cede the Falklands to Argentina as the geographically, politically, diplomatically and economically logical thing to do. The trouble was that the islanders did not see things that way, and although it would have been possible to reach an agreement with Argentina without their consent, this was regarded as too politically sensitive to attempt. But this left two issues, in particular, which, by the early

1980s, were becoming increasingly troublesome, namely the logistics and cost of supplying and defending the Falklands.

With regard to supplying the Falklands, the islands, as noted above, relied upon Argentina for sea and air transport. In the 1970s some suggestions had been made that the airport at Port Stanley, the Falklands' capital, be enlarged: it was thought that if it was 'capable of taking international traffic' it would reduce dependence on Argentina[58] and facilitate military support if necessary. This was a proposal made by the Shackleton Survey of the Falklands, which published its report in May 1976. The costs of such an expansion were, however, deemed prohibitive. Given the cost constraint, both the Callaghan and Thatcher administrations preferred the diplomatic option of seeking to lessen the tension with Argentina. At the same time, the Callaghan Government decided to maintain a token, but visible, British military presence in the South Atlantic, in the form of the ice-breaker and supply vessel HMS *Endurance*. This ship's military capacities were negligible, but as a 'statement' of British commitment it was deemed cost-effective. The fact that in November 1977 a larger force was deployed, made up of a nuclear submarine and two frigates within striking distance, is in some respects of marginal relevance, for if the aim were deterrence the Argentinians should have been informed, and it is not clear that they were.[59] Nevertheless, what is clear is that the increasingly assertive and aggressive stance of the Argentinian Military Government in the late 1970s was deemed a cause for concern. In this context it was somewhat surprising that the Defence Review of 1980 took the decision to withdraw *Endurance* as part of its reduction of naval commitments. The cost of maintaining *Endurance* on station was negligible in the overall defence budget, but, in spite of repeated requests from Carrington to John Nott, the Minister of Defence, the withdrawal of *Endurance* was not reconsidered.[60] This decision was greeted with some alarm in the Falklands, and a meeting of the Islands Councils informed Lord Carrington that it seemed that 'Britain appears to be abandoning its defence of British interests in the South Atlantic and Antarctic at a time when other powers are strengthening their position ... such a withdrawal will ... weaken British sovereignty in this area in the eyes not only of the Islanders but of the world.'[61] Nor was it only the Falklanders who saw the withdrawal as signifi-cant. The British Embassy in Argentina noted that a number of local newspapers had described the withdrawal of *Endurance* as a sign of Britain's 'abandoning the protection of the Falkland Islands.'[62] Furthermore, a British Intelligence report of September 1981 drew attention to the fact that the Argentinian Government saw the withdrawal 'as a deliberate political gesture ... [and not] as an inevitable economy in Britain's defence budget since the implications for the Islands and for Britain's position in the South Atlantic were fundamental.'[63] Given that the cost of *Endurance* was indeed nugatory,[64] and that the Thatcher administration, like its predecessors, had indicated that sovereignty was not immutable, the Argentinian Government's assumptions were not that surprising. Even the *Falkland Islands Review*, which was not critical of the government, concluded 'that it was inadvis-able for the Government to announce a decision to withdraw HMS *Endurance* and that, in the light of the developing situation in the second half of 1981, they should have rescinded their decision.'[65] If it was the case that a military regime either could not comprehend the British Government's deference to the wishes of 1,400 islanders or failed to see the domestic political-economic rationale of a minor defence cut, then part of the problem was a lack of clarity on the part of the British Government. It is not clear whether or not the misleading signals that the British gave out influenced the Argentinian decision to invade the Falklands, but what is clear is that those signals were easy to misinterpret.

In contrast to the British, the Argentinian Government's signals in the latter part of 1981 and early 1982 were marked by an increasingly aggressive clarity of word and deed. In the last two weeks of March 1982 an Argentine presence was established on South Georgia, and there was a steady build-up of Argentinian naval activity. Thus when Argentinian forces invaded and occupied the Falklands on 2 April 1982 it was not wholly surprising. The actual invasion was certainly no surprise to Thatcher herself. She had been in touch with Ronald Reagan, and on 1 April he informed her that he had spoken to the leader of the Argentinian Junta, General Galtieri, and had 'urged him to refrain from offensive action.' However, Reagan went on to say that Galtieri 'gave . . . no commitment that he would comply . . . spoke in terms of ultimatums and left me with the clear impression that he has embarked on a course of armed conflict.'[66] Given that this intervention by Reagan was made when the Argentinian forces were already off the coast of the Falklands, there was no real doubt as to their intentions. The only question was how the British would react.

The British response was rapid and unequivocal – the Argentinians were called upon to withdraw or face military action. This demand was in accordance with international law and was sanctioned by the United Nations. Equally important in terms of practicalities, it was a response sanctioned by the United States. Reagan had told Thatcher that 'we have a policy of neutrality on the sovereignty issue, [but] we will not be neutral on the issue involving Argentine use of military force.'[67] Reagan was distinctly more supportive of the British position than some senior members of his administration, notably his Secretary of State, Alexander Haig, and his Ambassador to the UN, Jean Kirkpatrick, who saw Argentina as an important element in US policy in South and Central America.[68] Reagan was aware of their desire to appear 'even-handed', and he told Haig, who sought to broker an Anglo-Argentinian deal, how 'difficult it will be to foster a compromise that gives Maggie enough to carry on and at the same time meets the test of "equity" with our Latin neighbors.'[69] Ultimately, Reagan's pro-British position overcame any hesitancy. Apart from the fact that it was politically reassuring to have the USA, with its influence in South America, supporting the British action, their practical support, even if tacit, was essential, given the logistical difficulties involved in sending a British force to the South Atlantic.

When the Argentinians made it clear that they had no intention of withdrawing, Thatcher was unhesitating about the need for a military response. A week after the invasion, following a meeting with Thatcher and the new Foreign Secretary, Francis Pym,[70] Haig told Reagan:

> The Prime Minister has the bit in her teeth, owing to the politics of a unified nation and an angry Parliament, as well as her own convictions about the principles at stake. She is clearly prepared to use force, though she admits a preference for a diplomatic solution. She is rigid in her insistence on a return to the status quo ante, and indeed seemingly determined that any solution involve some retribution.[71]

Haig's reference to the 'principles at stake' was an accurate summary of Thatcher's view of the 'ethics' of the situation, but he also noted that there was an important political aspect, namely that

> The Prime Minister is convinced she will fall if she concedes on any of three basic points, to which she is committed to Parliament … Immediate withdrawal of Argentine forces; Restoration of British administration on the islands; Preservation of their position that the islanders must be able to exercise self-determination.[72]

Again, this was an accurate description of Thatcher's, and indeed the general view, of the political implications of the Argentinian invasion. The Conservative Government had been experiencing low opinion-poll ratings and had suffered some severe by-election reversals over the course of 1981 and early 1982. These had been attributed to the economic downturn and rising unemployment, but the Falklands offered the prospect of a foreign policy humiliation to add to the government's domestic woes.

In the first week after the Falklands has been invaded, Thatcher's premiership and her government seemed to face disaster, but the outcome of the war saved and enhanced the reputations of both. The military campaign in the South Atlantic will not be discussed in this book, as it is concerned with Thatcher's political reputation, and here the details of the Falklands campaign are of little relevance. Once Thatcher and her government had decided to send the task force, the key decisions were in the hands of the military. In this context, the question of, for example, whether the decision to sink the Argentinian cruiser, the *Belgrano*, was a 'political' decision misses the key political point, which is that once a war starts it is the military who are largely in control. In terms of the political outcome of the war, one interesting feature of the campaign is how fortunate the British were. The US Defence Secretary, Casper Weinberger, remarked, 'If the British had not been lucky in several instances when Argentine … bombs struck six ships and did not explode, the outcome would have been much worse'. Moreover, Weinberger correctly noted that 'British logistics capabilities were severely stressed by the long distances involved', and he concluded that 'luck … played a significant role' in the British victory.[73] In so far as the Falklands triumph was to be crucial to

Thatcher's political standing, the fortunes of war favoured her as well as the British armed forces in 1982.

The general election of June 1983 saw the Conservatives gain an overall parliamentary majority of 144 seats, an increase of 101 over their majority in 1979. At the time of the election many commentators spoke of the Conservative success being driven by a 'Falklands Factor', that is, by a surge in their popular support produced by the war. But the fact that the Conservative vote had fallen by 1.5 per cent from its 1979 level, and as there had been signs of a revival in Conservative support before the Falklands crisis, some psephologists concluded that the 'Falklands Factor' was a political yeti – much talked about, but nonetheless mythical. Yet although the Falklands did not produce an increase in the Conservative vote, that does not rule out the existence of a more subtle Falklands Factor. As noted in chapter 5, the Conservatives benefited in 1983 from the division of the non-Conservative vote, brought about by the emergence of the SDP and its alliance with the Liberals. In early 1982 the rise of this 'third party' had threatened to cause more electoral damage to the Conservatives than to Labour. The SDP/Liberal Alliance at that point was taking votes in roughly equal proportion from both Labour and the Conservatives, but it was Conservative-held seats that it won at by-elections. This was because in many Conservative seats, especially in the south of England, there had been, since the 1960s, an effective three-way voting pattern, and the Conservatives had benefited from holding a larger, and *more stable*, vote than their rivals. But with the Alliance attracting both former Labour and Conservative voters in equal numbers, many Conservative seats were vulnerable. The electoral importance of the Falklands was that it halted the haemorrhage of Conservative votes to the Alliance, and allowed the Conservatives to take full advantage of the fact that they were the strongest of the three parties in what had become a three-party system.

The Falklands conflict began, in part, as an exercise in social imperialism by the Argentinian Junta and, in effect, ended as one for the Thatcher administration. Carrington noted in his memoirs that 'General Galtieri . . . needed some sort of diversion to unite a discontented and long-suffering Argentina',[74] which was an accurate description of the socio-economic and political background to the Junta's decision to invade.[75] But it was a description that could also have been applied to Britain in 1982. With unemployment high and rising, with serious disturbances having taken place in inner-city areas in 1981, and with her government deeply unpopular, Margaret Thatcher also needed a 'diversion', and the Falklands provided her with one. The political irony is that an adventure which Galtieri and the Junta hoped would secure their position ended with the collapse of their government and the end of military rule in Argentina, while in Britain, a government that had seemed very fragile was given new authority.

The Falklands marked a turning point for Thatcher herself as well as for the Conservative Party. In 1981 Thatcher had the lowest popularity rating of any prime minister since polling had begun, and this in turn had weakened her authority in the Cabinet. Although she had gradually been reducing the number of 'wets' in the Cabinet, they were still a significant presence in the spring of 1982. Indeed, when Carrington resigned as Foreign Secretary she replaced him with a leading 'wet', Francis Pym. In some respects, her choice of Pym, who was 'the most perfect epitome of the kind of Conservative politician Mrs Thatcher detested',[76] reflected the difficulty she was in immediately after the Falklands had been invaded, in that she felt she had to draw all elements of the party – even those she detested and, equally important, distrusted – behind her. The build-up to and outcome of the military operation to recover the Falklands served to confirm her distrust and prejudices with regard to the 'wets' and gave her the authority to remove them from the Cabinet. When Alexander Haig informed Reagan that Thatcher was committed to removing the Argentinians by force, he also noted that 'Her Foreign Secretary [Pym] does not share her position, and went surprisingly far in showing this in her presence.'[77] Pym's lack of deference was rewarded at the 1983 general election, when at party press conferences Thatcher treated him with a coolness that bordered on disdain; and then, soon after the Conservative victory, she removed him from the Cabinet and appointed her Thatcherite Chancellor, Geoffrey Howe, as Foreign Secretary. After the war against Argentina, Thatcher was 'no longer the political outrider'[78] and her post-1983 Cabinets contained only a residue of 'wets'. The Falklands gave Thatcher an authority within her party that she had not previously enjoyed.

That Britain was able to engage successfully in the Falklands operation when it faced significant logistical problems was in no small part due to the assistance it received, particularly in terms of intelligence, from the United States. For Thatcher this served to confirm a personal as well as diplomatic commitment to the 'special relationship', which was the central feature of her international outlook. Thatcher's 'discovery' of the United States came quite late. She first visited the USA in the spring of 1967 under the aegis of the US State Department, and then went again in 1969 on an English Speaking Union tour. But in her public statements she rarely mentioned the USA, and had no serious political contacts there until she met Reagan in April 1975. Reagan and Thatcher had an instant rapport, with the governor of California noting later, 'We found that we were really akin with regard to our views of government and economics'.[79] They also had in common a view of the international situation, which identified the USSR as an 'evil empire'. Nine months after her meeting with Reagan, Thatcher described the Soviet Union as a country 'ruled by a dictatorship of patient, far-sighted, determined men who are rapidly making the country the foremost naval and military power in the world', and she underlined their quest for world domination.[80] It was after she had made this speech that the *Red Army News* termed Thatcher 'the Iron Lady', a label she was to wear as a badge of honour. In 1977 she confirmed her firm 'cold war' stance on several occasions, but particularly when she visited the USA, and she told the US media, 'I watch with alarm the way in which the Warsaw Pact countries are increasing their expenditure on armaments', and she called for NATO to match that expenditure.[81] Shortly before she became prime minister, Thatcher spoke to a Conservative rally about Soviet expansion and imperialism, and argued that the direct Soviet invasion of Afghanistan had to be viewed alongside the emergence of a Marxist government in Ethiopia, the involvement of Cuban troops in Angola and – a quixotic connection – the overthrow of the Shah in Iran.[82] But it was her attitude to détente with the USSR that was crucial in terms of establishing a point of contact with Reagan.

In the summer of 1975 Thatcher told her home Conservative Association that 'throughout the decade of détente the armed forces of the Soviet Union have increased, are increasing, and show no signs of diminishing.'[83] In the spring of 1976, in an article in the Conservative Party's 'in-house' paper, Thatcher expanded on her by then much-publicized speech on the Soviet Union and explained why she was proud to be seen as an 'Iron Lady' by the Soviets. Her aim was to emphasize what she saw as the inconsistencies of the Soviet position, and she declared that 'Angola, not Helsinki, is seemingly the measure of Soviet belief in détente'.[84] That the leadership of the USSR preached peace and disarmament and practised expansionism was, Thatcher argued, consistent with their aims and beliefs. Quoting Alexander Solzhenitsyn and Arthur Koestler, two of her favourite anti-Soviet canon, she explained to a Conservative audience that communism and democracy were irreconcilable, that this demanded Soviet expansion and that there was 'no ideological détente' between East and West.[85] Hence, when she addressed the West German CDU Conference in 1976, she declared, 'We must add deterrence and defence to détente'[86] – indeed she argued that 'Strong defence, strong deterrents were the condition for successful détente.'[87] Without Western strength, especially within NATO, there could, Thatcher contended, only be 'an illusory détente',[88] with an ever-strengthening Soviet Union. Indeed, Thatcher stated at her 1978 Churchill Memorial Lecture that in 1946 the Soviet diplomat, Litvinov, had spoken of the interwar years not as years of peace but a 'prolonged armed truce', and she felt that it was 'far from clear that, for the Russians, the meaning of détente is any different.'[89]

In her second volume of memoirs, Thatcher stated that détente was 'one of those soothing foreign terms which carried an ugly reality that plain English would expose', and she concluded that 'It was difficult to see any difference between appeasement and détente.'[90] To liken any diplomatic initiative to 'appeasement' was, for Thatcher, the ultimate condemnation, and this summed up her view that, as practised in the 1970s, détente was a product of the West negotiating from a position of weakness, with the result that the USSR got stronger and more assertive. Here she was in complete accord with Reagan, who was very critical of Henry Kissinger's pursuit of détente. Speaking at Orlando in 1976, at the beginning of his unsuccessful campaign to oust Gerald Ford from the Republican nomination for the presidential election of that year, Reagan targeted the Nixon and Ford administrations' détente-based approach to the Soviet Union. He declared that 'Henry Kissinger's recent stewardship of US foreign policy has coincided precisely with the loss of US military supremacy', and he claimed that 'the Soviet Union will not stop *taking advantage of détente*' until a US president with a tougher approach was in the White House.[91] Thatcher clearly felt the same, for in 1978, shortly after her second meeting with Reagan, she met the then president, Jimmy Carter, and, finding him 'ill-suited for the presidency',[92] gave him a stern lecture on foreign policy and the need for vigilance with regard to the USSR. In terms of Thatcher's vision of the international climate, 'Central casting could not have produced a more compatible counterpart for Ronald Reagan.'[93]

Thatcher's commitment to the 'special relationship', her close personal friendship with Reagan and her gratitude for US support and assistance during the Falklands were marked and related features of her foreign policy outlook throughout her premiership. This did not mean, however, that Anglo-US relations were always harmonious in the 1980s. This was vividly illustrated in October 1983, when Reagan ordered the invasion of the Caribbean island of Grenada. Reagan's decision was driven by cold-war considerations. He told Thatcher that he was 'concerned by Grenada's recent drift into the Soviet bloc.' A coup d'état on the island had seen the rise to power of a hard-line Marxist faction, which Reagan saw as 'a group of leftist thugs who would likely align themselves with Cuba and the Soviet Union to an even greater degree than did the previous government,' and he decided to act so as not to allow time for 'Cuba and the Soviet Union to consolidate the position of the new regime.'[94] The problem was that Grenada was a member of the Commonwealth, the queen was the island's head of state and the US invasion took place without any consultation with, let alone the consent of, the British Government. This caused serious tension between the two governments[95] and the two leaders,[96] but by the end of the year fences had been mended, and Reagan was thanking Thatcher for her 'helpful and reassuring' statements in Parliament on Grenada.[97] It would be a mistake to ignore the differences between Thatcher and Reagan over US *conduct* in Grenada, but it would also be a mistake to overdraw them. Reagan's goal of preventing Grenada from becoming a 'Soviet satellite' was in keeping with Thatcher's critique of what she termed 'one-way' détente in the 1970s, which had led to Soviet expansion in Ethiopia and Angola. Her anger at the time of the Grenada invasion was over her not being informed and the fact that this had caused her some parliamentary and public discomfort, but it was not the product of any disagreement over the rationale for the invasion. The queen, as head of the Commonwealth, was appalled by the US action, but Thatcher did not see the Commonwealth dimension as crucial, and she had little concern for Commonwealth opinion on this or indeed any other issue. Thatcher's concern was that Reagan and the USA had acted more or less unilaterally, and thereby publicly undervalued Britain's status.

Grenada was not the only source of Anglo-American tension in the 1980s. In December 1984, following Reagan's re-election, Thatcher went to pay a 'congratulatory' visit on her friend. The US administration saw the meeting as a chance to confirm the president's 'close personal and consultative relationship with Mrs Thatcher,' and Reagan's staff were clear that 'Mrs Thatcher remains one of your staunchest personal supporters'.[98] But although it was agreed that 'the British pursue similar foreign policies',[99] it was also noted that this did not mean that all was smooth. In particular, issues with regard to nuclear arms and disarmament were deemed problematic. Thatcher had established herself as a key Reagan supporter in the early 1980s through her support of the deployment of cruise missiles in Britain and Europe in the face of strong domestic opposition. But in 1984–86 differences were to emerge as a result of Reagan's commitment to a new anti-missile programme, the Strategic Defence Initiative (SDI), and his simultaneous rapprochement with the new Soviet leader, Mikhail Gorbachev. With regard to the SDI, the White House, by December 1984, had reports that Thatcher was hostile to the idea, and the accuracy of these reports was confirmed by Thatcher's meeting with Reagan just before Christmas. It seemed for a while that this meeting had produced an accord, but in March 1985 a speech by Geoffrey Howe reopened the tensions, and in July Thatcher made clear her concern that the SDI would destabilize the international arms question.[100]

Thatcher's opposition to SDI was not rooted in an objection to the principles or technical feasibility of the project. She acknowledged the argument that US technical ascendancy meant that the Soviet Union would see SDI as rendering the USA invulnerable and able to attack without fear of retaliation, and that this, in turn, could give the USSR an incentive to launch a nuclear attack before the SDI became operative. But her fundamental objection was simpler. In her view, peace in Europe had been the result of nuclear deterrence, and NATO's nuclear arsenal had taken on an increased significance as the Soviet Union had established superiority in conventional forces. SDI opened the possibility of strategic nuclear weapons being rendered obsolete, and Thatcher saw this as destabilizing. In Washington in July 1985, Thatcher underlined at great length her view that the concept of SDI 'devalued' nuclear weapons and that its introduction would demand greater expenditure on conventional weapons in the West.[101] Her fears on this point were confirmed by Reagan's meeting with Gorbachev at Reykjavik in October 1986, when the two leaders came close to agreeing the 'zero option', that is, the elimination of all strategic nuclear weapons. This appalled Thatcher, in that she felt it would remove the US nuclear umbrella from Europe, leave the continent dependent on medium-range weapons (like cruise missiles), and the British and French deterrents, and would give the Soviet Union the opportunity to exploit their conventional superiority. In Thatcher's view, nuclear weapons were fundamental to deterrence, and a 'nuclear free Europe' could only result in a Soviet-dominated Europe.[102] It was this position that explains why one US adviser stated that 'Thatcher Loves the Bomb';[103] it also explains why Thatcher felt that, in terms of her relationship with Reagan, the SDI and the weapons issue produced 'the only real divergence we had.'[104]

Nuclear disarmament was the most important point of Anglo-US tension in the Thatcher–Reagan years, but there were others. One ongoing issue concerned the handling of members of the IRA by US courts. In December 1984, again in preparation for Thatcher's forthcoming visit, one of Reagan's advisers indicated that 'On December 14, Sir Geoffrey Howe passed me a hand-written note about a New York Federal district court's denial on political offense grounds of a UK request for extradition of IRA gunman and convicted murderer Joseph

Doherty.'[105] This was an issue where it was difficult for Reagan to be of assistance, for the US judiciary, as Howe had recognized, jealously guarded its autonomy.[106] Indeed, the White House staff argued that Thatcher should be persuaded to adopt a more open and flexible approach to relations with the Irish Government as the best means of addressing the Northern Ireland issue.[107]

Reagan was, however, able to offer significant assistance in a less sensitive legal area, which was on the troubled position of British Airways (BA). Before he met Thatcher in December 1984 Reagan was briefed that there were 'a number of chronic economic irritants' concerning US taxation of British companies and the export of US technology that Thatcher's staff had raised, but that 'Civil aviation ... [was] the source of our deepest difference.'[108] The key problem for Thatcher was a grand jury investigation into whether BA had entered into price-fixing arrangements with the major US airlines and helped bring about the collapse of Laker Airways. Thatcher had written to Reagan about this in March 1983, and had asked him 'to take it up personally and very quickly.'[109] Reagan, however, was reluctant to act. He told Thatcher that the issues raised by the case, such as 'fixing and raising air fares without the approval of our aeronautical authorities', were problematic, and that it was his 'clear obligation to see that our antitrust laws are enforced.' Reagan sought to soften his refusal by telling Thatcher, 'I value our personal relationship and the unique co-operation between our countries on important matters,' but he also stressed that 'in this case I feel that I do not have the latitude to respond to your concerns.'[110] The possibility that BA might face antitrust action, or a civil, 'triple-damages' action under the Clayton Act, hung over the company throughout 1983 and 1984, as US investigations proceeded. This was a matter of great concern to Thatcher, for she was planning to privatize BA and the threat of a substantial case against the company precluded any possibility of these plans being advanced. But immediately after his re-election in November 1984, and clearly in response to Thatcher's persistent requests, Reagan took the unprecedented step of calling off the grand jury investigation into BA's activities.[111] Furthermore, the following year, Reagan persuaded Laker Airways' leading US creditor, the Export Import Bank, to drop any potential civil action against BA. This decision led Laker's other US creditors to follow suit, and so BA was freed from the threat of civil as well as criminal action,[112] and the path to the privatization of BA was cleared.

With regard to the foreign affairs arena per se Reagan and Thatcher were in close harmony. The only real divergence was on the political economy of East–West relations, The attempt by the Polish Government to suppress the Solidarity movement led Reagan and the USA to impose a range of economic sanctions on Poland, and they hoped or expected their allies to do the same. But few, including Thatcher, were willing to toe Reagan's hard line. Thatcher was publicly supportive of Reagan, and was strong in her condemnation of the Polish military government under Jaruzelski, but she did not pursue, either unilaterally or in an EEC context, tougher sanctions.[113] Her reluctance was further underlined when she refused to endorse Reagan's policy of an embargo on technology exports to the USSR and non-cooperation with the Siberian gas pipeline to Western Europe. She stated in 1983 that she was 'absolutely all for stopping the latest technology from getting to the Soviet Union,' especially if such goods had a defence aspect, but she felt the pipeline was purely a trade issue.[114] This last point was particularly important for Thatcher, in so far as she argued, as she had in the South African context, that sanctions could damage the country imposing them. Hence, in 1981, she expressed 'strong hopes that the United States will not impose sanctions on John Brown Engineering of Clydebank, for supplying turbines to the Soviet-West European gas pipeline in defiance of an embargo by President Reagan.' She argued that such an action would only worsen unemployment on Clydeside, and she went so far as to state, 'I feel wounded . . . It is a difficult situation to have without it being brought about by a friend.'[115] Likewise, when she was asked if she felt that 'West Germany, France and the Benelux countries, in agreeing to the Siberian pipeline deal, in effect, sold their souls to the devil,' she was keen to 'point out . . . that one contract has come to this country that is very valuable to a particular development area'.[116] For Thatcher, military sanctions were necessary and relatively easy to enforce, but general sanctions were a double-edged sword and were easily circumvented.[117] On grounds of both principle and practice, Thatcher would not follow Reagan's lead on sanctions against the Soviet bloc, but offered only verbal backing.

But there were occasions when Thatcher offered both verbal and concrete support for Reagan when he would otherwise have been isolated. The prime example was the support she gave to the US decision to bomb targets in Libya in April 1986, an action which required the use of bases in Britain. There was a great deal of international, European and domestic criticism of the US raids, but Thatcher offered wholehearted support and was adamant that the action 'was not – I believe – illegal.'[118] Indeed, she argued that the US action was justifiable under UN Article 51 and was essential to break a pattern of the 'appeasement' of terrorism,[119] which, given that 'appeasement' was her ultimate foreign policy pejorative, was high praise for Reagan. In terms of practical assistance – British permission had been necessary for the USA to use their air-force bases in Britain – and both practical and public diplomatic support, 'Libya was the supreme occasion when Thatcher delivered for Reagan.'[120] With regard to practical matters, there were no other occasions when Thatcher was able to offer Reagan similar assistance, although his successor received an immediate commitment of British military support for what became the first Gulf War. However, Thatcher did offer welcome moral support when Reagan was politically beleaguered during his second term. When the Iran-Contra scandal was at its height, Thatcher sent a handwritten letter to Reagan in which she denounced media criticism of his Latin-American policy and told him, 'your achievements in restoring America's pride and confidence and in giving the West the leadership it needs are far too substantial to suffer any lasting damage.'[121] Five days after she had written this, Thatcher addressed the European Parliament. There she justified Britain's abstention on a UN motion critical of US policy towards Nicaragua, and stated that she was 'always very, very disturbed at any signs of anti-Americanism I find anywhere.'[122] Just as Carter's failure to prevent the victory of the Sandanistas in Nicaragua was, in Thatcher's view, a product of the 'Vietnam Syndrome' that had prevented the USA from exercising its power, so Reagan's policy represented 'America's Recovery' of assertive confidence. That Thatcher saw nothing untoward in the USA seeking to undermine the Sandanistas encapsulated her fundamental ideological harmony with Reagan. Ultimately, this was the key support that Thatcher and Reagan offered each other. They provided mutual confirmation of one another's instincts and shared each other's values and prejudices.

Thatcher's relationship with Reagan's successor, George Bush, was more problematic. Ironically, the main point of tension came about as a consequence of the collapse of the Soviet bloc. The fall of the Berlin Wall in November 1989 led to calls from within both East and West Germany for reunification of the country. Thatcher, however, was troubled by the prospect of a new German 'colossus' at the heart of Europe, and only a month after the wall came down she expressed extraordinary prejudices about the authoritarian German 'national character'[123] – and took up what John Campbell has accurately described as an 'Alf Garnett version of history'.[124] Bush and his Secretary of State, James Baker, took a different stance, which in part reflected the new president's view that Germany, and particularly a reunified Germany, would have to be the main focus of US diplomatic energy in Europe. The Reagan–Thatcher axis, which, in spite of their personal friendship, was not free from diplomatic tensions, was replaced by a relationship of which realpolitik was the public essence.

Thatcher defined international relations in binary, Manichaean terms. For her, the world was divided into camps that resembled characters from Ronald Reagan's westerns, in so far as there were the 'bad guys', who wore black hats, and the 'good guys', who wore white hats. In the big international picture, until the fall of the Berlin Wall, Reagan, herself and the Western allies were, of course, the latter, and the Soviet bloc the former. Indeed, the fact that she was able to 'do business' with Gorbachev seems, in part, to have stemmed from her view that he was part-way to becoming a 'white hat', while being surrounded by 'black-hatted' apparatchiks. If East and West – the main feature – were easily separated along these lines, so too were North and South – the support feature – with the two frequently overlapping in so far as the 'bad' elements in the South, even if members of the Commonwealth, would align themselves with the East. The division was further confirmed by political economy. The 'free world' was liberal market, because economic and political freedom were inseparable. Likewise, the unfree world was statist, with State intervention in the economy necessarily curtailing civil and political freedoms. Here, Thatcher's binary view of the world overlapped with her view of Europe's development, for she stated in her memoirs that there were *two* routes Europe could take, one of which was to a single, free market of nation states and the other to an interventionist, bureaucratic, federal Europe.[125]

Thatcher's view of Europe's polarity, as explored in chapter 7, was informed by her concern that continental Socialism had influenced the European Union's development in the 1980s and 1990s. But this concern was not *sui generis*: it was part of a more general anti-internationalist position. Speaking in New York in 1993, Thatcher lauded the watchful constitutional role of the US Supreme Court, and stated that, in the wake of numerous charters and directives from the European Commission, 'I have had cause to wonder whether our own Parliamentary Institutions might have been better protected by such a court than under our present system which permits more and more legislative powers to be passed to European institutions even though they are not accountable to the electorate.'[126] These thoughts were triggered by European federalists, but these tendencies were, she argued, not confined to Europe. For Thatcher, the international community's failure to control the conflicts in the former Yugoslavia in the early 1990s were a result of 'The mistake . . . of assuming that only the UN can confer legitimacy and moral authority to intervene in conflicts', and that it had to be recognized that 'nation states rather than the UN . . . [should] take the lead.'[127] This mistake was, in Thatcher's view, compounded by the aftermath of the Balkan conflicts, when President Clinton's Secretary of State, Madeleine Albright, called for the establishment of a standing international tribunal on war crimes so that all would be accountable to international law. Thatcher denounced this and argued, 'I do not think that "we are all accountable to international law."'[128] Warming to her theme, Thatcher asked,

> is international justice ever anything other than 'victor's justice'?. . . the answer to that question can be 'yes' – but only if the United States and its allies are [not] foolish enough to surrender power over their decisions and personnel to the proposed International Criminal Court at the Hague . . . [and] the victors of the Cold War . . . submit to an unelected, unaccountable, and almost certainly hostile body.[129]

For Thatcher, post-Gulf War 'robustness' had been 'diluted in the search for international consensus', which had seen the 'subordination of US national interests in favour of multilateralism.'[130] The only 'multilateral' organization that Thatcher ever spoke positively about was NATO, but that was effectively led by the USA and, in her terms, had no political agenda or rationale.

The word 'multilateralism' became, in Thatcher's vocabulary, almost as much of an epithet as 'appeasement', and it was small wonder that she felt that George W. Bush, the most anti-multilateral of recent US presidents, was right to reject all initiatives on international war crimes. Likewise, it was no surprise that Thatcher was critical of the Blair Government for agreeing to accept them,[131] that she saw the detention of General Pinochet in London as an example of their failings[132] and that *European* countries had been instrumental in bringing the case against the former Chilean dictator.[133] As far as Thatcher was concerned, all 'multilateral' or 'international' structures and ideals were either impractical or Left-leaning or both. For example, she saw the UN Charter on Human Rights as a fine statement of principles, but she was insistent that its implementation required the action of sovereign states as 'Constitutions have to be written on hearts, not just paper.'[134] Thatcher felt that a document like the European Charter on Fundamental Rights was equally worrying, again, not because its principles were wrong, but because it demanded 'the subordination of sovereign states, democratic decision-making and national law to international institutions.'[135] All of this Thatcher saw as driven by a specific and politically dangerous agenda, and she declared that 'Conservatives everywhere must go on the counter-offensive against the New Left human rights brigade.'[136]

Thatcher's Euroscepticism, her dislike of 'multilateralism' and her mistrust of international structures and institutions, including the UN and the Commonwealth, appear at first glance to confirm that she was a 'Little Englander'. To categorize her in these terms, however, would be simplistic. Thatcher was certainly a nationalist, and above all an *English* nationalist, but she also viewed nations and nationalisms generally as natural phenomena that, unlike international structures, had historical roots. This was the fundamental basis for her critique of what she described as the federalist tendency in Europe, which she contrasted with her own conception of Europe. Here Thatcher was described, and indeed described herself, as a 'Gaullist',[137] in so far as she felt that she and de Gaulle shared a view of 'a Europe of separate countries'[138] and not a fledgling United States of Europe. This 'Gaullist' vision informed the declaration in her 1988 Bruges speech that the 'willing and active co-operation between independent sovereign states is the best way to build a successful European Community,'[139] a point she underlined shortly afterwards to a US audience.[140]

It was this emphasis on inter-national, rather than international, association which led Thatcher to be so positive about NATO, which she described as the successful product of 'firm US leadership of *sovereign nations* in alliance.'[141] That the USA was the leading voice in NATO was crucial for Thatcher, for, above all else, she was an Atlanticist. In her second volume of memoirs she wrote an 'afterword', which presented a strong, general critique of European federalism, but one of her criticisms was that the Euro-federalists were not real internationalists because they were too Eurocentric in their outlook.[142] Of particular concern to Thatcher was that this Eurocentrism could manifest itself as anti-Americanism. In 1993 Thatcher argued that 'anti-Americanism . . . has too often been part of the thinking of some European governments – too often anti-Americanism has been regarded as the touchstone of loyalty to Europe.'[143] Nor was this a retrospective judgement. It had not been happenstance that, in December 1986, Thatcher chose the European Parliament as the venue to voice concerns about 'anti-Americanism'. In January that year she had been asked, in the context of the Westland affair, whether Michael Heseltine's backing for the European bid for Westland had revealed a latent anti-Americanism in Britain and Europe, and whether her support for the US bid had led to accusations of her being too pro-American. Thatcher's reply was, 'We are all in NATO and NATO consists of Europe and Canada and the United States, so I have never accepted that being pro-one is being anti-the other.'[144] In Thatcher's view, the problem was that not enough Europeans thought the same way, as they were either ungrateful about or resentful of the US role in liberating Europe in the Second World War and the presence of 300,000 US troops defending the 'frontier of freedom', that is, Western Europe, in the 1980s.[145]

For Thatcher, the politics of European anti-Americanism went hand in hand with its economics. The year after she left office, Thatcher warned a US audience that 'the nearer the EC approaches federalism, the further it departs from free trade – and the more it becomes fortress Europe.'[146] It was because of this that she had sought to reform the CAP, which was Europe's worst protectionist excess and made a nonsense out of genuine international trading agreements, like GATT.[147] But above all it was why she opposed any move towards anything that seemed closer to a federal Europe. Thatcher, as noted above, argued that a federal Europe would be a fortress Europe, and in 1990 she told a US audience, 'I am very much against fortress Europe as a protectionist club,'[148] which, she thought, could only end with 'Fortress Europe closing inwards ... against the rest of the world.'[149] Thatcher called for a more open Europe, which would look to 'tending our historic alliances, above all the United States to whom we owe so much, and understanding that Europe will never flourish as a fortress locked within the western peninsula of our continent'.[150] To Thatcher, the question of European union raised not only the question of whether Britain was part of Europe, but whether Europe was part of the Atlantic world and shared what she saw as the defining Anglo-American preference for open, economic and *therefore* political exchange. In 1991 she argued that 'the transatlantic relationship between Europe and the US has been eroded ... by Europe's selfishness on trade issues, its institutional obsessions, its growing isolationism.'[151] In this context she hoped that other Europeans would, like her, realize the economic and political benefits that had been and were to be gained from the Atlantic link. In stating her case she argued that if this meant 'being called a Trojan Horse' for the USA, 'then I would rather be a Trojan than a Greek.'[152] As a self-professed 'Gaullist', it was somewhat ironic that she thus described her role in exactly the terms that had led de Gaulle to veto Britain's first application to Europe. But Thatcher's Atlanticism was the dominant aspect of her international outlook, and the 'special relationship' overrode all others.

7

Thatcher and Europe

 During my lifetime most of the problems the world has faced have come
... from mainland Europe.[1]

When Margaret Thatcher was forced to resign in November 1990, a main cause was Europe. The challenge to her leadership by Michael Heseltine struck the fatal blow, but his challenge had been triggered by Sir Geoffrey Howe's resignation speech in Parliament on 13 November, and Howe's disagreements with Thatcher over Europe had prompted his resignation 12 days earlier. The issue of Britain's relationship with its European partners had been ticking under Thatcher's premiership for several years. She had been an enthusiastic signatory of the Single European Act of 1986, but she had seemed, almost immediately, to have second thoughts. These she expressed most forcibly at Bruges in September 1988, where she declared that 'We have not successfully rolled back the frontiers of the State in Britain, only to see them reimposed at a European level with a European super-state exercising a new dominance from Brussels.'[2] Thatcher perceived the European Union to be moving in a centralizing, federalist direction, and she was wholly opposed to this. In his memoirs, Howe states that he was appalled by Thatcher's Bruges speech, and increasingly perturbed by her hostile attitude towards other European leaders in general and officials of the European Union in particular.[3] Nor was Howe alone here, for Nigel Lawson, albeit for different reasons, was also increasingly frustrated by Thatcher's hostility towards closer European economic cooperation.[4] At the time of her resignation, and still more so during the 1990s, Thatcher's stance on European issues placed her firmly within what came to be known as the 'Eurosceptic' wing of the Conservative Party.

A recurring theme of this book has been that Margaret Thatcher's position on most issues was remarkably consistent throughout her political career, and Europe is no exception. Britain's relations with Europe did not figure in her public statements until she entered Parliament. Her personal knowledge of Europe was limited, for she had paid few visits to the Continent and spoke no European languages. During her first term in Parliament, however, it was not possible for Thatcher to avoid Europe, for the Macmillan Government submitted Britain's first application to join the EEC in 1961, the year she joined the government as a junior minister. Speaking at a meeting of her constituency party in August that year, Thatcher fulsomely presented the government's policy, and declared, 'We should be failing in our duty to future generations if . . . we committed this country to isolation from Europe for many years to come.'[5] She also addressed objections raised by Conservative opponents of the application. Many Conservatives felt that to embrace Europe was to abandon the Commonwealth, but Thatcher argued that 'to pose this as a choice between Europe and the Commonwealth is to put it falsely.'[6] She advanced two counter-arguments to the Commonwealth concern. First, she stated that the Commonwealth had gone through many changes, and that relations with leaders such as Kwame Nkrumah and Jomo Kenyatta were not as close as those with, for example, Robert Menzies. Second, she argued that 'unless our own economy flourishes we shall be unable to hold the Commonwealth together' and that Britain's membership of the EEC would enable it to provide more Commonwealth development aid. She also addressed the issue of sovereignty, and dismissed concerns on this issue by stating that, 'Looking at the European Community at present, it does not appear that its separate members have lost either their identity or their sovereignty.'[7] Not surprisingly, Thatcher supported Britain's application, and did so in terms that seemed to indicate enthusiastic endorsement rather than obligations of ministerial loyalty.

The failure of the 1961 application did not close the European question. The Conservative Party, above all its leadership, remained committed to entering the EEC. Thatcher followed the party's stance, and during the 1966 general election campaign she announced that 'Europe has become a cornerstone of our campaign.'[8] The intention to pursue an application was included in the 1970 Conservative manifesto, and negotiations proceeded through 1971. Thatcher continued to embrace the European cause, and used the hero of her teenage years to support the party's case when she told her constituency party that 'The great visionary of politics, Winston Churchill, had the idea to draw Europe together with a unity of voice and action.'[9] Thatcher supported the 1971 application in Parliament and, of course, voted for British entry into the EEC. The next time that Europe became a major issue was in 1975, when the referendum was held on Britain remaining a member of the EEC. Thatcher was by then leader of the Conservative Party, and 'she urged her supporters to vote Yes in strength.'[10] Her views from the time of her first entry into the upper echelons of politics to her first summer as Conservative leader seemed to indicate that she was a pro-European.

Thatcher's support for British entry into the EEC was clear, but it was by no means unequivocal. In February 1975, in the run-up to the referendum, there were indications that there were limits to her European 'idealism'. Tony Benn noted that 'Mrs Thatcher is anti-Europe,'[11] and his views were confirmed when he was informed that CCO had prepared a tremendous campaign in favour of Britain remaining in the Common Market and the constituency parties were being asked to work flat out to get a 'Yes' in the Referendum. But when Mrs Thatcher was elected she told them to drop the whole thing – this was the price demanded for the support of the anti-marketeers.[12]

Benn was perhaps overstating his case, but he was not alone in thinking that Thatcher was relatively quiet in the referendum debate. For example, the BBC put it to her that 'she had stood on the sidelines and given the impression that she would prefer Britain, too, to stay on the sidelines and not get too closely involved where Europe was concerned.'[13] She refused to accept this, but only a few days later she was confronted with a similar argument and again was forced to 'strongly reject . . . allegations that she had "abdicated" from the pro-Market campaign.'[14] To some extent the lady did protest too much. Although she was by no means invisible during the referendum campaign, Thatcher did not play an especially vigorous role. This may have been out of belated deference to Heath, the architect of Britain's entry, who chaired the Conservative 'Yes' campaign,[15] but at best this provides only a partial explanation. Thatcher's 'Europhilia' was not of the same order as Heath's, and, in the wake of the 'Yes' result, she was clear that she 'rejected the idea that the European Community should grow into a Federation . . . [and] did not regard the Community as an embryo United States of Europe.'[16] Thatcher trod a cautious path in 1975. She was keen to underline the practical, economic benefits of EEC membership, but she did not embrace the full European ideal. Indeed, only a year after the referendum, Keith Joseph was told by a leading industrialist, Boz de Ferranti, that 'During a discussion with Douglas Hurd and Peter Kirk at the CBI, they told me that Margaret Thatcher, whenever Europe was mentioned, always said that she "didn't want to be under the heel of the Europeans"'. Ferranti was clearly appalled, and told Joseph that it was 'important to feed in to her, and indeed many other people, the fact that we are not under their heel, but part of them, and we have to be so if we are going to export enough engineering products to pay for our food.'[17]

Thatcher's reference to the 'heel of the Europeans' is one of the earliest examples of her suspicion of, and latent hostility towards, Britain's European partners. This not only reflected her own outlook, but was also a product of the 'Euro-ambivalence' within her party, which was later to harden into more clearly defined camps. That there were divisions within the Conservative Party over Europe was evident in 1975, for leading backbench critics of the EEC made no secret of their position, and Edward du Cann, the chairman of the 1922 Committee, was a prominent campaigner for a 'No' vote. The number of *active* Conservative anti-marketeers was not great,[18] but there was concern about latent anti-EEC sentiment that was being held in check by the force of party loyalty.[19] Thatcher adroitly played the party loyalty card by presenting anti-EEC sentiment as a hallmark of the extreme Left: when she was challenged about du Cann's position and a 'Conservative split' over Europe, she countered that Labour was more divided, and that the anti-European views of Michael Foot and Tony Benn were more extreme than those held by any Conservatives.[20] Thatcher thus sought to turn the Europe spotlight onto Labour, and in so doing she emphasized Europe's political value to the Conservatives. Hence the Shadow Cabinet agreed, at its first meeting after the referendum, that although 'It was not an occasion for Party political controversy . . . a breakdown of the result showed that Conservatives had voted massively for Europe and that large numbers of people had voted against Mr Benn on this issue.' In these circumstances there was, it was thought, a real political opportunity for the Conservatives, in that 'Europeans feared that if Mr Wilson kept Ministers like Mr Benn and Mr Shore in the government, they would sabotage further progress in the Community.' It was suggested that this could be exploited, and 'Conservative back benchers at any rate should seize every opportunity to get Mr Benn to say something against Europe and thereby make it increasingly difficult for Mr Wilson to keep him in the government.'[21] In this way, Europe was to be used both to exacerbate Labour's internal disputes and, with careful handling, perhaps neutralize the Conservatives' bête noire on the Labour Left.

The notion that the Conservatives could present themselves to other EEC members as more 'Europhile' than Labour, and thereby enjoy easier relations when the party took office, was complemented by a strategy of developing links with continental Conservatives. In April 1976 the CRD's chief research officer, Chris Patten, began exchanges with the German CDU, on the basis that 'it would be a good idea for us to work closely with them in one or two areas.'[22] Two years later, at Shadow Cabinet, 'Mrs Thatcher reported that she and others were visiting Salzburg . . . to set up a new alliance with a large number of European parties of the centre-right.'[23] The aim of this alliance was 'to found a means of co-operation between centre and centre-right parties across Western Europe in order to influence the political future of the continent in our direction, in opposition to the Socialist international';[24] hence the European Democratic Union was created in the early spring of 1978 and, following the introduction of elections to the European Parliament, British Conservatives worked within this alliance. But Thatcher stated at the outset 'that there was no question of fusion with any of these parties; and that there naturally remained a number of points on which we had disagreements over emphasis.'[25] The Conservatives may have been anxious to demonstrate that they were better 'Europeans' than Labour, but there were still important limits, and even working with continental Conservatives posed problems. The formation of the EDU had presented difficulties in so far as

> It was not immediately clear in some countries as to who the most appropriate partner might be. In others the connotations of the word 'Conservative' still provoked hostile reaction. There was a feeling, too, that the [British] Party lacked a specifically Christian tradition. In one or two instances the obvious partner was simply non-socialist rather than anti-socialist, and indeed in government was often to be found in coalition with socialists.[26]

Thatcher was clear from the outset that the EDU was not

> a single monolithic party, but ... an alliance of autonomous parties co-operating for a common purpose. For many years there has been a Socialist International. We do not need to copy their barren doctrines or ideological arguments. But we must match them in organisational strength if we are serious in our purpose, and determined to achieve our victory.

Thatcher's troubled relations with the German CDU leadership in the 1980s were to demonstrate that her desire for autonomy outweighed moves to cooperation, and in this respect her view of the EDU was very similar to her attitude towards Europe as a whole.

The Conservative leadership became exercised by Europe again in 1978, when the question arose as to whether Britain should join the European Monetary System (EMS). When James Callaghan reported the plan for the EMS to Parliament in July 1978, he indicated that his government was cautious about Britain entering the system. Thatcher took a critical, 'communitaire' stance, and argued that 'we are more likely to get out of the problem of world recession by co-operating with our partners than we are by standing aside from the scheme which they have put up.'[27] She also declared, 'we welcome the concept of a currency sta-bilisation scheme', and suggested that Callaghan's caution was driven by political rather than economic considerations, in that 'his party would clearly never have allowed him to join.'[28] The date for the inauguration of the EMS had been set for 1 January 1979, and, at Thatcher's behest, a group of senior Conservatives held a series of meetings to shape the party's position. At an initial discussion they decid-ed the party should support sterling's entry for both political and economic rea-sons. Nigel Lawson and John Nott laid stress on the economic arguments, and the latter stated that 'the issue had little to do with "Europe" ... [but] it could become a step towards economic and monetary union.' Geoffrey Howe emphasized the political dimension, and argued that if sterling did not enter, 'we would be at the foot of a Franco-German high table', and that 'It was politically important to be in the big league if we could be.'[29] The group also thought, as Thatcher had argued with regard to the referendum, that there was domestic political capital to be gained from adopting a 'bipartisan' approach, in so far as the Labour govern-ment was divided and the Conservatives could help exacerbate that divide while gaining European diplomatic kudos.[30] Writing to Thatcher, Howe blended the economic and political arguments. He told her that 'This is not, and should not be presented as, a straight pro or anti-European issue,' and also that it was not a question of choosing between fixed and floating exchange rates. With regard to the economic case, he argued, 'we should pronounce in favour of the EMS – not as the ideal way ahead but nevertheless to be welcomed for providing greater cur-rency stability and encouraging convergence of economic policies.'[31] But Howe also concluded that there was a *political* economy to the EMS which was equally important. Howe argued that if Britain and sterling remained outside the EMS, this would mean 'surrendering the direction of the EEC and its policies to the Franco-German high table.' Moreover, he contended that 'unless we are participants rather than spectators of the EMS',[32] it would be difficult for Britain to influence reforms of the EEC Budget and the Common Agricultural Policy (CAP).[33] 'Labour's lukewarm attitude to Europe', Howe told Thatcher, 'has compounded the difficulties on every front'; he felt that a positive stance by the Conservatives would help create goodwill towards the party in Europe, which would be useful if and when they took office.[34] As a consequence of these discussions, the Shadow Cabinet decided that 'we should cautiously welcome the EMS proposals . . . and should emphasize that we were in favour of more co-operation on monetary matters between the European countries.' They also accepted Nigel Lawson's argument concerning the beneficial, disciplinary effects of the EMS, and noted that if the government chose to remain outside, this should be blamed on the Labour Left.[35]

The discussions on the EMS raised questions and themes that were to recur throughout the 1980s. These issues, and their contribution to Thatcher's demise, will be examined below. Here, we will turn to the European question that dominated the first phase of Thatcher's premiership – Britain's contribution to the EEC Budget. In 1979 Britain contributed £3.08 billion to the EEC Budget and received £2.04 billion,[36] which made Britain the second highest net contributor after Germany. Thatcher regarded this as unacceptable, and at the Dublin European Council (EC) meeting in November 1979, she was adamant that Britain should receive a substantial refund. This began a series of, at best, tense and, at worst, confrontational meetings between Thatcher, her ministers and their European counterparts. Thatcher's first Foreign Secretary, Lord Carrington, notes in his memoirs that 'The matter went on tediously long, dominating Community business . . . [and] overshadowed my first eighteen months as Foreign Secretary.'[37] Carrington also notes that because the Budget discussions took place at the European Council, the highest level of EEC governance, 'the row was conducted largely by Margaret Thatcher . . . no bad hand at conducting rows.'[38] The ongoing row saw Thatcher make herself 'exceptionally unpopular', especially at the EC meetings of 1979 and 1980 in Dublin and Luxembourg, where she bluntly said '"I want my money back", language which sent shudders down many a Continental spine.'[39] In terms of obtaining budgetary refunds, Thatcher was successful. At Dublin in November 1979, Britain was granted a £350 million rebate, and at Luxembourg in April 1980, £800 million, and the stage was set for further budgetary rebates and reform. Carrington came to the conclusion that 'Margaret's firmness and intransigence were the key factors in getting us a proper solution', but he also felt that 'the resultant atmosphere' clouded relations between Britain and its European partners.[40]

For Thatcher, the demand for the return of 'her money' was a means as well as an end. At the Dublin EC meeting she had stated that there were three related problems which needed to be addressed: the amount spent on the Common

Agricultural Policy (CAP), the calculation of contributions and the distribution of Budget receipts. There was general acceptance at the EC that these issues needed to be addressed, but Thatcher made it clear in April 1980 that 'we shall not get agreement on the agricultural price settlement, or any other major matter, unless our budget problem is satisfactorily settled.'[41] In June 1980, at a 24-hour meeting of EEC Foreign Ministers, Carrington and Sir Ian Gilmour negotiated a three-year agreement which confirmed ongoing, substantial repayments of Britain's contributions, but this by no means ended the dispute. At the EC meeting in Stuttgart in 1983, Thatcher and her team negotiated a 65.4 per cent refund of Britain's contribution. She had initially called for 65.9 per cent, but as the total sum involved came to £2.5 billion, she pronounced the agreement satisfactory, especially as the meeting agreed to address the question of long-term reform of the Budget.[42] But after the EC meeting, the French and Italian governments blocked the Budget refund, with the result that at the following EC meeting in Brussels in March 1984, another row took place.[43] This was only settled at the Fontainbleu EC summit in June 1984, when Britain was granted a 66 per cent refund, the previous year's was unblocked and a long-term rebate structure was put in place.[44] Indeed, at the Fontainbleu summit the EC agreed on the principle of 'juste retour' for payments, according to which Member States would never be required to sustain a budgetary burden considered excessive in relation to their relative prosperity. This marked a major shift, for the idea of the 'juste retour' had, from the outset, been the basis of the British case both for its rebates and for the reform of Budget calculation, and this approach had long been resisted by the other Member States. Thatcher clearly felt that the EEC had accepted the validity of her case, and, as a consequence, she had also reclaimed 'her money'. By early 1988 Thatcher thus felt able to consider the budgetary saga closed, and after an EC meeting in February that year, she told the House of Commons that with the Fontainbleu rebate formula in place, and the CAP reformed, the path was 'now clear for the Community to concentrate on its most important goal – the creation of a genuine single market by 1992.'[45]

Thatcher's reference to the single market indicates how far the budgetary issue was inseparable from broader developments in Europe. In November 1981 the German and Italian Foreign Ministers, backed by the European Commission, had drawn up a draft European Act which called for greater advancement towards European unity through an extension of the EC's powers into new areas, including foreign policy, defence, justice, culture and fundamental rights. This draft also proposed that EC decisions could be taken by majority rather than unanimous voting, but this was not agreed upon by the time of the 1983 Stuttgart EC. Nevertheless, Stuttgart did see the 'Solemn Declaration on European Union', which, although it was backed by no tangible measures, stated the intention of the EEC to move to closer economic and political cooperation. Intriguingly, Thatcher made only passing reference to the Solemn Declaration at the post-summit press conference, and instead focused attention on the fact that the EC had, in her view, produced a satisfactory Budget settlement.[46] This was an eloquent statement of her priorities, but her silence on the implications of the meaning of European Union was equally eloquent in terms of the shape of things to come.

The proposal presented by Genscher and Colombo at Stuttgart was a high-level manifestation of calls for EEC institutional reform emanating from the European Parliament (EP). A key base for these calls was the so-called Crocodile Group, formed in 1980 and coordinated by Altiero Spinelli, a former European Commissioner and founder of the European Federalist Movement. This group sought to extend the scope of Community activities, with an increasing procedural involvement of the European Parliament. Against them was ranged another group within the EP, the Kangaroo Group, which was set up in 1981 by less federalist-minded MEPs, supported by business groups, and which sought European integration through liberalization of the internal market. The Crocodile Group helped to draw up a 'Draft Treaty establishing the European Union' in 1984, which was explicitly designed to replace the Treaty of Rome. This draft proposed new common economic, monetary, social and foreign policies for the union, and called for the creation of a new two-chamber parliament and a union council for representatives of the national governments. The proposal was adopted by a large majority of the European Parliament, but there were no early indications that the EC and Member States would accept and ratify this proposal.

Thatcher, in effect if not in name, was a member of the Kangaroo Group, in that she saw the route to closer European relations in terms of the creation of a single market. Here she found a measure of accord with the German Chancellor, Helmut Kohl, who also wished to see greater European market liberalization. But Kohl, unlike Thatcher, was also in accord with the French president, François Mitterand, and advocated procedural and institutional reform to complement the market. These similarities and differences were thrown into relief when, in a speech at Strasbourg in May 1984, Mitterand endorsed the ideas put forward in the Crocodile Group's draft treaty, and argued for institutional reform of the EC and restricted use of the national veto. Mitterand's action ensured that the 'Crocodile' treaty did not simply disappear. In fact, he personally toured Europe in 1984, seeking support for the relaunching of the EC, and called for reform of the CAP, internal market reform and changes in Europe's decision-making procedures. Kohl supported Mitterand's efforts and a Franco-German alliance emerged as the fulcrum pressing for European Union. A further twist was given to this tale when Mitterand called for a conference on the future of the EC and stated that the Member States should confirm their commitment to closer union. If some States were uncommitted or hesitant, he raised the possibility of a Europe '*à géométrie variable*'. Mitterand again received support from Kohl, who announced that it was the right time to hasten the completion of the internal market and adopt majority voting at the EC. Mitterand and Kohl invited Member States to move in this direction, with or without consensus, and raised the possibility of a two-tier Europe ('*Europe à deux vitesses*') moving towards closer unity.

It was within the context of constructing the architecture of the European Union that Thatcher's own conception of European unity became clear and her differences with other European leaders and her own senior ministers crystallized. In her first volume of memoirs, Thatcher stated, 'I had one overriding positive goal ... to create a single common market.'[47] This had been one of her objectives in seeking to remove the 'obstacles' which the CAP and budgetary structure had placed in the way of European market relations. When the Single European Act (SEA) was introduced in 1986, and ratified by all the Member States of the newly renamed European Union, Thatcher was an enthusiastic supporter, and Britain was one of the first Member States to ratify the Act. In 1989 she expressed pride and pleasure in the fact that Britain was 'way ahead with implementation, in the Single Act',[48] and in preparing for the opening of the single market in 1992. But although she was enthused by the prospect of a European market with no internal trade barriers, Thatcher was alarmed by the fact that her interpretation of how this market was to function was not shared by many who had supported its creation.

In spite of her overwhelmingly negative response to the Delors Report and its endorsement by the EC, the Madrid summit saw Thatcher announce that Britain would join the European Exchange Rate Mechanism (ERM), albeit at an unspecified date.[49] The 'commitment' to join the ERM was not, however, an indication of Thatcher accepting the argument for closer European currency alignment. The ERM was essentially an outgrowth of the EMS that had been established in 1979, but with narrower bands permitted for currency fluctuation. As noted above, John Nott had thought in 1978 that the EMS could be 'a step towards economic and monetary union', and the ERM was designed to be precisely that. This was one of the main reasons why Thatcher resisted joining both the EMS and the ERM. In early 1985, when the ERM was being constructed as part of the background to the SEA, Thatcher had been willing to consider British membership, but by September of that year she had decided firmly against, and her opposition only grew stronger.[50] In 1980 Thatcher had stated that she was reluctant to join the EMS, as it would weaken the government's control of monetary policy and hence undermine its anti-inflation strategy. This seems to have been one cause of her hostility to the ERM, and Nigel Lawson contends that her thinking (and prejudices) on this question were reinforced by the advice she received from Alan Walters.[51] In contrast, Lawson, as had been the case in 1978, felt that exchange rate discipline could complement and reinforce internal monetary discipline and assist the fight against inflation. It was this that led him to 'shadow' the Deutschmark in 1987–88, and to support joining the ERM.[52] In short, Lawson saw the ERM in terms of its potentially beneficial economic effects, and saw Thatcher's concerns about the 'independence' of sterling and British monetary policy as evidence of her 'strong mercantilist streak'[53] – as if her philosophy could be expressed as 'monetarism in one country'. Geoffrey Howe, on the other hand, saw the ERM more in political terms. Unlike Lawson, Howe supported European Monetary Union and the idea of a single currency, and he saw both as commitments integral to the SEA. The commitment of Howe and Lawson, for different reasons, to the ERM, was crucial to her agreeing to join, for, at a meeting with her before the Madrid summit, they had both threatened to resign had she not agreed.[54] Thatcher's opposition to the broad goals of the SEA (which she had not questioned when she signed the Act), her rejection of the Delors Report (which gave concrete expression to SEA goals) and her hostility to the ERM soured relations with Britain's European partners and opened an irreparable breach between her and two of her closest colleagues.

The Delors Report of April 1989 brought many of Thatcher's latent concerns into the open. Her Bruges speech of the previous September had outlined her general concerns about what she perceived to be a centralizing, federalist, regulatory tendency at work in the European Commission and the European bureaucracy. The Delors Report confirmed her worst fears, for when the report was published she told Parliament that it 'aimed at a federal Europe, a common currency and a common economic policy, which would take many economic policies, including fiscal policy, out of the hands of the House'.[55] At the EC summit in Madrid, which discussed the Delors Report, Thatcher welcomed its 'stage 1' to European economic unity, which called for the abolition of exchange controls, the free movement of capital and a free market in financial services. This, she argued, would be an example of Europe following the path taken by Britain in 1979.[56] But 'stage 2' and 'stage 3' of the report, which called for the creation of a European Central Bank (ECB) and a single currency, were unacceptable to Thatcher. She informed a press conference at the Madrid summit that there was 'no need for a single currency in Europe',[57] and she stated in an interview with the BBC that the proposed ECB 'arrogates far more power from nation states to a central body of something like twelve bankers who are not publicly accountable to anyone'.[58] In the House of Commons she explained that her rejection of the report stemmed from her concern that 'stages 2 and 3 . . . would involve a massive transfer of sovereignty'[59] from the individual Member States to the European administration, and that this would lead towards centralization.

When Lawson resigned as Chancellor in October 1989, the immediate cause was his anger at Thatcher preferring the counsel of her personal economic adviser, Sir Alan Walters, to his own. Lawson and Walters had always had a tense relationship, but these tensions were exacerbated by Walters publishing and publicly voicing his criticisms of the ERM through 1989. For Lawson, Walters' criticisms were less about Europe and more about the exchange rate as a counter-inflationary tool. Walters (and here he both encouraged and influenced Thatcher's position) felt that an emphasis on exchange rate policy, which required an active use of short-term interest rates and the sale or purchase of currencies by the Bank of England, had inflationary effects on the money supply. Lawson did not accept this argument, which led some, including Thatcher, to blame his shadowing of the Deutschmark in 1987–88 for the rise in inflation.[60] The rift between Lawson and Thatcher found its focus in the figure of Sir Alan Walters, but underlying the personal tension was a conflict over the role that European as opposed to national economic policies could or should play in shaping a Member State's economic strategies and structures.

It was within this last context that Thatcher found herself in deep conflict with European leaders and party colleagues in late 1989 and 1990. A particular point of disagreement was the European Social Charter. At its Hanover summit of June 1988, the EC had stressed the importance of the social aspect of the single market, and in November that year the European Commission's Economic and Social Committee (ESC) had been instructed to formulate a charter of social rights for workers. The ESC's task was defined at the EC summit on Rhodes in December 1988, namely to show that the 'realisation of the single market should not be regarded as a goal in itself'. By February 1989 a draft social charter had been drawn up, and in March the EP passed a resolution calling for 'the adoption at Community level of the fundamental social rights which should not be jeopardised because of the pressure of competition or the search for increased competitiveness, and could be taken as the basis for the dialogue between management and labour.' The express aim was to ensure that there was a social dimension to the internal market. This goal was endorsed by the EC Madrid summit in June, and in October the European Commission published its draft 'Community Charter of Basic Social Rights'. The charter was passed by the EP in early December, with the result that workers were entitled to the protection of their newly defined rights by the European Court of Justice.

Thatcher was appalled by the social charter. Her goal in the United Kingdom had been to deregulate the labour market, through reducing the role of the State and removing the legal immunities and constraining the activities of trade unions. In the social charter she saw the embodiment of what she had spoken of at Bruges, namely the Brussels bureaucracy reimposing by the European back door the regulatory framework she had removed. When the social charter went through the EP she denounced it, and declared that 'the social charter . . . would regulate the labour market in a way which, far from creating jobs, would actually put them at risk, by raising costs.'[61] In her memoirs she was even more abrupt, and described the social charter as 'a Socialist Charter', which bore the imprint of the political background of the president of the Commission.[62]

Speaking in the House of Lords in 1993, Thatcher stated, 'I started out as an idealist on the European question';[63] but throughout her career she set strict limits on her European idealism, and these limits only grew stronger as the European ideal of others expanded. In her memoirs Thatcher argued that there were two conflicting visions of the European Union: one which saw Europe as a union of independent nation states linked by the bond of their mutual interest in the single market, and another which saw it as bureaucratic, interventionist and federalist.[64] This remark was not the product of post-retirement reflection. In October 1988 she had told the Conservative Party Conference that they faced 'The choice between two kinds of Europe: a Europe based on the widest possible freedom for enterprise or a Europe governed by Socialist methods of centralised control and regulation.'[65] The latter construction of Europe she described as the 'Babel Express,'[66] and she contended that it had become particularly pronounced in her second term as prime minister, when Europe had started sliding towards 'Statism and centralism.'[67] It was her anger and concern about this vision of Europe which led her in the 1990s to add a 'Eurosceptic' appendix to her second volume of memoirs, to engage in a series of 'provocative attacks on European integration and its leaders' and to be so critical of her successor.[68] Indeed, Thatcher's Euroscepticism became a focal point for the increasingly numerous core of Conservative MPs who, in John Major's words, engaged in 'trench warfare' over Europe and 'split the party' in the 1990s.[69] In 1992 Thatcher made one of her rare post-resignation Commons speeches to call for a referendum on the principle of a single currency, and, later in the year, having left the Commons, she urged Conservative MPs to vote against the Government's Maastricht Treaty Bill.[70] To say the least, it was unusual for a former prime minister to tell her party's representatives to vote against their government, but it reflected how deep her Euroscepticism had become. This was further confirmed when she chose to publish an article midway through the Conservative Party Conference which declared that 'Maastricht will hand over power to more unelected bureaucrats.'[71] Moreover, in 1995 she was studiously 'even-handed' when the Eurosceptic John Redwood challenged John Major's leadership, which in the circumstances was a thinly disguised attack on Major and a clear critique of Europe.[72]

But Thatcher reserved her most vitriolic criticisms, and indeed denunciations, of Europe for her last major publication. In *Statecraft* she notes that as prime minister she devoted a great deal of her time to Europe, but to no avail, as 'Europe as a whole is fundamentally unreformable.'[73] Europe, in Thatcher's view, was moving inexorably towards becoming a federal superstate, 'based upon the suppressing or, as the enthusiasts would doubtless have it, the surpassing of the concept of national identity.'[74] This nascent superstate she regarded, in theory and in practice, as a fundamentally flawed and dangerous concept, not least because 'Europe is, in truth, synonymous with bureaucracy. It is government by bureaucracy for bureaucracy ... [and] what makes Europe the ultimate bureaucracy is that it is *ultimately sustained by nothing else.*'[75] Rehearsing Europe's history in the 1980s and 1990s, Thatcher outlined the budgetary problems, the 'protectionist' CAP and the social charter as precursors of the creation of the ECB and the single currency. All these, she argued, were destructive of the economic and political liberty of the Member States, with the inauguration of the Eurozone and the ECB removing interest rate and currency control from the individual nations.[76]

That the bureaucratic, federal superstate had come into being and was threatening to eclipse nation-state democracy was attributable, in Thatcher's analysis, to two things. First, and here she engaged in an act of mea culpa, was the fact that politicians like herself had misjudged the outcome of the SEA. She had thought, she argued in *Statecraft*, that under the SEA the European Commission's powers would recede as the force of the single market increased. Instead, it had become increasingly clear that the Commission and many Continental governments saw the SEA in *political* rather than economic terms.[77] Second, she suggested that European politicians and bureaucrats were inherently predisposed (unlike the British!) to Empire building, as the evidence of the Hapsburgs, Napoleon and

Hitler had demonstrated.[78] This last remark, especially the reference to Hitler and his being twinned with Napoleon, was indicative of the less rational aspect of Thatcher's Euroscepticism. In August 1962, during the first application to Europe, Thatcher had told her constituents that if Britain remained outside 'we will leave the ascendancy to Germany,'[79] and her concerns on this front were to be constant, even increasing over time. Thatcher was by no means alone in seeing Germany as the dominant force in the European Community, but she seems to have had a particularly negative view of its influence. Nigel Lawson, for example, speaks in his memoirs of Thatcher's 'pathological hostility to Germany and the Germans which in the end came to dominate her view of the European Community.'[80] Indeed, Lawson felt that Nicholas Ridley's anti-German outburst in the *Spectator* in July 1990 reflected Thatcher's as well as his own visceral dislike of Germany.[81] Lawson argues that Thatcher was guilty of 'saloon-bar xenophobia',[82] a view echoed by Howe's reference to 'The scale and passion of Margaret Thatcher's anti-Germanism.'[83] Lawson and Howe's statements could be seen as necessarily parti pris, but George Urban, one of Thatcher's 'court' of advisers, also remarked upon her 'atavistic fear of Germany',[84] which he saw as at the root of her 'narrow and shortsighted conception of Britain's place in Europe.'[85] Exactly what the roots of Thatcher's anti-German views were it is difficult to tell. One senior Foreign Office official felt that Thatcher was 'a Little Englander through and through,'[86] which is in accord with Urban's sense of her 'unedifying moods of off-shore nationalism.'[87] Thatcher refers in her memoirs to the 'quintessentially un-English outlook displayed by the Community' during the 1979 EC discussions on the Budget in Dublin, which is a most uncosmopolitan remark.[88] Thatcher was profoundly nationalistic, and clearly found it difficult, if not impossible, to reconcile her form of nationalism with a 'European ideal' that was *not* couched in narrow nationalistic terms.

This narrow conception of the 'national interest' played a vital part in her downfall, for it was at the root of the damaging resignations of Lawson and Howe. In Lawson's case, the issue of the ERM was central. Thatcher's opposition to the ERM, as noted above, was tied to her view that it surrendered control of important realms of economic policy to Europe, and was a precursor to a single currency, which would mean, as she told her last party conference as leader, 'entering a federal Europe through the back Delors.'[89] She had stated two years earlier that 'A European Central Bank means Parliament and Government, giving up control ... of the way in which the economy is run,'[90] but in Lawson's view it was 'positively mind-boggling' that Thatcher had signed the SEA, which spoke of monetary union, and yet had not grasped that this implied the need for an ECB and pressure for a single currency.[91] For Lawson, who was not in favour of a single currency, the 'national' issue was largely irrelevant, but the ERM offered a route to greater currency and monetary discipline, which he felt were essential national interests. In Howe's case, the ERM was also important, partly for economic reasons, but more so because it was, as Delors had indeed stated, a route to the economic and monetary union that were part of the SEA which Britain had ratified in 1986. Howe simply found Thatcher's attitude towards Europe increasingly Europhobic. When proposals had been put forward for a Western European Union on diplomatic and military matters, Thatcher presented them as an intrusion on NATO's territory and discourteous to the USA, with the result that 'Margaret could never be trusted not to shout impatiently whenever the three letters WEU crossed her path.'[92] But if WEU had this effect, ERM was an acronym that evoked even more spleen. Both Lawson and Howe speak with a mixture of incredulity and embarrassment about an Anglo-Dutch summit at Chequers in April 1989, where they had both hoped the Dutch prime minister, Ruud Lubbers, would help soften Thatcher's opposition to the ERM. But when Lubbers opened the subject, Howe recalls that 'Margaret responded by laying into the Dutch with ferocious gusto.'[93] Such incidents had made Howe's last year as Foreign Secretary, when the pace of European integration had increased, very difficult.[94] Having been somewhat unceremoniously reshuffled in July 1989, Howe kept his peace, but in late October 1990, Thatcher's stance at the Rome EC summit and her parliamentary statement after the meeting proved unacceptable to him. In Parliament Thatcher declared, 'Mr Delors, said ... that he wanted the European Parliament to be the democratic body of the Community, he wanted the Commission to be the Executive and he wanted the Council of Ministers to be the Senate. No. No. No.'[95] For Howe, this was simply Europhobic anti-diplomacy and it prompted his resignation,[96] which in turn led Heseltine to challenge Thatcher.

For Thatcher, the fact that Howe made his wounding resignation speech would, in some respects, not have been a surprise. In her memoirs she states that when he went to the Foreign Office he fell into a 'misty Europeanism',[97] which informed his hostility towards her. This 'phenomenon' was not unknown to her. One early Thatcherite, Christopher Tugendhat, had been appointed a European Commissioner in the early 1980s, but by the mid-1980s she was seeking to replace him with 'One Of Us', as he had 'gone native' in Brussels.[98] His replacement was Frank Cockfield, another early Thatcherite, but by the end of the 1980s he too had become 'Europeanised' and 'the prisoner as well as the master of his subject.'[99] Other individual examples, such as Leon Brittan, were reinforced by the Foreign Office European specialists, whom Thatcher saw as 'Eurocrats' employed by the British Government. Thatcher summed up her experience in her memoirs when she noted, 'I have never understood why some Conservatives seem to accept that free markets are right for Britain but are prepared to accept dirigisme when it comes wrapped in the European flag.'[100] The 'culture' of European governments, and hence the European administration, was viewed by Thatcher as inherently Statist and interventionist, with the result that those who were absorbed into the Eurocratic structure absorbed its approach to governance.

It was the 'culture' of Statism which Thatcher saw as having undermined her vision of the single market. Her stance on the social charter and her position on the ERM were indicative of a perception of the single market as a large free trade area, in which the European institutional structures merely provided consistent legal and regulatory guarantees for all participants. Beyond that she saw no need for an active European bureaucracy or active European intervention. The single market was to be just that, and the role of the EC, the European Commission and the EP was to liberalize and ease the operation of the single market. Within that framework, economic and other policy decisions for each nation were to be the realm of the individual member States, with the only constraint being that they adhered to the common regulatory framework to which they had all consented and which ensured a level economic 'playing field'. This was her vision of 'a Europe based on willing and active co-operation between independent sovereign states, not a federal Europe'.[101] In contrast, she saw the Continental vision as informed by a dirigiste outlook. In *Statecraft* Thatcher refers to 'anti-liberal market' statements by the former French prime minister, Edouard Balladur, which led her to conclude that the French 'psyche' was much more pro-Statist than the British.[102] Likewise, she has described the German conception of the social market as 'corporatist',[103] and she thought that neither the French nor the German Government admired the economic policies pursued in the UK after 1979.[104] As a consequence of their different economic and political traditions, Thatcher felt that the 'Franco-German axis' at the heart of Europe's structures sought to use the SEA 'in order to push corporatist and collectivist social legislation upon Britain by the back door.'[105] *Le Figaro* once compared Margaret Thatcher to Charles de Gaulle. Thatcher stated, 'I liked the comparison',[106] but, ironically, Thatcher's view of the 'Continental' European ideal led her to confirm one of de Gaulle's prejudices with regard to Britain's international leanings. Thatcher concluded that the European social and economic ideal, as expressed in the social charter and the dirigiste conception of the single market, was wholly at odds with the British ideal, and that the economic traditions of Britain and the USA were closer than those of Britain and Europe.

Conclusion

The day after Thatcher resigned as prime minister and leader of the Conservative Party, the veteran Labour politician Tony Benn visited the Foreign Secretary, Douglas Hurd, to speak about a planned visit to Iraq. Thatcher's resignation was on many people's minds, and Benn was asked by a group of Foreign Office officials what her reputation would be. Benn responded by stating, 'Everyone drops into the darkest of all worlds between the headlines and the history books.'[1] Thatcher's world after her resignation was actually not that dark, for outside Britain, especially in the former Eastern bloc and in the USA, Thatcher was publicly feted. Moreover, in the early years of the new century she and her legacy were treated in Britain with renewed respect. The aim of this book has been to contextualize Thatcher and Thatcherism and to try to put in historical perspective what she and her party attempted to achieve. This has demanded critical engagement, with 'critical' here meaning not simply criticism, but appraisal. The goal has been to identify where Thatcher and Thatcherism came from and, in turn, to observe both the intentions and the outcomes of Thatcherite Conservatism.

Thatcher's legacy: the rise of New Labour

An essay question the author has asked undergraduates to address is why it was that Tony Blair succeeded where Hugh Gaitskell failed in reforming the Labour Party's constitution. One student responded by suggesting that Blair had an advantage, in that, unlike Gaitskell, Blair had had Thatcher 'to put the boot in on the trade unions'. This answer had a pleasing simplicity. 'New Labour' was a product of the 1980s and the political and electoral dominance of Thatcher and Thatcherism. Labour's initial response to Thatcherism was to move to the Left. In 1983 the Labour Party fought the general election on a manifesto that advocated withdrawal from the EEC, unilateral nuclear disarmament and extended nationalization – a strongly Socialist programme, referred to by one senior figure on the Right of the Labour Party as 'the longest suicide note in history'.[2] Labour suffered a humiliating defeat in 1983 as the Conservatives enjoyed a landslide, but, equally important, the then recently formed SDP-Liberal Alliance came close to matching the Labour vote. As a consequence, the Labour Left lost political credibility and Labour set out on a steady march to the political Right.

Labour's shift could at one level be attributed to their own split and the emergence of the SDP. But Labour's split was not inevitable, and in the late 1970s the Conservatives themselves had discounted the idea that such a division would take place. Since the Second World War there had been frequent tensions within the Labour Party, most notably between 'fundamentalists and revisionists', Bevanites and Gaitskellites, over Clause IV and nuclear weapons, and these tensions had reflected, for the most part, divisions between the Left and Right of the party. It was one of Harold Wilson's significant achievements as Labour leader that he managed to avoid an open rupture of the party, but then he, like Gaitskell before him, had enjoyed the support of the unions against the Left, and this had been crucial in allowing the Labour Right to outmanoeuvre the Left. But in the late 1970s and 1980s there was a significant swing to the Left among the unions, and this was decisive in shaping Labour policy, the construction of the 'suicide note' manifesto of 1983 and the near election of Tony Benn as deputy leader of the party in 1981. In the early 1980s the post-Wilson Labour Party had become identified by the public, largely as a result of the widespread industrial unrest of the 'winter of discontent' of 1978–79, as the political arm of the trade union movement. Furthermore, the trade unions were widely regarded, in the vocabulary deployed by Conservatives at the time, as 'overmighty subjects' or 'unruly barons', and left-wing extremists.

At the same time as being able to label the Labour Party the creature of the trade unions, the Conservatives also identified their opponents as the party of high taxation. With the Conservatives having presented reduced personal tax and public expenditure as the hallmarks of their own party's political agenda, Labour was portrayed as a 'tax and spend' party. This argument was central to the Conservative campaign of 1987 and continued to be crucial after Thatcher's resignation, with the idea that Labour would drop a 'tax bombshell' being the centrepiece of the Conservative general election campaign of 1992. As Labour sought to make itself electable, by recovering voters lost to both the Conservatives and the SDP-Liberal Alliance, it deemed it necessary to move away from both its close identification with the trade unions and its reputation as a high-tax party.

The first stages in the Labour Party's 'long march' were carried out under the leadership of Neil Kinnock, the Labour leader from 1983 to 1992. Kinnock himself embodied his party's shift away from the Left, for having been identified as a left-winger in his early political career, he was keen in the late 1980s to present himself as a scourge of the Left, most particularly the militant tendency. The local authorities denounced as 'loony Left' by Thatcherites were subject to powerful criticism by Kinnock and the Labour leadership, and indeed Kinnock sought to use his attack on Liverpool City Council to establish his credentials as a Labour critic of the extreme Left. But although he successfully overcame his own 'enemies within', and pulled the Labour Party away from withdrawal from Europe and unilateral nuclear disarmament, Kinnock was unable to convince the electorate that

Labour had abandoned its 'tax and spend' heritage. This was confirmed by the 1992 election campaign, when Labour's inability to assuage concerns over its tax policies cost the party the general election.

Kinnock's resignation did not slow the pace of Labour's reforming and rightward trajectory. John Smith's brief leadership saw the trade union bloc vote replaced at Labour conferences, which greatly reduced the institutionalized power of the unions in the party. But it was after Smith's death that the biggest symbolic change took place, for Smith's successor, Tony Blair, secured the reform of Clause IV of the Labour Party's constitution. Although this clause did not specifically refer to the unions, it had been the trade union movement which had always had most reverence for the 'mystical halo' of nationalization and which had defended it against Gaitskell's attempted reform in 1959–60. The 1994 reform thus sent an unequivocal public message that Labour had renounced nationalization, and over the course of the next 10 years Blair and his colleagues accepted, and apparently embraced, many liberal-market axioms. Hence, in May 1997 the language of the market took on an increased prominence in both Labour's internal discussions and its policy agenda. That only a minority of the Labour Party, and then rarely, advocated any renationalization was one thing, but the emphasis on public-private partnerships and the extension of market testing in the public services, along with its ongoing reform, were all redolent of a frame of thought that saw the economics of the private sector as intrinsically superior to that of the public sector.

Thatcher's goal of 'rolling back the frontiers of the State' was not matched, either in principle or practice, by a Labour counter-commitment to roll them forward again. Furthermore, the Labour government of 1997–2001 committed itself to following, in its first two years in power, the outgoing Conservative administration's expenditure plans. Although Labour subsequently decided significantly to expand public spending, they did so without raising the 'headline' basic rate of income tax. To achieve this end the 'New Labour' Governments adopted what their opponents labelled 'stealth' taxes, that is to say, alternative forms of both direct and indirect taxation. Thatcherite Conservatives were in a good position to recognize stealth taxes in so far as they had pursued this strategy in the 1980s, for although the basic rate of income tax had been reduced, the overall tax burden of the average taxpayer had increased. In terms of the political economy of personal taxation, Thatcher presided over the cementing of 'taxphobia' in Britain, whereby it became politically impossible even to suggest raising the basic rate of income tax.

Thatcher stated that one of her fundamental political goals was to bring about the death of Socialism, certainly in Britain, but also in the wider world. In terms of mainstream British politics she was successful. In order to overturn their electoral subjugation, the Labour Party felt obliged to adjust their ideological position in order to accommodate priorities laid out in the Thatcherite agenda. Here New Labour consciously chose to appeal to target groups that had been essential to Thatcherite Conservatism, namely the middle class and the skilled working class designated as social category C2. It was for this reason that the party chose to jettison key aspects of its institutional links with the unions and its 'tax and spend' reputation. In this context it would be a mistake to underestimate the importance of the 1992 general election result. Labour had thought it would win, but the balance of expectation among voters had been that Labour remained primarily committed to the interests of organized labour and likely to increase personal taxation. Public opinion surveys indicated that a majority of electors felt that it was better for government to fund public services than cuts in taxation, but similar surveys also showed that a majority felt tax reductions would benefit their personal interests more than increased expenditure on public services. The 1992 result seemed to confirm these findings, and this in turn appeared to indicate that the Thatcherite emphasis on individual as opposed to collective demands and rights was electorally more effective. Across the spectrum of political economy, the Labour Party hierarchy felt that if they were to achieve power they had to accommodate themselves to Thatcherite ideas and to the social groups that had been identified as the Thatcherite caucus. Ironically, Thatcher, who had set out to overturn a policy consensus between the elites of Britain's major political parties, herself instigated what could be seen as a 'new consensus', for in June 2002 Peter Mandelson, one of the principal architects of New Labour, announced that on economic policy 'we are all Thatcherites now',[3] and a year later the Marxist scholar Stuart Hall wrote, 'New Labour has picked up where Thatcherism left off'.[4]

For internal party and Left critics of New Labour it was rhetorically powerful to portray Tony Blair and his colleagues as 'Thatcherite', but it would be reductionist to accept the idea that Labour simply absorbed Thatcherism. Hall acknowledged this, for in his critique of New Labour he described it as a 'hybrid regime', in which Thatcherite neoliberalism was the predominant strand and older, social democratic Labour themes provided a subordinate element. In Hall's analysis, this accounted for the way in which the post-1997 Labour administrations engaged in a 'sneering renunciation of redistribution', with 'the new religion of managerial authoritarianism ... [and] the reversal of the historic commitment to equality, universality and collective social provision.'[5] Furthermore, Hall saw New Labour as having adopted the Thatcherite agenda of deregulation and market testing in the traditional Labour domains of the Welfare State in particular and public services more generally, with privatization an option and a choice that Blair and his colleagues were willing to consider and select. Hall also acknowledged that some New Labour policies, such as the introduction of the minimum wage, ran counter to liberal-market thinking, but he saw the core of the New Labour agenda as built upon Thatcherite foundations. Hall offered a pungent Left critique of New Labour, and, coming as it did from one of the first scholars to use the term Thatcherism, it carried some weight, but his notion of a 'hybrid' structure of political economy carries still more.

In terms of *basic* tax policy there was little difference between Thatcherite and New Labour strategy. In terms of stated goals and values, however, there was an important gap. For a Thatcherite Chancellor like Lawson, equality was '*the* great bug bear of our age',[6] which was a statement Gordon Brown would never have made. Arguably, this was a product of a difference between intention and outcome. Whereas Thatcher sought to allow the better off to become still better off and to provide incentives for others to join them, Brown and New Labour sought, unsuccessfully as it turned out, to be unobtrusively redistributive. But, as even Hall was willing to accept, there was after 1997 a fundamental change in the realm of family taxation, in that the Working Families Tax Credit marked a break in fiscal policy. In the same vein, the New Deal and other 'workfare' strategies adjusted the tax and benefits system in favour of the unemployed. Welfare strategy, and in particular child poverty, were central to early New Labour economic policy. For New Labourites, in contrast to Thatcherites, welfare enjoyed equal priority to and was inseparable from rather than an adjunct to economic policy.

The overlaps between New Labour and Thatcherism are apparent. Their roots lay primarily in the perceived electoral necessity for Labour of appealing to the interests of certain social groups, but there were also some interesting intersections in terms of economic ideas. At the 1983 Conservative conference, Thatcher famously waved what she declared was her own copy of the 1944 White Paper on Employment, and declared that the economic strategy and policies of her governments were the route to achieving the goal of a 'high and stable' level of employment. Thatcher's reading of the 1944 White Paper placed emphasis on what may be called its 'supply-side' concerns with regard to international competitiveness and productivity, and she downgraded the demand side. In similar fashion to Thatcher, Gordon Brown sought, in his 1999 Mais Lecture, to present his economic strategies, the clearest practical expression of New Labour economics, as the fulfilment of the 1944 White Paper. Brown, like Thatcher, stressed its 'supply-side' aspects, but melded rather than contrasted them with the demand side. This approach expressed Brown's underlying economic philosophy. Again, in his Mais Lecture, Brown acknowledged, in a manner that carried echoes of Thatcher, that post-war economic governance had been flawed, and he argued, it was 'undeniable that the shared economic purpose of 1945 broke down in fifty years of endless and sterile divisions between capital and labour, between state and market and between public and private sectors, denying Britain the national direction it needed.'[7] The New Labour approach was often given the shorthand the 'third way', in economic as well as other policy areas, in that it was based on a contention that the idea of a dichotomy of policy approaches was incorrect. For Brown, and many of the New Labour leadership, it was a rejection of policy polarity that underpinned their readiness to embrace, in Hall's terms, a 'hybrid' economic regime. This helps to explain New Labour's enthusiasm for public-private partnership, the second Blair Government's goal of establishing quasi-independent 'foundation-trust' hospitals, and ministers' usage of the language of 'customers' and 'clients' for those who use public services. In short, New Labour not only used the institutions and structures of the market, but also adopted its vocabulary of consumers.

In the light of the Labour Party's adoption of the language of the consumer society, Thatcher was, it seems, successful in terms of using the economy as a means to the end of changing the culture of British society and politics. Certainly, the language of Socialism largely disappeared from the mainstream of British politics. The irony was that Labour's internal institutional reforms and its ideological reconstruction, both driven by the Labour Party's perception of Thatcher's redefinition of the British political agenda, squeezed the political and electoral space available to the Conservatives. The Conservatives contributed to their own difficulties through their own factional disputes and their seemingly inexorable rightward drift on the economy as well as Europe. Nevertheless, New Labour, which was a product of the Thatcher years and Thatcherism, ended the Conservative Party's long hegemony and demanded that the Conservatives pursue an internal re-examination similar to that undertaken by Labour.

Thatcher's legacy: a conservative crisis

In the wake of their successive electoral defeats in 1997, 2001 and 2005, the Conservative Party has confronted a crisis similar in scale to that which it faced in the Edwardian period. Since 1997 the Conservatives have enjoyed their second-longest period of Opposition since 1906, but whereas in 1906 the Conservative politician Andrew Bonar Law stated, 'we may be in opposition for half-a-generation', in 2003 Kenneth Clarke declared the Conservatives could be in Opposition for a whole generation – it seems the early twenty-first-century party's crisis was twice as bad as that of the Edwardian party! Thatcher bequeathed a problematic electoral legacy to the Conservatives. The regional concentration of the Conservative vote under Thatcher rendered the party wholly dependent on votes in England – Welsh and Scottish Conservatism were endangered species by 1990 and, by the turn of the century, they were extinct in terms of parliamentary seats, and nearly so in terms of votes. Had the Labour government introduced rather than merely toyed with proportional representation, the chance of there being another Conservative government would have been extremely slim.

One major reason for the Conservatives' difficulties was/is their being so deeply split over the issue of Europe. The issue of Britain's relations with Europe had been a major point of tension in Conservative politics since Macmillan submitted Britain's first application to the EEC in 1961. Under Thatcher, and in no small part as a result of her actions and attitudes, the European fracture widened within the Conservative Party. Thatcher's own 'Little England' stance became increasingly pronounced during her final term in office, and still more so after her resignation. Thereafter, Little England Euroscepticism became a marked feature of Thatcher's interventions from the wings (or from the back seat!); it was fundamental to the outlook of the Conservative grass roots and played a central role in the election of Hague, Duncan-Smith and Howard to the party leadership. In 2001 Thatcher's successor, John Major, was asked whether he felt that the Conservative Party had been hampered at the general election of that year 'by an excessive emphasis on Thatcherism in the Tory party',[8] and provided, perhaps unsurprisingly, an ambivalent answer. But although Europe, and more particularly the Euro, were the issues on which Thatcher chose to make her most publicized interventions in the 2001 general election, neither the issues nor Thatcher's appearances provided the Conservatives with significant electoral assistance. The electoral troubles that racked the Conservative Party after 1992 were not simply a product of the effects of Britain's forced departure from the ERM. There had been an underlying fragility in the Conservative position in the 1980s which had been masked by the fact that they had faced fractured opposition.

Changes in the Conservative electoral position were accompanied by major changes in the nature of Conservatism as a political ideology. The most important of these concerned the Conservative view of the nature of society. Traditionally, Conservatives viewed society as an *organic* structure in which all units interacted. In 1947, in his pamphlet on 'The Conservative Faith in the Modern Age', the CRD officer, David Clarke, wrote that 'society is an organic whole in which the social atoms react in all their movements upon one another'.[9] Clarke's colleague at CRD, Michael Fraser, echoed this position in 1952, stating, 'It is a feature of Conservatism ... not to consider society as merely a haphazard aggregation of individuals in isolation ... We believe man to be a social animal, happiest when he is free to take part in the life of a variety of groups and communities within the nation.'[10] This was further underlined by the Young Conservatives' 1962 pamphlet, *Society and the Individual*, which denounced the notion of society as an aggregate of individuals as one of the most misleading and damaging ideas promulgated by the French Revolution,[11] an argument which was further underscored by Enoch Powell, who argued in 1965 that

> society is much more than a collection of individuals acting together, even through the complex and subtle mechanisms of the free economy, for material advantage. It has an existence of its own; it thinks and feels; it looks inward, as a community, to its members; it looks outward as a nation.[12]

For Conservatives the relationship between individuals and society was necessarily symbiotic, and the notion that one had primacy over the other was a misconception, in that it was only as a consequence of familiar rules and customs that had developed through social interaction and which were regulated and enforced by laws and social norms that individuality could be expressed.[13]

Thatcher's goal was to roll back the State to allow room for spontaneous, voluntary, civic associations to flourish.[14] Her strategy was, as she explained in 1980, 'to re-invigorate not just the economy and industry, but the whole body of voluntary associations, loyalties and activities which gives society its richness and diversity, and hence its real strength'.[15] According to the Conservative MP and former head of Thatcher's Policy Unit, David Willetts, 'the free market' may have been 'the cutting edge of modern Conservatism', but there was a broader civic goal. 'Civic Conservatism', he argued, 'places the free market in the context of institutions and values which makes up civil society'.[16] And the institutions and values which were the perfect exemplars of this civil society were the 'great and proud institutions such as voluntary hospitals . . . [and the] network of voluntary organisations . . . created by working-class self-help: friendly societies, mechanics institutes, local guilds', all of which had been 'weakened if not destroyed by the advance of the State'.[17] But whether as a consequence of a mismatch between intention and outcome, or as a result of a failure to anticipate where a liberal-market strategy could lead, Thatcher did not enhance, but instead depleted civic associational life. In 1997 David Willetts and the political philosopher John Gray co-produced a pamphlet entitled, *Is Conservatism Dead?* Willetts concluded, somewhat unsurprisingly, that it was not, but Gray argued that the emphasis in late twentieth-century Conservatism on market relations as a basis for social relations had acted as a solvent of social bonds, which had existed in the shape of varied and complex webs of associational activity.[18] The *individualist* logic of the liberal market, often explicitly embraced by Thatcher and her party, carried the intrinsic possibility of a tendency not only to *political* individualism, but also to social *individuation*, both of which placed question marks, in terms of theory and practice, against the importance of social action and social capital. That the emphasis on market relations which had informed much of the political, economic and social agenda of Thatcherism appeared to have brought about the possibility of such a fracturing of social cohesion was a matter of concern across the political spectrum, and it was a concern that was not confined to Britain.[19] But it presented particular problems for British Conservatives,[20] in that its implications stretched organicism, and, as a consequence, Conservatism itself, to breaking point.

Change and continuity

Thatcher called herself a revolutionary and many of her colleagues termed her and their own politics 'radical'. When she stated in 1978 that she had 'changed everything', she was referring to the Conservative Party, but it is a description that has been applied to her overall impact, with one generally critical commentator accepting that she was 'a leader with the courage of her convictions, who assailed the conventional wisdom of her day, challenged and overthrew the existing order, [and] changed the political map.'[21] With regard to the political map it cannot be gainsaid that the Thatcher era saw it redrawn. In his memoirs, Norman Tebbit, her one-time close colleague and party chairman, stated that the 1980s had witnessed 'a revolution whose chief casualties have been Socialism and the whole complacent Conservatism of the sixties and early seventies.'[22] Leaving aside the caustic vocabulary of his views on pre-Thatcherite Conservatives, his description was accurate, for the Thatcher era indeed saw Socialism banished and Conservatism redefined.

These changes in the ideological landmarks were accompanied by shifts in the institutional terrain of politics. Trade unions were reduced, especially after the miners' strike of 1984–85, to minor players on the political stage; local government was reshaped by the abolition of the metropolitan authorities and the imposition of central government controls over local taxation; 'tax phobia' in terms of personal direct taxation was embedded in British fiscal policy; the State was withdrawn from direct involvement in the real economy; Europe became a touchstone rather than a political side issue. These were all fundamental changes, and they can be attributed to Thatcher and Thatcherism.

Stuart Hall, as noted above, has seen New Labour as a political hybrid, but the same thing can be and has been said of Thatcherism. Hall himself, for example, described Thatcherism as 'authoritarian populism', in that it sought to strengthen the appeal of 'law and order' by mobilizing popular opinion against 'disruptive' groups, notably rioting ethnic minorities and militant trade unionists. Likewise, Gamble depicted Thatcherism as blending the 'free economy' with the 'strong state', the apparently paradoxical blend being necessary in so far as ensuring that the rules and often harsh outcomes of a free economy were enforced demanded firm governance. But these were by no means the only 'hybrid' aspects of Thatcherism.

With regard to local government, the Thatcher administrations frequently deployed the language of increasing the accountability of local authorities – ostensibly a central rationale for the introduction of the poll tax. But a feature of the 1980s was increased central government control over local authorities, most notably over spending and revenue raising, with rate-capping the most obvious example. In spite of the oft-stated Thatcherite goal of 'rolling back' the State, it was, in the sphere of local government, rolled forward. In some respects, the Thatcher administrations continued a trend in relations between central and local government that had begun in 1888, when central 'grants-in-aid' to local government were first introduced. Central government funding of local government had risen steadily thereafter, and the Thatcher era merely saw the trend accelerate. But for Thatcher, increased central subsidies of local government demanded greater control over the scale and the nature of local expenditure, for without such control, central government would simply be writing a blank cheque for Socialist councils. There was, however, another 'non-political' dimension to the issue of local expenditure, which, in turn, illustrates another dimension of Thatcherism. The Treasury regarded local government expenditure as a major problem, for it was an area of public expenditure which was not under their direct control, but for which, as a consequence of increased central government funding of local authorities, they bore the ultimate responsibility. Thatcher's governments, from her first administration on, signalled and acted upon their intention to bring local government spending under control. On this question, Thatcher and her colleagues were in administrative, if not always ideological, harmony with the Treasury, an institution where economic conservatism, on public expenditure especially, chimed with 'radical' Thatcherite priorities.

If central government control over local finance was one area which saw Thatcher's administration strengthen the State, another, related, area was the growth of quangos. Thatcher took office having denounced the proliferation of quangos under Labour and claiming that her government would reduce their number. In fact, they multiplied, not least in areas of local administration, where they were set up to fill the void left by the abolition of the GLC and the other metropolitan authorities. As a consequence of the train Thatcher laid, the explosion of quangos continued under her successor, and by 1996 £45 billion – approximately one-third of public expenditure – was being disbursed by these bodies. Given Thatcher and the Thatcherites' oft-repeated criticisms of the lack of accountability of left-wing local councils, this allocation of vast public funds to unelected organizations was an act of breathtaking inconsistency, and all the more so as it created a patronage network, in terms of government appointments, of a scale not seen since the ending of 'the old corruption' in the early nineteenth century.

The construction of the quango patronage network was not the only reversal of nineteenth-century administrative reforms undertaken by the Thatcher Governments. On taking office, Thatcher instituted the Efficiency Unit and called on Sir Derek Rayner, a prominent figure from the private sector, to suggest ways of streamlining the civil service. This was to lead to the cutting of over half a million civil service posts, but it was the next stage of reforms, known as 'The Next Steps', which led to the biggest change in the structure of the civil service. These reforms, again recommended by an adviser from the private sector, Sir Robin Ibbs, led to the creation of decentralized, quasi-autonomous 'executive agencies', which were headed by directors appointed on fixed-term contracts, rather than career civil servants. These directors were, as in the private sector, set targets and paid bonuses if they achieved them. Most directors were recruited from the private sector, and by the time Thatcher resigned, 60 agencies had been set up. The reforms continued after Thatcher resigned, and by the time Labour took office in 1997, 75 per cent of civil servants were acting under the supervision of executive agencies. The Thatcherite reforms of the civil service, like the expansion of quangos, moved the civil service towards a political patronage network. In part this resulted from the Thatcherite perception of the civil service as steeped in 'consensualist' assumptions. In December 1975 Keith Joseph noted 'how difficult it is politically to cut public spending substantially – and how great the resistance will be, not only from those affected outside but also from within the Civil Service',[23] and hence, in 1977, Thatcher's advisers and colleagues saw a key question to be, 'How does Mrs Thatcher identify suitable and sympathetic Civil Servants for top appointments?'[24] In office, Thatcher was able to identify some high-ranking officials who served her cause very effectively, such as Sir Robert Armstrong and Sir Robin Butler, but structural reform, both to redefine its operations and to open the 'Whitehall Village' to recruits drawn from the world of private enterprise, ensured that the system was built upon 'measures not men'. One of the least publicized but wide-ranging reforms Thatcher presided over was, through the parallel phenomena of the expansion of quangos and the remoulding of the civil service, the creation of what has been termed a 'new British State'. Yet this 'new' creation was, at the same time, a throwback, with the structure of appointments reminiscent of the situation that had existed before the Northcote-Trevelyan reforms of 1854.

There was also a strong blend of change and continuity in terms of the impact of Thatcherism on the British economy. Thatcher came to power with the stated aim of halting what she saw as Britain's economic decline and, further, of moving Britain out of what had come to known as the cycle of 'stop-go'. Decline, however, was a term that was politically rather than arithmetically defined, and her opponents, Conservative, SDP-Liberal and Labour, claimed as vocally as she had in the 1970s that 'decline' continued under her governments and, in fact, accelerated. In so far as decline was often equated with industrial decline, Britain's 'decline' *did* accelerate under Thatcher. The 1980s saw the structural shift from manufacturing to services, under way for over a century, accelerate dramatically. Sir John Clapham's 'great hinge', with economic activity, wealth and population swinging south, moved with a velocity previously unknown. The result of this was that the regional variations in Britain's wealth and living standards that had existed since the nineteenth century continued. The gap between England and what Thatcher – like nineteenth-century Conservatives – seemed to regard as 'the Celtic Fringe', between north and south, between inner cities and suburbs, broadened and deepened. Socially and economically, and, partly as a consequence, also ethnically, Britain was a more divided nation in 1990 than it was in 1979.

The divisions within British society were all the more apparent as a result of the fact that Thatcherism did not end the 'stop-go' cycle, but, as with many features of pre-Thatcher economic performance, continued and in crucial ways exacerbated it. Britain experienced a major recession between 1979 and 1983, recovery between 1983 and 1988 and then another recession in 1988, which was ongoing when Thatcher resigned. The regional and sectoral impact, as well as the severity, of the recession of the late 1980s was different to that of 1979–83, for it began with the stock-market crash of late 1987, which brought an end to the 'big bang' boom in the City and led to redundancies in the south-eastern service sector – the manufacturing districts that remained were less severely hit. But another additional feature of the late 1980s recession was that it ended the property boom that had begun in the mid-1980s. As property prices fell, the phenomenon of negative equity appeared. Thus, at the same time as Thatcher's then new 'flagship', the poll tax, foundered, her older ship-of-the-line, property-owning democracy, lost some of its lustre.

When Thatcher told Patrick Cosgrave in 1978 that she had 'changed everything', she was speaking about the Conservative Party, but after 1979, and especially after 1990, many commentators saw and described her as having changed many other things. This book accepts that Thatcher's time as Conservative leader and prime minister saw a great deal of change, but it would also conclude that she accelerated rather than inaugurated many of the changes that took place in the last quarter of the twentieth century. Thatcher was a product of, and indeed benefited from, political, economic and social trends that were under way long before she became a leading figure. To say this, is not part of an effort to belittle Thatcher, but rather it is to make the simple point that, like *any* historical figure, Thatcher was a creature of her time and not the creator of it. Thatcher's own positions help to underline this point, for they changed very little over time. At her adoption meeting in 1949 she addressed the state of the economy, and declared, 'The Government should do what any good housewife would do if money was short – look at the accounts and see what was wrong . . . produce things more cheaply and buy food and raw materials more economically.'[25] The analogy between government and household economics was, of course, to be central to Thatcherite economics in the 1970s and 1980s, as was her own identification with the figure of the housewife. Indeed, this presentation, and Thatcher's self-presentation as a prudent 'Domestic Chancellor of the Exchequer', earned her the title of 'the Iron Maiden',[26] which was later to be slightly altered and applied to the sphere of foreign relations by the Red Army newspaper. Thatcher's views on a variety of issues remained remarkably consistent over time – in the process of 'changing everything', Thatcher seems never to have thought it necessary to change herself or her views.

Notes

Introduction

1 Lord Salisbury's tenure was three years longer than Thatcher's, but he faced two interruptions.
2 I have used the gender specific usage in part because, as will become evident, it is a vocabulary the subject of the book would have chosen.
3 Urban, *Diplomacy and Disillusion*, p. 1.
4 P. Jenkins, *Guardian*, 4 May 1989.
5 *Sun*, 25 November 1972, in Lewis, *Margaret Thatcher*, p. 67.
6 Heseltine, *Life in the Jungle*, p. 160.
7 Castle, *Castle Diaries*, 22 January 1975, p. 291.
8 R.A. Butler, comment to C. Patten in Campbell, *Grocer's Daughter*, p. 299.
9 Castle, *Castle Diaries*, 11 February 1975, p. 303.
10 Benn, *Against the Tide*, 4 February 1975, p. 311.
11 Callaghan remark to B. Donoghue, 6 April 1979 in K.O. Morgan, *Callaghan: A Life* (Oxford, 1997) p. 697.
12 Clark, *Diaries*, 27 November 1979, p. 139.
13 Clark, ibid., 14 January 1981, p. 195. Brown had become an admirer of Thatcher, so this was not Labourite wishful thinking.
14 Hoskyns, diary entry, 23 July 1981, *Just In Time*, p. 321.
15 Junor, *Margaret Thatcher*, p. 198.
16 Clark, *Diaries*, 28 June 1988, pp. 218–19. The acquaintance was Sir Frank Cooper.
17 *Conservative Party Manifesto* (1979).
18 Ibid., p. 7.
19 Lawson, *View From No. 11*, p. 665.
20 Howe, *Conflict of Loyalty*, p. 201.
21 Ibid., p. 609.
22 Lawson, *View From No. 11*, p. 133.
23 E. Pearce, quoted in I. Gilmour, 'The Thatcher Memoirs', *TCBH,* v (1994), p. 263.
24 E.J. Tranter to J.P.L. Thomas, 14 January 1949, Conservative Party Archive, Bodleian Library, Oxford (hereafter CPA), CCO 1/7/397.
25 Ibid.
26 Miss Cook to J.P.L. Thomas, 1 February 1949, ibid.
27 S. Brace to CCO, 24 December 1949, Thatcher Papers, Churchill College, Cambridge (hereafter TP), THCR 1/1/1/.
28 E.J. Tranter to Mr Watson, 12 August 1949, CPA, CCO 1/7/397.
29 Miss Cook to Mr Watson, 14 February 1950, ibid.
30 Ibid.
31 Miss Cook to Mr Watson, 10 July 1951, ibid., CCO 1/8/397.

32 M. Roberts to Dartford Conservative Association, 30 October 1951, TP, THCR 1/2/1/40.

33 Note by Miss Cook to CCO, 19 November 1951, ibid., THCR 1/1/1.

34 M. Thatcher to D. Kaberry, 16 March 1956, ibid., THCR 13/1/1/1.

35 Unnamed sponsor's remark, n.d. attached to ibid.

36 In 1949 the Conservatives' chief organizational officer, Marjorie Maxse, had suggested that CCO, and in particular Lord Woolton, should assist their then young, single candidate to obtain a new post as an industrial chemist. M. Maxse to J.P.L. Thomas, 19 February 1949, ibid., THCR 1/1/1 and M. Maxse to Woolton, 17 March 1949, ibid., THCR 1/1/1.

37 J. Harris to D. Kaberry, 2 July 1958, CPA, CCO 1/12/375.

38 Thatcher's winning margin in the first round was 35 votes to 34, and in the second and final round 46 to 43. The voting figures were recorded in J. Harris to D. Kaberry 15 July 1958, ibid.

39 M. Thatcher to Miss Burgess, 18 September 1958, CCO 1/12/375.

40 Ibid.

41 Poole obliged. See O. Poole to Finchley Conservative Association, 22 September 1958, ibid.

42 Finchley was lost to the Liberal Democrats in 1997.

43 Miss J. Harris (CO Agent Home Counties North) to CCO, 20 March 1962, CPA, CCO 1/14/35.

44 J. Biffen in Dale (ed.), *Memories of Maggie*, p. 1.

45 Benn, *End of An Era*, 6 December 1990, p. 627.

46 M. Maxse to J.P.L. Thomas, 1 February 1949, TP, THCR 1/1/1.

47 Sir Waldron Smithers to J.P.L. Thomas, 5 February 1949, CPA, CCO 1/7/397.

48 J.P.L. Thomas to Sir Waldron Smithers, 9 February 1949, ibid.

49 Miss Cook to Mr Watson, 14 February 1950, CPA, CCO 1/7/397.

50 J.H. to the General Director, 19 June 1952, TP, THCR 1/1/1.

51 Miss Cook to J. Hare, 12 June 1952, ibid.

52 J.H. to the General Director, 19 June 1952, ibid.

53 Ibid.

54 M. Thatcher to J. Hare, 13 January 1954, ibid.

55 See J. Hare to M. Thatcher, 15 December 1954, ibid. This confirms the view, noted in the letter by J.H., cited above, that Thatcher wanted a seat in London or within a 30-mile radius of London, preferably in Kent. Thatcher's preference for Kent is noted in Campbell, *Grocer's Daughter*, pp. 96–7.

56 M. Thatcher to D. Kaberry, 16 March 1956, ibid.

57 W.H., Note of interview with Margaret Thatcher, sent to the General Director, 14 March 1956, ibid.

58 Thatcher, *Path to Power*, p. 94.

59 Unsigned note about a discussion with Mrs Thatcher, 23 April 1958, TP, THCR 1/1/1.

60 Extract from a memorandum from Mr Entwistle to Mr Kaberry, 18 March 1958, ibid.

61 Ibid.

62 M. Thatcher to D. Kaberry, 18 August 1958, ibid. Her ongoing concern may in part have stemmed from the fact that the selection vote in her favour was only 46 to 43 and that 'there were a handful of people who refused to give a unanimous vote at the end.' Miss Harris to D. Kaberry, 15 July 1958, ibid.

63 M. Thatcher, 'Wake Up Women', *Sunday Graphic*, 17 February 1952, ibid., THCR 1/17/1.

64 Thatcher, untitled article in *Onward*, April 1954, Collins, *Thatcher CD-ROM*.

65 M. Roberts to Bexley Conservative Women, Welling, 15 September 1949, ibid.

66 Thatcher in the *Evening Post*, 27 January 1950, ibid.

67 Thatcher, interview on Women in the House, *Daily Mail*, 23 October 1959, ibid.

68 MT to Finchley Women's Citizens' Association, 11 February 1961, ibid.

69 Thatcher, interview with the *Daily Express* on 'Women Candidates', 1 February 1965, ibid.

70 Thatcher, interview with the *Daily Telegraph*, 15 March 1966, ibid.

71 See Money, *Margaret Thatcher*, p. 60.

72 See ibid., p. 86, for a description of Thatcher as 'very good looking'.

73 Thatcher, interview with *The Times*, 22 April 1975, Collins, *Thatcher CD-ROM*.

74 Ibid.

75 Cosgrave, *Margaret Thatcher*, p. 14.

76 See Maddox, *Maggie*, pp. 169–72.

77 M. Thatcher to D. Kaberry, 18 August 1958, TP, THCR 1/1/1.

78 D. Hurd in Maddox, *Maggie*, p. 172.

79 Money, *Margaret Thatcher*, p. 81.

80 Thatcher to the Conservative Party Conference, Brighton, 10 October 1969, Collins, *Thatcher CD-ROM*.

81 Cosgrave, *Margaret Thatcher*, p. 14.

82 Thatcher, interview with the *Daily Express*, 17 April 1961, ibid.

83 Cosgrave, *Margaret Thatcher*, p. 14.

84 Thatcher, *Path to Power*, pp. 94–5.

85 L.W. Cradwick to M. Thatcher, n.d. January? 1975, TP, THCR 1/1/6/ (158–9) (original emphasis).

86 R. Thompson to M. Thatcher, n.d. February 1975, ibid., THCR 1/1/12 (3–4). Thompson addressed Thatcher as 'Peggy', the only person the author has found who used this abbreviation of Margaret.

87 W. Whitelaw quoted in Murray, *Margaret Thatcher*, p. 116.

88 Thatcher, interview with ITN, 4 February 1975, Collins, *Thatcher CD-ROM*.

89 Thatcher at Golders Green Brains Trust, 13 February 1964, ibid.

90 Thatcher, interview in the *Sun,* 10 April 1970, ibid.

91 Thatcher, interview with Brian Walden, 28 January 1981, ibid.

92 Thatcher to Finchley Conservative Women's Association, 23 March 1961.

93 Thatcher in Parliament, 20 May 1966, Collins, *Thatcher CD-ROM*.

94 Thatcher to Finchley Conservative Association, 4 March 1965, ibid.

95 Thatcher, interview with the *Evening Standard*, 18 October 1974, Collins, *Thatcher CD-ROM*.

96 Ibid.

97 M. Thatcher, 'My Kind of Tory Party', *Daily Telegraph*, 30 January 1975, ibid.

98 *Daily Express*, 3 February 1975, TP, THCR 1/1/6 (10).

99 Report of Thatcher's Press Conference after the lst Leadership Ballot, 4 February 1975, Collins, *Thatcher CD-ROM*.

100 Thatcher, article for the *Sunday Express*, 9 February 1975, ibid.

101 Thatcher, 'How Tories Will Face the Union', *Sunday Telegraph*, 15 May 1977.

102 Thatcher, interview with the *Sunday Times* magazine, 12 July 1978, ibid.

103 Lawson, *View From No. 11*, p. 255.

104 Thatcher, Keith Joseph Memorial Lecture, London, 11 January 1996, Collins, *Thatcher CD-ROM*.

105 Walker, *Staying Power*, p. 141.

106 Howe, *Conflict of Loyalty*, p. 280.

107 Minutes of the Policy Sub-Committee, 23 March 1976, TP, THCR 2/6/1/51(112).

108 Thatcher, *Downing Street Years*, p. 129.

109 Thatcher, Seoul, 3 September 1992.

110 Cosgrave, *Margaret Thatcher*, p. 87.

111 Joseph, *New Statesman*, 18 April 1975.

112 See Anderson and Nairn, *New Left Review*; Wiener, *English Culture*.

113 Benn, *Against the Tide*, 19 September 1975, p. 440.

114 Minutes of the Economic Reconstruction Group, 16 June 1977, TP, THCR 2/6/1/37.

115 Report of the Smaller Businesses Policy Committee, 22 July 1977, TP, THCR 2/6/1/160.

116 Lewis, *Margaret Thatcher*, pp. 152–3.

117 The term 'Churchillism' was used by Anthony Barnett in his 1984 publication *Iron Britannia*, but, intriguingly, he used it to describe Thatcher's nationalist stance during and after the Falklands conflict. See Barnett, *Iron Britannia*.

118 Sir Robin Day, interview with Thatcher, BBC, 8 June 1987, Collins, *Thatcher CD-ROM*.

119 Skidelsky, 'Introduction' to idem (ed.), *Thatcherism*, p. 2.

120 See Clarke, *Question of Leadership*, pp. 28–32, 318.

121 Money, *Margaret Thatcher*, p. 126.

122 Cosgrave, *Margaret Thatcher*, p. 20.

123 H. Wilson, quoted in Murray, *Margaret Thatcher*, p. 101.

124 Benn, *Against the Tide*, 19 September 1975, p. 440.

125 Campbell, *Grocer's Daughter*, p. 286.

126 Harrison, *TCBH*, v (1994), p. 211.

127 Thatcher, interview in *The Age*, 4 August 1988, Thatcher at Finchley, 19 October 1990, Collins, *Thatcher CD-ROM*.

128 For the influence of think tanks see Cockett, *Thinking the Unthinkable*.

129 Ranelagh, *Thatcher's People*, passim.

130 Urban, *Diplomacy and Disillusion*, p. 43.

131 Thatcher at the FCS Conference, Sheffield University, 24 March 1975, Collins, *Thatcher CD-ROM*.

132 Ibid.

133 Ibid. (my emphasis).

134 M. Thatcher to K. Joseph, 16 July 1975, CPA, CCO 20/8/19.

135 M. Thatcher to Baroness Young, 18 July 1975, ibid.

136 E. Koops, The Conservative Party and Academics, 1 July 1975, ibid.

137 Thatcher at the FCS Conference.

138 Ridley, *My Style of Government*, pp. 5–6.

139 J. Major, interview with the BBC, 17 June 2001.

Chapter 1

1 Day, interview with Thatcher, BBC, 8 June 1987, *Thatcher CD-ROM*.

2 N. Lawson, in P. Clarke, 'The Rise and Fall of Thatcherism', *LLB*, xx, No. 28, Dec. 1998.

3 See Hall and Jacques (eds), *Politics of Thatcherism*.

4 Thatcher to the Conservative Central Council, 15 March 1975, *Thatcher CD-ROM*.

5 Thatcher, interview with *Der Spiegel*, 22 April 1985, ibid.

6 Thatcher, interview with Sir Robin Day, BBC 1, 8 June 1987, ibid.

7 Thatcher, interview with *Der Spiegel*, 8 September 1987, ibid.

8 For these priorities see Thatcher, interview on Japanese television, 25 April 1988, ibid.

9 Thatcher, interview for Finnish TV, 28 August 1990, ibid.

10 See Gamble, *Free Economy*.

11 M. Roberts, Election Address, 3 February 1950, *Thatcher CD-ROM*.

12 Dartford Conservative Association AGM, 31 March 1949, ibid.

13 M. Roberts in Dartford, 13 August 1949, ibid.

14 Thatcher, Lecture on 'Economics and Progress', Stockholm, 28 August 1969, ibid.

15 Timmins, *Five Giants*, p. 361.

16 Ingham, *Kill the Messenger*, p. 225.

17 Thatcher, interview with ITN, 31 January 1975, *Thatcher CD-ROM*.

18 K. Joseph, Paper for the Policy Group Exercise, 10 July 1975, CPA, ACP 3/21 (73) 81.

19 Thatcher, Keith Joseph Memorial Lecture, 11 January 1996, *Thatcher CD-ROM*.

20 K. Joseph, 'Notes Towards the Definition of Policy', 4 April 1975, TP, THCR 2/6/1/156.

21 Thatcher, interview with *Svenske Dagblat*, 16 May 1988, *Thatcher CD-ROM*.

22 Thatcher, 'My Kind of Tory Party', *Daily Telegraph*, 30 January 1975, ibid.

23 Thatcher, CPC Lecture, 'What's Wrong With Politics', 11 October 1968, ibid.

24 Thatcher, 'Consensus or Choice', *Daily Telegraph*, 19 February 1969, ibid.

25 Thatcher, *Time and Tide*, 23 October 1969, ibid.

26 Thatcher, Menzies Lecture, Monash University, September 1981, ibid.

27 In this context, 1975 not only saw Thatcher become Conservative leader, but also witnessed the publication of Paul Addison's *The Road to 1945* – the germinal historical work on the origins of 'consensus'.

28 Her well-known statement, 'The Old Testament prophets did not say "Brothers, I want a consensus." They said "This is my faith and vision … If you believe it too, then come with me",' was a restatement of her 1968–69 position.

29 MT Edinburgh, 2 September 1987, *Thatcher CD-ROM*.

30 Ibid.

31 Thatcher, Keith Joseph Memorial Lecture, London, 11 January 1996, ibid.

32 See Cockett, *Thinking the Unthinkable* and Gamble, *Hayek*, pp. 100–25, 166–8.

33 For *The Constitution of Liberty* story see Ranelagh, *Thatcher's People*, ix.

34 Thatcher, interview with BBC Radio 3, 17 December 1985, *Thatcher CD-ROM*.

35 The Joseph Memorial Lecture and Lecture to the Bow Group on 'The Ideals of an Open Society', 6 May 1978, ibid., are particularly good examples.

36 Hayek, *Road to Serfdom*, passim, esp. pp. 54–75.

37 Hayek, *Constitution of Liberty*, p. 397; idem, 'Hayek on Hayek' in Gamble, *Hayek*, p. 100.

38 Thatcher, interview with ITN, 31 January 1975, *Thatcher CD-ROM*.

39 Thatcher, interview with BBC 1, 28 September 1977, ibid.

40 J. Nott, *Guardian*, 13 September 1982.

41 Thatcher, interview with BBC Radio 3, 17 December 1985, *Thatcher CD-ROM*.

42 Thatcher, Keith Joseph Memorial Lecture, London, 11 January 1996, ibid.

43 Thatcher, interview with BBC Radio 3, 17 February 1985, ibid.

44 Neoliberal economic ideas, notably monetarist and public choice economics, were also influential. They are discussed in chapter 2.

45 Thatcher, Seoul, 3 September 1992.

46 Tebbit, *Upwardly Mobile*, p. 94.

47 See Junor, *Margaret Thatcher*, p. 106.

48 Horne, *Harold Macmillan*, ii, pp. 616–20.

49 See in particular Garnett and Gilmour, 'Thatcherism and the Conservative Tradition' in Francis and Zweiniger-Bargielowska (eds), *Conservatives and British Society*, and Gilmour, *Dancing With Dogma* (1993).

50 See Pym, *Politics of Consent*, esp. pp. 111–30.

51 Walker, *Staying Power*, p. 236.

52 Thatcher at the Conservative Party Conference, Brighton, 14 October 1983, ibid.

53 Alfred Roberts at Dartford, 28 February 1949, ibid.

54 Howe, *Conflict of Loyalty*, p. 18.

55 Birch, *Conservative Party*, p. 34.

56 Hailsham, *Conservative Case*, p. 133.

57 Lord Home, interview with P. Murray in Murray, *Margaret Thatcher*, p. 138.

58 Whitelaw, *Whitelaw Memoirs*, p. 183.

59 Ibid., pp. 183–4.

60 For the minutes of the Selsdon Park Conference see CPA, CRD 3/9/92, 93.

61 E. Heath at Conservative Party Conference, 10 October 1970, in Campbell, *Edward Heath*, pp. 310–11.

62 The acronym for the latter, S.E.T., had been reproduced on a Conservative badge which stated, 'Abolish Socialist Economic Tyranny'.

63 See Seldon and Ball, Introduction, in idem (eds), *Heath Government*, and Campbell, *Edward Heath*, pp. 451–6, 468–83.

64 Young, *Enterprise Years*, p. 16.

65 Tebbit, *Upwardly Mobile*, p. 94.

66 Ibid., and see also Ridley, *My Style of Government*, pp. 2, 4.

67 Tebbit, *Upwardly Mobile*, p. 94.

68 See Joseph, *Reversing the Trend*.

69 K. Joseph at Upminster, 22 June 1974, in ibid., pp. 5–6.

70 K. Joseph at Preston, 5 September 1974, in ibid., p. 32. For a further statement of Joseph's views here see his *Stranded on the Middle Ground*.

71 Ridley, *My Style of Government*, p. 2.

72 Parkinson, *Right at the Centre*, p. 191.

73 The Chairman of the MCA was H.A. Price, a Conservative MP.

74 Cited in Ramsden, *Winds of Change*, pp. 219, 255.

75 See chapter 3.

76 Lawson, *View from No. 11*, p. 14.

77 Macmillan's comments are recorded in Walker, *Staying Power*, p. 138.

78 According to her assistant all but 12 came from Conservatives, and 6 of them were from ex-Conservatives who had been 're-converted' by her.

79 ? to M. Thatcher, n.d. January 1975, TP, THCR 1/1/6.

80 Lord Boyle to M. Thatcher, 16 February 1975, ibid., THCR 1/3/1.

81 Thatcher at Finchley, 31 January 1975, *Thatcher CD-ROM*.

82 Thatcher at Harrogate, 15 March 1975, ibid.

83 R. Thompson to M. Thatcher, n.d. February 1975, ibid., THCR 1/1/12.

84 I. Macleod to R.A. Butler, 6 August 1950, Butler Papers, Trinity College, Cambridge, H54, fos. 30–3.

85 These were, as noted above, sentiments which the young Margaret Roberts had espoused during her Parliamentary campaign in 1949–50.

86 Thatcher interview with Sir Robin Day, BBC 1, 8 June 1987, *Thatcher CD-ROM*.

87 The first use of the term seems to have been in Skelton's *Constructive Conservatism*, but it was first fully discussed at length on a course at the Conservative college at Ashridge in 1932, following a lecture on the topic by the Conservative MP, and later member of the Next Five Years Group, T.J. O'Connor. For this development see Berthezène, 'Les Conservateurs Britanniques'.

88 For the 'ramparts of property' theme see Offer, *Property and Politics*; Green, *Crisis of Conservatism*, pp. 121–2, 209–10, 215–19, 258–60.

89 Thatcher, interview on Japanese television, ibid. See also chapter 3.

90 See Ramsden, *TRHS*, xxxvii (1987).

91 See Smith, *Disraelian Conservatism*.

92 See Ranelagh, *Thatcher's People*, pp. 166–80 and Heffer, *Like the Roman*, pp. 680–792.

93 Geoffrey Howe has stated that *Change Is Our Ally* led him to see the importance of the concept of a 'social market economy': Howe, *Conflict of Loyalty*, p. 286.

94 For a full discussion of the links between One Nation and Thatcherism see Green, 'One Nation and the Ideological Origin of Thatcherism' (forthcoming).

95 Thatcher, interview for *Woman's Own*, 23 September 1987, *Thatcher CD-ROM*.

96 Ibid.

97 Thatcher, Lecture to the Bow Group on 'The Ideals of an Open Society', 6 May 1978, ibid.

98 Urban, *Diplomacy and Disillusion*, pp. 170–1.

99 Clarke, *Conservative Faith*, p. 17.

100 See Hogg, *Case For Conservatism*, p. 84.

101 R.A. Butler, 'Conservatism and Human Aspirations', *Information Please Almanac* (1949), in Conservative Political Centre, *New Conservatism*, p. 24.

102 White, *Conservative Tradition*.

103 J.E. Powell, 'Conservatives and Social Services', *Political Quarterly*, xxiv (1954), p. 166.

104 A. Maude, 'Modern Conservative Philosophy – 3', 3 October 1966, CPA, ACP 3/14.

105 On a less philosophical note, Maude had, in an article in the *Spectator* in January 1966, called on the Conservatives to 'stop pussy-footing' on trade union reform. Quoted in Denham and Garnett, *Keith Joseph*, p. 153.

106 Young Conservatives' Policy Group, 'Society and the Individual', June 1962, CPA, CRD 2/50/9.

107 Press release of the Conservative Political Centre, 24 March 1959, CPA, CCO 150/4/2/5.

108 One Nation, *Change*, p. 96.

109 See Green, 'Conservatism, the State and Civil Society in the Twentieth Century', in idem, *Ideologies*.

110 J.W. Hills et al., *Industrial Unrest* (1914), p. 3.

111 Hinchingbrooke, *Full Speed Ahead*, p. 21.

112 Beaverbrook to E.J. Flynn, 11 October 1945, in Taylor, *Beaverbrook*, pp. 728–9.

113 Freeden, *Ideologies*, pp. 385–93.

114 Thatcher, Nicholas Ridley Memorial Lecture, London, 22 November 1996, *Thatcher CD-ROM*. She went on to praise J.S. Mill as offering the best defence of this philosophy.

115 Thatcher, interview with James Naughtie, BBC Radio 4, 16 May 1990; interview with Jimmy Young, BBC Radio 2, 22 July 1988; Speech to CPS, 28 April 1988, *Thatcher CD-ROM*.

116 Quinton, *Politics of Imperfection*.

117 Ibid., pp. 12–13.

118 Ibid., p. 17.

119 Ibid., p. 16.

120 Ibid.

121 D. Clarke, *The Conservative Faith in a Modern Age* (1947), p. 13.

122 M. Fraser, 'The Ownership of Property', a lecture given in Oxford, 8 July 1952, enclosed with idem to R.A. Butler, 18 July 1952, Butler papers, H34 fos. 173–90.

123 Young Conservatives, *Society and the Individual*, p. 1.

124 J.E. Powell at Bromley, 24 October 1963 in Wood, *A Nation Not Afraid*, pp. 4–5.

125 M. Oakeshott, 'On Being Conservative' in idem, *Rationalism in Politics and Other Essays*, p. 407.

126 A notable example is the proposal for the privatization of health care put forward by the Adam Smith Institute.

127 Cecil, *Conservatism*, p. 195.

128 For a discussion of Cecil's position see Meadowcroft, *Conceptualizing the State*, pp. 90–106.

129 Cecil, *Conservatism*, pp. 176–80.

130 See, for example, the critique of the Conservative historical economists, which is discussed in Green, *Crisis of Conservatism*, pp.159–83. For a late twentieth century critique see Ormerod, *Death of Economics*, passim.

131 Myrdal, *Political Element*, p. 192.

132 Oakeshott, 'On Being Conservative', p. 415.

133 Willetts and Gray, *Is Conservatism Dead?*, pp. 3–65.

134 For a study of this phenomenon in the US context see Putnam, *Bowling Alone*. For Britain see Hall, *British Journal of Political Science*, 29 (1999).

135 One association which showed a marked decline in participation was, of course, the Conservative Party, the membership of which decreased significantly over the 1980s and 1990s. See Whiteley, Seyd and Richardson, *True Blues*, esp. pp. 219–38.

136 See Wickam-Jones, *TCBH*, viii (1997); Green, *TRHS*, xlviii (1998).

137 Willetts and Redwood entered politics through their work as members of Thatcher's policy unit.

138 The emphasis here is on the broad, generational and prosopographical nature of the 'class of 1959' rather than the impact of particular individuals.

139 Heath et al., *Understanding Political Change*, pp. 102–19, 136–55.

140 C. Hill to R.A. Butler, 11 February 1958, CPA, CRD 2/53/29.

141 Kilmuir to R.A. Butler, CPA, CRD 2/53/29.

142 D. Watt, *Financial Times*, 31 January 1975, in Cosgrave, *Margaret Thatcher*, p. 65.

Chapter 2

1 N. Lawson to M. Thatcher, 12 February 1979, TP, THCR 2/1/3/12A.

2 H. Wilson in Parliament, 19 November 1975, *Thatcher CD-ROM*.

3 Thatcher, 'Britain Awake', Kensington Town Hall, 19 January 1976, ibid.

4 Thatcher in Parliament, 11 October 1976, ibid.

5 Thatcher, 'Who are the dogmatists?', *Time and Tide*, 29 September 1978, ibid.

6 Thatcher, general election press conference, 2 May 1979, ibid.

7 Thatcher to Ulster Unionist Council, 19 June 1978, ibid.

8 Thatcher, general election press conference, 2 May 1979, ibid.

9 See chapter 3.

10 H. Macmillan at Bedford, 20 July 1957, in idem, *Riding the Storm*, p. 351.

11 For an example of Thatcherite scepticism of Phillips' ideas see Hoskyns, *Just in Time*, pp. 10–11.

12 J. Callaghan at the Labour Party Conference, Blackpool, 28 September 1976.

13 Thatcher herself was particularly insistent on this matter. See Minutes of the Shadow Cabinet, 15 July 1975, TP, THCR 2/6/1/92.

14 J. Biffen, D. Hurd, Finance Committee, 2 July 1976, ibid.

15 G. Howe to All Members of the Shadow Cabinet, 15 July 1975, ibid., THCR 2/6/1/156.

16 Discussion of 'Economic Prospects and the Party's Position', Minutes of the Shadow Cabinet, 16 February 1976, ibid., THCR (my emphasis).

17 Minutes of the Shadow Cabinet, 21 May 1975, ibid., THCR, 2/6/1/92.

18 ERG, Note by the Chairman, 24 July 1975, ibid., THCR 2/6/1/37.

19 ERG, 4 December 1975, 15 January 1976, ibid., THCR 2/6/1/37.

20 G. Howe, 'Liberating Free Enterprise', ibid.

21 N. Lawson to M. Thatcher, 12 February 1979, ibid., THCR 2/1/3/12A.

22 ERG, Note by the Chairman, 24 July 1975, ibid., THCR 2/6/1/37. Howe also noted that the ERG's initial work had 'devoted most … attention to inflation'.

23 G. Cardona, 'Inflation, Pay Determination and the Labour Market', 16 March 1978, ibid., THCR 2/6/1/96.

24 Ibid.

25 Powell, 'The Conservative Party', in Kavanagh and Seldon, p. 81.

26 Thatcher in Parliament, 1 November 1978, *Thatcher CD-ROM*.

27 H. Wilson in Parliament, 22 May 1975, ibid.

28 ERG, Note by the Chairman, 24 July 1975, TP, THCR 2/6/1/37 (original emphasis).

29 Ibid.

30 G. Howe, 'The Economic Prospects and the Party's Official Position', circulated with A. Ridley to Shadow Cabinet (with a handwritten note to M. Thatcher), 16 December 1975, ibid., THCR 2/6/1/158.

31 K. Joseph to M. Thatcher, 22 July 1976, ibid., THCR 2/1/1/37.

32 ERG, 4 December 1975, 15 January 1976, ibid., THCR 2/6/1/37.

33 G. Howe to M. Thatcher, 2 July 1976, ibid., THCR 2/1/1/30.

34 In December 1978 Adam Ridley of CRD arranged meetings with Minford and other monetarist economists. See G. Howe to M. Thatcher, 22 December 1978, ibid., THCR, 2/1/3/9.

35 Walters became Thatcher's personal economic adviser.

36 For an early critique of the DAE see A. Ridley to MT, 27 November 1975, ibid., THCR 2/6/1/94.

37 G. Howe to M. Thatcher, 29 May 1975, THCR 2/6/1/92.

38 G. Howe to All Members of the Shadow Cabinet, 15 July 1975, THCR 2/6/1/156.

39 Public Sector Policy Group, 23 July 1975, THCR 2/6/1/233.

40 N. Lawson to M. Thatcher, 12 February 1979, THCR 2/13/12A.

41 Lawson, *New Conservatism*, p. 4.

42 Ibid.

43 Alt, 'New Wine in Old Bottles', p. 224.

44 N. Lawson in Parliament, 13 March 1984.

45 N. Lawson in Parliament, 19 March 1985.

46 ERG, Note by the Chairman, 24 July 1975, ibid., THCR 2/6/1/37.

47 J. Prior, 'Counter Inflation Policy', 13 May 1975, TP, THCR 2/6/1/156.

48 Ibid. The Thatcherite ERG was politically cautious, and at a meeting in the summer of 1976 'It was agreed that wage-restraint was a crucial part of economic policy … This was not an area in which we should be seeking sharply to differentiate ourselves from the Government, except over the price of wage restraint.' ERG, 24 June 1976, ibid., THCR 2/6/1/37.

49 See chapter 4.

50 Cardona, 'Inflation'.

51 K. Joseph, 'Incomes Policy', 5 May 1976, TP, THCR 2/1/1/37.

52 Ibid.

53 See chapter 4.

54 K. Joseph to M. Thatcher, 22 July 1976, TP, THCR 2/1/1/37.

55 M. Thatcher, 'The Opposition View', *CBI Review*, THCR 2/6/1/19.

56 Thatcher to the Engineering Employers' Federation, 21 February 1978, *Thatcher CD-ROM*.

57 R. Harris to MT, 11 February 1976, TP, THCR 2/6/1/94.

58 K. Joseph, open letter to J. Callaghan, enclosed with R. Ryder to M. Thatcher, 1 October 1976, ibid., THCR 2/1/1/38.

59 Cardona, 'Inflation'.

60 Ibid. THCR 2/6/1/94 J. Douglas to MT and top leadership, 12 August 1975.

61 Minutes of a Meeting between M. Thatcher, K. Joseph, G. Howe, J. Prior and the CBI, 21 January 1976, ibid., THCR 2/6/1/19.

62 Joseph, 'Incomes Policy'.

63 Shadow Cabinet, 16 February 1976.

64 Ibid.

65 Joseph, 'Incomes Policy'.

66 K. Joseph to M. Thatcher, 22 July 1976, TP, THCR 2/1/1/37.

67 Joseph, 'Incomes Policy'.

68 Ibid.

69 A. Barber at the 4th Meeting of the Conservative Party Steering Committee, 8 April 1974, CPA, LCC 1/3/1.

70 K. Joseph, 'Inflation', 1 May 1974, ibid.

71 A. Ridley, 'Countering Inflation', 15 December 1976, ibid., THCR 2/6/1/37.

72 See Green, *TCBH*, xx (2001).

73 K. Joseph at Preston, 5 September 1974, in idem, *Reversing the Trend*, p. 19.

74 Cardona, 'Inflation'.

75 Thatcher to Conservative Central Council, 15 March 1975, to Conservative National Union, 11 June 1975, to Tory Reform Group, 19 September 1975, *Thatcher CD-ROM*.

76 Thatcher, interview with ITN, 11 February 1975, ibid.

77 Ibid.

78 K. Joseph, 'Inflation' (my emphasis).

79 Thatcher to FCS, 12 July 1975, *Thatcher CD-ROM*.

80 Lewis, *Margaret Thatcher*, pp. 152–3.

81 Ibid., p. 154.

82 Ibid., p. 152.

83 N. Lawson to M. Thatcher, 19 July 1978, TP, THCR 2/1/2/12A.

84 Thatcher to EEF, London, 21 February 1978, *Thatcher CD-ROM*.

85 Thatcher, MS draft of a speech, 'Time for a Message of Hope', n.d. January? 1975, TP, THCR 1/1/6.

86 Shadow Cabinet discussion of 'Background to the Budget', Minutes of the Shadow Cabinet, 11 April 1975, ibid., THCR 2/6/1/37.

87 Ibid.

88 THCR 2/6/1/37 ERG, 5 July 1975.

89 Minutes of a meeting, 8 July 1975, TP, THCR 2/6/1/92.

90 G. Howe to M. Thatcher, 29 May 1975, ibid.

91 Shadow Cabinet, 16 February 1976.

92 Thatcher on Tyneside, 11 September 1911, *Thatcher CD-ROM*.

93 Clarke and Trebilcock, *Understanding Decline*, p. xiii.

94 See Marrison, *British Business*, passim; Green, *Crisis of Conservatism*, pp. 27–58, 159–266.

95 See Tomlinson, *EcHR*, xc (1996).

96 For a brief summary of the extensive literature see Dintenfass, *The Decline of Industrial Britain*.

97 Unsigned document, n.d. (1978?), TP, THCR 2/6/1/96.

98 M. Thatcher, 'The Opposition View', *CBI Review*, p. 14.

99 Minutes of a meeting between M. Thatcher, K. Joseph, G. Howe, J. Prior and the CBI, 21 January 1976, TP, THCR 2/6/1/19.

100 M. Thatcher to H. Watkinson, 15 June 1976, ibid., THCR 2/6/1/19.

101 H. Watkinson to M. Thatcher, 16 June 1976, ibid., THCR 2/6/1/19.

102 John Methven at a meeting between M. Thatcher, K. Joseph, J. Prior and N. Ridley, 13 June 1977, ibid., THCR 2/6/1/19.

103 For this analysis see, for example, Meiksins Wood, *Pristine Culture*.

104 Small Businesses Policy Document, enclosed with A. Ridley to ERG, 13 June 1977, TP, THCR 2/6/1/37.

105 K. Joseph to N. Wingate, 1 August 1978, ibid., THCR 2/1/1/39.

106 Ibid.

107 K. Joseph to N. Cooper, 15 August 1978, ibid., THCR 2/1/1/39.

108 See Appendix A: Proposals for Press Conference during the General Election, ibid., THCR 2/7/1/14; and *Conservative Party Manifesto* (1979), p. 10.

109 W.J. Ashley to A.J. Balfour, 4 July 1904, Balfour Papers, British Library, Add MSS 49870, fos. 39–45.

110 Green, 'The Conservatives and the City' in Michie and Williamson.

111 Thatcher in the City, 7 February 1978, *Thatcher CD-ROM*.

112 Ibid.

113 Thatcher at the Guildhall, London, 16 November 1981, ibid.

114 Ibid.

115 See in particular Cain and Hopkins, *British Imperialism*.

116 One of them, the Midland, had also been taken over by an overseas bank, HSBC.

117 K. Joseph at Upminster, 22 June 1974, in idem, *Reversing the Trend* (1975), p. 5.

118 M. Thatcher at a Conference of Management in Industry, 9 January 1978, *Thatcher CD-ROM*.

119 Joseph, *Monetarism*, p. 5.

120 Lawson, *New Conservatism*, p. 6.

121 M. Thatcher at Roosevelt University, 22 September 1975, *Thatcher CD-ROM*.

122 M. Thatcher, interview with Independent Radio News, 31 December 1979, ibid.

123 Joseph, *Monetarism*, p. 5.

124 M. Thatcher to the American Chamber of Commerce, 20 October 1976; M. Thatcher, Interview with Radio 4, 15 December 1976, *Thatcher CD-ROM*.

125 Thatcher, interview in the *Sunday Times*, 22 February 1983, ibid.

126 Thatcher, interview in *The Times*, 3 May 1983, ibid.

127 TP, THCR 1/5/1.

128 Thatcher in Parliament, 6 November 1984, ibid.

129 In fact, the term 'full employment' was used only once in the White Paper.

130 See Lawson, *View From No. 11*, pp. 79–81.

131 Ibid.

132 In the interwar years Keynes made constant, critical appraisals of the actions of the financial sector, and during the war he expressed concern that 'the celebrated inefficiency of British manufacturers' could cause problems of international competitiveness after the war.

133 Thatcher to EEF, 21 February 1978, *Thatcher CD-ROM*.

134 N. Lawson, Budget Speech, Parliament, 19 March 1985, ibid.

135 Ibid.

136 Again, this raises the question of whether 1950s demand management was more expressive of Hawtrey's rather than Keynes' ideas, a point raised by Peter Clarke in his conclusion of *The Keynesian Revolution in the Making*.

137 The 'judge and jury' phrase was used by Lawson in his Mansion House speech of 1985, in which he also announced that monetary growth targets were no longer central to government policy.

138 Lawson, *New Conservatism*, p. 6.

139 Lord Boyle to M. Thatcher, 16 February 1975, TP, THCR 1/3/1.

140 Discussion by Shadow Cabinet members of CRD Paper, 'The Political Situation and Future Tactics', 20 May 1975, ibid.

141 See in particular Aglietta, *Theory of Capitalist Regulation*; Lipietz, *Towards a New Economic Order*.

Chapter 3

1 G. Howe, K. Joseph, J. Prior, D. Howell and A. Maude, 'The Right Approach to the Economy: An outline of the economic strategy of the next Conservative Government', 17 August 1977, TP, 2/6/1/161.

2 M. Thatcher to the Ulster Unionist Council 19 June 1979, *Thatcher CD-ROM*.

3 *Conservative Party Manifesto* (1979), p. 15.

4 The term 'privatization' was coined in 1969 by the American management specialist Peter Drucker, but I have found no Conservative politician using it before the 1980s.

5 M. Thatcher, interview with Jimmy Young, 8 October 1974, *Thatcher CD-ROM*.

6 Interview, *Sun*, 18 July 1978.

7 *Conservative Party Manifesto* (1983), p. 5.

8 *Conservative Party Manifesto* (1987), p. 7.

9 *The Industrial Charter*, pp. 24–5.

10 The pre-war Chamberlain Government had placed coal mineral royalties under State supervision, and Macmillan had advocated nationalization of the Bank in his 1938 publication, *The Middle Way*.

11 H. Macmillan in Parliament, 11 November 1946, in idem, *Tides of Fortune*, p. 81.

12 A. Eden at Dartford, 6 August 1949, *Thatcher CD-ROM*.

13 This was the campaign that produced the celebrated 'Mr Cube' character, who remained a feature of sugar advertising thereafter.

14 One Nation, *Change Is Our Ally*, p. 47.

15 Ibid., p. 86.

16 Ibid., p. 87.

17 Ibid., p. 96.

18 M. Roberts, Election Address, 3 February 1950, *Thatcher CD-ROM*.

19 M. Roberts at Erith, 7 April 1949, ibid.

20 For the origins of the PCNI see Chairman's Notes, 21 November 1956, CPA, CRD 2/6/3. The chairman was R.A. Butler.

21 PCNI, Terms of Reference, n.d. January? 1957, CPA, CRD 2/6/2.

22 Note by Mr Maudling, 25 March 1957, CPA, CRD 2/6/3.

23 J. Douglas to L. Urwick, 8 January 1957, CPA, CRD 2/6/2.

24 K. Joseph, Memorandum to PCNI on 'Efficiency Audit', 7 February 1957, CPA, CRD 2/6/2.

25 K. Joseph, Memorandum to PCNI, 25 April 1957, CPA, CRD 2/6/2.

26 Note by R. Maudling, 25 March 1957, CPA, CRD 2/6/3.

27 PCNI, Minutes of 5th Meeting, 13 February 1957, CPA, CRD 2/6/2.

28 The structure of BP was that the State owned 51 per cent of the company and appointed two directors, but all management decisions were based on the management's judgement of the company's commercial goals.

29 H. Watkinson Memorandum to PCNI, 'Making the Air Transport Corporations More Commercial', 13 March 1957, CPA, CRD 2/6/2.

30 J. Douglas to H. Watkinson, 13 March 1957, CPA, CRD 2/6/2.

31 PCNI, Minutes of 11th Meeting, 1 May 1957, CPA, CRD 2/6/3.

32 R.A. Butler to H. Macmillan, 12 September 1957, CPA, CRD 2/6/2.

33 J. Douglas to M. Fraser, 22 February 1957, CPA, CRD 2/6/2.

34 J. Douglas to P. Dean, 27 May 1957, CPA, CRD 2/6/2.

35 Ibid.

36 PCNI, Minutes of 2nd Meeting, 18 November 1956, CPA, CRD 6/2/3.

37 D. Heathcoat-Amory to H. Macmillan, 21 November 1958, PRO, PREM 11/2669.

38 Hailsham to H. Macmillan, 24 November 1958, ibid.

39 Report of the Committee on 'Wider Ownership of Shares in Industry', 13 March 1959.

40 T. Low et al., *Everyman a Capitalist* (1959).

41 Report of the PGNI, May 1968, CPA, CRD 3/17/2.

42 Ibid.

43 Ibid.

44 N. Ridley, 'Denationalisation', 14 May 1969, CPA, ACP 3/19 (69) 62 – (70) 71.

45 Ibid.

46 Ibid.

47 Ibid.

48 Ibid.

49 Ibid.

50 Report of the PGNI, May 1968, CPA, CRD 3/17/2; and this in spite of the fact that at the Conservative Party Conference in 1968, Heath had spoken of the need to 'reintroduce private ownership into the Nationalized Industries', and Joseph had called for the use of risk capital and commercial management discipline in the State sector.

51 John Eden was another 'denationalizer'.

52 M. Fraser to J. Douglas, 18 May 1970, quoted in Taylor, 'The Heath Government' in Seldon and Ball, p. 146.

53 'Report of Policy Group on Nationalized Industries and the Consumer', 8 April 1976, 2/6/1/158.

54 Ibid.

55 Ibid.

56 Ibid.

57 M. Heseltine, 'Nationalised Industries', 13 July 1976, 2/6/1/159.

58 A. Bulloch, 'Small Business Consultative Document', 23 August 1977, 2/6/1/161.

59 Economic Reconstruction Group, Discussion of the Final Report of the Nationalized Industries Policy Group, 8 July 1977, KJP, 10/7.

60 Ibid.

61 Ibid.

62 See Report of Policy Group on Nationalized Industries and the Consumer, 8 April 1976, ibid., 2/1/6/158.

63 N. Ridley, 'Policy for the Nationalised Industries', 28 June 1978, ibid., 2/1/6/163.

64 Minutes of the Economic Reconstruction Group Meeting, 8 July 1977, TP, 2/6/1/37.

65 Interim Report of PGNI, 9 July 1976, ibid., 2/6/1/159.

66 Ibid.

67 M. Heseltine, 'Industrial Policy Recommendations', 3 June 1976, ibid., 2/6/1/158.

68 Ibid.

69 Ibid.

70 M. Heseltine, 'Nationalised Industries', 13 July 1976, ibid., 2/6/1/159. At a Shadow Cabinet meeting at the end of the month it was noted that the Conservative MP Ian Gow was to introduce a private member's bill to denationalize the National Bus Company on 2 August. Shadow Cabinet Minutes, 28 July 1976, no fo.

71 Economic Reconstruction Group, Discussion of the Final Report of the Nationalized Industries Policy Group, 8 July 1977, KJP, 10/7.

72 Ibid.

73 M. Heseltine, 'Nationalised Industries', 13 July 1976, 2/6/1/159.

74 Economic Reconstruction Group, Discussion of the Final Report of the Nationalized Industries Policy Group, 8 July 1977, KJP, 10/7.

75 N. Lamont, British Steel Corporation, 13 January 1978, TP, 2/6/1/162.

76 Interim Report of PGNI, 9 July 1976, ibid.

77 Minutes of Economic Reconstruction Group Meeting, 14 July 1977, ibid., 2/6/1/37.

78 Interim Report of PGNI, 9 July 1976, ibid., 2/6/1/159.

79 Ibid.

80 Minutes of Economic Reconstruction Group Meeting, 14 July 1977, 2/6/1/37.

81 Economic Reconstruction Group, Discussion of the Final Report of the Nationalized Industries Policy Group, 8 July 1977, KJP, 10/7.

82 Interim Report of PGNI, 9 July 1976, 2/6/1/159.

83 Economic Reconstruction Group, 4th Meeting, 18 July 1975, 2/6/1/37. See also J.A.

Redwood, untitled paper on the nationalized industries, n.d. August 1975, TP, THCR 2/6/1/55 (100–7).

84 Ibid.

85 Interim Report of PGNI, 9 July 1976, ibid., 2/6/1/159.

86 M. Heseltine, 'Nationalised Industries', 13 July 1976, ibid.

87 Interim Report of PGNI, 9 July 1976, ibid.

88 N. Ridley, 'Policy for the Nationalised Industries', 28 June 1978, ibid., 2/6/1/163.

89 Ibid.

90 'The Right Approach to the Economy'.

91 Ibid.

92 M. Heseltine, 'Nationalised Industries', 13 July 1976, ibid.

93 Interim Report of PGNI, 9 July 1976, ibid.

94 J. Prior, Employment Policy: Interim Report, 5 July 1976, ibid., 2/6/1/159.

95 Shadow Cabinet Meeting, 28 February 1977, ibid., 2/6/1/233.

96 At the Shadow Cabinet meeting of February 1977 when share-ownership was discussed, it was seen as a complement to a paper by David Howell on 'Property-Owning Democracy', ibid.

97 Shadow Cabinet, 16 January 1978, no. fo.

98 A. Maude, R. Boyson, D. Howell, N. Lawson and N. Tebbit, 'Themes', 13 February 1978 2/6/1/233.

99 M. Thatcher in Parliament, 30 July 1981, *Thatcher CD-ROM*.

100 M. Thatcher in Parliament, 4 February 1982, ibid.

101 The change in terminology is itself interesting. 'Denationalization' was deemed, or so it seems, to carry a negative tone, with perhaps 'anti-national' overtones, whereas 'privatization' implied positive perceptions of the private sector.

102 G. Howe in Parliament, 10 March 1981, *Thatcher CD-ROM*.

103 Georgetown University, 27 February 1981, ibid.

104 Report of Policy Group and the Nationalized Industries and the Consumer, 8 April 1976, TP, 2/6/1/158.

105 Heseltine, 'Nationalised Industries'.

106 Minutes of the Shadow Cabinet Finance Committee, 2 July 1976, TP, 2/6/1/92.

107 N. Lamont, British Steel Corporation, 13 January 1978, ibid., 2/6/1/162.

108 C. Gratton Lavoie, 'Essays on Privatization', unpublished Ph.D. thesis, Virginia Polytechnic and State University (2000), p. 155.

109 Ibid., pp. 136–7.

110 M. Thatcher, interview with Sir Robin Day, BBC 1, 17 February 1986, *Thatcher CD-ROM*.

111 M. Thatcher to Congress, Washington, 20 February 1985, ibid.

112 M. Thatcher at the Conservative Party Conference, 10 October 1986, ibid.

113 M. Thatcher in London, 10 November 1986, ibid.

114 N. Lawson in Parliament, 18 March 1986, ibid.

115 Lawson's tax reforms of the mid-1980s, especially the reduction of stamp duty on the purchase of equities, were designed as a complement to privatization. See N. Lawson, *Tax Reform, The Government's Record* (1988).

116 Conservative Party general election press conference, 4 June 1987, *Thatcher CD-ROM*.

117 M. Thatcher at the Fraser Institute Toronto, 8 November 1994, ibid.

118 M. Thatcher at a Conservative Party rally, Harrogate, 9 June 1987, ibid.

119 Ibid. The same claim about One Nation was made by Nigel Lawson at a general election press conference that year, N. Lawson at CCO, 2 June 1987, ibid.

120 M. Thatcher, interview with BBC Radio 4, 31 May 1987, ibid.

Chapter 4

1 M. Roberts at Belvedere, 9 February 1950, *Thatcher CD-ROM*.
2 M. Roberts at Dartford Conservative Club, 28 August 1950, *Dartford Chronicle*, 1 September 1950, ibid.
3 M. Roberts to Conservative trade unionists, Dartford, 15 November 1950, ibid.
4 M. Roberts at Dartford, 8 October 1951, ibid.
5 Ibid.
6 M. Roberts at Belvedere, 17 October 1951, ibid.
7 Ibid.
8 See Roberts, 'Walter Monckton and the Retreat from Reality' in idem, *Eminent Churchillians*.
9 See, for example, the motions by P. Clarkson (Wakefield) and R. Mawby (Rugby), NUCA Conference, Scarborough, 10 October 1952, Microfiche Cards 8–9.
10 See the Industrial Relations Debate, NUCA Conference, Llandudno, 12 October 1956, Microfiche Cards, 16–17.
11 I. Macleod, 'Trade Union Legislation', 2 July 1958, CPA, CRD 2/53/31.
12 I. Macleod, Paper for the 6th Meeting of the Steering Committee, 23 July 1958, ibid., CRD 2/53/34.
13 I. Macleod, Minutes of the 6th Meeting of the Steering Committee, 23 July 1958, ibid., CRD 2/53/31.
14 Hailsham, ibid.
15 See Green, 'The Conservative Party, the State and the Electorate, 1945–64' in Lawrence and Taylor.
16 For Macleod's caution see Shepherd, *Iain Macleod*, pp. 122–50.
17 I. Macleod, 'Trade Union Legislation', 24 September 1958, CPA, CRD 2/53/31.
18 I. Macleod, 'Trade Union Legislation', 2 July 1958, ibid.
19 I. Macleod, 'Trade Union Legislation', 24 September 1958, ibid.
20 Minutes of the 7th Meeting of the Steering Committee, 5 November 1958, ibid.
21 Shepherd, *Macleod*, p. 149.
22 Conversation with Lord Howe.
23 M. Thatcher, Finchley adoption meeting, 31 July 1958, *Thatcher CD-ROM*.
24 M. Thatcher to Finchley Young Conservatives, 12 November 1958, *Finchley Press*, 21 November 1958, ibid.
25 M. Thatcher to Finchley Chamber of Commerce, 4 May 1964, ibid.
26 Ramsden, *Winds of Change*, p. 218. The Monday Club proposal was exactly what Macleod had rejected in 1958, namely a return to Taff Vale and the pre-1906 situation.
27 A. Maude, *Spectator*, January 1966, in Campbell, *Edward Heath*.
28 M. Thatcher at Finchley Conservative Association, 10 March 1966, *Thatcher CD-ROM*.
29 M. Thatcher in Finchley, 14 March 1966, ibid.
30 M. Thatcher at Friern Barnet Conservative Association, 27 February 1970, ibid.
31 M. Thatcher at Finchley Conservative Association, 23 June 1969, ibid.
32 M. Fraser, Political Assessment, 23 January 1970, CRD 3/9/92.
33 Briefing Paper for the Shadow Cabinet, Priorities for Government Action, 20 January 1970, ibid.
34 Selsdon Park Shadow Cabinet Conference, Minutes of the 7th Session, 1 February 1970, CRD 3/9/93.
35 M. Thatcher at Finchley Conservative Association AGM, 4 March 1971, and to Finchley Conservative Women's Association, 25 March 1971, ibid.
36 This figure is taken from R. Richardson, 'Trade Unions and Industrial Relations' in Crafts and Woodward (eds), *British Economy*.
37 Ramsden, *Winds of Change*, p. 333.

38 Taylor, 'The Heath Government and Industrial Relations', in Seldon and Ball, p. 166.

39 Ramsden, *Winds of Change*, pp. 330–2. This helps to explain why a number of senior Conservatives in the 1970s argued that the party should implement the proposals contained in the Wilson Government's abandoned reform programme, In Place of Strife.

40 Shadow Cabinet Steering Committee, Minutes of the 2nd Meeting, 25 March 1974, CPA, LCC 1/3/1.

41 M. Thatcher, *The Times*, 10 February 1975, *Thatcher CD-ROM*.

42 See Taylor, 'The Party and the Trade Unions' in Seldon and Ball, pp. 527–33.

43 Minutes of the Shadow Cabinet, 17 December 1975, TP, no fo.

44 G. Howe to M. Thatcher, 5 August 1977, TP 2/1/3/9.

45 Minutes of the Economic Reconstruction Group, 27 June 1975, TP, 2/6/1/37.

46 J. Prior to the Industrial Society, 29 May 1975, in J. Prior to K. Joseph, 24 July 1975, TP, 2/6/1/157. The Labour Government passed these two measures in 1974 and 1975.

47 M. Thatcher to Conservative Trade Unionists Conference, Manchester, 28 February 1976, *Thatcher CD-ROM*.

48 N. Lawson to M. Thatcher, 1 March 1976, TP, 2/1/1/42A.

49 M. Thatcher to N. Lawson, 2 March 1976, ibid.

50 J. Prior, Employment Policy: Interim Report, 5 July 1976, ibid., 2/6/1/159 (original emphasis).

51 Ibid.

52 G. Howe, notes for a speech on trade unions, n.d. December 1977, ibid., 2/1/3/9.

53 M. Thatcher, handwritten notes, ibid. (original emphasis).

54 K. Joseph and A. Maude, 'Notes Towards the Definition of Policy', 4 April 1975, ibid.

55 Minutes of a meeting in the leader of the Opposition's office, Parliament, 8 July 1975, KJP, KJ 10/11.

56 Minutes of the Economic Reconstruction Group, 20 November 1975, ibid., 2/6/1/37.

57 Minutes of the Economic Reconstruction Group, 20 November 1975, ibid.

58 Ibid.

59 Minutes of the Shadow Cabinet, 16 February 1976, ibid., no fo.

60 CRD, 'The Pay Deal', 10 May 1976, ibid., 2/6/1/158.

61 G. Howe to the Economic Committee, Bow Group, Carlton Club, 12 May 1976, ibid., 2/1/3/9.

62 G. Howe to K. Joseph, 13 October 1976, TP, 2/1/3/9. For further contemporary praise for West German 'Concerted Action' see the CBI publication, *The Future of Pay Bargaining*, pp. 40–1.

63 Hoskyns, *Just in Time*, p. 110.

64 N. Lawson to M. Thatcher, 1 March 1976, TP, 2/1/1/42A.

65 M. Thatcher to N. Lawson, 2 March 1976, ibid.

66 M. Thatcher, handwritten notes on A. Ridley, 'The Economic Education of the Public: Proposals for Concerted Action and Fighting Inflation', 16 May 1977, ibid., 2/6/1/96.

67 G. Howe to M. Thatcher, 26 May 1977, ibid., 2/1/3/9.

68 G. Howe, 'Our Attitude Towards Pay Policy', 6 March 1977, ibid., 2/6/1/233.

69 Ibid.

70 'The Right Approach to the Economy'.

71 Ibid.

72 Minutes of a meeting to discuss pay bargaining, 15 February 1978, ibid., 2/6/1/96.

73 Ibid.

74 See, for example, Thatcher's warnings about, respectively, Britain becoming a 'corporate state' under Labour, and the emergence of a 'socialist, corporate Europe'. M. Thatcher at Finchley, 2 May 1979, interview with the *Daily Mail*, 17 May 1989, *Thatcher CD-ROM*.

75 See search results for 'corporatism' and 'corporate' used in the political, i.e. non-business, sense, ibid.

76 M. Thatcher, comments on G. Howe, outline notes for a speech on trade unions, n.d. December 1977, TP, 2/1/3/9.

77 Ibid.

78 M. Thatcher, interview with *New Yorker*, 30 September 1985, *Thatcher CD-ROM*.

79 M. Thatcher in Parliament, 5 February 1980, ibid.

80 M. Thatcher in Parliament, 13 March 1980, ibid.

81 M. Thatcher to Birmingham Chamber of Industry and Commerce, 21 April 1980, ibid.

82 M. Thatcher in Parliament, 17 June 1982, ibid.

83 M. Thatcher in Parliament, 26 April 1984, ibid.

84 Thatcher, *Downing Street Years*, p. 93.

85 Cardona, 'Inflation'.

86 Ibid.

87 Ibid.

88 Hoskyns, *Just in Time*, p. 40.

89 J. Hoskyns, 'The Stepping Stones Programme', 19 January 1978, TP, 2/6/1/233.

90 Ibid.

91 Shadow Cabinet, Minutes of a Special Meeting on 'Stepping Stones', 30 January 1978, TP, 2/6/1/233.

92 Hoskyns, diary entry, 22 May 1978, in idem, *Just in Time*, p. 67.

93 Hoskyns, diary entry, 29 November 1977, ibid., p. 46.

94 Ibid., p. 179.

95 Ibid., pp. 202–6.

96 The Clegg Committee had been set up by the previous Labour Government.

97 Hoskyns, *Just in Time*, pp. 280–3.

98 G. Howe, notes for a speech on trade unions, n.d. December 1977, ibid., 2/1/3/9.

99 L. Brittan to K. Joseph, 24 July 1975, KJP, 26/3.

100 J. Prior, Employment Policy: Interim Report, 5 July 1976, TP 2/6/1/159.

101 Ibid.

102 'The Right Approach to the Economy'.

103 The 1982 Act made these compulsory every five years.

104 J. Prior, Employment Policy: Interim Report, 5 July 1976, TP, 2/6/1/159.

105 M. Thatcher in Parliament, 28 February 1980, ibid.

106 Minutes of the Shadow Cabinet, 15 January 1979, TP.

107 *Conservative Party Manifesto* (1979), p. 10.

108 For a rehearsal of this argument see M. Thatcher, interview with Robin Day, BBC 1, 25 February 1980, *Thatcher CD-ROM*.

109 M. Thatcher, interview with Brian Walden, London Weekend Television, 6 January 1980, ibid.

110 The one, indirect exception was at the government's electronic intelligence centre, GCHQ, at Cheltenham. After 1984 GCHQ staff were forbidden to be trade union members and effectively prevented from organizing industrial action.

111 Minutes of the Shadow Cabinet, 17 December 1975, TP, no fo.

112 Employment Policy Committee, 'Industrial Relations: The Rights of the Individual', n.d. July 1976, TP, 2/6/1/159.

113 For Thatcher's views on this issue see M. Thatcher, interview with *Illustrated London News*, 3 April 1980, and to Birmingham Chamber of Commerce, 21 April 1980, *Thatcher CD-ROM*.

114 M. Thatcher, interview with Jimmy Young, BBC Radio 2, 30 April 1980, ibid.

115 Confidential Annex to the Final Report of the Nationalized Industries Policy Group, 8 July 1977, KJP 10/7.

116 See Hoskyns, *Just in Time*, pp. 139–43, 308–12.

117 See Parker, *Thatcherism and the Fall of Coal*, pp. 13–16.

118 Lawson, *View from No. 11*, p. 140.

119 Ibid., pp. 141–9.

120 Parker, *Fall of Coal*, pp. 12–13.

121 Ibid., p. 45.

122 Parker, *Fall of Coal*, pp. 34–7.

123 Ibid., pp. 37–8.

124 Parker, *Fall of Coal*, p. 48.

125 Lawson, *View from No. 11*, p. 160.

126 Thatcher, *Downing Street Years*, p. 340.

127 M. Thatcher to 1922 Committee, 19 July 1984, *Thatcher CD-ROM*.

128 Lawson, *View from No. 11*, p. 161; Thatcher, *Downing Street Years*, p. 378.

129 This choice was in part forced upon him in so far as the Myron Report had led, in 1982, to the ending of national pay settlements for the industry and the introduction of local pay settlements based on productivity targets.

130 Hendy, *Conservative Employment Laws*, p. 13.

131 Deakin, 'Labour Law and Industrial Relations' in Michie, p. 176, Table 8.1.

132 Taylor, 'The Party and the Trade Unions', in Seldon and Ball, p. 527.

133 Hailsham, *Sparrow's Flight*, p. 407.

134 Thatcher, interview with Brian Walden, London Weekend Television, 6 January 1980, *Thatcher CD-ROM*.

135 Ibid.

136 Lawson, *View from No. 11*, pp. 713–18.

Chapter 5

1 Heath's party gained 46.4 per cent of the electorate in 1970.

2 G. Howe, 'Party Strategy, Policy and Organisation', n.d August 1976, TP, THCR 2/1/3/9.

3 Thatcher also saw university academics as crucial. See pp. 22–4.

4 Howe, 'Party Strategy'.

5 CRD, 'Summary: 29 March or 5 April', 11 July 1978, ibid., THCR 2/7/1/25.

6 Shadow Cabinet, 17 April 1978, ibid., THCR 2/6/1/162.

7 Thatcher at the Conservative Trade Union Conference, 28 February 1976, *Thatcher CD-ROM*.

8 CRD Public Opinion on Some Key Issues, n.d. August 1978, TP, THCR 2/7/1/25.

9 Thatcher at Newcastle, 23 April 1979, *Thatcher CD-ROM*.

10 Thatcher at the Conservative Party Conference, Brighton, 8 October 1982, ibid.

11 Thatcher at the Young Conservatives Conference, Eastbourne, 14 February 1981, ibid.

12 N. Lawson, 'Thoughts on Implementing Our Strategy', 15 January 1978, TP, THCR 2/1/2/12A.

13 W. Whitelaw to Leicester Conservative Federation, 17 September 1977, TP, THCR 2/6/1/39.

14 Adam (Ridley?) to M. Thatcher, 16 February 1978, enclosing speech to be made by Powell in Coventry, 18 February 1978, ibid., THCR 2/6/1/141.

15 A. Neave to M. Thatcher, 16 June 1976, ibid., THCR 2/6/1/39.

16 Ibid.

17 E. Leigh to M. Thatcher, 2 July 1976, ibid., THCR 2/6/1/39.

18 Ibid.

19 D. Smith to M. Thatcher, 20 January 1978, ibid., THCR 2/6/1/141.

20 G. Howe to M. Thatcher, 20 October 1975, ibid., THCR, 2/1/1/30.

21 G. Howe to M. Thatcher, 27 October 1975, ibid., THCR, 2/1/1/30.

22 Ibid.

23 A. Rowe to Thorneycroft, 23 October 1975, ibid., THCR, 2/1/1/30.

24 Ibid.

25 A. Rowe, 'Immigration Policy – the Way Ahead', ibid., THCR 2/6/1/141.

26 Ibid.

27 Ibid.

28 A. Rowe, 'The Conservative Party and Race Relations', 17 January 1978, ibid., THCR 2/6/1/141.

29 Ibid.

30 Ibid.

31 R. Ryder to A. Rowe, 6 February 1978, ibid., THCR 2/6/1/141.

32 CRD, Summary: 29 March or 5 April, 11 July 1978, ibid., THCR 2/7/1/25.

33 Rowe, 'The Conservative Party and Race Relations'.

34 Note on Immigration, n.a., n.d. July? 1977, ibid., THCR 2/6/1/139.

35 W. Whitelaw, Control of Immigration (A Supplementary Note), n.d. May 1976?, ibid., THCR 2/6/1/162.

36 N.S. Saroop to E. Leigh, 29 July 1976, ibid., THCR 2/6/1/39.

37 Note on Immigration, n.a., n.d. July? 1977, ibid., THCR 2/6/1/139.

38 CRD, Manifesto: Background Briefing, 12 April 1978, ibid., THCR 2/7/1/5.

39 See Zweiniger-Bargielowska, *HJ* (1993).

40 Thatcher at a meeting of the Shadow Cabinet, 3 May 1974, Minutes of the Shadow Cabinet, CPA, LCC 10th Meeting.

41 Ibid.

42 See Butler, Adonis and Travers, *Failure in British Government*.

43 Devon Ratepayers Association, evidence to Layfield Committee on Local Government Finance, 24 February 1975, enclosed with R. Maxwell-Hyslop to K. Joseph, 2 July 1975, KJP, KJ 8/13.

44 Ibid.

45 Minutes of the Shadow Cabinet, 3 May 1974, CPA, LCC 10th Meeting.

46 Ibid.

47 T. Raison, Local Government, 18 March 1975, TP, THCR 2/6/1/156.

48 Minutes of the Shadow Cabinet, 3 May 1974, CPA, LCC 10th Meeting.

49 Ibid.

50 Report of the Local Government Finance Policy Group, 21 July 1976, TP, THCR 2/6/1/159 (original emphasis).

51 Ibid. (original emphasis).

52 Ibid.

53 Minutes of the Shadow Cabinet, 11 July 1977, ibid., THCR 2/6/1/233.

54 See Butler, Adonis and Travers, *Failure in British Government*, pp. 29–33.

55 Ibid., pp. 61–5.

56 Lawson, *View from No. 11*, p. 572.

57 Ibid., p. 577.

58 See Butler, Adonis and Travers, *Failure in British Government*, pp. 61–5.

59 Baker, *Turbulent Years*, p. 118.

60 Lawson was not the only member of Cabinet who queried the poll tax. See Lawson, *View from No. 11*, p. 562.

61 Ibid., pp. 133–7, which emphasizes Thatcher was not 'running a one-person campaign'.

62 Thatcher, *Downing Street Years*, p. 677.

Chapter 6

1 Stephenson, *Mrs Thatcher's First Year*, p. 77. This was certainly the case for a Conservative PM, where Neville Chamberlain stands out as the only comparable example.

2 Remark by Thatcher to Frank Cooper, n.d. 1977, in Clark, *Diaries*, 28 June 1988, pp. 218–19.

3 M. Thatcher at Sleaford, 25 June 1945, *Thatcher CD-ROM*.

4 See M. Thatcher, General Election Addresses, 1950, 1951, ibid.

5 M. Thatcher, interview in the *Daily Sketch*, 3 December 1965, ibid.

6 M. Thatcher, *Any Questions*, BBC Light, 10 June 1966, ibid.

7 M. Thatcher to Bath Conservative Women's Association, 13 November 1968, ibid.

8 M. Thatcher, Delhi, 24 September 1976, ibid.

9 M. Thatcher in Parliament, 26 August 1977, ibid.

10 Minutes of the Shadow Cabinet, 4 October 1978, TP, 2/6/1/163.

11 Minutes of the Shadow Cabinet, 31 October 1978, ibid., 2/6/1/163.

12 Ibid.

13 M. Thatcher to W. Churchill, 9 November 1978, *Thatcher CD-ROM*.

14 The former Conservative Colonial Secretary, Alan Lennox-Boyd.

15 M. Thatcher in Parliament, 25 July 1979, *Thatcher CD-ROM*.

16 Ibid.

17 The *Daily Telegraph*, for example, noted a marked difference between Thatcher's enthusiasm and the Australian Government's response; see *Daily Telegraph*, 2 July 1979, report on M. Thatcher at the National Press Club, Canberra, 1 July 1979, ibid.

18 Carrington, *Reflect on Things Past*, pp. 298–9.

19 Ibid.

20 Ibid., p. 292.

21 Thatcher, *Downing Street Years*, p. 78.

22 Campbell, *Iron Lady*, p. 440.

23 G. Fitzgerald at a press conference with Thatcher, London, 15 November 1985, *Thatcher CD-ROM*.

24 M. Thatcher in Parliament, 29 October 1985, *Thatcher CD-ROM*.

25 M. Thatcher, interview with *Beeld*, London, 29 November 1988, ibid.

26 M. Thatcher, interview with the *Sowetan*, 2 October 1989, ibid.

27 See, for example, M. Thatcher, interview with Channel 4, 15 October 1985; interview with *Corriere della Sera*, 19 February 1990, ibid. The author, who was an employee of BP in 1985–6, attended talks given by the firm's public affairs department, at which the company's large-scale involvement in South Africa was explained/excused in terms of 'constructive engagement'.

28 M. Thatcher, interview with BBC 1, Nassau, 20 October 1985, ibid.

29 Howe, *Conflict of Loyalty*, p. 483.

30 M. Thatcher, interview with BBC World Service, 17 October 1987, *Thatcher CD-ROM*.

31 M. Thatcher in Brisbane, 5 August 1988, ibid.

32 M. Thatcher in Parliament, 26 October 1989, ibid.

33 M. Thatcher, interview with the *Guardian*, 8 July 1986, ibid.

34 Ibid.

35 Ibid.

36 M. Thatcher, interview with the *Sunday Telegraph*, 19 July 1986, ibid.

37 M. Thatcher in Parliament, 5 June 1984, ibid.

38 M. Thatcher to Finchley Conservative Women's Advisory Committee, 25 October 1985, ibid.

39 M. Thatcher, interview with the *Guardian*, 8 July 1986, ibid.

40 M. Thatcher in Parliament, 22 October 1987, ibid.

41 Ibid.

42 Thatcher publicly cited Buthelezi's opposition to sanctions on 23 occasions during her time as prime minister, ibid.

43 M. Thatcher, interview with *Johannesburg Star*, 16 July 1990, ibid.

44 *Finchley Press*, 31 October 1985, ibid.

45 M. Thatcher, interview with IRN, Nassau, 20 October 1985, and press conference in New York, 24 October 1985, ibid.

46 R. Reagan to M. Thatcher, 23 June 1986, Ronald Reagan papers, copy in TP.

47 Thatcher, *Downing Street Years*, pp. 516–31.

48 D. Abbot in Parliament, 26 October 1989, ibid.

49 Carlisle argued that denunciation of South Africa was used by black African states as a veil for their own abuse of human rights.

50 M. Thatcher, interview with Channel 10, Sydney, 4 August 1988, *Thatcher CD-ROM*.

51 M. Thatcher, interview with BBC World Service, 17 October 1987, ibid. The figures she used in this context fluctuated, for in 1986 she told the *Sunday Telegraph* that 3 million workers came to South Africa from black African states; M. Thatcher, interview with the *Sunday Telegraph*, 19 July 1986, ibid. (my emphasis).

52 M. Thatcher, interview with *Johannesburg Star*, 16 July 1990, ibid.

53 M. Thatcher in Portsmouth, 11 February 1977, ibid.

54 Carrington, *Reflect on Things Past*, p. 348.

55 *Falkland Islands Review*, 1983, Cmnd. 8787, pp. 4–34.

56 N. Ridley to Carrington, 20 July 1981, cited in ibid., p. 27.

57 Ibid.

58 Sir Frederic Bennett in Parliament, 5 February 1976, *Thatcher CD-ROM*.

59 *Falkland Islands Review*, p. 18.

60 Carrington, *Reflect on Things Past*, pp. 359–60, 364–5.

61 Falkland Islands Councils Meeting to Carrington, 26 June 1981, *Falkland Islands Review*, p. 33.

62 *Falkland Islands Review*, p. 34.

63 Ibid.

64 Approximately £3 million.

65 *Falkland Islands Review*, p. 78.

66 R. Reagan to M. Thatcher, 1 April 1982, Reagan Archive, copy in TP.

67 Ibid.

68 Freedman and Gamba-Stonehouse, *Signals of War*, pp. 159–62.

69 R. Reagan to A. Haig, 9 April 1982, Reagan Archive, copy in TP.

70 Lord Carrington had resigned after the Argentinian invasion.

71 A. Haig to R. Reagan, 9 April 1982, Reagan Archive, copy in TP.

72 Ibid.

73 C. Weinberger to R. Reagan, 19 July 1982, ibid. Freedman and Gamba-Stonehouse, *Signals of War*, pp. 359–61 confirm the good fortune of the British forces.

74 Carrington, *Reflect on Things Past*, p. 358.

75 Freedman and Gamba-Stonehouse, *Signals of War*, pp. 62, 68, indicate that domestic pressure was a factor in the Junta's decision to invade, but was not decisive.

76 Young, *One of Us*, p. 266.

77 A. Haig to R. Reagan, 9 April 1982, Reagan Archive, copy in TP.

78 Barnett, *Iron Britannia*, p. 19.

79 Smith, *Reagan and Thatcher*, p. 1.

80 M. Thatcher at Kensington Town Hall, 19 January 1976, *Thatcher CD-ROM*.

81 M. Thatcher, interview with *US News* and *World Report*, 4 September 1977, ibid.

82 M. Thatcher to a Conservative Party rally, Birmingham, 19 April 1979, ibid.

83 M. Thatcher to Chelsea Conservative Association, 26 July 1975, ibid.

84 M. Thatcher, *Conservative News*, 1 March 1976, ibid.

85 M. Thatcher to a Conservative Party rally, Dorking, 31 July 1976, ibid.

86 M. Thatcher to CDU Conference, Hanover, 25 May 1976, ibid.

87 M. Thatcher, interview for Central Office of Information, 20 December 1979, ibid.

88 M. Thatcher to a Conservative Party rally, Birmingham, 19 April 1979, ibid.

89 M. Thatcher, 'Europe: the Obligation of Liberty', Winston Churchill Memorial Lecture, 18 October 1979, ibid.

90 Thatcher, *Path to Power*, p. 348.

91 R. Reagan in Orlando, n.d. January 1976, in Hayward, *Age of Reagan*, p. 465 (my emphasis).

92 Thatcher, *Downing Street Years*, p. 68.

93 Hayward, *Age of Reagan,* p. 532.

94 R. Reagan to M. Thatcher, 25 October 1983, Reagan Archive, copy in TP.

95 See Williams, *TCBH*, xii (2001).

96 The British Ambassador to the US was in the Oval Office when Reagan received a call from Thatcher about the invasion, and he recalls that Reagan held the earpiece away as Thatcher shouted at him.

97 R. Reagan to M. Thatcher, 23 December 1983, ibid.

98 R. MacFarlane, Paper on 'Meeting With British Prime Minister Margaret Thatcher', 22 December 1984. Reagan Archive, copy in TP.

99 Ibid.

100 See Smith, *Reagan and Thatcher*, pp. 146–59.

101 Ibid., pp.165–6.

102 For Thatcher's concern about a nuclear-free Europe see Sharp, *Thatcher's Diplomacy*, p. 200.

103 K. Adelman, quoted in Smith, *Reagan and Thatcher,* p. 166.

104 Ibid., p. 168.

105 R. Kimmitt to P. Sommer and P. Thompson, 18 December 1984, Reagan Archive, copy in TP.

106 Ibid.

107 R. MacFarlane, Paper on 'Meeting With British Prime Minister Margaret Thatcher', 22 December 1984, ibid.

108 Ibid.

109 M. Thatcher to R. Reagan, 29 March 1983, ibid.

110 R. Reagan to M. Thatcher, 6 April 1983, ibid.

111 Smith, *Reagan and Thatcher*, p. 144.

112 Ibid., p. 165.

113 Ibid., pp. 65–6.

114 M. Thatcher, *Daily Telegraph*, 16 February 1983, *Thatcher CD-ROM.*

115 M. Thatcher in Glasgow, 1 September 1982, ibid.

116 D. Atkinson and M. Thatcher in Parliament, 23 February 1982, ibid.

117 M. Thatcher, *Daily Telegraph*, 16 February 1983, ibid.

118 M. Thatcher, interview in *Newsweek International*, 28 April 1986, ibid.

119 M. Thatcher, interview with Granada Television, 21 April 1986, ibid.

120 Smith, *Reagan and Thatcher*, p. 197.

121 M. Thatcher to R. Reagan, 4 December 1986, Reagan Archive, copy in TP.

122 M. Thatcher in the European Parliament, 9 December 1986.

123 Urban, *Diplomacy and Disillusion*, p. 83.

124 Campbell, *Iron Lady*, p. 633.

125 Thatcher, *Downing Street Years*, p. 61.

126 M. Thatcher to National Legal Center for the Public Interest, New York, 20 September 1993, *Thatcher CD-ROM*.

127 M. Thatcher to Aspen Institute, 4 August 1995, ibid.

128 Thatcher, *Statecraft*, pp. 259–60.

129 Ibid., p. 262.

130 Ibid., pp. 30–1.

131 Ibid., p. 265.

132 Ibid., pp. 267–74.

133 Ibid., p. 274.

134 Ibid., p. 256.

135 Ibid., p. 279.

136 Ibid., p. 280.

137 Thatcher, *Path to Power*, p. 500.

138 M. Thatcher on BBC Radio 2, 27 July 1982, *Thatcher CD-ROM*.

139 M. Thatcher at the College of Europe, Bruges, 20 September 1988, ibid.

140 M. Thatcher, interview with *New York Times*, 27 September 1988, ibid. When asked by her interviewer if she was a 'Gaullist', Thatcher accepted the label.

141 M. Thatcher at the Hoover Institute, Washington, 1 March 1991, ibid. (my emphasis).

142 Thatcher, *Path to Power*, pp. 470–1.

143 M. Thatcher, 'Europe: Quo Vadis': Speech at Europ-Assistance 25th Anniversary Dinner, Milan, 24 May 1993, *Thatcher CD-ROM*.

144 M. Thatcher at a press conference for American Press, London, 13 January 1986, ibid.

145 M. Thatcher in the European Parliament, 9 December 1986, ibid.

146 M. Thatcher, Clare Booth Luce Lecture, Washington, 23 September 1991.

147 M. Thatcher in Parliament, 12 July 1990, ibid.

148 M. Thatcher, interview with *US News* and *World Report*, 6 December 1988, ibid.

149 M. Thatcher to Newspaper Press Fund, 3 February 1989, ibid.

150 M. Thatcher, 'Europe: Quo Vadis': Speech at Europ-Assistance 25th Anniversary Dinner, Milan, 24 May 1993, ibid.

151 M. Thatcher to Foreign Relations Council of Chicago, 17 June 1991, ibid.

152 Ibid.

Chapter 7

1 Thatcher, *Statecraft*, p. 320.

2 M. Thatcher in Bruges, 20 September 1988, *Thatcher CD-ROM*.

3 Howe, *Conflict of Loyalty*, pp. 537–50.

4 Lawson, *View from No. 11*, pp. 784–9, 890–900, 909–18.

5 M. Thatcher in Finchley, 14 August 1961, *Thatcher CD-ROM*.

6 Ibid.

7 Ibid.

8 M. Thatcher in Finchley, 18 March 1966, ibid.

9 M. Thatcher in Finchley, 7 August 1971, ibid.

10 M. Thatcher at a Referendum Press Conference, 3 June 1975, ibid.

11 Benn, *Against the Tide*, 18 February 1975, p. 319.

12 Ibid., 23 February 1975.

13 M. Thatcher, interview for BBC 2, 2 June 1975, *Thatcher CD-ROM*.

14 M. Thatcher, *Financial Times*, 7 June 1975, ibid.

15 See, for example, her speech at the meeting, chaired by Heath, which marked the opening of the Conservative campaign, St Ermin's, Westminster, 16 April 1975, ibid.

16 M. Thatcher, interview for BBC 2, 2 June 1975, ibid.

17 Boz de Ferranti to A. Frodsham, cc. K. Joseph, 29 November 1976, KJP, KJ 8/21.

18 The number of openly anti-EEC MPs was in the mid-20s.

19 Du Cann claimed that half of the Conservative Party was really anti-EEC, but did not want a damaging split in the party.

20 M. Thatcher, interview with BBC 2, 2 June 1975; M. Thatcher, open letter to T. Benn, 21 April 1975; M. Thatcher, *Financial Times*, 7 June 1975, *Thatcher CD-ROM*.

21 TP 2/6/1/233.

22 C. Patten to K. Joseph, A. Maude and J. Douglas, 7 April 1976, KJP 8/15.

23 Shadow Cabinet Minutes, 19 April 1978, TP, 2/6/1/162.

24 'The European Democratic Union (EDU)' (A Note by Douglas Hurd and the Baroness Elles), 12 April 1978, ibid., THCR 2/6/2/162.

25 Shadow Cabinet Minutes, 19 April 1978, TP, 2/6/1/162.

26 'The European Democratic Union (EDU)' (A Note by Douglas Hurd and the Baroness Elles), 12 April 1978, ibid., THCR 2/6/2/162.

27 M. Thatcher, House of Commons, 10 July 1978.

28 Ibid.

29 G. Howe, N. Lawson, C. Soames, J. Nott and F. Pym, Meeting on the EMS, 25 October 1978, 2/1/3/9, TP.

30 Ibid.

31 G. Howe to M. Thatcher, 31 October 1978, ibid. Lawson argued that the EMS would provide an added 'external discipline' over domestic monetary policy for all participants. N. Lawson to M. Thatcher, cc. G. Howe, F. Pym, Lord Thorneycroft, C. Soames, J. Nott, D. Hurd and A. Ridley, 30 October 1978, ibid., 2/1/2/12A.

32 Ibid. This echoed Lawson's view that staying outside the EMS 'would risk abdicating for good the leadership of Europe, and more precisely the EEC and its policies to a Franco-German axis.' N. Lawson to M. Thatcher, cc. G. Howe, F. Pym, Lord Thorneycroft, C. Soames, J. Nott, D. Hurd and A. Ridley, 30 October 1978, ibid., 2/1/2/12A.

33 G. Howe to M. Thatcher, 31 October 1978, ibid., 2/1/3/9. The CAP was a particularly important issue for Howe and Thatcher, for they saw it as 'protectionist and an obstacle to GATT negotiations with the USA'. See G. Howe to M. Thatcher, 9 June 1977, ibid.

34 Ibid.

35 Minutes of the Shadow Cabinet, 15 November 1978, ibid., 2/6/1/163.

36 House of Commons Select Committee on European Legislation, 1980.

37 Carrington, *Reflect on Things Past*, pp. 316, 318.

38 Ibid., p. 319.

39 Ibid.

40 Ibid.

41 M. Thatcher, Parliamentary Statement on the Luxembourg EC, 29 April 1980, *Thatcher CD-ROM*.

42 M. Thatcher, interview with the BBC, 19 June 1983; and at the post-meeting press conference, 19 June 1983, ibid.

43 M. Thatcher, interview with the BBC, 20 March 1984, ibid.

44 M. Thatcher, interview with the BBC, 26 June 1984, ibid. The summit also agreed that Member States should increase the proportion of their internal VAT receipts contributed to the Community from 1 to 1.4 per cent.

45 M. Thatcher, Parliamentary Statement on the Brussels EC, 15 February 1988, ibid.

46 M. Thatcher to press conference, Stuttgart, 19 June 1983, ibid. See also Sharp, *Thatcher's Diplomacy*, p. 160.

47 Thatcher, *Downing Street Years*, p. 553.

48 M. Thatcher, press conference in Strasbourg, 9 December 1989, *Thatcher CD-ROM*.

49 Ibid.

50 See Lawson, *View from No. 11*, pp. 486–95, 651–2.

51 Ibid., pp. 495–6.

52 Ibid., pp. 784–9.

53 Ibid., p. 548.

54 Ibid., pp. 931–4; Howe, *Conflict of Loyalty*, pp. 579–83.

55 M. Thatcher in Parliament, 27 April 1989, ibid.

56 M. Thatcher at a press conference in Madrid, 27 June 1989, ibid.

57 Ibid.

58 M. Thatcher, interview with the BBC, 27 June 1989, ibid.

59 M. Thatcher, parliamentary statement on the Madrid EC, 29 June 1989, ibid.

60 M. Thatcher, interview with BBC Radio 4, 14 May 1989, *Thatcher CD-ROM*. Thatcher did, however, offer Lawson an 'almost unique' apology for this. See Lawson, *View from No. 11*, p. 920.

61 M. Thatcher in Parliament, 12 December 1989, *Thatcher CD-ROM*.

62 Thatcher, *Downing Street Years*, p. 750.

63 M. Thatcher in the House of Lords, 14 July 1993, ibid.

64 Thatcher, *Downing Street Years*, p. 61.

65 M. Thatcher at the Conservative Party Conference, 14 October 1988, *Thatcher CD-ROM*.

66 Ibid., pp. 727–67.

67 Ibid., p. 536.

68 See Thatcher, *Path to Power*, pp. 470–507; Urban, *Diplomacy and Disillusion*, p. 3; Major, *Autobiography*, pp. 274–5, 361–2.

69 Ibid., p. 27.

70 Ibid., pp. 350–1.

71 M. Thatcher, *The European*, 11 October 1992, *Thatcher CD-ROM*.

72 Major, *Autobiography*, p. 636.

73 Thatcher, *Statecraft*, p. 321.

74 Ibid., p. 323.

75 Ibid., p. 324.

76 Ibid., p. 351.

77 Ibid., pp. 374–5.

78 Ibid., pp. 326–7.

79 M. Thatcher in Finchley, 10 August 1962, *Thatcher CD-ROM*.

80 Lawson, *View from No. 11*, pp. 274–5.

81 Ibid., p. 900.

82 Ibid. The 'saloon bar' being the natural location for what John Campbell has called Thatcher's 'Alf Garnett' vision of Germany's role in European history.

83 Howe, *Conflict of Loyalty*, p. 632.

84 Urban, *Diplomacy and Disillusion,* p. 99.

85 Ibid., p. 12.

86 F. Cooper, remark to A. Clark, 28 June 1988, Clark, *Diaries*, pp. 218–19.

87 Urban, *Diplomacy and Disillusion*, p. 12.

88 Thatcher, *Downing Street Years*, p. 81.

89 M. Thatcher, Conservative Party Conference, 12 October 1990, *Thatcher CD-ROM*.

90 M. Thatcher, interview with Channel 4, 23 September 1988, ibid.

91 Lawson, *View from No. 11*, p. 904.

92 Howe, *Conflict of Loyalty*, p 544.

93 Ibid., pp. 577–8, and Lawson, *View from No. 11*, pp. 913–14.

94 Lawson also noted that Thatcher's confrontational behaviour and tone at European meetings often led the Europeans to unite against the British position. Ibid., pp. 898–9.

95 M. Thatcher, parliamentary statement on the Rome EC summit, 30 October 1990, *Thatcher CD-ROM*.

96 Howe, *Conflict of Loyalty*, p. 643.

97 Thatcher, *Downing Street Years*, p. 309.

98 Howe, *Conflict of Loyalty*, p. 405.

99 Thatcher, *Downing Street Years*, p. 547.

100 Ibid.

101 M. Thatcher to the Conservative Central Council, 18 March 1989, *Thatcher CD-ROM*.

102 Thatcher, *Statecraft*, pp. 329–30.

103 Thatcher, *Downing Street Years*, p. 750. Lord Howe told the author that Thatcher did not distinguish between social market and Socialism.

104 Thatcher, *Statecraft*, p. 330.

105 Ibid., p. 375.

106 Thatcher, *Downing Street Years*, p. 82.

Conclusion

1 Benn, *End of An Era*, 21 November 1990, p. 613.

2 This remark is usually attributed to the Labour frontbencher Gerald Kaufmann.

3 P. Mandelson, *The Times*, 10 June 2002.

4 S. Hall, 'New Labour Has Picked Up Where Thatcherism Left Off', *Guardian*, 6 August 2003.

5 Ibid.

6 N. Lawson to M. Thatcher, 3 October 1975, TP, THCR 2/1/1/42A (original emphasis).

7 G. Brown, Mais Lecture, London, 19 October 1999.

8 J. Major, interview with the BBC, 17 June 2001.

9 Clarke, *Conservative Faith*, p. 13.

10 M. Fraser, 'The Ownership of Property', a lecture given in Oxford, 8 July 1952, enclosed with idem to R. A. Butler, 18 July 1952, Butler papers, H34, fos. 173–90.

11 Young Conservatives, *Society and the Individual*, p. 1.

12 J.E. Powell at Bromley, 24 October 1963, in Wood, *A Nation Not Afraid*, pp. 4–5.

13 Oakeshott, 'On Being Conservative', pp. 432–3.

14 On this see above, pp. 44–50, and see also Green, *Ideologies of Conservatism*, pp. 240–79.

15 Thatcher, Airey Neave Memorial Lecture, 3 March 1980, ibid.

16 Willetts, *Civic Conservatism*, pp. 15, 18.

17 Ibid., p. 16.

18 Willetts and Gray, *Is Conservatism Dead?*, pp. 3–65.

19 For a study of this phenomenon in the US context see Putnam, *Bowling Alone*. For Britain see Hall, *British Journal of Political Science*, 29, 1999.

20 One association which showed a marked decline in participation was, of course, the Conservative Party, the membership of which decreased significantly over the 1980s and 1990s. See Whiteley, Seyd and Richardson, *True Blues*, esp. pp. 219–38.

21 P. Jenkins, *Guardian*, 4 May 1989.

22 Tebbit, *Upwardly Mobile*, p. 267.

23 K. Joseph to J. Rootham, 10 December 1975, KJP, KJ 10/11.

24 Highly Confidential Draft Questions for Mrs Thatcher, to be first considered by Mr Whitelaw, n.d. July 1977?, ibid., KJ 8/22.

25 M. Roberts at Erith, 28 February 1949, *Thatcher CD-ROM*.

26 M. Proops, *Daily Mirror*, 5 February 1975.

Bibliography

Place of publication is London, unless otherwise stated.

Primary sources

Baldwin Papers, Cambridge University Library.
Balfour Papers, British Library.
A. Bryant Papers, King's College, London.
Butler Papers, Trinity College, Cambridge.
N. Chamberlain Papers, Birmingham University Library.
Conservative Party Archive, Bodleian Library, Oxford.
Hailes Papers, Churchill College Library, Cambridge.
Joseph Papers, Bodleian Library, Oxford.
Macmillan Papers, Bodleian Library, Oxford.
Thatcher Papers, Churchill College, Cambridge.

Collins, C. (ed.), *The Complete Public Statements of Margaret Thatcher 1945–1990 on CD-ROM* (OUP, Oxford, 2000).

Falkland Islands Review, 1983, Cmnd. 8787.

Books

Addison, P., *The Road to 1945: British Politics and the Second World War* (Jonathan Cape, 1975).
Aglietta, M., *A Theory of Capitalist Regulation: the US Experience* (New Left Books, 1979).
Baker, K., *The Turbulent Years: My Life in Politics* (Faber and Faber, 1993).
Barnett, A., *Iron Britannia: Why Parliament Waged its Falklands War* (Allison & Busby, 1982).
Benn, T., *Against the Tide: Diaries 1973–1977* (Hutchinson, 1989).
Benn, T., *The End of An Era: Diaries 1980–90* (Hutchinson, 1992).
Bentley, M. (ed.), *Public and Private Doctrine: Essays in British History Presented to Maurice Cowling* (CUP, Cambridge, 1993).
Berrington, H. (ed.), *Britain in the Nineties: The Politics of Paradox* (Frank Cass Publishers, 1998).
Birch, N., *The Conservative Party* (1949).
Blake, R., *The Conservative Party From Peel to Thatcher* (Fontana Press, 1985).
Boyd-Carpenter, Lord, (J.), *Way of Life: The Memoirs of John Boyd-Carpenter* (Sidgwick & Jackson, 1980).
Bryant, A., *The Spirit of Conservatism* (1929).
Bryant, A., *History of Britain and the British People: Set in A Silver Sea* (Grafton Books, 1985).

Butler, D., Adonis, A. and Travers, T., *Failure in British Government: the Politics of the Poll Tax* (Oxford, 1994).

Butler, Lord (R.A.), *The Art of the Possible* (Penguin, 1973).

Cain, P. and Hopkins, A.G., *British Imperialism, 1688–1990*, 2 vols (Longman, 1993).

Campbell, J., *Edward Heath: A Biography* (Jonathan Cape, 1993).

Campbell, J., *Margaret Thatcher*, 2 vols, *The Grocer's Daughter* and *Iron Lady* (Jonathan Cape, 2000–3).

Carrington, Lord, *Reflect On Things Past: the Memoirs of Lord Carrington* (HarperCollins, 1988).

Castle, B., *The Castle Diaries, 1974–1976* (Weidenfeld & Nicolson, 1980).

CBI, *The Future of Pay Bargaining* (CBI, 1977).

Cecil, H., *Conservatism* (1912).

Charmley, J., *A History of Conservative Politics, 1900–1996* (Palgrave Macmillan, Basingstoke, 1996).

Clark, A., *The Tories: Conservatives and the Nation State, 1922–1997* (Weidenfeld & Nicolson, 1998).

Clark, A., *Diaries: Into Politics* (Weidenfeld & Nicolson, 2000).

Clarke, D., *The Conservative Faith in a Modern Age* (1947).

Clarke, P., *The Keynesian Revolution in the Making: 1924–36* (Clarendon Press, Oxford, 1988).

Clarke, P., *A Question of Leadership: From Gladstone to Thatcher* (Hamish Hamilton, 1991).

Clarke, P., *The Keynesian Revolution and its Economic Consequences* (Edward Elgar, Cheltenham, 1998).

Clarke, P. and Trebilcock, C. (eds), *Understanding Decline: Perceptions and Realities of British Economic Performance* (CUP, Cambridge, 1997).

Cobham, D. and Artis, M., *The Labour Government's Economic Policy, 1974–79.*

Cockett, R., *Thinking the Unthinkable: Think-tanks and the Economic Counter-revolution, 1931–83* (1994).

Conservative Central Office, *The Industrial Charter* (Conservative Central Office, 1947).

Conservative Party Manifesto (Conservative Political Centre, 1979).

Conservative Party Manifesto (Conservative Political Centre, 1983).

Conservative Party Manifesto (Conservative Political Centre, 1987).

Conservative Political Centre, *Conservatism 1945–50* (Conservative Political Centre, 1950).

Conservative Political Centre, *The New Conservatism: An Anthology of Post-War Thought* (Conservative Political Centre, 1955).

Coopey, R. et al. (eds), *Britain in the 1970s: The Troubled Decade* (Palgrave Macmillan, Basingstoke, 1996).

Cosgrave, P., *Margaret Thatcher: A Tory and Her Party* (Hutchinson, 1978).

Crafts, N.F.R. and Woodward, N. (eds), *The British Economy Since 1945* (OUP, Oxford, 1991).

Dale, I. (ed.), *Memories of Maggie: A Portrait of Margaret Thatcher* (Politico's Publishing, 2000).

Denham, A. and Garnett, M., *Keith Joseph* (Acumen Publishing, Chesham, 2001).

Dintenfass, M., *The Decline of Industrial Britain: 1870–1980* (1991).

Eccleshall, R., *English Conservatism Since the Restoration* (Routledge, 1990).

Elliot, W., *Toryism and the Twentieth Century* (1927).

Feiling, K., *What Is Conservatism?* (1930).

Floud, R. and McCloskey, D. (eds), *The Economic History of Britain Since 1700*, 3 vols, 2nd edn (CUP, Cambridge, 1994).

Francis, M. and Zweiniger-Bargielowska, I. (eds), *The Conservatives and British Society, 1880–1990* (University of Wales Press, Cardiff, 1996).

Franco, P., *The Political Philosophy of Michael Oakeshott* (Yale University Press, New Haven, 1990).

Freeden, M., *Ideologies and Political Theory: A Conceptual Approach* (Clarendon Press, Oxford, 1996).

Freedman, L. and Gamba-Stonehouse, V., *Signals of War: Falklands Conflict of 1982* (Faber and Faber, 1990).

Gamble, A., *The Free Economy and the Strong State: The Politics of Thatcherism* (Palgrave Macmillan, Basingstoke, 1988).

Gamble, A., *Hayek: The Iron Cage of Liberty* (Polity Press, Cambridge, 1996).

Garnett, M., *Alport: A Study in Loyalty* (Acumen Publishing, Teddington, 1999).

Gilmour, I., *Britain Can Work* (Blackwell Publishers, Oxford, 1983).

Gilmour, I., *Dancing With Dogma: Thatcherite Britain in the Eighties* (Simon & Schuster, 1992).

Gilmour, I., *Whatever Happened to the Tories?: The Conservative Party Since 1945* (Fourth Estate, 1997).

Green, E.H.H., *The Crisis of Conservatism: The Politics, Economics and Ideology of the British Conservative Party, 1880–1914* (Routledge, 1995).

Green, E.H.H., *Ideologies of Conservatism: Conservative Political Ideas in the Twentieth Century* (OUP, Oxford, 2002).

Green, F. *The Restructuring of the United Kingdom Economy* (Prentice-Hall, 1989).

Greenleaf, W.H., *The British Political Tradition*, 3 vols (Routledge, 1983–7).

Gorst, A. et al. (eds), *Britain, 1945–64: Themes and Perspectives* (Continuum International Publishing, 1989).

Hailsham, Lord (Q. Hogg), *The Conservative Case* (Penguin, 1959).

Hailsham, Lord (Q. Hogg), *A Sparrow's Flight* (HarperCollins, 1990).

Halcrow, M., *Keith Joseph: A Single Mind* (Macmillan, 1989).

Hall, P., *Governing the Economy* (Polity Press, Cambridge, 1986).

Hall, S. and Jacques, M. (eds), *The Politics of Thatcherism* (Lawrence & Wishart, 1983).

Hames, T. and Adonis, A. (eds), *A Conservative Revolution* (Manchester University Press, Manchester, 1993).

Hayek, F.A., *The Road to Serfdom* (1943).

Hayek, F.A., *The Constitution of Liberty* (Routledge, 1960, 1976 edn).

Hayward, S., *The Age of Reagan: The Fall of the Old Liberal Order, 1964–1980* (Prima Lifestyles, California, 2001).

Heath, A. and Jowell, R., *Understanding Political Change: The British Voter, 1964–87* (Butterworth-Heinemann, Oxford, 1991).

Heffer, S., *Like the Roman: The Life of Enoch Powell* (Weidenfeld & Nicolson, 1998).

Hendy, J., *The Conservative Employment Laws: A National and International Perspective* (Institute of Employment Rights, 1989).

Heseltine, M., *Life in the Jungle: My Autobiography* (Hodder & Stoughton, 2000).

Hickson, K. (ed.), *The Political Thought of the Conservative Party Since 1945* (Palgrave Macmillan, Basingstoke, 2005).

Hills, J.W., *Managed Money* (1937).

Hinchingbrooke, Viscount, *Full Speed Ahead: Essays in Tory Reform* (1944).

Hogg, Q., *The Case For Conservatism* (1947).

Honderich, T., *Conservatism* (Hamish Hamilton, 1990).

Hoover, K. and Plant, R., *Conservative Capitalism in Britain and America* (Routledge, 1989).

Horne, A., *Macmillan*, 2 vols (Palgrave Macmillan, Basingstoke, 1989).

Hoskyns, J., *Just in Time: Inside the Thatcher Revolution* (Aurum Press, 2000).

Howe, G., *Conflict of Loyalty* (Palgrave Macmillan, Basingstoke, 1995).

Ingham, B., *Kill the Messenger* (Fontana Press, 1991).

Jeffreys, K., *Retreat from New Jerusalem: British Policies, 1951–64* (St Martin's Press, 1997).

Jenkins, P., *Mrs Thatcher's Revolution: Ending of the Socialist Era* (1987).

Jessop, R. et al., *Thatcherism* (Polity Press, Cambridge, 1988).

Jewkes, J., *Ordeal by Planning* (1948).

Jewkes, J., *The New Ordeal by Planning: The Experience of the Forties and Sixties* (Macmillan, 1968).

Jones, H. and Kandiah, M. (eds), *The Myth of Consensus: New Views on British History, 1945–64* (Palgrave Macmillan, Basingstoke, 1996).

Joseph, K., *Reversing the Trend* (B Rose, 1975).

Joseph, K., *Stranded on the Middle Ground* (CPS, 1975).

Joseph, K., *Monetarism Is Not Enough* (B Rose, 1976).

Junor, P., *Margaret Thatcher: Wife, Mother, Politician* (Sidgwick & Jackson, 1983).

Kelly, S., *The Myth of Mr. Butskell: The Politics of British Economic Policy, 1950–55* (Ashgate, 2002).

Lawrence, J. and Taylor, M. (eds), *Party, State and Society: Electoral Behaviour in Modern Britain Since 1820* (Scolar Press, Aldershot, 1996).

Lawson, N., *The New Conservatism* (Centre for Policy Studies, 1980).

Lawson, N., *The View from No. 11: Memoirs of a Tory Radical* (Bantam Press, 1992).

Lewis, R., *Margaret Thatcher: A Personal and Political Biography* (Routledge, 1975).

Lipietz, A., *Towards a New Economic Order: Postfordism, Ecology and Democracy* (Polity Press, Cambridge, 1992).

Low, T., *Everyman a Capitalist* (Conservative Political Centre, 1959).

Macmillan, H., *The Middle Way: Study of the Problems of Economic and Social Progress in a Free and Democratic Society* (EP, 1938, 1978 edn).

Macmillan, H., *The Middle Way: 20 Years After* (Conservative Political Centre, 1958).

Macmillan, H., *Tides of Fortune, 1945–55* (Macmillan, 1969).

Macmillan, H., *Riding the Storm, 1956–59* (Macmillan, 1971).

Macmillan, H., *Pointing the Way, 1959–61* (Macmillan, 1972).

Macmillan, H., *At the End of the Day, 1961–63* (Macmillan, 1973).

Maddox, B., *Maggie: The First Lady* (Hodder & Stoughton, 2003).

Major, J., *The Autobiography* (HarperCollins, 1999).

Marlow, J.D., *Questioning the Post-War Consensus Thesis* (Aldershot, 1996).

Marrison, A., *British Business and Protection, 1903–32* (Clarendon Press, Oxford, 1996).

Meadowcroft, J., *Conceptualizing the State: Innovation and Dispute in British Political Thought: 1880–1914* (Clarendon Press, Oxford, 1995).

Meiksins Wood, E., *The Pristine Culture of Capitalism: A Historical Essay on Old Regimes and Modern States* (Verso Books, 1991).

Michie, J. (ed.), *The Economic Legacy, 1979–92* (Academic Press, 1992).

Middlemas, K., *Power, Competition and the State*, 3 vols (Palgrave Macmillan, Basingstoke, 1986–91).

Minogue, K. and Biddiss, R. (eds), *Thatcherism: Personality and Politics* (Palgrave Macmillan, Basingstoke, 1987).

Money, E., *Margaret Thatcher: First Lady of the House* (Taylor & Francis, 1975).

Morgan, K.O., *The People's Peace: British History 1945–1989* (OUP, Oxford, 1990).

Murphy, P., *Party Politics and Decolonization: The Conservative Party and British Colonial Policy in Tropical Africa, 1951–64* (Clarendon Press, Oxford, 1995).

Murray, P., *Margaret Thatcher: A Profile* (WH Allen, 1980).

Myrdal, G., *The Political Element in the Development of Economic Theory* (Routledge and Kegan Paul, 1953).

Northam, R., *Conservatism: The Only Way* (1938).

Oakley, A. and Williams, S. (eds), *The Politics of the Welfare State* (Routledge, 1994).

Offer, A., *Property and Politics, 1870–1914: Landownership, Law Ideology and Urban Development in England* (CUP, Cambridge, 1981).

One Nation Group, *One Nation* (Conservative Political Centre, 1950).

One Nation Group (chief authors Macleod, I. and. Powell, J.E.), *The Social Services: Needs and Means* (Conservative Political Centre, 1952).

One Nation Group (chief authors Maude, A. and Powell, J.E.), *Change Is Our Ally: A Tory Approach to Industrial Problems* (Conservative Political Centre, 1954).

One Nation Group, *The Responsible Society* (Conservative Political Centre, 1959).

Ormerod, P., *The Death of Economics* (Faber and Faber, 1994).

O'Sullivan, N., *Conservatism* (Everyman, 1976).

Parker, M.J., *Thatcherism and the Fall of Coal: Politics and Economics of UK Coal, 1979–2000* (OUP and Oxford Institute for Energy Studies, Oxford, 2000).

Parkinson, C., *Right at the Centre: An Autobiography* (1992).

Peden, G.C., *The Treasury and British Public Policy, 1906–1959* (OUP, Oxford, 2000).

Pierson, P., *Dismantling the Welfare State? Reagan, Thatcher and the Politics of Retrenchment* (CUP, Cambridge, 1994).

Powell, J.E., *A Nation Not Afraid: The Thinking of Enoch Powell* (1965).

Powell, J.E., *Freedom and Reality* (1969).

Powell, J.E., *Still To Decide* (Batsford, 1972).

Powell, J.E., *No Easy Answers* (Sheldon Press, 1973).

Putnam, R.D., *Bowling Alone: The Collapse and Revival of American Community* (Simon & Schuster, New York, 2001).

Pym, F., *The Politics of Consent* (Hamish Hamilton, 1984).

Quinton, A., *The Politics of Imperfection* (Faber and Faber, 1975).

Raison, T., *Tories and the Welfare State* (Palgrave Macmillan, Basingstoke, 1990).

Ramsden, J., *The Winds of Change: Macmillan to Heath, 1957–75* (Longman, 1996).

Ramsden, J., *An Appetite for Power: New History of the Conservative Party* (HarperCollins, 1998).

Ranelagh, J., *Thatcher's People* (HarperCollins, 1991).

Riddell, P., *The Thatcher Government* (Blackwell, Oxford, 1985).

Riddell, P., *The Thatcher Era* (Blackwell, Oxford, 1991).

Ridley, N., *My Style of Government: The Thatcher Years* (Hutchinson, 1991).

Roberts, A., *Eminent Churchillians* (Weidenfeld & Nicolson, 1994).

Schoen, D.E., *Enoch Powell and the Powellites* (Macmillan, 1977).

Scruton, R., *The Meaning of Conservatism* (Penguin, 1980).

Seldon, A. (ed.), *How Tory Governments Die: Tory Party in Power, 1783–1987* (Fontana Press, 1996).

Seldon, A. and Ball, S. (eds), *Conservative Century: The Conservative Party Since 1900* (OUP, Oxford, 1994).

Seldon, A. and Ball, S. (eds), *The Heath Government, 1970–74: A Reappraisal* (Longman, 1996).

Seldon, A. and Kavanagh, D. (eds), *The Thatcher Effect: A Decade of Change* (Clarendon Press, Oxford, 1989).

Sharp, P., *Thatcher's Diplomacy: The Revival of British Foreign Policy* (Palgrave Macmillan, Basingstoke, 1997).

Shepherd, R., *Iain Macleod* (Hutchinson, 1994).

Shepherd, R., *Enoch Powell* (Hutchinson, 1996).

Skelton, N., *Constructive Conservatism* (1924).

Skidelsky, R. (ed.), *Thatcherism* (Chatto & Windus, 1988).

Smith, G., *Reagan and Thatcher* (WW Norton & Co, New York, 1991).

Smith, P., *Disraelian Conservatism and Social Reform* (Routledge, 1967).

Stephenson, H., *Mrs Thatcher's First Year* (J Norman, 1980).

Supple, B. and Furner, M.O. (eds), *The State and Economic Knowledge: The American and British Experiences* (CUP, Cambridge, 1990).

Taylor, A.J.P., *Beaverbrook* (Hamish Hamilton, 1972).

Taylor, R., *The Trade Union Question in British Politics: Government and the Union Since 1945* (Blackwell Publishers, Oxford, 1993).

Tebbit, N., *Upwardly Mobile* (Weidenfeld & Nicolson, 1988).

Timmins, N., *The Five Giants: A Biography of the Welfare State* (Fontana Press, 1996).

Thatcher, M., *The Revival of Britain* (Aurum Press, 1989).

Thatcher, M., *The Downing Street Years* (HarperCollins, 1993).

Thatcher, M., *The Path to Power* (HarperCollins, 1995).

Thatcher, M., *Statecraft: Strategies for a Changing World* (HarperCollins, 2002).

Thorpe, D.R., *Alec Douglas-Home* (Sinclair-Stevenson, 1996).

Tiratsoo, N. et al. (eds), *The Wilson Governments, 1964–70* (Continuum, 1993).

Urban, G., *Diplomacy and Disillusion at the Court of Margaret Thatcher: An Insider's View* (I.B. Tauris, 1996).

Walker, P., *Staying Power* (Bloomsbury, 1991).

White, R.J., *The Conservative Tradition* (Kaye, 1950).

Whitelaw, W., *The Whitelaw Memoirs* (Aurum Press, 1989).

Whiteley, P., Seyd, P. and Richardson, J., *True Blues: The Politics of Conservative Party Membership* (OUP, Oxford, 1994).

Wiener, M., *English Culture and the Decline of the Industrial Spirit, 1850–1980* (CUP, Cambridge, 1981).

Willetts, D., *Civic Conservatism* (The Social Market Foundation, 1994).

Willetts, D. and Gray, J., *Is Conservatism Dead?* (Profile Books, 1997).

Young, H., *One of Us: Life of Margaret Thatcher* (Pan, 1990).

Young, Lord, *The Enterprise Years: A Businessman in the Cabinet* (Headline Book Publishing, 1991).

Young Conservatives, *Society and the Individual* (1962).

Essays and articles

Alt, J., 'New Wine in Old Bottles: Thatcher's Conservative Economic Policy'.

Anderson, P. and Nairn, T., 'The Origins of the Present Crisis', *New Left Review*, 23 (1964).

Bevir, M. and Rhodes, R.A.W. 'Narratives of Thatcherism' in H. Berrington (ed.), *Britain in the Nineties: The Politics of Paradox* (Frank Cass Publishers, 1998).

Biddiss, M., 'Thatcherism: Concept and Interpretations' in K. Minogue and M. Biddiss (eds), *Thatcherism: Personality and Politics* (Palgrave Macmillan, Basingstoke, 1987).

Booth, A., 'Inflation, Expectations, and the Political Economy of Conservative Britain, 1951–64', *HJ*, xliii (2000).

Brown, G., Mais Lecture, London, 19 October 1999.

Clarke, P., 'Keynes, Buchanan and the balanced budget doctrine' in idem, *The Keynesian Revolution and its Economic Consequences* (Edward Elgar, Cheltenham, 1998).

Clarke, P., 'The Rise and Fall of Thatcherism', *Historical Research*, lxxii (1999).

Cowley, P. and Bailey, M., 'Peasants' Uprising or Religious War? Re-examining the 1975 Conservative Leadership Contest', *British Journal of Political Science*, xxx (2000).

Deakin, S., 'Labour Law and Industrial Relations' in J. Michie (ed.), *The Economic Legacy, 1979–92* (Academic Press, 1992).

Findley, R., 'The Conservative Party and Defeat: The Significance of Resale Price Maintenance for the Election of 1964', *TCBH*, xi (2001).

Francis, M., '"Set the People Free"? The Conservative Party and the State, 1920–60' in M. Francis and I. Zweiniger-Bargielowska (eds), *The Conservatives and British Society, 1880–1990* (University of Wales Press, Cardiff, 1996).

Garnett, M. and Gilmour, I., 'Thatcherism and the Conservative Tradition' in M. Francis and I. Zweiniger-Bargielowska (eds), *The Conservatives and British Society, 1880–1990* (University of Wales Press, Cardiff, 1996).

Gilmour, I., 'The Thatcher Memoirs', *TCBH*, 5 (1994).

Gould, J. and Anderson, D. 'Thatcherism and British Society' in K. Minogue and M. Biddiss (eds), *Thatcherism: Personality and Poltics* (Palgrave Macmillan, Basingstoke, 1987).

Green, E.H.H., 'The Conservative Party, the State and the Electorate, 1945–64' in J. Lawrence and M. Taylor (eds), *Party, State and Society: Electoral Behaviour in Modern Britain Since 1820* (Scolar Press, Aldershot, 1996).

Green, E.H.H., 'Thatcherism: an Historical Perspective', *TRHS*, 48 (1998).

Green, E.H.H., 'The Treasury Resignations of 1958: A Reconsideration', *TCBH*, 20 (2001).

Green, E.H.H., 'Conservatism, the State and Civil Society in the Twentieth Century' in idem, *Ideologies of Conservatism: Conservative Political Ideas in the Twentieth Century* (OUP, Oxford, 2002).

Green, E.H.H., 'The Conservatives and the City' in R. Michie and P. Williamson (eds), *The British Government and the City of London in the Twentieth Century* (CUP, Cambridge, 2004).

Hall, P.A., 'Social Capital in Britain', *British Journal of Political Science*, 29 (1999).

Harrison, B., 'Mrs Thatcher and the Intellectuals', *TCBH*, 5 (1994).

Hayek, F.A., 'Hayek on Hayek' in A. Gamble, *Hayek* (Polity Press, Cambridge, 1996).

Jarvis, M., 'The 1958 Treasury Dispute', *CBH*, xii (1998).

Johnmann, L., 'The Conservative Party in Opposition, 1964–70' in R. Coopey, S. Fielding, and N. Tiratsoo (eds), *The Wilson Governments, 1964–70* (1993).

Joseph, K., 'Is Beckermann Among the Sociologists?', *New Statesman*, 18 Apr. 1975.

Leys, C., 'Thatcherism and Industry', *New Left Review*, 159 (1985).

Oakeshott, M., 'On Being Conservative' in idem, *Rationalism in Politics and Other Essays* (Liberty Fund, Indianapolis, 1991 edn).

Phillips, A.W., 'The Relation Between Unemployment and the Rate of Change of Money Wage Rates in the United Kingdom, 1861–1957', *Economica*, xxv (1958).

Powell, J.E., 'The Conservative Party' in A. Seldon and D. Kavanagh (eds), *The Thatcher Effect: A Decade of Change* (Clarendon Press, Oxford, 1989).

Ramsden, J., 'A Party for Owners or a Party for Earners? How Far did the British Conservative Party Really Change After 1945?', *TRHS*, 37 (1987).

Ringe, A. (ed.), 'Witness Seminar: The National Economic Development Council, 1962–7', *CBH*, xii (1998).

Roberts, A., 'Walter Monckton and the Retreat from Reality' in idem, *Eminent Churchillians* (Weidenfeld and Nicolson, 1994).

Rollings, N., 'Poor Mr. Butskell: A Short Life Wrecked by Schizophrenia', *TCBH*, iv, (1994).

Rollings, N., 'Butskellism, the Post-War Consensus and the Managed Economy', in H. Jones and M. Kandiah (eds), *The Myth of Consensus: New Views on British History, 1945–64* (Palgrave Macmillan, Basingstoke, 1996).

Taylor, A., 'The Party and the Trade Unions' in A. Seldon and S. Ball (eds), *Conservative Century: The Conservative Party Since 1900* (OUP, Oxford, 1994).

Taylor, R., 'The Heath Government, Industrial Policy and the "New Capitalism"' in A. Seldon and S. Ball (eds.), *The Heath Government, 1970–74: A Reappraisal* (Harlow, 1996).

Tomlinson, J., 'Inventing Decline: The Falling Behind of the British Economy in the Post-War Years', *EcHR*, 99 (1996).

Tomlinson, J., 'Conservative Modernisation, 1960–64: Too Little, Too Late?', *CBH*, xi (1997).

Turner, J., 'The British Conservative Party in the Twentieth Century: From Beginning to End', *CEH*, viii (1999).

Webster, C., 'Conflict and Consensus: Explaining the British Health Service', *TCBH*, i (1990).

Webster, C., 'Conservatives and Consensus: The Politics of the National Health Service, 1951–64' in A. Oakley and S. Williams (eds), *The Politics of the Welfare State* (Routledge, 1994).

Weiler, P.,'The Rise and Fall of the Conservatives' "Grand Design" for Housing, 1951–1964', *CBH* (2000).

Wickham-Jones, M., 'Right Turn: A Revisionist Account of the 1975 Conservative Party Leadership Election', *TCBH*, 8 (1997).

Williams, G., '"A Matter of Regret": Britain, the 1983 Grenada Crisis and the Special Relationship', *TCBH*, 12 (2001).

Zweiniger-Bargielowska, I., 'Rationing, Austerity and the Conservative Electoral Recovery After 1945', *Historical Journal*, 37 (1993).

Unpublished theses

Berthezène, C., 'Les Conservateurs Britanniques dans la Bataille des Idées. Le Ashridge Bonar Law Memorial College: des "Conservateurs Fabiens" à la Conquête des Esprits, 1929–54', unpublished Ph.D. thesis, Université de Paris III – La Sorbonne Nouvelle (2003).

Dewey, R.F., 'British National Identity and the First Application to Europe', unpublished D.Phil. thesis, Oxford University (2003).

Gratton Lavoie, C., 'Essays on Privatization', unpublished Ph.D. thesis, Virginia Polytechnic and State University (2000).

Jones, H., 'The Conservative Party and the Welfare State, 1942–55', unpublished Ph.D. thesis, London University (1992).

Index